JOURNAL
1955–1962

MOULOUD FERAOUN

# JOURNAL
## 1955~1962
Reflections on the French-Algerian War

*Edited and with an introduction by* JAMES D. LE SUEUR
*Translated by* MARY ELLEN WOLF *and* CLAUDE FOUILLADE

*University of Nebraska Press*
LINCOLN AND LONDON

Publication of this translation was
assisted by grants from the French
Ministry of Culture and the National
Endowment for the Arts.

Originally published as *Journal,
1955–1962*

∞

Library of Congress
Cataloging-in-Publication Data
Feraoun, Mouloud.
[Journal, 1955–1962. English]
Journal, 1955–1962 : reflections on the
French-Algerian War / Mouloud
Feraoun ; edited and with an
introduction by James D. Le Sueur ;
translated by Mary Ellen Wolf and
Claude Fouillade.
p.   cm.
ISBN 0-8032-2002-2 (cl : alk. paper) —
ISBN 0-8032-6903-X (pa : alk. paper)
1. Algeria—History—Revolution, 1954–
1962—Personal narratives, Algerian.
2. Feraoun, Mouloud.   I. Le Sueur,
James D.   II. Title.     .
DT295 .F3814   2000
965'.046'092—dc21
[B]                          99-053747

# CONTENTS

## Editor's Acknowledgments

I wish to thank many people for their gracious support in helping to bring this project to fruition. To begin, I applaud Mary Wolf and Claude Fouillade for their magnificent rendering of Feraoun's *Journal* into English and for their ability to work with me on key concerns of the translation. I would especially like to acknowledge the University of Nebraska Press's commitment and assistance—without which this project would not have been possible. I am enormously indebted to my friend and colleague John Ruedy, whose guidance and careful reading of the introduction and translation were indispensable. William A. Cook and Julia A. Clancy-Smith also provided important, critical suggestions for the introduction, and I am deeply thankful for their contributions. I am grateful to Germaine Tillion and Isabelle Deblé for allowing me to consult their private papers in Paris and for showing me such unlimited hospitality. I appreciate the countless hours of help from Donna Bentley and the superb staff at Wilson Library at the University of La Verne. I owe a special debt to Loukia K. Sarroub for her encouragement and conversations, which inspired me to work even harder to bring Feraoun's unique vision and wisdom to light. Finally, I would like to thank the University of La Verne for its much-appreciated support.

JAMES D. LE SUEUR
*La Verne, California*

## Translators' Preface

"Can words express the horror that grips us?" Mouloud Fera-oun has purposely inserted such agonizing questions throughout his *Journal*. Feraoun was, after all, acutely aware of the inadequacy of language, the difficulties of creating a personal yet accurate record of the French-Algerian war. He offers readers his voice, a voice that is interwoven with the voices of all those willing or unwilling actors—whether French or Algerian—who participated in one of the longest and most brutal conflicts of the twentieth century.

Our translation, since it is a collaborative effort, puts two more voices into play. We have focused our effort on preserving the polyphony of the text as well as the various styles and levels of language in Feraoun's text. It is our hope that readers will hear with clarity both the conversational quality of the street dialogues and the more formal tones of one of the more prominent Algerian intellectuals of that era.

To this end, we have retained, wherever possible, the poetic rhythms of fragmentary sentences, the winding prose that is so natural to the French language, and the original French spelling of Algerian place-names and customs.

We had to be certain that our own two voices could be successfully combined with those already present in Feraoun's *Journal*. Therefore we started out by each translating the same excerpt. We then compared our individual translations and eventually merged them into what became our first draft. This has been the process to which we adhered throughout the project. Thus, we share equally in any inadequacies that the reader may encounter.

The endnotes found in this edition include the translation of those footnotes authored by Feraoun and Roblès in the French edition as well as those compiled by the editor and by ourselves.

We are grateful to James Le Sueur and the editors at the University of Nebraska Press for inviting us to participate in this project and for making this text available to a global audience. We are also indebted to Leslie Coutant for her thorough reading of the manuscript and valuable feedback. Finally, this translation could not have come to fruition without the patience, support, and encouragement of Sharon, Sarah, Dick, Judith, Emilienne, and Louis.

MARY ELLEN WOLF *and* CLAUDE FOUILLADE

## Introduction

The French-Algerian war was probably the most violent anticolonial war of the twentieth century. For seven of eight years, Mouloud Feraoun kept a journal of this conflict, which began on November 1, 1954, and ended on March 18, 1962. As a personal record of the war, Feraoun's *Journal*—here published for the first time in English—is a shocking, firsthand account of France's bitter and long overdue withdrawal from its most prized colonial possession, Algeria.[1] The protracted decolonization of French Algeria is not a pleasant story, and Feraoun's depiction of it requires sensitivity on the part of the reader. This is no doubt the case because the *Journal*'s candor and honesty was meant to represent the war as Feraoun saw it, without illusions and without self-censorship. Feraoun believed that this was the only way to affect future generations in Algeria, North Africa, France, and the world. Feraoun, as an intellectual and a writer, certainly understood the importance of honestly capturing the war from the inside, from personal experience, and he noted the ethics of such a recording toward the end of his *Journal* on August 17, 1961, less than a year before his murder:

> I have spent hours upon hours rereading all my notes, newspaper articles, and small clippings that I have kept. I have become reimmersed in a sad past, and I am leaving it overwhelmed. I am frightened by my candor, my audacity, my cruelty, and, at times, my blind spots and prejudice. Do I have a right to tamper with what I have written, to go back, to alter or rectify it?
>
> Did I not write all of this day by day, according to my frame of mind, my mood, the circumstances, the atmosphere created by the event, its reverberations in my heart? And why did I write it like this, bit by bit, if it was not to witness, to stand before the world and shout out the suffering and misfortune that have stalked me? Granted, I was very awkward and headstrong the day when I decided to write. Whom do I know that would have been willing to do it in my place? And would I have been able to remain blind and deaf just to silence myself, just to avoid the risk of being suffocated by my anger and despair? Now that it is done, now that everything has been recorded—good or

bad, true or false, just or unjust—now that we can foresee the end of this nightmare, must I keep all of this for
myself? Must I forget, look ahead, look toward those who
will build our future, preach oblivion, hope, brotherhood,
and all the rest? That would be a fine program for future
moralists. Alas! I am not one of them, and my faith in man
has been shaken enough that, from here on, I might become a hypocrite or a victim of my own naïveté.

    The reason I did all of this is simple: it is appropriate
that my journal supplement what has already been written
about the Algerian war—good or bad, true or false, just
or unjust. Consider it one more document in an extremely
poignant dossier. Nothing more. And the time has come
to add it to the rest. It is either now or never. (294–95)

Feraoun and the other five unfortunate educators who
were working for the French educational apparatus known as
Service des Centres Sociaux Éducatifs in Algeria did not live
to see postcolonial Algeria, but the effects of the eight years of
warfare on Feraoun have left us with a deeply personal, intelligent, and profound account of the French-Algerian war. As
he said, it was his respect for the war itself—with its suffering and destruction—that mandated he not alter his reflections
after the fact, preferring genuine thoughts to doctored recalcu-
lations. This very fact, his desire to preserve his notes as true
artifacts of history, certainly tells us as much about his character
as it does about his sensitivity to the importance of lived history. This means that, in many ways, Feraoun is for the French-
Algerian war what Thucydides was for the Peloponnesian war,
and just like Thucydides, Feraoun faithfully recorded the war
with such anthropological and historical precision—consult-
ing informants and compiling documents—that his account remains unparalleled. In other words, Feraoun was keenly aware
that he was preserving a record of something unique, a personal
experience molded by the very historical processes over which
he had little control and of which he was both witness and victim. However, unlike Thucydides, Feraoun did not live to see
the end of the war. He met his death at the hands of the fascist
*Organisation Armée Secrète* (oas) mere days before the cease-fire
ended the French-Algerian war.

    Feraoun's reflections and his murder undeniably mark the
end of an era for France: the end of Franco-Muslim reconciliation and the end of France's so-called *epic grandeur*, which

thrived on imperialism and universalism yet was marred by racism and inequality. For Feraoun, the collapse of French power in Algeria and North Africa was indeed bittersweet in that he welcomed the right of Algerians (and indigenous populations) to reclaim their soil and their identity from the French occupiers, and in that he recognized that the future of an *Algerian* Algeria would be built on the lost lives of the sacrificed. Feraoun also realized that French and Algerian cultures and intellectuals were deeply intertwined (he, himself, wrote in French) and that it would take generations to untangle the knots of more than a century of colonization. This is why Feraoun believed that his writings could make a difference by instructing future generations, starting with his children's compatriots, as they labored at the painful and difficult task of reconstructing their war-torn nation. Ultimately, Feraoun's writings went totally unheeded by subsequent generations in his beloved Algeria, and there is no doubt that he would be saddened by (if not a victim of) the tragic turn of events in postcolonial Algeria now commonly referred to in France and Algeria as the "Second Algerian war." The failure to heed his sage advice was certainly no fault of Feraoun's; it would be more accurate to say that the future generations and the leadership (uniparty government and the Islamic Fundamentalists) in Algeria failed him and the nation, and miserably so.

But just who was Mouloud Feraoun? And what kind of war was the French-Algerian war? Without answering these questions in some detail, a reading of the *Journal* may appear too cryptic. These questions will be addressed first by outlining Feraoun's life and his career, by highlighting the main historical points of the French-Algerian war, and then by turning to an examination of some of the central themes of his *Journal*.

### AN OUTLINE OF MOULOUD FERAOUN'S CAREER

Mouloud Feraoun was one of the most respected intellectuals and novelists in colonial Algeria. His first book, *Fils du pauvre*, published in 1950 and republished by Éditions du Seuil in 1954, earned him the respect and friendship of an entire generation of French and North African writers, including Albert Camus and Emmanuel Roblès. His other works, *Terre et le sang* (1953), *Les Chemins qui montent* (1957), and *Les poèmes de Si-Mohand* (1960), as well as his three posthumous works and edited works, *Lettres à ses amis* (1969), *L'Anniversaire* (1972), and, of course, his *Journal, 1955–1962* (1962), only highlight his profound intellect. Before he was assassinated, Feraoun's publisher in Paris (Éditions du Seuil) already had plans to publish his reflections on the war, but after his death Roblès edited Feraoun's many individual notebooks and oversaw their publication under the title *Journal, 1955-1962*.

But to really understand Feraoun, one has to think of him above all as a committed teacher and a Kabyle (a Berber Muslim) who was equally proud of his profession and his cultural heritage. Both of these aspects of his personal history directly colored how he perceived the war and what he wrote about it. He was born on March 8, 1913, in Tizi-Hibel, a village in Kabylia about thirteen miles from Tizi-Ouzou. His parents emphasized his education from an early age during a time when very few Muslims had the opportunity to pursue even primary education. A talented primary school student in the 1920s, Feraoun was quickly noticed and was given a scholarship to study at the Collège de Tizi-Ouzou (a French version of high school). In 1932, he was admitted to the prestigious École Normale d'Alger-Bouzaréa. It was there that he studied and made a lifelong friendship with such Frenchmen as Emmanuel Roblès, the man who would eventually edit the French edition of the *Journal*.

When Feraoun was writing his *Journal*, Algeria was no longer considered a colony by France because it was officially considered French soil. Hence, as part of Algeria's indigenous Muslim elite, Feraoun received his education entirely within the French system. He wrote in French and spoke Tamazight, a Kabyle language, but he did not speak or write Arabic. Importantly, although Feraoun did often mention that he was writing about Kabylia and that there were still cultural and political differences between the Kabyles and the Arabs in Algerian society, he did tend to see the non-French population as a unified bloc that rejected the colonial status quo.

These factions, especially the divisions between the Arabs and the Kabyles, predated the French occupation in 1830. However, the French used them to perfection during the colonial period. As a result, the "Kabyles" and the "Arabs" were further separated as distinct populations by the French, and the effects of these representations (Kabyles sympathetic to France, Arabs antagonistic) solidified as racial or ethnic categories. These categories were thus socially constructed to make room for the "divide and conquer" practices (along with the *mission civilisatrice* ideology of European colonialism), which the French used to maintain hegemony in Algeria. Arabs in Algeria were identified with feudalism, whereas the Kabyles were seen as being more democratic and open to modern political transformations. The issue of finding the appropriate legal codes for indigenous society also led the French to make further distinctions between the Kabyles and the Arabs; this, in turn, fueled the rivalry between the two groups.[2] This rivalry played itself out during the French-Algerian war in important ways. In the *Journal*, however, Feraoun very seldom makes direct references to this rivalry, though it was something to which he often alludes.

After leaving the École Normale in 1935, Feraoun spent the rest of his life teaching in Algeria, mostly in Kabylia. He began his teaching career in 1936 at Taourirt-Auden in the Grand Kabylia, located about forty miles east of Algiers. From Taourirt-Auden, Feraoun moved to Taboudrist in 1937, to Aït-Abdel-Moumen in 1945, where he stayed until 1946, and then to Taourirt-Moussa from 1946 until 1952. Just after he went to Taboudrist, he followed the Kabyle custom and married his cousin, Dehbia, who, by most accounts, was a traditional wife, was deeply connected to her Kabyle customs, had no formal education, and spoke only Berber. Also, while in Taboudrist, Mouloud Feraoun was not mobilized to fight for France against the Axis powers.[3] In 1952, he requested that he be assigned to Fort-National instead of Algiers, and he was at Fort-National on the day the Algerian revolution started in November 1954. In July 1957, Feraoun asked to be transferred to École de la Cité Nador in Clos Salembier, a suburb of Algiers. He had asked for this teaching post in order to be nearer to his friend Roblès and to escape from the heat of the conflict. His final educational move came in October 1960, when he accepted a post as an inspector for the French educational organization in Algiers known as the Centres Sociaux.

### AN OUTLINE OF THE FRENCH-ALGERIAN WAR

During the first year of the war, between November 1954 and November 1955, Feraoun and his compatriots witnessed several important events, but he wrote nothing about the war in his *Journal* during this time. When the rebellion first broke in November 1954, it was not at all clear that it would have lasting importance, but most observers felt that the colonial status quo could not continue. For example, the French government's

Ordinance of March 7, 1944, which allowed more than 65,000 Algerians (out of a population of about 8.5 million) to become French citizens without renouncing their adherence to Islamic law (as they had to after the *sénatus consulte* of 1865), only widened the divisions between Muslims and Europeans in Algeria.[4] And although it was true that Muslims could now elect representatives to the newly created Muslim College in the Algerian Assembly, political segregation was officially endorsed.

Two important nationalist leaders, Ferhat Abbas and Messali Hadj, rejected this segregationist plan and called for the intensification of political action. As a result, Ferhat Abbas created the *Amis du Manifeste et de la Liberté* (AML), and Messali Hadj's followers in *Parti du Peuple Algérien* (PPA)—which had been outlawed by the French—were encouraged to join the AML by Messali. Messali himself was placed under house arrest. The activities of these groups culminated with the nationalist public demonstrations against France spearheaded by the AML in and around Sétif on VE Day, May 8, 1945. The French response to this upsurge in Algerian nationalism was swift and brutal. After the demonstration turned violent and the Muslims unveiled the Algerian nationalist flag, thousands of Algerians were slaughtered by the French troops. (Some estimates of casualties run as high as 45,000.) Following the Sétif repression, traditional divisions between the French colonial community and the Algerian Muslims grew even more pronounced, and some Algerian nationalists set out on a course for unconditional independence.

From 1945 to 1954, there were several factions that emerged within Algeria and competed for power. Messali Hadj, who was still under watch but who had been set free by the French authorities, created the *Mouvement pour le Triomphe des Libertés Démocratiques* (MTLD), a new political organization to replace his outlawed PPA. While the MTLD operated on a legal basis to pursue independence primarily as an Islamic and Arab movement, the PPA unofficially continued its course underground and created the *Organisation Spéciale* (OS) as a paramilitary resistance organization. Among the first members of the OS were Ahmed Ben Bella (an Arab who became Algeria's first president in 1962) and Hocine Ait Ahmed (a young Kabyle militant who took over the leadership of the OS after Mohamed Belouizdad and who was quickly replaced by Ben Bella). Eventually, as divisions among the MTLD leadership became too severe, the *Comité Révolutionnaire d'Unité et d'Action* (CRUA) was created. In 1952,

CRUA started to plan its attack on the French government in Algeria. CRUA initially tried to regenerate a sense of unity among the various factions (especially the Arab-Kabyle divisions), but by the summer of 1954 it was thought that only open revolution could reunite the various factions.

While CRUA continued to plan for insurrection during 1954, that year was an important, if not catastrophic, year for the French Empire or "Greater France," as it was called. Antoine Pinay had come to power as prime minister in the wake of national political chaos. A classic liberal politician, he had very little support from the powerful socialist lobbies in France. After a momentary effort by René Meyer, Pinay was followed in 1953 by Joseph Laniel. Laniel's more conservative government had to react first to money scandals and then, most importantly, to the growing nationalist forces in Indochina. At the same time, René Coty was elected to the French presidency. French policy in Asia took a decisive turn with the defeat of the French forces in Indochina at Dien Bien Phu on May 7, 1954. A stern critic of Pinay and Laniel, Pierre Mendès France was invested as prime minister on June 17, 1954. As fate would have it, Mendès France would be the one to negotiate for France in the Geneva Conference, which set the stage for a peace treaty and the extraction of the French troops from Indochina. In July, Mendès France confronted yet another colonial problem, this time in Tunisia, where he resolved to move the Tunisian protectorate gradually toward independence, achieved in 1956.

When war finally broke out in Algeria, the territory had long been considered by the French government to be France. In other words, the country was nothing less than metropolitan France itself and was divided into the three French *départements* (administrative districts) of Constantine, Oran, and Algiers. In fact, when the nine historic chiefs of CRUA gave the order to commence the uprising on November 1, 1954, France's then minister of interior, François Mitterrand (as well as Mendès France), stated confidently that Algeria was France: "Algeria is France. And France will recognize no authority in Algeria other than her own." [5] This claim that Algeria was France and therefore that all disturbances within French sovereign territory were domestic issues was a card frequently played by France on the international scene, especially as it struggled to keep the United Nations from interfering in the conflict.

When CRUA initiated its call to arms on November 1, it

also declared the creation of a new revolutionary organization, the *Front de Libération Nationale* (FLN). From the very beginning of the conflict, the FLN's principal objective was the liberation of Algeria, but it articulated its future orientation by stating that it would fight for a sovereign state based on Islamic principles, and it pledged to respect Algeria's "basic liberties" without distinctions of race or religion. And although Messali's MTLD still existed, its members were frequently subject to arrest by the French authorities. The FLN immediately benefited from these arrests of MTLD members because many centrists moved into the arms of the FLN during the first months of the revolution.

During the summer of 1954, Messali Hadj split from the directing committee of the MTLD and formed the second most powerful revolutionary political group in Algeria, the *Mouvement National Algérien* (MNA). The MNA drew much of its support from Kabylia, Feraoun's region. The FLN and the MNA became bitter rivals; each was supported by its own militia, with the *Armée de Libération Nationale* (ALN) representing the FLN forces. Feraoun states often in his *Journal* that this vitriolic conflict between the MNA and the FLN-ALN placed the Algerian population and their chief foe, the French military, in a deadly tug-of-war. The daily skirmishes between these factions were often exploited by the French military and took a heavy toll on Algerian populations in secluded rural villages. The worst symbol of this violent conflict was by far the massacre at Mélouza, when in May 1957, over three hundred men in this war-torn part of Algeria were massacred in a most grotesque fashion: throats slit, genitals cut off and stuffed in mouths of corpses, and so forth. The massacre had an immediate effect on Algerians as well as on the metropolitan French population, especially the intellectuals. As Feraoun indicates in his *Journal*, it was not clear who (the French military, the FLN, or the MNA) engineered the atrocity.[6]

Back in Paris, three months after the Algerian revolution began in 1954, French politicians turned to Jacques Soustelle —a well-respected liberal intellectual and politician—to help bring the situation in Algeria under control. Soustelle was nominated to the post of governor general of Algeria on January 25, 1955, by Prime Minister Pierre Mendès France and was later confirmed by Edgar Faure. By the end of his term as governor general in February 1956, Soustelle had done more to shape discussions over Franco-Muslim reconciliation than any other political figure during the first year of the war. Because Jacques Soustelle possessed a reputation for being a left-wing, antifascist intellectual, he seemed a logical choice for the post in Pierre Mendès France's government. However, the right-wing French settlers (the Ultras) in Algeria protested Soustelle's appointment because he had a reputation as a radical and because he had come to Algeria as a reformist.

Soustelle's reforms attempted to win over support for France among Algerians by instituting economic and political programs that would clear the path for continued cooperation between the French and Algerians. Concentrating his attention on the implementation of the Organic Law of 1947, which recognized the civic personality of Algeria and its financial autonomy, he dubbed his program for the Muslims *assimilation*. According to Soustelle, assimilation would acknowledge the distinct character of Algeria but keep the territory French.

In reality, Soustelle was ill-equipped to deal with the realities of the Algerian conflict, especially the violence. For example, just three months before Feraoun began recording his reflections on the war, the FLN decided to massacre Europeans and Muslims (71 out of a total of 123 victims were Europeans) on August 20, 1955, in the coastal city of Philippeville. According to John Ruedy, the decision to massacre French and Muslims was largely the FLN's attempt to stir up mass support for the revolution by creating a climate of intercommunal tension.[7]

Soustelle played into the FLN's hands by sanctioning massive reprisals against the adversaries. The overzealous reactions of the French military to Philippeville destroyed the last chances of political moderation, forcing many of the remaining Algerian Muslims who had formally supported continued cooperation between France and Algeria to part company with Soustelle. Although Soustelle had played into the hands of the FLN by increasing the collective repression against the Muslim population, on September 26, the Algerian Muslims, who were elected to the Second College (the Muslim representative body in the Algerian Assembly), issued their "Declaration of 61," which condemned the French government's "blind repression." Ironically, Soustelle left Algeria universally detested by Muslim leaders and adored by the French Ultras, the very people who originally opposed his nomination.

Before Soustelle left his post as governor general in January 1956, he created two important organizations that went on to play critical roles during the course of the war: the Centres Sociaux d'Algérie, which was assembled by Germaine Tillion and first directed by Charles Arguesse, and the *Sections Administratives Spécialisées* (SAS), which was created by Vincent Monteil. Each organization, the former tied to the Ministry of National Education in Paris and Algiers and the latter rooted in the military, was designed to cater to the central ideal of Soustelle's liberal reformism, the creation of Franco-Muslim solidarity through education, and other forms of aid. By tending to very real educational and material needs, each group cultivated a committed squad of educators who worked on traditional forms of education—domestic, agricultural, and mechanical—in order to enhance the living standards of Algeria's underdeveloped population. While Feraoun seemed to trust the aims of the Centres Sociaux, he openly distrusted the role of the SAS in the Algerian conflict and comments on it frequently. The Centres Sociaux and the SAS remained important aspects of French policy in Algeria, and Feraoun himself finally joined the Centres Sociaux in October 1960.

At the end of 1955, Edgar Faure requested authority from President René Coty to dissolve the National Assembly and call for new elections. General elections were held in France on January 2, 1956, and the new left-center coalition known as the Republican Front won the election. Soon thereafter Guy Mollet, the secretary-general of the Socialist Party (SFIO), formed a new government. One of his first acts was to name General Georges Catroux as Soustelle's successor. This turned out to be an extremely unfortunate decision, because on February 2, when the unpopular Mollet appeared for a scheduled visit to Algeria, he was met with hostility by settlers who pummeled him with insults, tomatoes, and rotten fruit. Very unwisely, on February 6, 1956, Mollet bowed to the settlers' demands to withdraw Catroux. A new post of resident minister was created that expanded on the former governor general's powers and allowed the new resident minister to report directly to the prime minister in Paris. Robert Lacoste was selected as the first resident minister by Mollet, who increased the military presence in Algeria to over five hundred thousand soldiers. In March 1956, the French National Assembly formally granted the French military full police powers in Algeria by approving the Special Powers Act. A month later, on April 11, 1956, Lacoste dissolved the Algerian Assembly.

While Algerian Muslims were increasingly being crushed in the vise composed of rival nationalist groups and the French military, a series of important international events transpired. In April 1955, Algeria's FLN sent a delegation to the Bandung Conference, the first major showing of Third World countries expressing a common desire to cast off the yoke of colonial oppression. In April 1955, the UN adopted Egypt's resolution to hear the Algerian question of independence, and by the fall of 1955 the Algerian question was placed on the UN agenda. Not surprisingly, the French delegates (including Jacques Soustelle) walked out of the session. In March 1956, both Tunisia and Morocco were granted independence. Meanwhile, in July 1956, Gamal Abd el-Nasser of Egypt nationalized the Suez company.

In the meantime, in August and September of 1956, in the mountains near the Soumman Valley in Kabylia, a group of about fifty "internal" leaders of the FLN met to reorganize their movement. It was during this Soumman Congress that the FLN created the *Conseil National de la Révolution Algérienne* (CNRA). According the John Ruedy, this was "in effect Algeria's first sovereign parliament."[8] A month later, on October 22, 1956, the French military broke international law and seized the king of Morocco's private aircraft carrying important "external" leaders of the Algerian revolution (Ben Bella, Budiaf, Khider, Ait Ahmed, and a well-known intellectual, Moustapha Lacheraf). The next week, on November 1, the Soviet army made its way into Hungary and crushed the Imre Nagy's revolt in Budapest. Almost simultaneously, Israeli, French, and British forces struck against Abd el-Nasser's troops in Egypt. Fortunately for Egypt, President Eisenhower refused to allow this aggression to continue, and the three countries were forced to withdraw their troops from Egypt.

Once in power, Lacoste pursued his own reforms, the most important of which was the *loi-cadre*. In practical terms, the *loi-cadre* looked something like federalism and drew intense fire from the hard-line Ultras in Algeria because they feared that it was moving too close in the direction of statehood. Not surprisingly, Jacques Soustelle (now back in the National Assembly in Paris) and Jacques Chevallier (the mayor of Algiers) rejected the plan. The basic idea of the *loi-cadre* was to grant a limited degree of autonomy to Algeria, which would be separated into about a half-dozen administrative districts. The *loi-cadre* was voted on in the French National Assembly, where its supporters met resistance from the pro-settler lobby, and it was defeated by a vote of 279 to 253. Soustelle had been decisive in engineering its defeat. In May 1957, Guy Mollet's government collapsed, and Maurice Bourgès-Maunoury formed his government in France, which lasted until September 1957. Completely unable to provide stability and weighed down by the Algerian question, successive French governments continued to fall in Paris while Robert Lacoste remained loosely in control of the French administration in Algeria, ever working on the *loi-cadre*. In concrete terms, Lacoste's *loi-cadre* was probably the last opportunity to keep Algeria French, and it triggered the collapse of Bourgès-Maunoury's government. Following Bourgès-Maunoury's turn as prime minster, Félix Gaillard finally nudged the National Assembly on November 5, 1957, into accepting a different version of the *loi-cadre*. This version, however, rendered it useless in the eyes of the Muslim population because it kept intact the settlers' status quo.

Meanwhile, the French government and its military control of the Algerian situation would command a heavy price for the civilian population. For example, following the French Ultras' decision to use bombs to terrorize innocent Muslims, the FLN's commander of the Algiers region, Saadi Yacef, quickly followed suit and orchestrated a series of attacks on French civilians on September 30, 1956. Two of the three bombs went off as planned, but the third bomb placed in the Air France terminal did not detonate. The use of bombs against the civilian population in Algeria changed the nature of the war and set the stage for the French to draw up plans for the Battle of Algiers. Directed by Commander Raoul Salan and General Jacques Massu, the man in charge of the Tenth Paratroop Regiment, the Battle of Algiers was an all-out assault on the FLN structure in Algiers and lasted throughout most of 1957. Extremely brutal methods put an end to the general strike called by the FLN. By the end of 1957, the French army successfully destroyed many of the extensive FLN networks within the city and had almost entirely disabled the FLN within Algiers.

By mid-1958 the French military numbered about half a million soldiers. Also by 1958, the French military had all but perfected its time-honored system of control called *quadrillage*, which created three separate zones within Algeria: "forbidden," "pacification," and "operational." The forbidden zones were mostly isolated areas from which populations were forcefully relocated in order to ensure a safe zone for French military personnel. The relocation of the rural Muslim populations from these so-called forbidden zones had dramatic consequences. By 1960, 2,157,000 Algerians (about one-fourth of the entire Muslim population) were forced into more than two thousand concentration camps and were held there for the duration of the war.⁹ Within the pacification zones, the French kept a running record of Algerian inhabitants' movements, and all Algerians were required to keep identification papers with them at all times. Finally, within the operational zones, which were more populated areas, the French conducted random and frequent searches. Central to this *quadrillage* technique was the use of *harkis* (Algerian Muslims in the service of the French military).¹⁰ Although effective in military terms, *quadrillage* often fostered pro-nationalist sentiments because it increased resentment among the Muslims for the French troops.

In addition to *quadrillage*, the French military decided to cut off the supply routes for the FLN-ALN coming from the east and west by building an elaborate defensive border along the frontiers of Tunisia and Morocco. The fortified zone along the Moroccan border was nearly ninety miles and was called the *Pedron line*. The *Morice line*, which ran along Tunisian border, was more sophisticated (hence deadly) because in addition to the over two hundred miles of electrified fences and flood lights, French troops were stationed about every mile or so apart along the entire length of the line. The border patrols along these two boundaries effectively isolated Algeria from the support that came easily over the borders at the beginning of the war.

The strangling of supply routes was not the only means at the army's disposal to cut back on so-called rebel activities. The French military began to use torture as a routine method of interrogation. There were literally thousands of cases of torture against Algerian Muslims during the war, but perhaps the most notable cases were those that involved Maurice Audin, Henri Alleg, and Djamila Boupacha. Audin, a young French mathematics professor, was accused of collaborating with the FLN. During his "questioning" in June 1957, Audin was reported to have escaped, but his body was never recovered. News of his "disappearance" sent shock waves throughout the French intellectual community, especially after his case was publicized by Pierre Vidal-Naquet and others in metropolitan France. News of the use of torture by the French authorities was already widely known, but at the end of 1957, when Henri Alleg—a French-man, a friend, and a fellow Communist intellectual of Audin—successfully smuggled out of prison *The Question* (*La Question*), his personal testimony of suffering torture at the hands of the French military, the world took notice. Jean-Paul Sartre quickly denounced the use of torture and wrote a review of the Alleg book, which was immediately republished (outside of France) and included Sartre's review as the book's introduction. Although *The Question* (which Feraoun mentions in his *Journal*) was suppressed in France, the French people finally acknowledged the hideous reality of the continued French presence in Algeria. The full hideousness came into the open with the case of Djamila Boupacha, a young Algerian girl who was arrested by French authorities and who lost her virginity while being raped with a bottle by the French soldiers. The case became a national scandal after Simone de Beauvoir and her lawyer, Gisèle Halimi, published a description of the torture and the maneuverings of the French military judicial system under the title of *Djamila Boupacha* (1962).

Meanwhile, the volcanic eruptions in Algeria finally spewed over into French politics in May 1958 after a conflict between the government in Paris and the military stationed in Algeria. Pierre Pflimlin, the leader of the *Mouvement Républicain Populaire* (MPR), tried to check the military's power by creating a new government in Paris, but his efforts were immediately jeopardized when a group of hard-line French colonists known as the *comité de Vigilance* (Vigilance Committee) tried to take control of Algiers. Eventually, even the military itself became uncomfortable with the French settlers' radicalism, so on May 13, 1958, Generals Jacques Massu and Raoul Salan created the moderate and military-backed *comité de Salut Public* (Committee of Public Safety) in Algiers. In the wake of these events, the National Assembly in Paris was unable to regain control over the situation in Algiers, and the military's loyalty to the Fourth Republic was dubious at best. Robert Lacoste, who had since flown to Paris, did not return to Algiers.

Not surprisingly, the former Governor General and procolonist intellectual Jacques Soustelle watched these events with delight, and after escaping from house arrest, he rejoined the French Ultras and the military in Algiers on May 17. A committed Gaullist, however, Soustelle helped convince General Salan to support de Gaulle's return to power. Charles de Gaulle immediately stepped up and stated he was prepared to assume control of the French government. Such unconstitutionality frightened the majority of the French politicians, but Mouloud Feraoun—perhaps realizing what de Gaulle's ultimate plans were—expressed his satisfaction regarding de Gaulle's leadership. Finally, on May 29, de Gaulle began to create the new Fifth Republic.

Guided by Michel Debré, France worked out a new constitution that was finished in August. De Gaulle formally presented it on September 4, 1958. The new constitution, which expanded the president's powers, passed in a referendum by a large margin on September 28. The Fifth Republic was close to complete, but the parliamentary elections of November 23 and 30 solidified de Gaulle's government, and in December de Gaulle was elected president of the Fifth Republic. De Gaulle entered the Elysée Palace on January 8, 1959; Michel Debré replaced him at the Hôtel Matignon as prime minister. Since the French military (especially Generals Salan and Massu) had helped make de Gaulle's capture of power possible, they expected de Gaulle to keep Algeria French.

However, to keep the Fifth Republic from suffering the same fate as the Fourth Republic, de Gaulle quickly replaced the officers in Algeria whom he suspected were too sympathetic to the French Ultras. Even General Salan was reassigned to the position of the military governor of Paris, and his position in Algeria was handed over to General Maurice Challe. All actions by de Gaulle on the Algerian question began to point to a fundamental reconsideration of France's role in the territory. On September 16, 1959, de Gaulle delivered his famous "self-determination" speech to the French nation. In effect, by openly advocating self-determination, de Gaulle acknowledged that he was considering the possibility of complete independence for Algeria. But de Gaulle had also made it clear that he preferred integration to self-determination for Algerians, and in response, on September 19, the FLN announced in Egypt that it was creating the *Gouvernement Provisoire de la République Algérienne* (GPRA). This new provisional government of Algeria would henceforth be located in Tunis. Ferhat Abbas, a pharmacist from Sétif and the creator of the AML, and Ben Bella were chosen as president and vice-president, respectively.

De Gaulle's fear of his own troops in Algeria proved to be well warranted when the extremist forces in Algiers began to provoke the government. General Massu publicly expressed his dissatisfaction with de Gaulle's policy and was immediately recalled to France. In response, French colonists threw up barricades in Algiers on January 24, 1960, and took control of the city. Once again, Paris was at the mercy of the military in Algeria. Some of the French troops mutinied against the government, but fortunately for de Gaulle, his address to the military on radio and television helped end the barricade revolt.

In June 1960, de Gaulle moved even closer to Algerian independence when he invited the GPRA to meet French representatives in the French city of Melun. Later that month, the FLN restated its demand that it would discuss a cease-fire only after the issue of independence was resolved. The Melun Conference, held June 25–29, 1960, underscored an impending move away from French colonial interests and was the first important step in arriving at the cease-fire eventually secured by the Evian Accords. In 1961, after the Melun Conference and before the Evian Accords in February–March 1962, it was already clear that de Gaulle was preparing to affirm Algerian sovereignty. De Gaulle made this clear when he stated publicly that France was willing to negotiate with the GPRA. However, because de Gaulle demanded a conditional cease-fire before talks could begin, the Melun Conference was quickly abandoned by the FLN-GPRA.

Unfortunately, the suppression of the barricade revolt in Algiers in 1960 did not end de Gaulle's troubles, because his public willingness to negotiate with the rebels only increased the stakes for the French colonists and the extremists within the military. As a result, the army in Algeria once again mutinied in April 1961. Led by a group of four generals—Maurice Challe, Edmond Jouhaud, Raoul Salan, and Marie-André Zeller—this putsch against de Gaulle ended badly for its organizers. De Gaulle was able to thwart this mutiny only by appearing on television in full military uniform and asking that French servicemen not follow orders from their renegade commanders. Although de Gaulle did succeed in staving off the rebellion in April 1961, his opposition took their movement underground.

Generals Jouhaud, Paul Gardy, and Salan—as well as Colonels Joseph Broizart, Yves Godard, Charles Lacheroy, and Antoine Argoud—all went into hiding and were sentenced to death *in absentia*. Many of these men quickly regrouped in mid-May 1961 to form the notorious fascist group, the OAS. The purpose of the OAS was to prevent the removal of France from

Algeria and to aid in the overthrow of de Gaulle's government. The OAS also started its bombing campaigns within France and Algeria. By this time, former Governor General Jacques Soustelle, with a warrant out for his arrest, had gone into hiding and was said to be meeting with his absentee comrades to plot a coup d'état against de Gaulle. To this end, de Gaulle and France realized that the OAS would do anything in its power to destroy Algerian independence and to provoke the demise of what it called the Gaullist dictatorship.

Meanwhile, events concerning Algeria developed quickly. In March 1962, in Evian, Switzerland, the definitive cease-fire was being negotiated. Aware of this, the OAS went on a murderous rampage, killing prominent Algerians in an attempt to disrupt negotiations. On March 15, Mouloud Feraoun and five other educators were machine-gunned by a group of OAS commandos during the last planning session of Centres Sociaux. Despite this heinous crime, on March 18, the Evian Accords were signed, and just three days after Feraoun's execution the cease-fire was declared. Finally, on July 5, 1962, Algeria became fully independent.

## THE JOURNAL AND THE WAR

Watching the war's events unfold in succession, Feraoun often anguished over the intellectual responsibilities that had been forced upon him. Keenly aware of his status as a leading Kabyle intellectual, he felt the constant intrusion of the war into his life. It was something from which he could not escape, even when he went to France to distance himself from the conflict. He writes about his anxiety on December 12, 1955:

The only reason that I flew to Paris was to be with people who had other concerns. But, unfortunately, the very worries that I wanted to escape resurfaced over there, as did the same confusion and the same anxiety. That is what everyone was talking about. My friends began to talk to me about Algeria; my editor demanded that I talk to him about it; and when I got a room at a hotel, the manager wanted to discuss Algeria. When I was obliged to see some compatriots, they were inevitably Algerian. I decided to take two weeks off in order to break loose from my perspective, my friends, my routine, my troubles. The image of my country in full revolt followed me like an obsession. It was a country determined to cry out its pain, its rage,

and its hatred. Although proud to hear its voice, I was terrified that it would not be understood and that the raucous
cries erupting from its throat would seem incoherent to
the very people who were ready and willing to listen. (24)

Haunting him like a ghost, the war troubled yet excited
Feraoun; wisely, he both feared and welcomed the cultural and
political destruction it would leave in its wake. Feeling the burden of speaking for a revolution and about revolutionary methods that he did not wholly approve, Feraoun knew that he was
somewhat out of step with the war. In fact, on the same day
as he wrote about his desire to "break loose from his perspective," he also lamented in the same journal entry how Algerian
nationalists had distorted the revolution and the situation to suit
their own ends. Anticipating the comments of intellectuals such
as Frantz Fanon and responding to criticisms of his contempo-
raries, he writes:

> My characters as well as all of their expectations are sup-
> posedly Western oriented. . . . Yet, it is a fact that my com-
> patriots expect or would have expected my books to have
> more backbone. They expect nationalist works that call
> for nothing short of a divorce, a divorce from a marriage
> in which we are the only partner to foot the bill. They gave
> me reasons why it should be so. But I know some facts
> as well. Unfortunately, these young people have nothing
> to teach me about this area. I am the elder. Moreover, the
> split between Arabs and Kabyles still exists. It is just local
> politics, they tell me.
>
> Besides, the "leaders" are all more or less open to
> criticism and are indeed criticized. All of this leads us to
> wonder who, in the future, might be capable of guiding
> the nationalist party. Who might this virtuous political
> leader be? (24–25)

Unquestionably critical of the revolutionary leaders and not
willing to relinquish his "elder" status to speak about his own
people, Feraoun's vision of the war is, therefore, extremely complex and far more nuanced than other theoreticians such as
Fanon. He questions whether Algeria can find decent future
leaders within the nationalist party because, in part, he realized
that they are beginning to sound more and more like Robespierre and the Jacobins during the Reign of Terror. It is no accident that he frequently returns to the danger of revolutionary
mythology, especially the absurd notion that all remnants of

colonialism, good or bad, could and should be destroyed because they are products of an exploitative system.

There are other aspects of nationalism that Feraoun explored in his notes. For instance, even though he seemed to have supported the rebels' actions during 1955, he realized in 1956 that another authoritarian beast (perhaps as dangerous as French colonialism) was developing. "The rebels' expectations are both excessive and disappointing. They include prohibitions of all kinds, nothing but prohibitions, dictated by the most obtuse fanaticism, the most intransigent racism, and the most authoritarian fist. In a way, this is true terrorism" (53). At this point, in 1956, Feraoun shied away from a complete condemnation of the FLN because he also knew that the French army was to blame and that violence was part of wartime dynamics.

There is no question that Feraoun was the elder and that he did, indeed, have little to learn from revolutionaries, especially from Frantz Fanon, who would become the revolution's principal theorist and the primary mouthpiece of the FLN. However, Fanon, who was neither Algerian nor Muslim but rather a black psychiatrist from Martinique in the French West Indies, believed that the French-Algerian war represented a chance to enact complete (African) revolution. Not surprisingly, Fanon in his *A Dying Colonialism* (*L'An cinq de la révolution algérienne*), published in 1959, acknowledged that the war had brought unprecedented violence to Algeria. And like Feraoun, Fanon declared that this violence was a legitimate reaction against the French army's violence and the settlers' intransigence. However, Fanon and Feraoun held antithetical views on violence. For Feraoun, the question was not whether violence could be used, when need be, as a response to colonial oppression but was a matter of when violence should stop and what the effects of violence were. Here, it is important to keep in mind that Fanon was a theoretician and a revolutionary outsider in the Algerian conflict while Feraoun was living through (and eventually died because of) the war's extraordinary violence.

Fanon thought that the essential task at hand was to determine the degree to which the Algerian nation had been born during the revolution. At every level, Algerian society was being remade. Families, women, traditions, dissemination and production of information, settler politics, medical practices, and even metropolitan France, he argued, were each now being "colonized by Algerian activists." [11] It was Feraoun's fear of a new "colonization" by Algeria's FLN leadership that separated him from Fanon's optimism concerning revolutionary violence. Consider what he writes on March 9, 1956, after the news of a massacre committed against Algerian peasants by rebel troops:

> Can people who kill innocents in cold blood be called liberators? If so, have they considered for a moment that their "violence" will engender more "violence," will legitimize it, and will hasten its terrible manifestation? They know that the people are unarmed, bunched together in their villages, immensely vulnerable. Are they knowingly preparing for the massacre of "their brothers"? Even by admitting that they are bloodthirsty brutes—which in any case does not excuse them but, on the contrary, goes against them, against us, against the ideal that they claim to defend—they have to consider sparing us so as not to provoke repression. Unless liberation means something different for them than it does for us. We thought that they wanted to liberate the country along with its inhabitants. But maybe they feel that this generation of cowards that is proliferating in Algeria must first disappear, and that a truly free Algeria must be repopulated with new men who have not known the yoke of the secular invader. One can logically defend this point of view. Too logically, unfortunately. And, gradually, from suspicions to compromises and from compromises to betrayals, we will all be declared guilty and summarily executed in the end. (84–85)

Again, while Fanon was theorizing violence and adjusting it into a revolutionary framework, Feraoun felt its immediate effects and realized that it was setting Algerian society up for inescapable violence.

In speculating about and celebrating the revolution's effects, Fanon truly believed that the future for postcolonial Algeria would free Algerians, especially the women, from an oppressive familial traditionalism, even Islamic traditionalism.[12] Fanon underscored revolutionary action, not the traditional aspects of Algerian culture, and his analysis displayed general suspicion of traditionalism because it had been so deeply contaminated by colonialism. In this sense, Fanon believed that traditional Algerian society posed a tremendous obstacle to true revolutionary activity. For instance, Fanon argued that Algerian men and women would be freed from the rigid formalism of paternal authority because both men and women had participated in the struggle to liberate Algeria. Algerian women had not been able to fulfill an important political function in traditional Algerian society but were now free to enter the revolution. Hence, despite the protests of anxious and honor-bound fathers, Algerian women now left oppressive paternalistic protection to join the maquis (resistance fighters). Couples, Fanon emphasized, found even more freedom as they moved away from the ever-watchful eyes of their families. Feraoun tended to see these changes in negative terms and frequently criticized the FLN's use of women (even sexual use) in his *Journal*. In other words, where Fanon saw positive structural changes transpiring as a result of the revolution, Feraoun recorded the solemn destruction of his society.

Feraoun and Fanon did both agree, however, that the ideal of the Algerian nation had been so firmly implanted in the Algerians' minds that it had become an essential aspect of Algerian identity. "The Algerian nation is no longer in a future heaven," Fanon wrote. In fairness, Fanon did warn against Pan-African, Pan-Arab, or Pan-Islamic culture, as he did against the development of tribalism and the national bourgeoisie. Yet, what was most important for him were the psychological transformations of nationalism on the Algerian people. As he wrote, "[Algeria] is no longer the product of hazy and phantasy-ridden imaginations. It is at the very center of the Algerian man. *There is a new kind of Algerian man*, a new dimension to his existence." [13]

Hence, unlike Feraoun, who denied that the war would suddenly transform Algerian Muslims, Fanon argued that revolutionary action created a "new man." For Fanon, the genius of revolutionary action rested on its ability to fundamentally and swiftly erase ingrained psychological dimensions of an Algerian identity that had suffered generations of colonial usurpation. The revolution's power resided "henceforth in the radical mutation that the Algerian has undergone." [14]

In 1961, Fanon published his masterpiece, *The Wretched of the Earth (Les Damnés de la Terre)*.[15] Curiously, Feraoun makes no reference to the book, which was widely discussed in Europe and elsewhere. Perhaps he did not feel a need to since he likely thought it was brilliant but dangerous. Without question, Fanon's work and Sartre's preface to it are two of the most negatively influential works on violence written during the war; unfortunately, they have had lasting implications in postcolonial Algeria and throughout the world. Sartre certainly helped

xxix

Fanon's vision along in claiming that the "Third World" found "*itself*" and spoke "*itself* through his voice" (emphasis in original). What most captured Sartre's attention was Fanon's belief that the process of decolonization created a tabula rasa for Algerian (read "revolutionaries' ") identity. As Fanon said, the revolution meant a "veritable creation of new men." Not surprisingly, Fanon also wrote that violence would be a fundamental aspect of the tabula rasa: "At the level of individuals, violence is a cleansing force. It frees the native from his inferiority complex and from his despair and inaction; it makes him fearless and restores his self-respect." [16]

Jean Daniel, a French-Jewish journalist from Algeria, noted that after hearing of Fanon's death, he felt *The Wretched of the Earth* was obviously the work of a man who was "condemned" to death and who cared little about the effects of his theories on the living. "So Fanon was able to work sufficiently in order to leave something that is not himself, which was already not him, a useful presence for others which is not his own." [17] This was not to say that Daniel did not respect Fanon; in fact, he admitted that he did. Regrettably, however, Daniel went on to correctly predict that Fanon would become a "saint" in Algeria.[18]

Daniel found Fanon's text troubling and felt Sartre's preface was even more bothersome. Concerning Sartre's celebration of the violence—the killing of Europeans that was to affirm the Algerians' rights to be men—Daniel responded that it was nothing short of "verbal masturbation!" "What mortal frivolity!" he continued. "If I kill, if I could, I would be denied, I would deny all men. This would include the rebel Aimé Césaire who presents himself thus: 'My name, offended; my first name: humiliated; my state: revolted; my age: stone age.' " [19]

Yet, there was something more important and more troubling in the marriage of Fanon and Sartre. According to Daniel, this Fanon-Sartre "phenomenon" was as important as the phenomenon of Georges Sorel, who "reoriented the reflections of Mussolini and Stalin." If he was correct, he warned, *The Wretched of the Earth* could throw the entire Third World into "convulsions." The outcome of this would be mass killing because "[a]fter having found it necessary to kill the colonist, they will find it indispensable to kill those among them who refused to kill. The redemptive assassin will be worse than the crimes of Stalin." Therefore, despite his respect for Fanon, Daniel wrote that Fanon's work was a "terrible book, terribly revealing, and terribly foretelling of barbaric justice." What Fanon and Sartre had done was to provide terrorists with a motive for killing based solely on the assassin's desire to affirm himself by killing others.[20]

Feraoun's *Journal* was certainly out of fashion among many leftist intellectuals when it was published in Paris in 1962. This was at the height of Marxist revolutionary rhetoric, which desensitized intellectuals to the lasting residues of revolutionary violence. That Feraoun held antithetical views from Fanon (and members of the French left such as Sartre) on the emancipatory and medicinal functions of violence cannot be questioned. But that does not allow one to assume that Feraoun was naive—or, even worse, a colonial sellout—as he reflected on the war, for there is a unique, timeless wisdom in his words. In fact, while he criticized the shift in the attitudes of his French colleagues teaching with him in Algerian schools, he also anticipated the impending rise of fascism coming from the ranks of the French Ultras and the military as well as the dangers inherent in the FLN's authoritarian stance. Unlike Fanon, Feraoun openly wrote about his concern for the FLN's abuses of revolutionary power. For example, on March 11, 1956, he warned that Algerians would grow to despise the nationalists if the nationalists began to act like the French soldiers whose malice was neither shocking nor new. "Do not consider yourselves powerful men or administrators. You have no right to do that. And if you insist on it, we will hate you. When the country begins to fear and detest you, you will no longer amount to anything. You will be nothing more than bandits, just as you are already called, or criminals who deserve to be hanged. And when they execute you, the country will breathe a sigh of relief" (87).

For Feraoun, colonial history was more complicated than simply breaking identity into the two camps of the colonizer and the colonized, and his *Journal* shows that he was a man trapped by the infernal logic of colonial warfare. He admits that he became a hybrid of sorts—part Kabyle, part French, part Muslim. He frequently confesses his pain at being placed in the no-man's land of colonial identity during the war: "When I say that I am French, I give myself a label that each French person refuses me. I speak French, and I got my education in a French school. I have learned as much as the average Frenchman. What am I then, dear God? Is it possible that as long as there are labels, there is not one for me? Which one is mine? Can somebody tell me what I am! Of course, they may want me to pretend that I am wearing a label because they pretend to believe in it. I am very sorry, but this is not enough" (65–66). And, on March 14, 1956, he writes: "The French, the Kabyle, the soldier, and the *fellagha* [rebels] frighten me. I am afraid of myself. The French are inside me, and the Kabyle are inside me. I feel disgust for those who kill, not because they want to kill me, but because they have the backbone to kill. Then, on either side, one legitimizes the crime and justifies it. Thus, crimes are rendered necessary, like acts of faith or worthy deeds" (90). Afraid of the dangers of a revolutionary mythology, which he knows could legitimize any crime by covering it with the veil of respectable ideology, Feraoun also knows that he was being watched with equal vigilance by French authorities (he mentions General Olié) as well as Algerian nationalists. To no surprise, he admits that he could have easily become a victim of either side's extremism because revolutions call into question the behavior of people who, like himself, understand nuances and refuse to see through Manichean lenses.

However, it would be entirely wrong to interpret Feraoun's equivocation on the FLN's tactics as an endorsement of colonialism. Nothing could be further from the truth. He agrees with the basic tenets of Algerian nationalism (independence and equality) and realizes that the Muslims had been backed into a corner by the French, who left them no alternative other than armed resistance. Hence, on December 18, 1955, he notes the effects of systematic brutality, rapes, and murders of Algerians: "From this point on, positions are straightforward and clear in these scores of villages where people feel frustrated and let down: the Frenchman is the enemy and will show no leniency. We have to outfox him and, when the situation presents itself, give him back a dose of his own medicine. It is truly over. There is no room for anything except force" (34). Although reconciliation may have been possible in the past, the French abuses—especially the common use of torture against Algerians (which he mentions throughout the *Journal*)—have brought definitive closure to this idea. However, as Feraoun wrestles with the failure of French-Muslim reconciliation, unlike Fanon, he does not celebrate the end of reconciliation. "A metallic, ice-cold bridge," he writes on June 12, 1956, "has been thrown over a century of Franco-Algerian history. This bridge is similar to the Sirat that leads to the resting place of the chosen; it is as fragile as a rope, as sharp as a sword, and it is being stained little by little with the dark blood of the sinners. A blade on fire stands poised over this century; it is stained with the blood of men: that of the fighters and the victims; it will form a bloody line of retribution across a useless page" (118).

As much as Feraoun distrusts the FLN's growing power, he trusts the French government and the French Ultras even less. In fact, on January 31, 1957, Feraoun writes of a shocking confrontation between the military (a captain and chief of police) and the educators when they were visited in the midst of an FLN education strike. In no uncertain terms, Feraoun and his colleagues were derided by the army captain, forced to listen to grave insults, and threatened that if they did not go back to work they would be arrested and fired from their jobs. This, according to the strident captain, was how the Special Powers were intended to be used, to force the Algerians to once again accept the rule of French colonial force. After this warning, Feraoun states that he would rather play the "game" to the benefit of the rebels but would follow the military's orders for "fear of being shot" by the French (130). In other words, Feraoun rightfully feared that the French had turned fascist in Algeria and would use all means available (torture, execution, rape, and coercion) to subdue any resistance.

In the end, this excessive violence that was used to crush nationalist opposition led Algerians to a dead end. Furthermore, French military and police violence (torture and indiscriminate killing) could be used by the FLN to create hegemony in Algeria. As Feraoun writes: "The brutal executions, the arbitrary ransoms, the arrogance of a brand-new, narrow-minded, and scornful authority will, little by little, look like a yoke that will become more unbearable than the one from which we claim to be breaking free. All this cannot last long and will act against the tyrants' apprentices once we figure out that we are allowing ourselves to be led by men with neither scruples nor education. They are bandits who should go back to jail, not leaders or guides for a people suffering and thirsty for dignity, ready to die in order to gain men's respect" (118–19). Finally, during a visit to his native Tizi-Hibel, Feraoun admits his growing curiosity with regard to the rebel forces and states that he went to discover for himself if they could be respected. Unfortunately, he writes, he found "much

suffering and little enthusiasm, much injustice and little devotion, and cruelty, egoism, ambition, arrogance, and stupidity"
(133).

On July 2, 1957, Feraoun announced his decision to move
from Fort-National in Kabylia to Algiers in order to secure a
safer environment for his family. Terrorism and reprisals had destroyed all remnants of peace in Kabylia. It was in Fort-National
that he heard of the murder of his brother-in-law by the French
military. As the war continued, however, the destruction of the
French-created schools by the Algerian resistance and the FLN's
student strikes against educational institutions wore heavily on
Feraoun. As an educator, he believed that the youth were unnecessarily victimized by Algerian nationalists in being denied educational opportunities. Although he understood that the French
military provoked the FLN to burn down schools by quarter-
ing French troops in school buildings, he saw the destruction of
schools as a tremendous waste of very limited resources. This is
especially true when he records on January 29, 1956, his stupe-
faction at hearing that his own childhood school in Tizi-Hibel
had been burned to the ground. "I am angry at my people. I am
angry at all those who did not know how to prevent this, who
could not prevent it. Shame on all of us forever. Poor kids of
Tizi, your parents are not worthy of you" (64).

Education was one aspect of life under colonialism, according to Feraoun, that should not be jettisoned and that needs
to be protected because it possesses intrinsic merit, regardless
of its colonial origins. In fact, education had a unique value for
him. It was not a negative product of the colonial regime but a
life-affirming example and lasting value that France brought to
Algeria. Education, as Feraoun saw it here, was no longer part
of France's *mission civilisatrice* but was something Algerians had
learned to use and could continue to use for themselves — with or
without the French. Feraoun notes with irony how this change
had left many of his French colleagues stranded. For the first
time, he writes, "they are . . . on their own with their hearts, their
will, their consciences. For once, they must decide for themselves" (35).

Although he maintained no illusions about France's benevolence, to a certain degree Feraoun felt some nostalgia for
the selflessness of individual French educators who had come to
Kabylia during the nineteenth century and early twentieth century to teach the young. These first education pioneers had "no

concern for comfort or material rewards," but they were able to do something unique because they "captured" the Kabyles' "hearts and inscribed themselves into the minds and memories of their students" (36). Unfortunately, he goes on to comment, "times have changed" because now these French educators rush to Algeria in search of a solution to an unsolvable problem. In other words, the once noble dream of helping to educate the Kabyles for education's sake has been tainted by a façade of good will, which is nothing less than the desire to subdue the revolution and quiet the disturbance. Consequently, the wall between indigenous and French educators continued to grow as the two sides realized the stakes. This "rupture that both sides deplore but also endure" brought closure to the profitable era of collaboration since neither side could trust the other (37). As he states sadly later in the text: "The only thing left to do is to harvest this mutual indifference that is the opposite of love" (42).

Moreover, Feraoun also records his growing frustration with his French colleagues as they begin to realize that their traditional, racist privileges in Algeria were losing currency. Importantly, while there is no doubt that he wanted some sort of Algerian independence, the death of colonialism forced him to wrestle with the paradox of his own identity, which led him to feel, in many ways, "more French" than the French. But what does he mean by that, to be "more French" than the French? Feraoun uses the notion of French identity throughout the text in order to express disappointment with France and as an indicator that he still believed in the once cherished but now largely abandoned universal ideals of liberty, equality, and fraternity.

But, although on the one hand he argues that he is "more French" than the French, on the other hand he is equally insistent that French intellectuals and friends such as Albert Camus and Emmanuel Roblès finally understand that Algerians no longer wanted to be French and had a right to reject French rule as illegitimate. After all, Camus's controversial and ambivalent position during the war cost him many friendships and eventually forced him to suffer humiliation at the hands of his many critics, both French and Algerian alike.[21] As Feraoun states, Roblès and Camus

> are wrong to talk to us when we are waiting for generous hearts if there are any; they are wrong to talk to us when they cannot express their thoughts completely. It is a hun-

dred times better that they remain quiet. Because, in the end, this country is indeed called Algeria and its inhabitants are called Algerians. Why sidestep the evidence? Are you Algerians, my friends? You must stand with those who fight. Tell the French that this country does not belong to them, that they took it over by force, and that they intend to remain here by force. Anything else is a lie and in bad faith. (71)

Perhaps the worst sign of this "bad faith" came during the Hungarian crisis when almost all French intellectuals sided with Imre Nagy (the Hungarian prime minister) as he tried unsuccessfully to fend off the Russian advance on Budapest. Although Feraoun acknowledges that the Russians were committing a grave crime, he detects the hypocrisy of French intellectuals (Camus, for example) who were more than willing to defend the Hungarians' right to self-determination but who also supported the French military occupation of Algeria. What makes the Algerian case any different, he asks? "Is it because the world that sees us suffer is not convinced that we are humans? It is true that we are only Muslims. That may be our unforgivable crime. That is a question I would like to discuss with Sartre or Camus or Mauriac" (153).

Feraoun also strongly resented the way in which the French and European presses wrote about the Algerian situation as if it were the sudden, dialectical awakening of a slumbering, exploited people. "To talk, like the press, about an awakening of the Algerian consciousness is frivolous. . . . There were no miraculous phenomena that suddenly opened their eyes, whispered in their ears the magical word *patrie* [fatherland], distending their hearts with militant enthusiasm and captivating crowds behind a flamboyant banner. No, the time for Jeanne d'Arc is over for Algeria because there has already been La Kahena" (43–44).

Perhaps the most egregious example of France's fundamental inhumanity, Feraoun noted, was Lacoste's policy of pacification. Although Feraoun clearly thought that Camus and Roblès (and other French intellectuals) frequently acted in bad faith and that the FLN's call for strikes in schools hurt the Algerian youth, he despised Lacoste's oppression even more and commented that Lacoste's *loi-cadre* had no bearing on reality. He particularly resented the French efforts to keep the Algerian question from coming to the floor of the United Nations.

Importantly, as things continued to take a turn for the worse in Algeria, Feraoun understood by March 1958, earlier than most, that Charles de Gaulle's return to power was nearly inevitable. "People are looking openly to de Gaulle," he writes on March 3, "whose long silhouette outlines the horizon" (240). Feraoun put great faith in de Gaulle and believed that he could resolve the Algerian crisis. Not completely willing to abandon hope for some sort of reconciliation but optimistic enough to think this would come after independence, Feraoun hoped that de Gaulle could bring closure to the war. "De Gaulle is a wise man. That is what I think" (250).

Feraoun, however, did not harbor illusions about the French settlers' willingness to relinquish control of Algeria. He watched de Gaulle with curious admiration as the latter took power in May 1958 and later when the general began to take on the settlers during the barricade episode in January and February 1960. About three months after de Gaulle's troops defeated the organizers of the barricade revolt in the streets of Algiers, Feraoun confessed that the war was sapping his energy. Indeed, one undeniable feature of the war as reflected in his notes is its effects on Feraoun's zest for reflection. As the war drummed on, his entries become leaner, and he is less willing to record his impressions because, in his words, "it was childish to narrate—for myself and in my own style—what the front page of the press from all sides throw at us everyday" (270). Furthermore, although impatient with the slow pace of de Gaulle's policies, he understood very clearly that de Gaulle's self-determination referendum on Algeria in January 1961 was sure to unleash a violent flurry on the part of the French Ultras in Algeria.

Here, there can be no question that the war tore his spirit apart. The violence and the murder of friends and family members by the French military began to destroy his compassion to the point that he became generally indifferent to the misery he witnessed, especially as the French escalated their modernization efforts through education. For example, when he entered the service of the Centres Sociaux, Feraoun even harbored ambivalent feelings concerning his position as an administrator in the Centres. In a letter to Emmanuel Roblès dated April 8, 1961, Feraoun writes:

> The atmosphere of Algiers is depressing. It stinks of lies and hypocrisy from all sides. . . . It is as if a deplorable

xxxvii

epidemic threatens to descend on the people, soon to feed on us and leave nothing. . . . At the Centres Sociaux, I do boring work for which I do not give a damn and that will not interest anyone. It is the most sterile bla-bla-bla, but I also realize that every academy is bla-bla-bla. The only true work is that of the teacher. All the others, who call themselves the patrons, are in reality only parasites who exist because of him [the teacher] and spend their time pressing him like a lemon.

If there were ever a good book to be written, it would certainly be that; to render justice to the teacher.[22]

In a letter to another friend, Paul Flamand, Feraoun deepened these criticisms on August 6, 1961:

Where am I? I have left the school in order to become an inspector in the Service des Centres Sociaux Éducatifs which is an institution for basic education charged with providing a comprehensive assistance that allows the rural masses access to the modern world: literacy for adolescents and adults, men and women, hygienic education, rural development, professional, social, and civic education. In principal, a very grand program, very interesting: the old job as a teacher in the village systematized, codified, officially encouraged, supported. . . . Three times over, alas! It should have been done in '50 and now no one believes in it: neither the administration, nor the educators, nor the users. Maybe we should come back to it when the killing and self-deception have stopped. In itself, it is great, even a *coup*. But all is divided by the incertitude that fogs the street and fills it with the most general agony and the most narrow-minded hatred. No one wants to do good any more. For my part, I simply miss happy times when I had a cow at Taourirt-Moussa, a class of 50 students, and my school notebooks where I recounted the history of "Madame" [from his novel *La Terre et le Sang*].[23]

In another letter on August 15, 1961, Feraoun announced to a friend that he had just changed positions within the Centres, moving to the agriculture section. If he did not find that position satisfactory, he wrote, he would definitively leave the Centres in June 1962, at the end of the academic year.[24]

Although Feraoun certainly harbored doubts about working for the Centres Sociaux, he did not question the integrity of the institutions themselves as the Ultras did. For example, in 1957, a group of educators was accused of conspiring to work on behalf of the FLN, and many of those brought to trial by the French courts were Centres Sociaux employees. Then, on July 11, 1959, the Algerian newspaper *Dépêche quotidienne* reported that the police discovered a metropolitan-based FLN network within the Centres. This new scandal caused more problems for the Centres. By July 27, 1959, the Centres counted nineteen apprehended members. Unlike the scandals of 1957, most of those accused in 1959 were Muslims. Only one European figured among two Centres directors, three adjuncts to the director of the Centres, thirteen monitors, and one monitor-aide who were arrested. Moreover, despite the de Gaulle government's claims that torture by police in Algeria had ceased, a handful of the nineteen arrested claimed to have been tortured. By July 27, 1959, six had been released, six indicted, and seven cases remained undetermined.[25] The principal charge against the members was that they had been aiding the rebels by illegally providing them with pharmaceutical supplies and medical equipment from the Centres.

On July 28, the Ultra paper, *Sud-Ouest,* did its utmost to damage the apolitical reputation of the Centres Sociaux by printing a story titled "The Centres Sociaux of Algiers was infiltrated by the FLN." Since the 1957 arrests, the article claimed, the man responsible for the proper functioning of the Centres Sociaux (Charles Aguesse, the director) had been " 'maneuvered' by people within the FLN." With a dozen of its members convicted, the *Sud-Ouest* story continued, the police have found a "real organization aiding the rebellion. . . . The importance of the Centres Sociaux, their dispersion, their materials, the medication at their disposition, their contacts with the population constitute an important stake for the rebellion. The problem is now to get it under control because its direction lacks surveillance."[26] The accusation was clear: the Centres Sociaux's attitude toward the Algerian rebellion had forced it across the French-Algerian divide into the arms of Algerian nationalism.

Then, in December 1960, during the trial of those who had taken part in the barricades fiasco, the French officers testified that the Centres had initiated subversive activities. The cardinal accusation came from Colonel Gardes during his defense. *L'Echo d'Alger,* on December 13, 1960, reported Gardes's testimony, "We [the army] saw the Service des Centres Sociaux peppered with agents whom we knew perfectly well to be men from the FLN, and among them, important leaders of the FLN." After discovering this, Gardes recounted that the military had the secret police investigate the Centres by placing one of their agents inside the Centres. According to Gardes, the man who was charged with secret intelligence (Colonel Ruyssen) eventually left his position in Algiers because the investigation of the Centres Sociaux, where the "infiltration" of the FLN was "known by all intelligence officers," had not been taken seriously by the French authorities.[27]

As Feraoun reconsidered his personal future and his decision to work for the Centres Sociaux, the key elements of the French military establishment were beginning to cast doubt on the Centres. Moreover, the French Ultras were putting pressure on the military to stop de Gaulle's plans in Algeria. Feraoun could see the tension building and predicted that the French Ultras would increasingly use violence to keep the Algerian nationalists from claiming victory. He noted that the failure of the generals' putsch in April 1961 would only further intensify indiscriminate French violence against Muslims, and yet, ironically, his first impression of the actions of the OAS (his eventual assassins) on July 20 was that they were "amusing, a bit stupid" (290). After the creation of the OAS, he saw how the rest of the war would be played out in Algeria as the potential cease-fire was being negotiated: absolute terror would reign. As a result, people would become too comfortable with death and destruction. Hence, he warns on September 26, 1961, that "[t]his is no longer hysteria but an endless and desperate scream that stirs even the most callous among men" (305–6). On December 30, 1961, he commented on the OAS decision to turn its murderous rage against all those who oppose its policies, Muslims and French alike: "No, the OAS feels that the Europeans must form a block and fight to the death against us, if we do not agree to live under their law. This is true fascism" (307).

Feraoun was correct about the OAS becoming a fascist organization and understood that, should de Gaulle be assassinated by the OAS (which it was trying to do), the "stage is ripe for a dictator" (309). Four days later Feraoun makes a rather powerful observation, albeit sardonically, that the French in Algeria had always practiced fascism. "In Algeria, more than a century ago," he writes, "another practice was adopted; a minority, blessed by God, holds all the power in its hands and uses it impudently to its own advantage. For generations, people here have been unable to distinguish between democracy and fascism. But their fascism was applicable only to us, and we, the Muslims, ended up mistaking it for their democracy. This is why our fine scholars and theologians have always claimed that nothing in the world is more liberal than the Qur'an and Islam. In fact, Qur'anic doctrine is more progressive than that of Salazar and Franco. End of discussion" (310).

The remainder of the *Journal,* the last two months of Feraoun's life, is a catalog of killing at a rate of "eight miles per hour" (January 20, 1962). With the OAS certain that France was going to abandon Algeria, it would stop at nothing to prevent the easy transfer of power. Its reign of terror in Algiers climaxed on March 15, with the assassination of the six officials from the Centres Sociaux. Aware that violence was the only way to destroy the peace process, the OAS's commando squads instituted a policy of absolute terrorism against Muslims. According to one OAS member: "We began by hitting low-level Moslem employees—those who most likely belonged to the FLN. . . . Orders were given to hit all Moslems standing at bus stops who were wearing ties. We killed them [*on les flinguait*]. The next day we would go after Moslem pharmaceutical employees. . . . The lads were very efficient [*très opérationnels*]. . . . [the objective was to] empty the European quarters of Moslems."[28] With these murderous policies underway, the OAS had specific reasons for targeting the Centres Sociaux. It was truly the last remaining institution capable of providing a bridge between the two communities, which had been ripped apart by one hundred and thirty years of colonization and eight years of warfare, leaving about eleven thousand soldiers dead on the French side and a million dead (so the FLN claimed) on the Algerian side.[29]

On 15 March, at El Biar, a suburb just outside Algiers, a meeting of the administration of the Centres Sociaux was underway. At 10:45 A.M., OAS commando squads, Delta 5, led by Gabriel Anglade, and Delta 9, led by Joseph Rizza, burst into the conference room brandishing machine guns and locked the door. The leader of the commandos, machine gun in hand, announced that Marchand, Basset, Aimard, Hommoutene, Feraoun, Ould Aoudia, and Petitbon were to follow him outside.[30]

Leaving behind the other members of the Centres, the OAS commandos ushered the six men present outside into the hot sun of the Chateau-Royal's courtyard. Within seconds, as some

xli

of the victims' children watched, the six were forced against the wall, and the commando squads opened fire. Three were French; three were Algerians: Marcel Aimard (French), an inspector and chief of the Bureau of Studies; Marcel Basset (French), an inspector and chief of personnel training, Max Marchand (French), inspector of the academy and director of the Centres Sociaux Éducatifs; Ali Hamoutène (Algerian), inspector for Algiers; Salah Ould Aoudia (Algerian), inspector for Algiers; Mouloud Feraoun (Algerian), adjunct to the director. With this execution by the OAS, both the leadership and the Centres Sociaux Éducatifs' project of Franco-Muslim solidarity simultaneously died.

The reaction to the murders of the six men was outrage and disbelief. All commentators interpreted it as an attempt to destroy the possibility of reconciliation between the two populations. On March 15, 1962, *Le Figaro* published an article by Jean-Marie Garraud entitled "The Shame. . . ," which compared the assassination of the six men by the OAS to "Hitler's executioners" and to the "throat-slitting [FLN] rebels." [31] Garraud, however, did not miss the opportunity to restate that it had been the FLN terrorists who first provoked these types of violent crimes, and it was now up to the French community in Algeria, unlike the ignoble Algerians, to distance itself from criminals of this sort. François Mauriac, in his "bloc-notes" of that week, wrote: "El Biar. What to write and for whom to write? What commentaries merit the crimes of El Biar?" Importantly, Mauriac, who had long fought for a reconciliation between Christians and Muslims, hoped that France would be able to recover from this disgrace and that the Algerian Muslims would recognize the true face of France: "There is no another choice for you [the French] between subversion—the true face of which is shown in the crimes of El Biar—and the admirable work of the victims who have been murdered by Salan's men: the reconciliation of the two races depends on mutual acceptance. . . . That August and serene France will endure in order to become that which Islam loves, despite what the other France can accomplish." [32] Like Mauriac, Albert Memmi—the well-known Tunisian writer—deplored the violent attack against the six partisans of peace. According to Memmi, the murder was intended to be symbolic, especially the murder of Feraoun. Aside from being one of Algeria's greatest literary talents, "[h]e was also a teacher," Memmi wrote, "a teacher and then a director of a

xlii

school: he very sincerely believed in the mediation of the French language, in a cultural rapprochement, and [he] is now dead in the exercise of his functions." So why was it necessary to kill him, Memmi asked, if Feraoun was not an extremist? "Men like Feraoun, old-fashioned during crises, become indispensable, irreplaceable afterward when it is necessary to reconstruct. His assassins, did they not want to express their desire to forbid the possibility of a common future between the two populations?"[33]

In *Le Monde* on March 17, two more outspoken critics of the war, Jules Roy and Jean Amrouche, wrote commentaries on the assassination. Amrouche, the Algerian intellectual whom Feraoun had once harshly criticized for being more French than Algerian, cited the courage to fight for a new Algeria as the provocation for the murder. "The French and Algerians," Amrouche wrote, "who worked together in the same project of light and human friendship have died together under the blows of the same fascist enemy."[34] Roy said of Feraoun: "We loved each other. . . . Just words? Certainly not. He had members of his family massacred by the French, just as mine were massacred by the FLN. But neither he nor I could cede to the blind desire for revenge. We knew that after that long and tragic misunderstanding that a fraternity could be reborn, because despite it all, we stayed brothers. It is the best part of France that has been assassinated with him. . . . The last victory of Mouloud Feraoun would be to help us in not despairing."[35]

Perhaps the most moving eulogy for those assassinated came from the original creator of the Centres Sociaux herself, Germaine Tillion, when she published her indictment of the OAS entitled "The Stupidity That Coldly Assassinates" in *Le Monde*.[36] Tillion focused on her friendship with Feraoun and praised him as a man who was "full of life." "This honest man, this good man, this man who never did wrong to anyone, and who devoted his life to the public good, and who was one of the greatest writers in Algeria, has been assassinated. . . . Not by accident, not by mistake, but called by his name and killed with preference. And this man who believed in humanity, moaned and agonized four hours,[37] —not by the fault of a microbe, of car breaks that did not work, or of a thousand accidents that are on the lookout for our lives, but because it [his assassination] entered into the imbecilic calculations of murdering monkeys who make the law in Algeria." Feraoun and the others, Tillion continued, despite their diverse backgrounds and religions, were united by the noble and common goal of fighting for the "protection of children" in Algeria. According to Tillion, this was their sole crime in the eyes of the OAS.[38]

On March 18, the very day that France and Algeria signed a peace agreement, the rector of the University of Algiers, Meyer, the delegate general, Morin, the minister of public works, Guillaumat, and the minister of national education, Paye, all attended the funeral services at the cemetery of El-Alia, a town on the outskirts of Algiers. Paye, in paying homage to the six men assassinated, expressed the shame of the French people that their name would be associated with the murder of the six innocent men: "That such a crime can have been inspired, decided, and committed by men who claim to be part of France seemed not so long ago impossible."[39]

Yet, despite the public honor rendered to the victims of the "imbecilic" killing, the time had not come for reconciliation between the two communities. The French of Algeria faced a questionable future. While schools were temporarily suspended and while people were observing silence out of respect for those assassinated by the OAS, the General Association of the Students of Algeria, a rightist student organization, issued a communiqué in Algiers on March 21. The association took it upon itself to denounce the "odious exploitation of the death of the six members of the Centres Sociaux." They reminded their audience that "several dozen students and teachers have fallen under the blows of the FLN without the Minister of National Education or the rector of the University of Algiers having dreamed to denounce the guilty or to associate the University with the mourning which strikes the families of the victims."

By the time the more than one million French and non-French men, women, and children fled Algeria after the Evian accords, all realistic hopes of a lasting Franco-Muslim solidarity had been abandoned. In France and Algeria, the roaming OAS squads continued to seek out victims, and it was not until 1963 that most of its leaders were captured. When 90 percent of the European population left Algeria immediately following the war, they feverishly destroyed Algeria's hospitals, schools, agricultural resources, communication networks, and existing administrative fabrics. In short, if they could no longer enjoy their former lifestyle, they would ensure that the newly constituted Algerian nation also could not. For the next several years, first under the leadership of Ahmed Ben Bella and then Houari Bou-

medienne, Algeria faced the task of reconstructing its histori-
cally distorted economy and identity, but it was not long before
the dictatorial techniques of the FLN that Feraoun had warned
against repeatedly in his journals began to mar the Algerian political process.

Feraoun's account of the war and its outcomes presented
in his *Journal* has perhaps never been more relevant than today.
Having been eclipsed by the deeply flawed but no less persua-
sive analysis of the war written by Frantz Fanon, Feraoun's testament—now in English—should help restore balance to the
study of postcolonial Algeria and also postcolonial studies in
general. That Fanon profoundly misread the Algerian conflict
and how history would proceed following independence can
hardly be questioned today. But what is indeed troubling is that
few (if any) of the contemporary theorists and historians who
have fastened themselves to a Fanonian interpretation of identity and violence have really gone back to consider alternative
explanations of identity and violence written by Algerian intellectuals. This is where Feraoun's *Journal* fits into today's discussion. Because he was alive and writing throughout the war, his
insights into the apocalyptic violence of decolonization are far
more revealing than theories written about the conflict out of
harm's way, especially the observations written by Fanon in *The
Wretched of the Earth* and celebrated by Sartre in his preface to
that book. Both Sartre and Fanon, as non-Algerians and non-
Muslims living outside the actual conflict itself, had few of the
day-to-day insights into violence that Feraoun's observations af-
ford. In fact, I would argue that they knew little about the events
they described and that they saw in the Algerian revolution a
chance to achieve their revolutionary utopia and the opportunity to sculpt their "new man" through complete and unmitigated violence.

The FLN realized also that its hegemony could be wielded
during and after the war into a political platform. It is little
wonder that as the FLN labored to regenerate society, the quest
for the so-called authenticity of the "new man" has often gone
astray and has been riddled with violence. But this cannot be
blamed uniquely on Algerians. Unquestionably, the initial revolutionary violence of the French-Algerian war was borne of the
history of Franco-Algerian relations dating from the conquest
of Algeria in 1830, relations that Feraoun has rightfully diag-
nosed as racist and reprehensible. Nevertheless, Feraoun was

xlv

right to worry about the FLN's increasing authoritarianism and to say that it could not be excused by writing it off as a product of French colonialism. Here it would be wise to remember the question he posed in his *Journal* on August 30, 1957, concerning the Mélouza massacre: "Gentlemen of the FLN, gentlemen of the Fourth Republic, do you think that a drop of your blood is really worth anything more than a drop of anyone else's blood — blood that, because of you, is being shed on the scorched soil of Algeria?" (223).

As the war moved from a war between the French military and Algerian resistance in general to a quadrangulated war among the FLN, the MNA, the French military, and the OAS, Feraoun — though still an undeniable humanist — began to despair regarding the possibility of a future without violence. By September 1961, according to Feraoun, this possibility had all but been destroyed by the successive histories of terrorism and revenge of the OAS and the FLN. "Even if France is successful in removing itself and its soldiers, the game is underway between the indigenous people and the Europeans, and it will terminate to the advantage of one or the other of the protagonists. It is therefore time for France to decide to use all of its might to defeat one or the other of the adversaries. Because these adversaries, in the end, are devouring each other little by little and, in the first place, are coldly putting to death innocent people. Pity the innocents! Except remember, there are no innocents" (304).

There were acts of violence that destroyed Algerian society on a daily basis. The assassination of Mayor Frappoli, the murder of "Rabbit" in February 1956, the killing of all the village dogs in March 1956, the treatment of women by the resistance and the rape of the Kabyle women by the French military (1959), the murder of Feraoun's brother-in-law and other relatives by the French military, all destroyed Algeria little by little. All of these small acts of violence compounded the universal misfortune of a nation. These were neither the means for constructing a new identity, nor a license for unmitigated revenge. Furthermore, alongside the French criminal activities, there were also unexpected humane acts such as the SAS captain's decision to notify Feraoun from Béni-Douala that Feraoun's father had died. As insignificant as this might appear, it touched Feraoun deeply and evoked from him a certain sense of bitter sympathy for a French officer whom he considered a criminal. All of these unique experiences were recorded by Feraoun and combine to give readers an incredibly personal but no less profound account of the war.

The message of the *Journal* is clear: war is hell, even justified wars of liberation with all of their psychological, political, military, and racist repercussions. But it also has another, more powerful message: those who live by the dialectic of violence shall feel its blows sooner or later. And so we are able to use the *Journal* to compare the utopian revolutionary violence to the everyday, lived, ethical anxieties of a nation in the process of forming. Above all, the *Journal* sends us a clear warning against the type of "recolonization" that would occur within a Hegelian dialectical philosophy, which Fanon openly advocated. This philosophy places undue authority in the state (the FLN), which has always seen itself after independence as the concrete embodiment of all claims of national authenticity. By the end of the *Journal*, there is no doubt that the French military and the Algerian *maquis* have each engaged in a war that will have lasting psychological, moral, and political repercussions on both nations. This is not to suggest that Feraoun condemned both sides in the conflict equally. In fact, his condemnation of France is unequivocal, and he left no room to doubt that France with its "civilizing mission" was morally bankrupt. According to Feraoun, France's more than one hundred and thirty years of racist domination of the Arabs and the Muslims in Algeria were the cause of the French-Algerian war. It forced the Algerian *maquis* to fight with any means they could against the French.

Ironically, the odds are today that Feraoun would encounter a similar threat to his safety—from the old guard of the FLN, the current Algerian military-backed government, or the Islamists—had he survived the massacre at El Biar on March 15, 1962. There is also no doubt that he would have protested against the Algerian government's crackdown on the Kabyle protesters in 1980, which killed hundreds as they rallied behind efforts to have the Algerian government recognize their language and culture. Nor can there be any doubt that he would be protesting against the government's brutal methods of fighting the Islamic fundamentalists—the same methods of terror and random execution used by the French against Algerian nationalists—and against the Islamic fundamentalists' hideous acts of terrorism. This speculation aside, Feraoun's *Journal* offers an alternative perspective to current views of colonialism and post-

xlvii

colonialism. His voice is that of a realist, an insider and teacher, one whose identity was made more complex as the war progressed. In effect, Feraoun represents the best of two irreconcilable worlds, and his writing is a testament of what could have been, had not the inhumanity of war and the arrogance of two peoples violated all that was good and possible. It is time, finally, that the voice of this ambassador of peace echoes loudly in the workshop of humanity.

## Preface to the Original French Edition

During the morning of March 15, 1962, in El Biar, on the hills above Algiers, Mouloud Feraoun was taking part in a work session in his function as inspector of Centres Sociaux. He was inside one of the barracks of an estate where the director's office of this division was located. Soon after 11:00 A.M., armed men rushed inside the room and ordered those present to go stand along the walls with their arms up. Once everyone had been checked, they called seven names. One of the people they had selected was not there. Feraoun was among the six others. The leader of the group of assassins assured them quite casually that no harm would come to them, that all that was required was to record a statement on a tape recorder. People thought that it was a "pirate broadcast" of the OAS.

The six victims were led outside, single file, to the corner of two buildings where other armed men were waiting for them. They took their ID cards from them. Then the massacre started. Feraoun was the last one to fall, his chest crushed by a burst of machine gun fire. His body fell over that of his friend, Ould Aoudia.

It was 11:15 A.M. In a nearby field, an old woman and some children were witnesses to the killing.

It is very difficult for me to speak of him now that he is no longer with us. In any case, what portrait of him could be better than the one that emerges from these pages? Yes, here he is as he was, patient, generous, stubborn, imbued with all the virtues of the people of the Kabylia Mountains, filled with honor and justice. Here he is with his human kindness, his confidence in people as well as the anger and the heartbreak that he used to express to me during our meetings or in his letters, and that so specifically answered mine!

He was a wonderful storyteller; we could spend entire nights listening to him. When the insurrection began, he brought us so many facts, so many anecdotes, that I strongly urged him to write them down. Indeed, it seemed to me regrettable that such a wealth of information might be lost. I ended up convincing Feraoun to do so, and he undertook this task primarily with the aim of later using these memories in an elaborate text.

He had to leave Fort-National where he was teaching after some bad business with a civil servant who was known for his cruelty. He agreed to become the principal of a school in the suburbs of Algiers, at the Clos Salembier, because it brought us closer together. I lived in a nearby neighborhood.

Despite the friendship we extended to him, he missed Kabylia. He did not like Algiers, where he felt literally uprooted. It was during this time that, in order to calm his nostalgia some-what, he wrote an essay on Si-Mohand, whose poems he also translated.

To be safe, he would write his "journal" inside student notebooks that he mixed with those of his own students. He was well aware of the naïveté of this strategy. Like all the other lib-erals who, at that time, lived under the threat of house searches, he had a lot of reasons to be careful. From time to time he entrusted me with some of the notebooks he felt were more compromising. I would hide them in my garden with my own documents. At that time, I was a militant in the Espoir-Algérie committee and was under scrutiny. Then the first letters con-taining threats started reaching Feraoun and all of us. Far from being intimidated by them, those anonymous letters seemed to strengthen his convictions, his hope for an Algeria where there would be no winners and no losers, but only men freed "from a century-old injustice." Yet his convictions increased his anguish. They were the very sign of the insanity that was to kill him on the threshold of a spring of death. In any case, these threats forced him to act and bear witness. He was seen in Algiers on the plat-form at a demonstration organized by liberals. In Paris, we read lucid and well-thought-out texts that he had written. He had al-ready defined his position toward the insurrection in an open letter dated and sent to the Ligue de l'Enseignement on Febru-ary 22, 1956. Here are a few excerpts from it: "For Kabylia, I feel the tenderness a son feels, and it is this tenderness that I have tried to express in my books. The image I have given of Kabylia is sympathetic not deceitful. What can I write about now, when anguish is knotting my throat? Will I speak about its suffering or about its revolt? (. . .) All that matters is understanding why there is such unanimity in favor of the rebellion and why the divorce is so definitive and brutal. The truth is that there never had been a marriage! No, the French have remained aloof. Scornfully aloof. The French lived apart from us. They have always believed that they were Algeria. (. . .) What should we have done to get along

1

with each other? First of all, get to know one another. We have been coexisting for a century without the slightest curiosity. The only thing that is left to do is to harvest this mutual indifference which is the opposite of love. (. . .) By accountability, we mean recognizing our right to live, our right to learn, to make progress, and our right to be free."

This will to act and to bear witness also gave him the idea to publish his *Journal*. But people at the Seuil publishing house were hesitant, fearing that such a publication, at a time when passions were exacerbated more than ever, would bring retaliation against the author. I shared this fear, and Feraoun wrote me a letter to push for publication: "If this Journal is not published now, people will accuse me later of cowardice. If that were to happen, it would be better if it was never published."

When he sent me this letter, death was already standing very close to him, ever watchful, like in those oriental tales where death is waiting for some mysterious signal. He had such a strong premonition that, on March 14, before finishing the evening with his son Ali, he led his wife to the end of their garden and gave her his most pressing recommendations in case something bad should happen to him.

He is buried in Tizi-Hibel, the village of his birth, inside the small cemetery that I know well and that he described himself, across from the room in which the Soeurs Blanches gather to do their work, "where the paved road ends. . . . And his tomb will become one with all the others because it will not bear any special inscription. When early spring comes, it will be covered with graminae and white daisies."[1]

EMMANUEL ROBLÈS

# JOURNAL
1955–1962

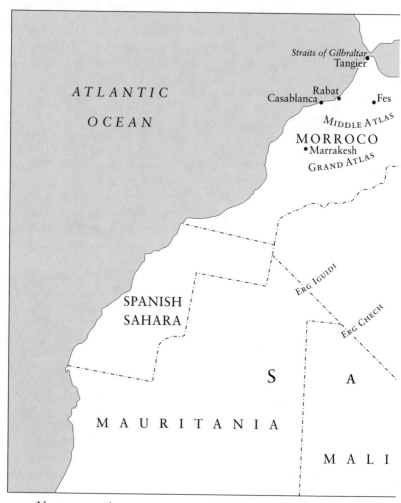

ATLANTIC

OCEAN

*Straits of Gilbraltar*
Tangier

Rabat
Casablanca • Fes

MIDDLE ATLAS

MORROCO
• Marrakesh
GRAND ATLAS

ERG IGUIDI

ERG CHECH

SPANISH
SAHARA

S          A

MAURITANIA

MALI

NORTHWEST AFRICA

2

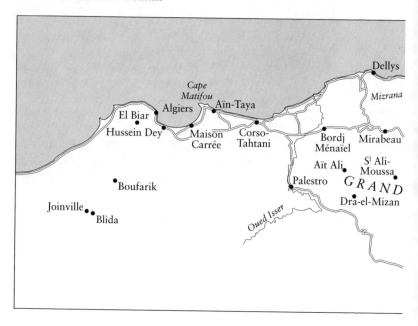

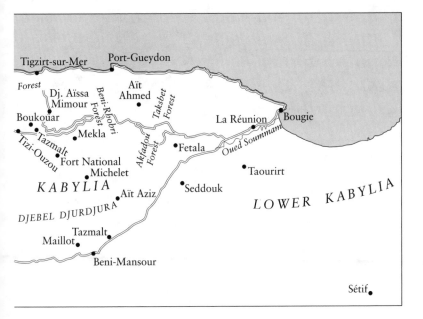

Tizi-Ouzou

Aït Mannsour

Irhil Bouzerou
Aguamoun

*Tamedjout Forest*

Irhil-bou Rioul

Aït Ouanech

S^t Mannsour

Beni-Douala

Taguemount-Azouz

Aït Ahmed

Tizi-Ameur

S^l Ali Moussa

Ouadhja

Pirette

Boghni

Mechtras

Dra-el-Mizan

GREATER KABYLIA REGION

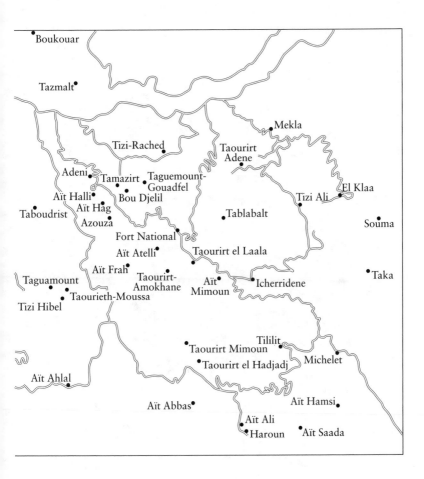

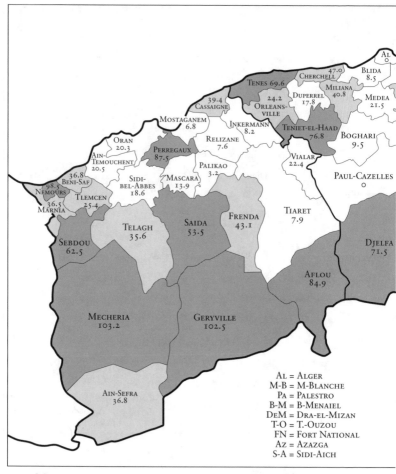

MUSLIM AREAS TARGETED FOR RELOCATION BY FRENCH
AUTHORITIES DURING THE FRENCH-ALGERIAN WAR

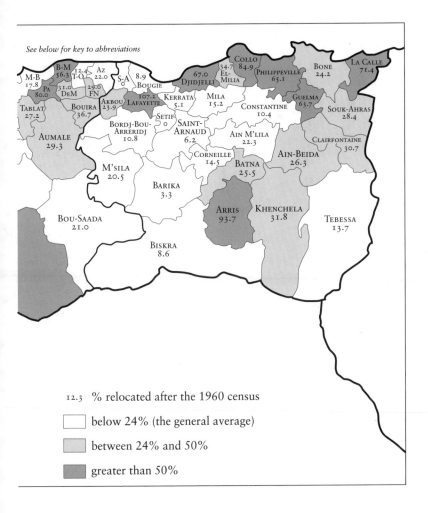

See below for key to abbreviations

M-B
17.8
B-M
56.3
PA
80.0
T-O
31.0
DeM
12.4
AZ
22.0
FN
29.0
S-A
8.9
BOUGIE
TABLAT
27.2
BOUIRA
36.7
AKBOU
23.9
LAFAYETTE
107.2
KERRATA
5.1
MILA
15.2
DJIDJELLI
67.0
EL-MILIA
34.7
COLLO
84.9
PHILIPPEVILLE
65.1
BONE
24.2
LA CALLE
71.4
CONSTANTINE
10.4
GUELMA
63.7
SOUK-AHRAS
28.4
AUMALE
29.3
BORDJ-BOU-ARRERIDJ
10.8
SETIF
SAINT-ARNAUD
6.2
AIN M'LILA
22.3
CORNEILLE
14.5
BATNA
25.5
AIN-BEIDA
26.3
CLAIRFONTAINE
30.7
M'SILA
20.5
BARIKA
3.3
BOU-SAADA
21.0
ARRIS
93.7
KHENCHELA
31.8
TEBESSA
13.7
BISKRA
8.6

12.3   % relocated after the 1960 census

☐  below 24% (the general average)

☐  between 24% and 50%

■  greater than 50%

9

# 19**55**

1    **November 1, 1955,** 6:30 P.M.

"It is raining on the city." The streetlights have been on for two hours, lighting up the closed shutters and doors of silent façades. The city is still and secluded, cunning, hostile, and frightened . . .

This was a calm day, a sad autumn day. Until 4:00, it had not rained; let us say that it was nice. A sun pale with autumn, a sky smutty with melancholic days. The stubborn peal of the All Saints' Day bells cannot wake the village. Although the bells ring for the dead, neither they nor the living can hear them. Hushed and hurried like conspirators, the faithful slip into the church through a half-opened door. Other conspirators who pass by and hastily exchange a weary and meaningless greeting do not see them. The Muslims, like the Christians, have nothing to say to one another. The "Kabyles," like the "French," are not thinking about anything. This morning, it seems that everyone has lost the desire to speak, joke, laugh, drink, come or go. It is as if each person feels trapped and sealed in an airtight bell jar. Vision is still possible, but any attempt at communication, even on the most ordinary and superficial level, is futile. No, really, they have nothing to say to each other today, the 1st of November. This is a sad day—the dead are indifferent, the living anxious, the French are not willing to understand, and the Kabyles refuse to explain.

It is a day off for the civil servant who will spend the morning in bed. At 8:00 he sleeps peacefully. Today there are no humming motors, prattling children, shouting dealers, passersby discussing just beneath his window. Silence! The street above is just as deserted as the street below. The main street, the village's one and only street, is also empty. Yet, there are shadows moving about, slow or rapid, shadows that move aside at each turn so as not to disturb the deep sense of peace. Day of the dead, day of mourning, day of the living who—like the dead—are silent, their faces beyond reach, like impenetrable graves.

**November 3**

A trip to Algiers, yesterday. They received me with kindness.

—It is really serious over there? Look, be careful, extremely careful.

—Why, what happened at home?

—Don't you read the papers or listen to the radio?

Of course, there are times when I do not read the papers or listen to the radio. They are saying that on the night of the 31st, Fort-National was attacked twice. They discovered weapons and a body in the field. His soul is with God. This corpse must have vaporized since no one saw it. What did I see when I left at 11:00? People on edge and hesitant about talking to one another. Stores, boutiques, and cafés, all closed. Everything shut down, barricaded, locked up. Mr. L. opened one side of his front door: three or four clients look at each other while young clerks go from one end of the store to the other, pretending to be busy and at the call of a numerous clientele.

—That is why, he explained to me, I wanted to close. At first, I did close. But from my post, the counter, I saw the clients coming, and I had them reopen the store. You must understand, I was keeping an eye out.

I understood that he feared an attack. He had sent for two laid-back policemen with the delusional plan that they would protect him. He showed me some official telegrams, which refer to putting the ringleaders of the general strike under house arrest. But, my God, where are the agitators? Everybody follows the lead and is capable of going wherever one chooses to lead them.

I went back to my place, tired and bored. There was nothing for me to do; nothing held my interest. When I took a nap that afternoon I was reconnected in my dreams to that sense of community that we experienced last Tuesday night.

Yesterday, just as I started out for Algiers, Fort-National was swarming with life. Like a hive, it took in the Kabyles of the region, selling them fabrics, vegetables, spices, and kabob meat. After reading the newspaper, the citizens were able to think of themselves in slightly heroic terms: the Kabyles because they had threatened and scared off the French, the French for having driven back the shadow of the enemy, and the soldiers who carried out the noble mission entrusted to them. The only exception is the humble sentry who spread the alarm and refuses to be decorated for the resounding errors in the headlines. This is how the press honors us.

## November 6

However, there is one matter: the atmosphere is no longer what it was. You can feel and see this change, which is brutal only in appearance. This is how that appearance translates: a year ago, when the revolt erupted, we did not want to gauge its importance. Indeed, it really was not important. We were settled into a truly orderly and peaceful existence, a tolerable life structured by small necessities, needs, and daily tasks. We took care of illnesses, surmounted difficulties, and held reasonable expectations. We experienced bad manners without scandals, disputes without aftermath, and friendships without roots. We deserved this peaceful time. It was necessary—that each of us feel useful both to ourselves and to others and worthy of living. It was inconceivable that this quiet life might be threatened from one day to the next. We thought it unjust that this respect for life be questioned.

## November 9

So we were at ease, poking a little fun at the fellagha.[1] "Woman, make some bread," as Rostram would say. It seems that right at the start, the administrator of the school called his assistants together one night, to tell them in his hollow voice: "Gentlemen, France is in danger: The Arabs have rebelled!" He did not believe what he was saying.

While showering his older students with kindness, the school inspector would sometimes tell me things on the sly:
—And to think that the one who might slit my throat is among them!

This kind of prospect always left me speechless.

Quite often, I have been obliged to discuss "incidents" with French people who were worried about the future of Algeria and, in particular, about their own future. But neither the other party nor I have experienced these incidents firsthand. We were quite far from Aurès.[2] From time to time, the telephone poles were cut, but nothing else happened. We used to call it sabotage—simple kids' pranks that miffed the postmaster.

—These people are the first to suffer the consequences, Mr. F., he told me. This morning someone came by to telephone a boy who lost his mother. The kid is in Algiers. They buried his mother before he could see her. It is stupid, sir, isn't it? There are certain things that bother the poor lads, things that people should not do.

How could I not agree?

All those who choose to discuss such incidents recognize that there is a lot to be done in this country, that mistakes have been made, and that, after all, the guerrillas are right to want to teach a lesson to the profiteers, to the people who are happy and in good situations. For they are happy because the masses are miserable—so miserable, I swear, that it is shockingly evident that they have suffered enough. The only problem is that I exchange my ideas with people who never, for one second, think that they could possibly be these profiteers, these fortunate, affluent people. It is probably because each one in his own little world persists in thinking that he is disadvantaged. He believes that by rights, society still owes him for everything that he does not have and that if he is not rebelling, he is, in fact a revolutionary in spirit and heart.

### November 10

As the days and weeks went by one after the other, everything appeared to be normal. Life at school continued at a slow pace. The older, *cours complémentaire* students seemed to act more freely: they had grown up and become daring.[3] They had to work hard for the exam. They did reasonably well, but just the same, I realized that they were more interested in what was happening outside school. I felt that they would no longer accept my habitual noninvolvement; they wanted to see me take a position, show some kind of commitment to an ideal that had to be mine. I will be careful not to disappoint them too much. That is all. That is it.

Outside of school, life in the city is nothing special: the usual raveling and unraveling of local intrigues, spreading of anecdotes, whispers of minor scandals and small deals wrapped up. There are the customary, and rather more than customary, official visits to Fort-National—the minister of the interior accompanied by the governor, then the new governor, and, finally, the new minister of the interior.

### November 12

The newspapers and radio put out periodic accounts of isolated attacks: the killings of some village policemen considered to be spies, a forest ranger, a Moorish café owner.[4] This

14

usually occurred in neighboring regions so it did not really disturb us. All the same, people would say:

— Well, the fellagha follow through with their ideas. These people know what they want.

The end of the school year was in sight—first the primary certificate and the other exams afterward. Everything was normal. But on the last day, we should have taken certain precautions before leaving Taourit-Moussa.[5] We had a frank discussion about the danger we were risking in returning separately. But in the end, everything went well.

For the past few days there had been talk of an armored division that was to leave France and occupy Kabylia: ten thousand men. On my way to Algiers on June 16th, I encountered hundreds of vehicles carrying soldiers all along the 75-mile route from Oued Aïssi to Hussein Dey. This impressive parade of green soldiers and equipment brought to mind the 1942 disembarkation, an event that left me quite indifferent. But that day on the road, I had to admit that we were in for new times.

In Algiers, the strikes against tobacco and alcohol had begun.[6] I not only had to hide to smoke but also had to steer clear of the cafés. The indigenous Algerians are very disciplined. During a chat, a journalist mentioned that some young men were assaulting smokers. He wanted to know my opinion. But even after our discussion, he will still be in the dark about my thoughts. What do I think of all this? Nothing. Our French colleagues are all worried about a situation that promises to become extremely complicated. I am at the point of wondering: "Is this good or bad?" What concerns me is the end result. Will we gain anything from all of this? If so, then yes it is, at whatever cost. Too bad for individual cases like my own.

### November 13

At Fort-National the French have been disgruntled since June 20th. This is because the Kabyles have quit frequenting cafés and getting drunk in public. The age-old order of things is in immediate danger of collapse. With Wednesday's profits about to disappear, those employers who had built their futures on the unsteady shoulders of disloyal Kablyes beheld the approaching specter of bankruptcy. Mayor Frapolli was summoned to intervene at the same time as the Kabyle advisers. The former is putting forth explanations to console the wine merchants. Although jubilant inside, he makes sure to be seen in the cafés with one or another of his advisers from the technical school. Every time that I go to have a drink, people greet me with a sign of relief and shake both my hands. A certain French school principal from France has started inviting us over out of pure patriotism. We do take advantage of this unexpected stroke of luck. The townspeople only smoke and drink in the evening after the visitors have left. In short, we are living in a climate of suspicion without knowing for sure if the future will drive us apart or, on the contrary, dispel this thin cloud.

It was a joyful July 14th. The dance on the town square lasted until 2:00 A.M. Under the mindful eyes of their mothers, young girls went from soldier to soldier. Yet there were soldiers walking in front of the square and tanks parked by the school and the officers' mess hall. Some sacks blocked the vision of a crowd of Kabyle onlookers who came to gawk. This gray cloth suggested a sad and sinister barrier between two worlds all too ready to hate each other.

The following week I went to Tizi-Hibel to spend my vacation.[7] I stayed fifteen days. I had not been there for two years. Everything seemed exactly two years older. My eyes can now perceive quite precisely the passage of years. And in a sense, these eyes are content to claim that everything happens according to an immutable order of things, an order that simply follows its path and could not stop to please anyone . . . But this is not my purpose. All along the route, I was looking at stunted chestnuts and frail fig trees, eroded shale and sand. The landscape that welcomed me screamed its nakedness, poverty, and near hostility. It said to me: "What are you doing here? You managed to escape." I understood it, agreed with it, and despised it with all of my heart.

At Béni-Douala on the slope where the market is held behind tangles of twisted barbed wire, soldiers, in shorts blackened by dust and sun, busy themselves around jeeps, trucks, and tanks. It seems that the cannons and machine guns pointed at the sky are there to convince you that you are not lost, that you are with fine people who know how to live and proclaim the benefits of a motorized and armored civilization. They are trying to reassure you and will undoubtedly succeed unless, on the road immediately below, there happens to be some Kabyles, shaken and afraid, who slip by quickly like ghosts. As for myself, my interests lie with my compatriots. I have wanted to read their faces, guess their impressions, and know what they think. Their response to my greeting is solemn, as if to imply that we have nothing to say to each other. In fact, there is nothing to say. Why would I want to make them talk when, if I myself were forced, I would not have a clue as to how to do it. It is so much easier to keep quiet. But come on! Enough of this hypocrisy. I am too much like these people to need them as confidants. What do I think? I am not thinking anything at all. Let us say that I would have to dig quite deep down into myself. Then I would not be able to stop or control the endless surge of ideas, opinions, and conclusions that have always been a part of me and that would surely surface. If indeed these ideas found a way to escape, all of them would emerge like very dense vapors that, as legends have it, wait patiently for a hand to come and loosen the cover of the copper pot in which they have been imprisoned by a powerful genie for centuries. Just like these vapors, the contents of my insides would compress and, once outside of prison, would appear like a crippled, ridiculous devil to the puzzled eyes of those people who think that they know me. An astute and nasty devil whose accusing sneers would know nothing about pity or gratitude, a dreadful character who, immovable and insensible, would demand atonement. What one could hear from the mouth of such a demon will be exactly what I and my compatriots think. Just like legendary devils, he would limp, having lost some of his vapors: the most understanding and generous parts, the only part capable of friendship and forgiveness. With these parts scattered to the winds, there would be nothing left but hatred.

However, I was able to have a discussion with a fellow passenger in a taxi. The chauffeur said to him with a knowing look:

—So you found him? He is in Blida? You see.

The old man's face was drawn, his eyes bewildered, his demeanor dull and insipid just like his entire appearance and his clothes. Completely common. These are the type of men from this area who act like imbeciles in order to hide their real motives. Just the same, there was something more. He began to speak with the chauffeur.

—Ah yes, I saw him! I like people who keep their word. You promised me a place in this car. And here I am. That is what I like. I would never say to you: Save me a place and then look for another one and take off. No, I picked your taxi, and here I am. We have to be men. Look here—if you had left, I would not have spent the night in Tizi-Ouzou. Not for anything in the world. I would have taken another taxi to go see the old woman and tell her that I saw him. Just saw him. It is enough for her that he is alive. Her son looked at me and spoke to me just like I am looking and talking to you. I have been on the outside for eight days. You are right to believe that his lawyer is a pro.

—His lawyer is a pro?

—Yes. You do not have to say it, I know it. That is how the lawyer found him. He went to see the prosecutor and said: "I want to defend him." And without any debate, the prosecutor gave him the address: the Blida Prison!

—Who is his lawyer?

—Maître T.

—So, he is a pro.

—You are quite right. But you have to pay. And that is how it is.

When I asked for an explanation, he looked at me, his eyes more dense than ever, and merely shook his head while sliding over closer to the chauffeur in order to give me a little more room. This indicated that I would get nothing more from him. I took advantage of it by stretching out my legs, which up until then I had crossed—a position that was ruining my new pants.

—Oh, he is from your area, the chauffeur said.[8] You can talk, he is a teacher.

This time, I saw clearly the glint of malice in his eyes that is so typical of the fellagha in our region. For them, the teacher is both educated and naive, a man with good advice who can inform you about laws and regulations and yet believes everything that you tell him.

The time was right, so the fellow started talking to me.

—Ah, yes! Listen, my friend, he did not do anything. They flat out arrested him, just like that.

—So whom did they arrest?

—My nephew and myself. But I am another case. I said to the NCO [noncommissioned officer], "Don't hit me." I was also an NCO during the war in Italy and Germany. If I had stayed in the army since 1945, I would now be a sergeant major. That is certain. Do not hit your sergeant. So he did not beat me. He just threatened to douse my face with a quart of fresh water, but that was before I told him. When it was clear that the police were going to let me go, he even offered me a cigarette. I did not take it, of course. I was glad to know that they take into account certain circumstances. You have to put yourself in these people's place. If they are told to arrest someone, they do it. To hit someone, they do it. The army is about taking orders. So when I saw them beating my nephew, my blood started to boil and I yelled at him:

—Take it, you son of a gun, take it. Show that you are a man.

But how do you stick it out, brother? He was bent over and they were whipping him on the buttocks. Seeing his genitals made me wish that the earth would just swallow me up. We were both disgraced—uncle and nephew. And I ask you, could you take that, being horsewhipped on the testicles—excuse my being so blunt. No, the boy did not hear me. It was a blessing for both of us when he passed out.

At that point the administrator came by, saw us, and stopped. He undoubtedly knew me.

—What are you two doing here? he asked me.

—They arrested us.

He was shocked, even a bit outraged.

—You were beaten? he said.

—Yes, see what condition my nephew is in . . .

—That is what you get for causing trouble.

—But we did not do anything.

—Okay, I am going to take care of you.

I never saw him again. But I really believe that he is the one who rescued me from the soldiers. He could not do anything for the boy. As for myself, I had fought in the war. Surely, he must have recognized me.

Later, I [Feraoun] was to find out bit by bit about the dreadful experience that this fellow [the old man] had just lived through. Dreadful but routine because, at last, we instinctively knew that our peaceful times were over. Once again, everyone is a suspect; you have to take the beating. (When someone beats you, you have to bend your head down.)

When I saw the administrator again, he told me himself that the culprits who had murdered the village policeman had confessed and given up all of their accomplices. A whole bunch of scoundrels.

—But sir, what about the coercion, the beatings . . .

—Do you see me beating someone to make them talk? Come on, Mr. F., we know each other . . . Sure the soldiers, the police, they will do whatever. But me, I made them talk. You see they confessed, and besides, I released one because he hadn't done anything.

—I understand, but he does have a nephew.

—That is not the same, Mr. F. That is simply not the same.

—They were picked up together in a field. Besides, he was sure that you had nothing to do with it, that you were completely in the dark about it. You were there to save him . . .

—Well, Mr. F., I had them arrested because I am sure that they are guilty. Crimes of this sort have to be punished . . .

As in dozens of cases, this crime will not go unpunished but since we cannot get the assassin himself, we punish people at random.

—Everything's going well except that I cut my neighbor's fig trees.

—Yes, you do that well, but do you also cut down telephone poles?

—I do when I am broke.

—Who pays you?

—This same neighbor who. . . that . . .

—Who?

—Who does not want to pay me any more. Besides, he is a fellagha, a rebel, a bandit.

—He is the one who killed the village policeman.

—Correct.

—He was not alone?

—No, he was not.

The police fingered the least likely person in the village. An irresponsible drunk, a near idiot who, when faced with the Socratic method, supplied the police with every detail they wanted. Once they got the information, they spread terror throughout the village. A terror like this turns people into idiots, and I could read it in the face of my fellow passenger, a face full of rancor and hatred.

Fortunately, it was going better in my native village. It is three miles from Béni-Douala, and the troops are there. We are among ourselves and free to speak. I have simply noticed that, just like myself, the people and things here have aged two years. I want to repeat that, in my case, this observation is neither bleak nor alarming. It is only a bit sad. We all grow old. And afterward? What is important at the present time is that the possibility of growing old is still a sure thing.

## November 28

I have to admit that, in the beginning, everybody used the same formalities with me as with the administrator. My friends, cousins, and peers were paying me far too much respect.

—No, I said, and tried to make them understand. It could be that you are proud of me, that you consider me powerful and respected. That is okay . . . I will not forget it, you know. And here is the proof: I am living here among you while I try to fix up my tiny rundown house. So, as matters stand, I intend to stay. To be sure, you can again make room for me in your circle, draw me into your plans, your politics, your passions. You can envy me, get sore with me, love me, or hate me. But do not let me stay off by myself. That is truly too much honor . . .

I would have been able to speak this way with them, and it would have touched them. It seemed that they heard it come from my mouth, but out of respect they were careful not to let anything show. Just as if I had never left them, we began to live together again—to chat, joke, discuss, and, at times, argue. Any favorable treatment would have insulted them and, more so, myself. They loved me too much to insult me.

### December 4

An insidious and nearly invisible fear had crept in everywhere. People kept calm, but everyone knew that the police posed a threat that weighed heavily on them. It hovered over the villages and, at times, materialized in the form of a policeman, a soldier, or something else. Go figure! People no longer lingered outside. By dusk, the village streets were deserted, haunted by cries and mysterious sounds. You could identify the cries: barking dogs that soon became frightened and, after retreating into the silence of men, listened to the jackals' screeches, which came to jeer us under our windows. As for the noises, we never did recognize them. In the distance, we heard the droning of motors (trucks, jeeps, motorcycles, planes?) and up close, the sound of steps, a rustling noise, and pebbles tumbling about. Wait, there is a faint knock at the door. Someone is turning the knob, whispering. Should I get up and see? No, it is an illusion. Have I not been warned?

In the morning, they say to you:

—Yesterday, so-and-so had a nasty night. Someone tapped at his door and then they threw a big rock into the courtyard.

—I found my dog tied up with his paws bound. I cut him free. I am sure he did not bark. I was not asleep.

—You did not hear anything? You know it is the soldiers. They must have lured and petted him, thrown him a piece of meat. Instead of barking, he started to wag his tail and that is how it happened.

The imagination runs wild. One fact that no one doubts is that at night anyone who answers a knock at the door will find themselves face to face with soldiers bearing machine guns who have come to shove them around a bit for sport.

—Why did you open the door?

—Well, it seems that you knocked.

—Yes, I knocked like the others. You answered just like you do for others, for the rebels who come here to get supplies from you. You answered because this is the time they arrive. Out you go! Follow us.

So, the fellow clad in a mere gandoura is transported to Béni-Douala.[9]

When I ask the guy about the identity of this compatriot who was taken away, he admits that it did not exactly happen here but in the next village.

—But what I told you about the knocking is true. You will see, they will surely tap at your door. But, be careful, do not answer. Sleep, all of you, sleep. They'll knock, listen for a minute and then be on their way.

That is why I did not open my door when they knocked and turned the handle, and I heard whispering.

In the brilliant light of the following day while listening to my deepest intuition, I coolly decided that my neighbor was jealous that I was building a new house. He was undoubtedly capable of climbing over the small wall between our properties in order to welcome me and secretly express his neighborliness. So, as soon as I saw him in the square, I put on a pleasant smile and went to shake his two hands.

—He did that so I would not start up again, he probably thought. He did not bother me.

**December 8**

I have decided to go home for this vacation in order to spend l'Aïd Kébir with my family, something I had not done for a decade . . .[10] It would do me good to be back in my element for the holiday! But this time people had lost their spirit. They have guilty consciences and not much appetite for celebrating. They are generally avoiding taking their little ones to the market. When the time came to slaughter the sheep, it was done quickly and with some apprehension. For some time now it has been rumored that "ritual sacrifice" is forbidden. There are other equally plausible and tedious rumors in the air. In the end, I had to admit that my Aïd with the family was quite sad, and as a result, I spent a good deal of the day outside.

In a café I saw some young people whose hats bobbed as they toasted each other over bottles of red wine. They were railing against the "fellagha fanatics" who, they perceived, wanted to put an end to their "good times." They left the village to drink their wine, and in the evening I saw them again, yelling at the top of their lungs that they were going to capture the maquis and send everyone packing—France, her soldiers, and her policemen.[11]

### December 9

After Aïd, I returned to Fort-National and rediscovered my friends and my routine. The Kabyles were joking among themselves about French behavior. On the one hand, the French are suspicious and full of unspoken hatred for us, and on the other, they continually smile and make all sorts of overtures. It is as if all of us are equally threatening, cunning, and decidedly Machiavellian. On my walks with Q. O., we would objectively assess the delicacy of our situation. Our French friends or, simply, our pals would prefer to see us express our warmth and affection for them in public. Not so long ago, they would never have wanted such a thing. They have also been ready to show us their brotherly feelings, which, in another period of time, would have deeply touched us and truly won us over. We did not feel that their efforts concealed any hypocrisy whatsoever. Our compatriots were clearly after "peace among brothers," a truly impossible peace. So with utter objectivity Q. O. and I understood that, in spite of appearances, not all situations are alike.

During our walks he would say to me:

—Do you see this tormented country, these deep valleys, these mountains covered by thick bushes and shrubs pressing together one behind the other like hordes of barbarous warriors? Do you see these shabby villages, watching out from the mountain tops? All of this is just now waking up from a hundred years of inertia. How can we explain this to those who are bewildered and afraid? How can we make them understand that nothing can subdue this awakening and that no one can contain its fire, for the rage is so great.

Enraged and full of premonitions, the country is waking up—its power, still undefined, is slowly rising from within. This power, which continues to frighten beyond measure, will soon be fully understood. The country will use it and demand that those who have prolonged its deep sleep vindicate themselves.

Every time that we passed through the city's walls on our way to the center, we would encounter French people and exchange the customary greetings, smiles, and friendly chatter. Occasionally a group of us went for an anisette. We convinced each other that nothing had or ever would change. We not only took pleasure in fooling our friends, but with the utmost humility, we willingly fooled ourselves. It was to be like that until the month of August. That is when the violent break occurred unexpectedly.

11    **December 12**

The only reason that I flew to Paris was to be with people who had other concerns. But, unfortunately, the very worries that I wanted to escape resurfaced over there, as did the same confusion and the same anxiety. That is what everyone was talking about. My friends began to talk to me about Algeria; my editor demanded that I talk to him about it; and when I got a room at a hotel, the manager wanted to discuss Algeria. When I was obliged to see some compatriots, they were inevitably Algerian. I decided to take two weeks off in order to break loose from my perspective, my friends, my routine, my troubles. The image of my country in full revolt followed me like an obsession. It was a country determined to cry out its pain, its rage, and its hatred. Although proud to hear its voice, I was terrified that it would not be understood and that the raucous cries erupting from its throat would seem incoherent to the very people who were ready and willing to listen.

In La Goutte d'Or, I saw a young accountant who has openly criticized my work. It seemed to me that Mammeri's work had taken a harsher beating and that I was faulted for preaching assimilation.[12] My characters as well as all of their expectations are supposedly Western oriented. These criticisms remained imprecise for I was a guest, and they were buying my aperitif. Yet, it is a fact that my compatriots expect or would have expected my books to have more backbone. They expect nationalist works that called for nothing short of a divorce, a divorce from a marriage in which we are the only partner to foot the bill. They gave me reasons why it should be so. But I know some facts as well. Unfortunately, these young people have nothing to teach me about this area. I am the elder. Moreover, the split between Arabs and Kabyles still exists. It is just local politics, they tell me.

Besides, the "leaders" are all more or less open to criticism and are indeed criticized. All of this leads us to wonder who, in the future, might be capable of guiding the nationalist party. Who might this virtuous political leader be?

People generally think that the posing of such questions will provoke anxiety when the time comes. Right now, each and every effort must bend toward freedom, above all, freedom from an incredibly persistent and tyrannical yoke. In my opinion, the very persistence of this yoke makes everyone lose sight of any and all advantages that they might have gained, past or prospective. So they say, "Let today's joys be tomorrow's bitter regrets, It is just too bad. Now, as far as we are concerned, it is only a question of dignity." In a world that is trying to forget such talk, I am happy to see that our young people are discovering it and are, somewhat naively, claiming to use it for themselves.

### December 13

The people from my region whom I was able to meet in Paris or in the North all know that their suffering is tremendously unjust. No longer unaware of their predicament, these victims are also knowledgeable about its origin and those responsible for it. The problem is the Frenchman for whom they work. He is the reason for their misery. From this point on, an insurmountable gap separates us from the French who are no longer masters, models, or equals, but rather enemies.

They have always been our enemies. Their manner is so nonchalant; their words and actions exude such confidence and candor. They have conquered us not with hatred but with goodness, a goodness that was essentially a veiled hatred. But their hatred was so clever that we could not understand it and mistook it for kindness. They were good, we were bad; they were civilized, we were barbaric; they were Christian, we were Muslim; they were superior, we were inferior. This is what we were made to believe. This is why we construed their little acts of charity as expressions of kindness. Similarly, the most sincere and intelligent people among us honored the French with infinite gratitude and unbounded admiration. So we, in our turn, ended up by solidifying their belief in their honesty, goodness, and superiority in relation to us. Now they have to sing a different tune. They must know the truth: they no longer control us, so why delude themselves?

## 1955

### December 17

I was in Dunkerque on August 22nd when I learned of F.'s death.[13] We can credit the rebels with this deed because that same week some very serious problems (terrorism and repression) cast a dark cloud over the skies of Algeria and the hearts of Algerians. I had been observing, with some distance, what was happening all over Algeria. This distance vanished with F.'s death—I felt it right here. If I had not been hundreds of miles away on a plane, I would have left him just a few minutes before his death. On the eve of my departure for France, he came to say good-bye and wish me bon voyage.

—I did not want to let you leave without shaking your hand. Have a good trip, my friend. Write to us. And do not worry about your kids . . .

The next day, just when I was getting into H.'s car, I saw him up on the square that looks out over the school. There was something soft and sad about his expression, something suggesting that he regretted not accompanying me to that country where one takes vacations. He raised his hand and waved good-bye. This is the last image I have of him: quite small, a smile on his slender and slightly pale face, a face dominated by a large forehead and his extremely intelligent expression. But[14]

It was this image that came to me at Malo-les-Bains and blurred his obituary—a few lines dancing before my eyes, lines that I could not manage to read. I cut my trip short and returned at once.

I was not able to attend F.'s state funeral. After the burial there was a sense of absolute emptiness at Fort-National. It was indeed a dead city that I found one morning. Although impatient to see L. and O. and present the necessary condolences, I was prevented from going out by a sort of reticence that, like shame, remained unprofessed. I no longer knew how to approach people or what to talk about. I had a fear that in their remorse I would read a vague reproach, an insinuation that my escape made me somewhat responsible. I was ashamed to be in good health in front of this family that had lost everything. I shared the disgrace of my compatriots who were perhaps fated to be collectively responsible for this crime. No, I was not in any hurry to go out. I waited until the following day. I knew that my friends would understand me, that they were also patiently waiting—waiting for me to come out.

December 18

Passing through the village like a sleepwalker, I did not see the shopkeepers on their stoops, the village policemen on the road, the taxi drivers in front of their cars, the idlers on the sidewalk. I went directly to express my sympathies to F.'s grief-stricken family. The children, with heart-rending smiles, acted a bit like orphans, as they showed me the black mark of the bullet hole in the wall. Even though I asked for no explanations, they would not spare me any of the details. I was anxious to leave, for neither words nor tears were forthcoming. Perhaps the orphans were waiting for me to say something, to lie or even cry. I do not know what they were looking for. I was waiting for this painful visit to be over.[15]

I stopped at old L.'s place. A good guy. What must he be feeling? He is tall, stocky, heavy, and crippled. His expression exudes bourgeois malice and egoism. Yet it is also gentle, foolish, and smart. He is not brave, and he knows it. He even says so to discourage anyone from thinking that he is and to make sure that those who exploit this will at least know that he is not a fool. Mr. L. is sixty years old. For the last thirty years he has been, when circumstances demanded it, a city councilman or mayor or deputy-mayor. At the moment, he is the highest-ranking councilman, and with F.'s death, he has automatically taken on the mayor's responsibilities. For two years, he has been eager to play his true role in a municipality where one man has been doing only what he saw fit. Now that the position is empty, he is going to fill it. The job apparently sits well with him. While not proud of the delight he takes in the job, he still cannot help showing it. His pleasure is like that of the small child who clutches a newly inherited toy to his chest while his parents grieve over his older sibling lying in a corner.

When he shook my hand, I had the impression that Mr. L. was clutching this toy. After leading me into the dining room, he began to speak to me in that familiar confidant tone of his, which I personally like very much. He is completely trusting, tenacious in the way that he disarms you by opening himself up and pouring his heart out as if in the confessional. He does not demand any absolution in return. He proves that his conscience is clear by disclosing everything and allowing you to be the judge.

Mr. L. has spent his entire life behind his counter. He has acquired a passion for chatting nonstop with the client about everything that goes on in the village. Regardless of the client, the mood, or the kind of gossip offered, he rattles on in a perpetually monotonous and slightly nasal tone. The secrets that he broadcasts are shared by all those who frequent the shop, which simply means everyone since there is nothing that you cannot find in his shop: a small bar in the corner, a haberdashery, foodstuffs, newspapers and books, trinkets, tobaccos . . . For years, he has lived behind this counter taping everything in detail. So he is capable of making you listen to all sorts of recordings: scandals, heroics, politics, slander, love, rape, war, and peace. Ask him anything; he has a story for it. I have always known about the special friendship that ties him to the eldest of his boys and, at times, to other boys. This has been the case for decades, and so now the scandal is gone. In fact, his friends do not even think about it. People readily agree that his "weakness" is the source of his absolute integrity in business. He is an example that no one wants to follow. His vice has made him not only a coward but an honest man. They poke fun at him for his timidity and yet agree that he is honest, as if he could not be otherwise.

We were heading toward the dining room. While he waddled in front of me on his sore foot like a big, overstuffed turkey, I was thinking about the man whose place he was going to take — the little mayor, sharp, nervous, and full of life and finesse. Inside myself, I was telling him:

—Poor guy! Your dream is coming true a bit late. You are going to play the fool a while longer. Are there any respectable men left to pity you?

He began to speak.

—You understand, Mr. F., I did not know anything. I did not suspect what was going to happen. Yes, there was a lady. You know her, of course. She had just bought a piece of cheese. She left and then came back in a hurry, her eyes ablaze. You understand—I do not have a refrigerator. Only a freezer. A refrigerator costs 500,000 francs. If I had the money, I would have bought one. I said to myself: That is how it's going to be: the cheese got soft. She does not want it, she is bringing it back to me . . .

It was not the cheese, you understand! . . .

Yes, it was not the cheese, it was the mayor. Someone had just assassinated him in front of his villa. The lady had heard the shot, and people had immediately grasped what had happened. But Mr. L. did not hear it and vacillated. The village panicked;

people rushed home and locked their doors. Mr. L. asked for his jacket and enough time to slip it on. Ten minutes passed. As soon as he went out into the street, a frightened and suspicious employee from city hall approached. O. was already on his way to the villa at the edge of town. No longer indecisive, L. and the others went together to find F. They found him lying on the pavement. He had tumbled down the front steps. His wife was dry-eyed, covered with blood, her teeth clenched and her eyes cold. She was trying to get him up. He was no longer alive.

L. described for me the entrance to the villa that I saw every day. He pointed out the assassin's position, explaining how he must have hidden himself either behind the acacia or the signpost and tried to decipher F.'s movements.

—You understand, he must have turned around like this because the other one may have coughed or made some noise. So the bullet hit the chest and went right to the heart. Did you see it? The children showed you.

Yes, the children showed me: after passing through his chest, the bullet hit below the window. This mark is stuck there like a black rubber suction cup on a white wall. It is deep and will be there a long time.

Then he began to hold forth on this brutal death.

—He died without suffering.

Such is Mr. L.'s dream! To die without suffering! His obsession.

—Once you reach sixty, it is over. We know we have to die. I do not disagree with this, but am I capable of suffering, Mr. F.? Can I tolerate pain in the state that I am in? In a sense, I am envious of the way he died.

—Let us not exaggerate, Mr. L.

—No, I know what I am saying. You have to understand, I really want to die in my bed. Not by a bullet in my heart. That would be awful. All that blood. If you had seen all the blood. And he was quite small. And then I told them to be careful, not to simply lay him down like that on the bed. Can you imagine? All of that blood drenching everything until it trickled down onto the floor. No, it is awful. And what do I need? An embolism. Yes, that is a quick way to go. But only if it catches me unawares, surprises me while I am sleeping in my bed. Then I will not mind.

It was endless. I could not wait for him to get to the point, to tell me what he thought about this crime and where the investigation stood. L. was right. He filled me in scrupulously. He told me everything he knew. And I went back to my place where, once again, I was swept up by the village. Once I knew the latest gossip, I became caught up in the atmosphere, and my brief absence did not matter.

I have to say that it was a nasty atmosphere. No one doubted that the assassin was a Kabyle. L. had his suspicions, and so did the police as well as all the local Frenchmen. And the Kabyles as well. The unanswered question was who had armed this man? Was it a clan? Was it this other clan? A very shaken L. informed me that the soldiers and the prosecutors had been immediately alerted but had taken two hours to get to the body. I learned from my compatriots that a very zealous captain, rather than rushing toward the terrified family, stationed himself near the side of the church and proceeded to line up every Kabyle who passed by—for he was certain that the commander would order a summary execution. While the French excuse the captain because he is a drunkard, the Kabyles thank Providence that the commander prevented the captain from shooting them. From now on we no longer dare to freely approach one another. We exchange greetings but with reticence. And in order to avoid saying hello, we avoid each other. At times, we just bluntly turn away. Yet, when circumstances force us to spend a few moments together, we exchange words about something pathetically trite as if we had nothing to say to one another, except what can be said in a friendly tone, as if to suggest that nothing had happened. From time to time a shrewd and vexed observer can read, in the expression of either a Frenchman or a Kabyle, a desperate pleading, an appeal that comes from a heart in shackles. And, without mincing words, it says: "Good Lord, why shouldn't we care for each other? Why do we turn our backs on each other? I know that you understand me. You don't? I am sorry, really sorry."

Then the expression changes to indifference, and they leave one another with a lukewarm handshake, a small but discreet gesture. We also part by simply turning away without so much as a handshake or a nod of the head. Damn it, we have had enough. It seems that this is the chorus sung by everybody here all at the same time. Go to hell! In this case, the Kabyle who immediately runs into one of his peers or the Frenchman who meets another Frenchman after leaving a Kabyle flashes his compatriot a complicit smile, so as to clearly demonstrate that he has just snubbed the enemy; in a nutshell, he has done his duty.

More and more, you see a few French civilians gathering in front of one of their cafés devoid of Kabyles. Walking up and down the main street with a serious air and even more serious expression, they tend to stroll in groups of three or four, their greetings increasingly strained and in short supply. They walk together, pretending to have forgotten their rivalries, the basis of their friendship with the Kabyles.

—As soon as they start getting along, it is because they are united against us. As the Kabyles say among themselves, their hearts are steeped in hatred.

Besides, as soon as it is legitimate to judge them as a group, it is no longer troubling for anyone to point out their faults. It is no longer a question of Mr. Eugène or Jojo but of the triumphant Frenchman who has taken over his place and gotten rich off our backs. Once you buttress yourself with generalities, you are amazed to discover some very broad horizons. You feel equal to every man on the planet, and you wonder what aberration, what delusion, what apathy has kept all of us in servitude and misery; why have we tolerated leaders, masters, bosses, managers coming from God knows where. They just look down on us and hoard up scornfully and effortlessly all the pennies that we earn by the sweat of our brows.

We see things clearly and at a distance. At such a distance that our vision pierces all of the mirages, the reflections that they are still trying to manipulate in order to deceive us. At such a distance that we no longer want to debate because, at last, we have mastered our truth, and it cannot be up for discussion. Yes, this truth is different from others' truth. But are we trying to discuss theirs? So leave us alone, for God's sake! . . .

The higher-ups, used to having it good and easy, to being on familiar terms with the people, were either fearful or angry, depending on people, places, and circumstances. They were determined not to understand. We have to put ourselves in their place. When you have settled into a situation, woven your web of habits and practices, built a life on a solid past with a reasonable future in mind, it is difficult to imagine that the structure might crumble. It is difficult to allow men with whom you have had easy dealings, who are peaceful and satisfied with their lot as you are, to suddenly ask you to justify yourself, to put your past into question, and to threaten your future. No, you have to keep a cool head and trust the powers that be, even if you do not really approve of their leniency, which suggests weakness. We have to believe in our soldiers. The looting will soon stop, and peace will be restored. And once again, life will be beautiful. What is happening now will serve as a lesson. We will surely not forget it. "A bad man will return evil for good!"

Yes, there are those who hang on, who are scared stiff but who continue to cling to the old privileges, to speak and act like masters in spite of the Kabyles and their sly manner. And the latter believe that the night of August 4th is to a great extent obsolete mainly because they want nothing more do with it.[16]

—What is the use? This is our home, right?

Still behaving like leaders, the director, the judge, and the notary continue to patronize and grant their protection to those with whom they have dealings; Joseph the policeman uses the familiar *tu* with a school principal when he asks to look at his papers.[17] This is simply because the principal is Kabyle, and he is there with his veiled wife. On our way to Mekla one day, L. saw a road sign at an intersection that shocked him. Written on the sign in large letters was "Djemaâ Saharidj 2½ miles," and underneath in small characters was written "Mekla 1¼ miles." Whereas Mekla is a small colonial center with three or four European families, Djemaâ is a large village with five thousand residents, all of them Kabyle. The tiny letters for Mekla went straight like darts into his heart, causing it to bleed. And yet this public works road sign is a few years old and is not a product of recent events.

Like a big pumpkin in a jar full of oil, L. has been shutting himself up for years in his store. Although distressed by everything that he sees, he quit thinking about it a long time ago. He cannot accept the fact that Mekla, however small it is, is playing second fiddle to Djemaâ Saharidj, however large it is. His sense of shock came from the heart and is something that I shared. We both anguished over a disintegrating situation. It was precisely to Djemaâ that we were heading. An old aga [general] whom I knew quite well had just been assassinated. It was a few weeks after F.'s death . . .

Before the beginning of October, we found ourselves in a country in jeopardy. Military vehicles plowed through the streets, swooped down into the valleys, crawled up to the villages, stopped in fields, rounded up "suspects," and, at times, came under gunfire. As for the terrorists, they displayed more daring by setting fires to bulldozers, laying ambushes, getting even with informers, and disclosing their own identities to a population that was ready and willing to give them sympathy and support. We were beginning to take them seriously, and that gave us new strength.

Here are a few facts:

End of September: a schoolmate, H. A., principal and president of the Centre died right under the noses of some policemen who had come to investigate an attempted arson at the town hall. The principal investigator along with some colleagues who were very familiar with H. A., the country, and the situation said that the latter was a nervous wreck because he was being threatened by both clans. They blame his suicide on human frailty and depression. What do I know? All of them have supplied me with some graphic details. Poor guy. Was it really suicide?

October: An employee of the mixed community went home one night, got out of his taxi, and was put on trial and executed just like that only a mile from Fort-National.[18] He was a family man about forty years old.

A former president of the Centre d'arrondissement was nabbed by the police one evening at his house.[19] That night soldiers shot him six miles from his house. The following day's communiqué: an armed rebel was killed. It is normal to be armed when you are a rebel. What is not normal is to offer this explanation. In reality, there was no rebel and no weapon.

My colleague B. told me how his cousin was picked up and murdered. They say he was an informer. Even though B. is devastated at losing his cousin, he does not seem to look upon him as an innocent victim.

They are periodically cutting down poles on the road to Michelet. One morning, the police discovered an identity card lying at the base of a pole. Either they found it or someone turned it in. The result? The police went to the person's home. He had taken up with the maquis, so they waited to pick up the father instead. But the father killed one of their men and, like his son, joined the maquis. They tell me that some time later, the over-eager snitch who turned in the card had to negotiate with the rebels. For the time being, he has saved his skin for a price.

It was at that very moment that I heard about a horrible raid at Ighil Imoula. Men shot, shacks burned, and women raped. The reign of brutality and barbarism has replaced the reign of submission, hypocrisy, and hatred, whether it be half-hidden or suppressed. From this point on, positions are straightforward and clear in these scores of villages where people feel frustrated and let down: the Frenchman is the enemy and will show no leniency. We have to outfox him and, when the situation presents itself, give him back a dose of his own medicine. It is truly over. There is no room for anything except force.

I also found out that a journalist from *L'Observateur* was able to contact and interview the leaders of the maquis.[20] Everyone who spoke to me about it was proud and reinvigorated by it. Politics, perspective, conduct, and philosophy—all of this is irrelevant with respect to the maquis. Hearts are indeed conquered as soon as this group pits itself against its oppressors, a role that fits the French.

Surprise attacks and skirmishes are proliferating; the rebels are organizing and becoming aware of their strength. They make a practice of reassuring the people from the mountains. And with more contact, the latter, like children, are overjoyed to discover that a dream once thought impossible is in the process of coming true.

III  The beginning of the fall school term took place without incident at Fort-National. A few days before, there was talk of an order that was going to prevent parents from sending us their kids. It did not happen. The first of October was a feast day. As usual, there was a big crowd. I managed to please everyone and find a place for all school-age children. Everyone, myself included, was satisfied. Our big factory got going right away: teachers met, we distributed supplies, classes, and syllabi, and we set up schedules. All of this did not take more than two days.

We hear that a few schools in the area are still without teachers and remain closed. A matter of days, we are thinking. Not so. They are closed because nobody wants to reopen them. Young normal school graduates from France are beginning to arrive with the commendable intention of doing a good job.[21] Their faith and devotion is unequivocal. We lavish advice on them whenever they ask for it. But this passionate generosity disappears as soon as they meet the administrative officer.

He is what you might consider an alarmist. I am convinced

that his fear borders on madness, but I also believe that he enjoys demoralizing the most enthusiastic teachers. At all costs, he wants to be relieved of a commitment that no one has ever assigned him: responsibility for his schoolteachers' lives.

—I cannot guarantee your lives, he tells them bluntly.

Although no one expects him to be responsible for them, the teachers believe that their lives are seriously in danger as soon as the administrator refuses responsibility.

So, they repack their barely opened suitcases and rush to Algiers, where a reasonable withdrawal indemnity awaits them. They say that this compensation will allow them to live in the capital without dipping into their regular teacher's salary.

This indemnity is indeed legitimate in the case of a rational withdrawal, but it could easily become the cause for it. This is the mildly scornful assumption of those of us who remain in our jobs out of loyalty to the administration.

The leader of the next village is more daring than our own. He simply closed all the schools in his territory. He immediately reassured our colleagues that they cannot be accused of either taking off or going after that notorious indemnity.

It can be said that, in general, the colleagues born in France have lost all feeling for the work. Put yourself in their place! Everyone who works with me is applying for this discharge, and in the midst of the stampede, the school inspector keeps a cool head and postpones all requests. Together with the grade school inspector and preceded by the secretary of the Teaching League and the trade union secretary, he has begun to explore Kabylia. Colleagues think that this is surely poor timing, even if the region boasts a wild beauty that a visitor as refined and attentive as he can appreciate, in spite of the general situation. In just eight days he has visited Fort-National twice. While spending time chatting with teachers and officials in very remote minor schools, he got the idea that teachers who are working at peaceful tasks cannot be harassed. Nevertheless, he gave his subordinates a free choice in the matter: he approves whoever remains and refuses to blame whoever leaves.

The question posed for the teachers from France is very serious. They are alone in this affair—on their own with their hearts, their will, their consciences. For once, they must decide for themselves. If need be, they can remember the settlers.

As for the indigenous teachers, they supposedly have nothing to fear, except for the few who foolishly became involved with the offices in ethnically mixed villages. If the situation presents itself, they can be evacuated and given positions in Algiers. Their insecurity is understandable.

I was not given the opportunity to witness many French colleagues invoke the memory of the settlers and follow their example. For those settlers opened the minds of young Kabyles in very tough conditions. They had no concern for comfort or material rewards and no assurance of living in peace in villages that at times were openly hostile—or so it seemed. In fact, in no time at all they captured hearts and inscribed themselves into the minds and memories of their students. Times, indeed, have changed. Nowadays, the schoolteacher who arrives from afar does not always come as an apostle. He is usually a civil servant who holds dear his colonial supplement, who ran to Algeria in order to straighten out a critical situation, who volunteered for the backcountry so that he could save money, get a fast promotion, and, without much delay, land an important administrative position. Even so, he may consider himself indispensable, worthy of representing France and the elders with whom he identifies—the heir apparent of those eternal values for which they sacrificed themselves.

But this heritage is truly too much of a burden for those who, now that they have tenure and promotion, dream of little else but getting out. They have no feeling left for the job.

Some of them, by their speech or actions, have "outraged" the grade school inspector. He accuses them of having "cold feet."

Up to now, the same school inspector saw things differently. He too believed that the teachers from France were the guardians of the ideals of the old school. Whether he was aware of it or not, he also treated them as if they were superior to us, the natives. Oh, I know he was very diplomatic about it, but even the least perceptive among us saw it very clearly. The most scrupulous among us anticipated no less from him than a measure of paternal benevolence—a protective regard that would sustain us morally, promote and elevate us, as is fitting for our superior rank. Once again, these attitudes emerge unconsciously, out of habit. The inspector would be quite surprised to find himself judged so severely by our oversensitive and feeble outlook. This man believes himself to be so unbiased, so objective, and so unprejudiced to the extent that deep within himself he allows those of his own kind the right to criticize him precisely because of his attitude toward us. He keeps us in place and treats us "exactly" as he does his compatriots.

To use one of his pet expressions, the inspector is now "singing a different tune." As for us, we are hardly proud of the cool image that we project. Even though we are as fearful as anyone else, we know that it does not pay to broadcast it. At times, those who want to show us that they understand tell us that we are between a rock and a hard place. But I also think that our quiet indifference tends to make them wonder whether we are capable of sincerity or whether our detached manner does not simply prove that we are double-dealers and covert rebels.

Whatever this colleague's thinking is, there is now an impassable breach between us; a rupture that both sides deplore but also endure, knowing that it is inevitable. We avoid talking politics. Our French colleagues are, however, quite tactful. When they comment on a crime, a bomb, an attack, or when they speak about their fears, they always assume that we are on their side, that our fates are identical, in short, that we are just as French as they are. We tolerate the assumption, and everyday life remains bearable.

From time to time, news reaches us that such and such a school was burned. Always schools that had been shut down. Moreover, the daily papers take pleasure in printing spreads about the rebels' barbarous and fanatical deeds. All this drives the people crazy with fear, without motivating the rebels to behave in a more rational and prudent manner. If one believes the press, one must assume that the outlaws are the only perpetrators of horrors and atrocities. When the forces of repression, the so-called governmental forces of order, shoot down a Kabyle, it is always a case of a "rebel bearing arms," as if one could encounter an unarmed rebel. Maybe it is possible, for there are both armed and completely unarmed revolutionaries. But I fear that the latter category is the more numerous and that it covers the entire Kabyle population. In this sense, the soldier considers himself inside enemy territory. He simply waits for an order to shoot at anyone without discrimination. He is ready for the door-to-door search, the scorched earth—total war.

To get back to the subject, each time a school is burned down, we find explanations. We have to admit that the rebels are smart. By torching a school, they prevent the soldiers from taking the students' place. Or one could view this action as a response to those who would prevent the children from learning.

We are gradually realizing that the rebels are not against teachers. Not only do they recognize and appreciate the true value of our work as educators, but they consider us allies in the fight against ignorance, poverty, and everything that stands in the way of human growth. Working with the same high ideal in mind, we are the descendants, biological and spiritual, of the *sans-culottes* and the brothers of the outlaws of Kabylia.[22]

—Ah, if only we could talk to them, here, face-to-face! We would surely come to an understanding and draw up a *modus vivendi*. Try to contact them, suggested my friend M., of the Teaching League.

M. is a kind of lay friar whose asceticism and appearance remind me a bit of Gandhi. He feels that it is within his power to reform society, to blow up the planet, and to do away with the human race in order to replace it with a true universal brotherhood. He is an apostle of nonviolence. I love him like a brother.

M. has contaminated me with his enthusiasm. I too believe that life is still possible for schoolteachers in the boondocks. As long as nothing is forced on us, as long as we are not openly criticized or threatened, we must continue to educate the children. That is why they pay us. We are spending October talking about serious events either nonchalantly or with great pessimism, depending on the day. It is our steadfast hope that everything will turn out all right. Naive educators that we are, we do not attach any importance to either the mayors' increasingly imperious statements or the progress of the rebels' call for insurrection that, slowly but surely, is penetrating the minds and hearts of all peasants. We take note of this progress every Wednesday when the town is filled with silent people rushing to finish their errands in order to return to their villages. Shuffling back and forth, apparently avoiding the French pubs, this "Ramadan" crowd, in which nobody is seen smoking or taking snuff, appears indifferent and almost arrogant in front of the tanks and trucks packed with soldiers.[23] You feel that this crowd is wrapped in a new dignity as stiff as a new suit. A suit cut and made to measure, for which everyone is determined to pay the price. For the uneasy observer, the unanimous strike on November 1st was not at all unexpected.

IV    **November–December**

Two months of war, gloom, and agony. Every morning there is something new. A taxi driver cut down, a father of six, a baker machine-gunned in broad daylight, right in the middle of town, a village policeman who had already retired . . .[24] A bus burned, railroad tracks sabotaged, bulldozers set on fire . . . The press never misses the chance to fill us in immediately, if not sooner. When they make a blunder and situate a village or tribe within a neighboring municipality or *département*, the people who know shrug their shoulders but continue to read their newspaper, whose credibility remains intact. Willing to pay any price for information, they forgive their newspaper its mistakes. For the Kabyle reader, the effect of these errors is remarkable. They double his apprehension. If up to now he has displayed the naive tendency of believing anything in print, he certainly knows from now on what is and is not true. So he separates fact from fiction and pushes the commentary aside. So that is it. With suspicions aroused, he will pounce on the colonist's newspaper as if it were the colonist himself. After manufacturing his own commentary, he will feel equal to the lying colonist, and because his strength is ignored, he will feel stronger.

—So-and-so was killed? Mind you, I am certain that he received some threatening letters. He was a snitch. No, the maquis know exactly what they were doing.

—Speaking about T.'s skirmish, did they say that there were five rebels killed and only one soldier in the regular army wounded? Well, let them say it. Did you know that an eyewitness gave me the actual details? The rebels were locals who were working in their fields when they were shot. It was to make up for losses. Losses? A canvas-covered truck was full of soldiers, dead or wounded. Let them say what they want. Before dying a fellagha kills at least ten soldiers. You have got to know that. Besides, it is easy to understand: the fellagha hides and waits, showing himself only when he is ready. It's just like a hunter waiting for a covey of partridges. Why don't you think about it a minute? Didn't you go to school?

Yes, I did go to school. So, now I feel that it is time for my compatriots to educate themselves, and all these events are putting them to the test. They want to understand and they are quickly getting the idea. From now on, when they become part of a clan, they will be fully aware that the other clan is an enemy that must be destroyed. They accept those who fight for them, those who make it possible for them to hope. In spirit they are with these courageous and committed brothers; those who wish to wash away with their blood our shame at being inferior men.

39

They are becoming aware of their unbearable circumstances. They see the need to throw off this yoke that can no longer be worn lightly. It suddenly seems to be very heavy, so heavy that it crushes you, so heavy that you are ready to die in order to free yourself from it.

Last November, I found out specific details regarding future contact between the rebels and the community.

In A. K., the village council received the rebels in the mosque at night. The men listened politely to their hosts, who gave them a warm welcome.

—Winter is coming, the rebels said. It will no longer be possible to live outside, in the bush. At times, our people will come by. You must put them up. They will need food and a place to rest. The elders will arrange things. We trust them. We are a hospitable race with a very keen sense of honor. . .

Everyone was won over. They promised that further down the road, they would come back to chat, to get the young people together, train them how to handle guns, etc.

They settled into Taourirt-Moussa several weeks ago, even months ago. A building is available for their use. They benefit from the useful discretion of the entire community, which does not fear them but loves and looks after them.

At Tizi-Hibel, they were introduced by a fellow who had disappeared for years in France and then returned specifically as a liaison officer. That is all the information I have. They began by sending threatening letters demanding a specific ransom to be paid by the fat cats. These outrageous sums provoked the fat cats to seek contact. There was a rendezvous in a mosque. This is what the rebels told them:

—You people of Tizi-Hibel, you deserve to be burned alive. You are nonbelievers. You have neither faith nor law. You are all drunkards. In your midst, there are people who are not true Algerians and people who believe in another God. You have never done anything for the cause.

The people of Tizi-Hibel were greatly confused. It was all true. They were going to have to make Mohammed popular again, along with prayers and marabouts.[25]

—We are guilty.

—We forgive you. You are brothers. Redeem yourselves.

Now, since that day, there are new leaders at Tizi-Hibel as well as in all the other villages. They are calling upon the people to create cells that are headed up by a few people who must in turn be in constant contact with an outside leader. We who have been so distrustful of foreigners—now, here we are following these brave men. They are determined to die for the good cause and to drag you along with them. And this happens after they have made your houses burn and perhaps raped your women. In the beginning, you gradually get adjusted to the idea that the bridges have been burned, that the reign of cowardice and hypocrisy is over, and that there is nowhere left to turn except toward violence. Then each person reaches down into the deepest part of himself to get the strength he needs to accept a new life. Included in this life is a bitter taste for risk, a stubborn and heartless will to surrender everything you have up to now either loved or endured, and a neophyte's enthusiasm, which pushes aside once and for all your sense of doubt. Compelled to commit the worse excesses, you become, in the interim, a model partisan who forsakes all discussion and blindly executes orders. We tell each other that, in any case, this fight concerns us and that we are willing to fight. We are willing to do so with as much bitterness and wrath as the other side. Our anger is equally great, with rage, injustice, brutality, and a hatred that foments humiliation and engenders an even more violent anger.

Coming from our ranks, the rebels behave like true Kabyles and are careful not to hurt us. Depending on the circumstances, they either praise our fanaticism, our pride, our expectations, or they partake of our ideas, our democratic social concepts, our humanitarian sentiments. They are of all kinds. Anyone would feel at ease in the maquis because he would know that he was among brothers, that he could discuss and defend his point of view while challenging others. All of us long to fulfill the same mission, reach the same ideal: to be free. To feel that we are indeed free and equal to all men. The people in the maquis have already realized this ideal. Whoever remains in power is also their adversary, an enemy to be expelled and sent back to his home where he will inevitably lose his arrogance.

It was indeed a long time ago when our ancestors fought against the invaders and tried in vain to resist them. They were beaten and they capitulated. The invader became their master and our ancestors his subjects. Then power, like servitude, was passed down from father to son. Now everything is open to discussion again. What has been going on for the last one hundred years? What sort of relations have we maintained with our masters?

Of course, the problem is quite vast, and to really examine it would require an extremely detailed explanation. In order to look at it from every angle, you would first have to establish all of the facts. But this is not what it is about. It is simply a question of trying to understand the reason behind this unanimous rebellion. Why is it that all of a sudden an entire population recognizes the existence of a sizable rift and stands by ready to make it even larger? Why have such peaceful, undemanding, and reasonable people become unruly overnight? Why is the divorce so definitive and brutal? Why is it that the weakest and the most backward of people—in a word, those who truly benefit from the alliance—why are they the ones who are insisting on this divorce in spite of the threats hanging over their heads and the horrible suffering that they tolerate?

The truth is that there has never been a marriage. No, the French have remained aloof. Scornfully aloof. The French have remained foreigners. They have always believed that they were Algeria. Now that we feel that we are rather strong or that we see them as a bit weak, we are telling them: No, gentlemen. We are Algeria. You are foreigners on our land.

What should we have done to get along with each other? First of all, get to know one another. But we have not done this. Just ask a Kabyle woman for her definition of a Frenchman. She will answer that he is a nonbeliever, a man who is often handsome and strong but heartless. He might be intelligent, but he gets this, like his power, from the devil. What does she expect from a Frenchman? Nothing good; neither his justice, which cuts like a knife, nor his charity, which is overbearing and never without insults. How does a European define a native? A common laborer, a maid. A bizarre creature with ridiculous customs, peculiar dress, and an impossible language. A more or less dirty, tattered, and unpleasant character. At any rate, a person on the fringe, quite alone, and let us leave him where he is. It is almost childish to revert to these clichés so quickly. But this is the source of the injustice, and it is useless to look elsewhere. We have been co-existing for a century without the slightest curiosity. The only thing left to do is to harvest this mutual indifference that is the opposite of love.

In December 1955, this item appeared in the weekly news: "Have our political leaders sometimes worried about this Algerian administration that, according to Governor General Soustelle, has managed the country poorly? Who has ever taken it upon themselves to start mobilizing French young people to educate that 80 percent of Algerian children who are not in school? Who talked about integration when it was still possible about thirty or forty years ago? Has any economist ever proposed a realistic plan to industrialize Algeria? Is there a French farmer who has ever considered Algeria as anything but an annoying rival? Finally, how many French people have really gone out of their way to welcome Algerian workers who, driven by dire need, have come to France?"

Sure, now they recognize their mistakes. Is that really the case? We cannot be sure. You do not recognize anything, you do not regret anything. It is still bad faith to speak about mistakes. From the very beginning, they knew what had to be done in order to be on good terms with the natives. They also knew what was required in order to be the only ones to benefit from colonization, much to the detriment of the native. They had to exploit him, make him sweat, beat him, and keep him ignorant. In the beginning, there was still a choice to be made, and they made it. Why talk about mistakes at this point? Because now we are demanding accountability? Come on, accountability is more than confessing one's guilt. We could not care less about this confession. We do not gain any ground by it. By accountability, we mean recognizing our right to live, our right to learn and make progress, and our right to be free. If the right moment had not presented itself, we would have remained silent. If they manage to squash the revolution, then it is highly likely that all promises, projects, and good intentions will be squashed along with it. So the positions are quite clear: the fight between two different peoples has begun—the master and the slave. That is all there is to it. To talk, like the press, about an awakening of the Algerian consciousness is frivolous. That is a completely illogical statement. A man does not have to have gone to school to be a man. The Algerians did not wait for the twentieth century to realize that they were Algerians. The best proof of this is that right away they got together behind the liberators. They gathered together because they thought that they were strong enough to fight or die a meaningful death. They united because they expected to succeed. There were no miraculous phenomena that suddenly opened their eyes, whispered in their ears the magical word *patrie*, distending their hearts with a militant enthusiasm and captivating crowds behind a flamboyant banner. No, the time for Jeanne d'Arc is over for Algeria because there has already been the La Kahena.[26]

The tourist has always regarded the people of the villages with amusing curiosity and no sense of human compassion. Gazing at this multitude of ants from the paved highway, he has never sought to enter their domain. When the rebels made contact with villages, things unfolded simply and cautiously. The Kabyles and rebels immediately found common ground. The French master was far away in the city, his usual surveillance headquarters. The informer was either done in or set straight. The country belonged to her children, and they understood right away that it was time to unite and that the age-old truce was over. Why even talk about fanaticism or barbarity? Neither fanatics nor barbarians, these people simply wanted to get rid of distant and arrogant guardians. They have never needed someone to organize them on the local level or to teach them about dignity and good citizenship. They have never demanded policemen or built prisons. These people have always considered their honor more sacred than their lives. Why should they have to wake up when they have never fallen asleep? Why are they accused of self-denial when they are faithful to themselves? Of course, there was a time when the most progressive among them could, for example, identify themselves as Kabyle, just as a Breton believes that he is Breton and a Corsican or a Savoyard. If you can no longer identify yourself like that, whose fault is it today? To be completely objective about it, we understand that this is impossible. Well, perhaps it is better that way. The time of hypocrisy is truly past because it was illogical. It engendered an era of violence because logic needs violence to prevail. In the course of this tragic confrontation, the natives and the French will surely come to know one another.

Yet it is legitimate to say that it was the violence of terrorism that jolted a good number of us out of our complacency and our reluctance to think about things. It demanded that each one of us take a close look at the problem, examine our conscience, and fear for our hides, because the hide of a Kabyle is not worth much to a terrorist. Suspects are being killed as they turn a corner in the road, get out of buses, inside buses, in villages, markets, cities. They are dying left and right. Nobody is condemning the executioners except their relatives and children who weep over their deaths and fear for themselves.

From this moment on, the rebels' orders are as welcome as any official decree. There are no cigarettes on the shelves; smokers give up tobacco and no longer have any desire to smoke on the sly at home. Everybody has deserted the French cafés, and you no longer see any drunks stumbling in the streets. "A welcomed measure in which the drunks find consolation—May God grant them power." In the wait for God to grant power to the fellagha, He grants fear especially to everyone else. The Moorish cafés do good business and give you a brotherly welcome. These cafés are filled with silent patrons who remain straight-faced as they whisper in your ear the latest gossip of the day. Yes, a cordial but slightly stiff ambiance dominates the Moorish cafés as it does the markets. People approach each other with apprehension. They portray themselves as people who think, people who weigh the importance of events and accept their own responsibility. It is clear that everyone is participating in the fight in spirit. When fear becomes intelligence, it evolves necessarily into obedience, and as soon as it is necessary to obey, one must also become a partisan. So everyone comes together, tries to understand their reasons for joining, discovers the evil that they already know and that they would not previously acknowledge. The mind takes giant steps; the most frustrated among us discuss politics or strategy or combat. We talk about the past and envision the future. We finally feel like men. We are comfortable. We feel that we are free or in the process of freeing ourselves. Everything has yet to be built? It does not really matter. We are confident. The future can only be an improvement. The Kabyle has everything to gain. He has absolutely nothing to lose. So he gets into the game.

The French, being aware of our fear, do not blame us for obeying the rebels' orders. Out of friendship for us, they seem to believe that we are playing both sides against each other in order to avoid the worst. When they see a colleague give up drinking, smoking, and suddenly put on a chéchia—nobody would object to the burnoose[27]—they shake their heads and say:

—You are doing the right thing. If I were you, I would do the same.

But their sunken smiles break our hearts just as we break their hearts when we suddenly change our attitude. If we have a discussion, they generally acknowledge France's mistakes and no longer comprehend why racial distinctions and the whole gamut of inequities persists. Oh! We see eye to eye right away.

—We are all brothers, aren't we? Good God, why all this?

They are truly distressed and so are we. Do we really have to point out that there are quite a few things that we are keeping for ourselves and that they do the same? It is quite natural since we are no longer on the same side.

For example, when a substantial military convoy passes through here, we read a sense of boundless joy on our neighbors' faces. Some of them even discretely applaud it. A woman in a window happens to make a friendly gesture. An elated soldier responds with a kiss from his fingertips. At the same time the tank grinds over the road, and the Kabyles' faces cringe undoubtedly at the deafening sound of the engines.

If, one morning, we find out that a telephone line has been sabotaged over a considerable distance, if a few erratic jeeps pass by, and we learn that military planes are monitoring the surrounding area, and that a helicopter with its stretcher in plain view is grazing roofs, the Kabyles modestly avoid making any commentary, keeping their glee to themselves. But the French make it clear that sabotage is stupid, that the plane is doing a good job, and that the helicopter is transporting a seriously injured person who must have "shot a few."

The choice of our newspapers is another sign that escapes neither camp but that, by mutual consent, completely tacit as well, we avoid pointing out.

However, since they did away with the Communist newspaper, we are left with only two dailies—both mouthpieces for the colonists and the rich French bourgeoisie.[28] And that is the way it is. Since one of these dailies is more moderate than the other, all the Kabyles read it, while the French buy the most reactionary. Whereas we indulge ourselves with *L'Observateur*, *L'Express*, and *Le Canard*, our fellow-citizens ostensibly prefer *Paris*, *Présence française*, and even more violent periodicals if they are available. In a brotherly fashion, anyhow.

More than ever, we are secluding ourselves within our respective worlds, both of which are distinct and hostile. They have their nostalgia for the past, for which they have decided to fight. We maintain the crazy hope of a better future, for which we have decided to die. But as their confidence wavers and discouragement sets in, our self-assurance and courage get stronger.

Tracts calling for resignations began to circulate in the beginning of December. They were drawn up in order to prevent early elections in Algeria from taking place at the same time that they were scheduled in France. The patriots' objective was to prove that, contrary to the government's claims, Algeria is not a French territory. Threatened by violence, the administration backed off, and toward the 10th, I believe, we were given official notice that early elections would not take place. Sigh of relief. But the resignations? Was the tract obsolete, dead in the water? Of course not! The word was to resign, and it was necessary to comply. It is impossible to penetrate the plans of the higher-ups. The courage of the elected officials is more or less manufactured, and you cannot fault them for it. Their patriotism is indisputable. We have all resigned within the required time.[29] And since then we have our diploma in good citizenship, and at the same time, we have saved this miserable life that we value so little.

Here is the tract in question:

### Front de Libération Nationale
*Elections for the Renewal of the French National Assembly*
People of Algeria,

The French government has just decided that you will vote on January 2, 1956.

This follows an extensive study of the situation in our country and in the world and against the obstinacy and blindness of French colonialism, which endeavors to make us French regardless of the many opposed. Not only would this be an insult to all the martyrs to the Algerian cause, but it would also entail a repudiation of ourselves, our past, our civilization, and our history.

Accepting once again its responsibilities before God, men, and history, the FLN hereby resolves:
1. An abstention that will be manifested by:
   a. the continuous activity of all patriots (those who fight for the ALN, militants, and sympathizers of the FLN) during the entire electoral campaign;
   b. the use of force on Election Day;
2. The execution of candidates regardless of which side they represent;
3. The execution and throat slashing of all electoral agents;
4. The resignation of every sitting official, whether he be a deputy or merely a member of the djemaâ.[30] They are invited to resign from their positions before January 1, 1956.

Any official (there will be no exceptions) who refuses to

47

resign will be considered a traitor to the homeland and will be executed without a trial.

The officers of the ALN in charge of operational sectors and zones and the political commissioners of the FLN will be held personally responsible for the carrying out of these orders.

The FLN is asking all of its militants and sympathizers to arm themselves and proceed to direct action.

Each patriot will make it his duty to execute a traitor.

Long live the fight for freedom.

Long live the Armée de Libération Nationale.

Long live the Front de Libération Nationale.

The city councilmen at Fort-National held an unforgettable meeting at which L. was the only speaker. For two hours he talked about bits and pieces of his life with which we were already familiar. He was scarlet, sweating profusely, feeling sorry for having led such a dull life and in a panic over his impending future. He begged us to think things through and to fear the administration, which might penalize us. But at the same time, he washed his hands of what would undoubtedly happen to us if we persisted in our wish to remain in power.

—You understand that when I leave here someone could kill me. If only I could die right away like Mr. F. Nothing is less certain. He was lucky. So, gentlemen, if you feel threatened . . . What do you expect? The authorities are powerless and can no longer defend us. Under these conditions, we are all going to be leaving . . . So what do you say Mr. O. . . . What you are proposing is dangerous, very dangerous. I am asking you to think long and hard about this.

We agreed to think it over. At noon, they posted letters containing threats. There was one for L. and one for each of the most intransigent councilors. Two days later, we drafted our collective resignation.

Throughout Algeria there was an avalanche of resignations. The rebels' orders were obeyed by everyone, especially in Kabylia.

Right after the resignations, the "guns" affair came up. Who started it? The administration or the rebels? It was undoubtedly the former, which, by this gesture, wanted to demonstrate a general trust in the Kabyles. This was a wise precaution on the part of the administration because it proved that they were privy to the people's state of mind. Orders were given to confiscate all arms held by the villagers in the mountains, who possessed special authorizations. As far back as we can remember, these authorizations were meted out after detailed checks on financial status, respectability, and loyalty. The authorizations were, moreover, frequently sold by caids, the office clerks of the mixed communities, the secretaries, and more recently by village policemen and center presidents.[31] By and large, there might be from ten to one hundred hunting guns in each village, depending on its importance. They decided to confiscate them, and they wanted to do it quickly. So it became an arms race:

The police came during the day, the rebels at night. Whoever arrived last was politely told that it was too late and that the weapons had already been handed over to the enemy.

One has to admit that the Algerian patriots behaved properly. Each time that they found weapons, they provided receipts with an authentic seal and a number. This paper is kept in a portfolio with other authentic papers.

There was also the "taxes" incident. A few villages were bold enough to do their duty as good citizens, which consists of paying their contribution. It is a duty that we, as teachers, are required to teach to children. As petty civil servants, we perform this duty punctually and graciously. Well, they should not have paid. Not for anything in the world. The people quickly realized that they should not have paid and that, in fact, this money was going to be used to fatten the French budget, just like the money taken in by indirect taxes—notably, alcohol and tobacco. They understood, but it was too late. There was nothing left to do except to apologize for their unfortunate deed. Since apologies never suffice, they were taxed yet again. So while neighboring villages reveled in patriotic joy, these villages were paying taxes. And it came from the bottom of their hearts. It is for a good cause, of course! Shame on the . . . unintentional . . . traitors.

The tax collector also understood without delay. He prudently called back his agents whom he had sent into the douars.[32] Since then, he has been waiting behind his desk for the peasants to come and settle their debts. He is liable to wait a long time . . .

As 1955 comes to a close, we are certain that 1956 will be the year of radical changes. The maquis appear to be so solidly organized that they have gained the Kabyle people's trust and admiration. They are becoming the guardian of all of our illusions, our extravagant hopes. They are the ones who right all the wrongs that we have suffered for a century, the ones that must avenge our private grudges and our collective degradation. Each individual is exposing his reasons for discontent, reasons for justifying his anger or his hatred, reasons that motivate the maquis to destroy, burn, kill, or die especially for him. So what happened just a short time ago in France is now happening here: people change opinions overnight to become patriots, conspirators in Moorish cafés. They like to think of themselves as part of the action, as serving the cause. It is a duty that they can fulfill without any real compromise and simply through dispassionate affiliation.

Speak to any one of the rebels, and he will tell you that he is informed: he knows the maquis, they know and appreciate him. But do not kid yourself about him. He intimates that his role is minor. A minor but important role. The more important it is, the more mysterious. Even if you put him to the test by expressing some imaginary fear, by telling that you feel threatened, he will graciously offer his assistance, guarantee your precious life, and thereby prove to you that you are indispensable, almost as indispensable as he. Knowing that the zone leaders are at his beck and call, you leave with your mind at ease.

This kind of naïveté does not shock the man on the street. Yet, it is insufferable for the "administrative" doctor who, known and labeled, excuses himself pretentiously for the rebels who are wounded and sick in the rural areas. He considers himself to be the most enthusiastic disciple in the hinterlands. He howls with the wolves, bleats with the sheep, and is always ready to betray the loser. But the doctor is not the only one. There is also the former caid, the rich businessman, and any one of a batch of corrupt officials.

These people are politicians. Given that we are living in an era in which they are carving words into the flesh of men, this word *politician* makes us feel like vomiting.

# 19**56**

**January 2**

The newspaper is reporting the arrest of a Kabyle who traveled from Egypt to the Nememcha in order to complete an important mission. He had with him instructions and a logbook. The daily paper called it an important capture. The same newspaper mentions the Fox Movietone movie of which *L'Express* had already published a review and photos. There is also Governor Soustelle's interview with *Combat* . . .

I hear that there was an important military confrontation last night in Tamazirt. They say that several soldiers were killed or wounded. (?) There was a surprise attack right here during the night. One dead soldier. (?)

Mrs. F. has received a threatening letter and is considering leaving the country. Mr. R. has closed his café and is leaving tomorrow, and Mr. L. has decided to either pay what he has been asked to or agree to a settlement. (?)

**January 4**

Market day. Kabyles. Nothing else. People are quiet and in a hurry. Conspiracy is in the air. It is cold, and the streets are filled with people. The French cafés may have customers, but the doors remain closed. In the evening, I learn that, back home, the bridges of the V.O. 1 have been blown up. There is no traffic beyond Béni-Douala.

**January 5**

I found out that the Moorish cafés have been ordered to prohibit any kind of gambling: dominoes, cards, lotto, etc.[1] Of course, these games go against the teachings of Islam. And further, it is a well-known fact that gambling leads to laziness, dissipation, and neglect of family duties. One must be honest and hardworking to make sure that there is enough bread on the table to feed one's children. Alcohol is bad, tobacco is bad, and gambling is bad. Bad! Bad! It is time to return to austerity. It is an absolute duty to blindly obey the Decalogue. B. comes to me with a broad smile and a high, deep-red fez with a tassel on the side, which brightens up his hair. From now on, the fez will be required apparel for us. Our visible rallying sign.

The primary school inspector spent the morning here. He sounded rather pessimistic for a change. What is the solution? he asked.

—Oh! It is time for one!

—For instance?

—The policeman.

—Do you think so?

—Yes, I do. The police could bring peace back. So let us go back to the beginning. A century ago, they tried to conquer hearts. If we started from ground zero, if we went back to conquering hearts, this time with sincerity, maybe we would achieve our goal in a century from now. The children of our children would become assimilated. Nobody would have any objections. But it is too late for us.

—Because you do not want to make it work.

—You have never wanted to. We do not want it anymore. It is not quite the same.

At city hall, Mr. L. told me that the purchaser at the market had come to resign. He will no longer be able to levy the city toll. Just like people are prevented from paying their taxes.

The newspapers are talking a lot about the twelve soldiers taken by the rebels into the Bouzegza (Palestro) Mountains. They found three. Their bodies were covered with wounds, telling of their pitiful odyssey, and they have their puffed up faces and their half-slit throats photographed. It is horrible to look at.

No one is excused from this act. An answer to Fox Movietone. But Fox is not telling all there is to be told, and the rebels do not own a newspaper.

### January 6

Yesterday, while I was writing (6:30 P.M.), my wife happened to hear on the radio a message near the Kabyle frequency: important skirmish at Taourirt-Moussa. Four rebels killed including a leader, Adila, who was carrying documents. One soldier is dead and five are wounded . . .

I find out something else in the newspapers: my colleague Dupuy, from Maâtkas, was kidnapped on the road to Tizi-Ouzou at 9:00 yesterday.

At 10:00, I meet a man from Tizi-Hibel; he says that there

were no victims among the fellagha during yesterday's skirmish at Taourirt-Moussa. He adds that there were over fifty dead or wounded soldiers. It took place quite near the village. Several houses were burned to the ground, and there was a woman among the four people from the village who died. It seems that the soldiers had received information and that they were trying to encircle the village. However, someone warned the rebels in time, and they were able to organize and defend themselves.

Here my colleagues are becoming more and more demoralized. L. B. is thinking about going back to France without any further delay. Nobody wants to go outside anymore. The village is horribly deserted by 6:00 P.M.

**January 7**

There are big headlines in the newspapers about my colleague who was kidnapped last Thursday. His two assistants have been freed, so to speak, but he was taken away by the rebels. He told one of his assistants: "I am the one they want." What did the poor fellow do? So far the patrols have remained helpless. To arrest suspects? Evidently. (?)

I have more information about Taourirt-Moussa. It is rumored now that nine houses have burned down and two women are dead instead of one.

This morning, from Azouza to Tamazirt all the telephone poles have been sawed off, and the road is blocked.

**January 8**

Still no trace of Dupuy. I hear that the army surrounded some villages in the vicinity at 2:00 A.M. Identity checks start at daybreak. They arrested a few suspects in Azouza. By 11:00, it is all over. Supposedly, some Kabyle women mentioned some first names (like Boussad) and those with these first names have been arrested.

Abrous is giving me more details about the meetings at the T. A. mosque. The rebels' expectations are both excessive and disappointing. They include prohibitions of all kinds, nothing but prohibitions, dictated by the most obtuse fanaticism, the most intransigent racism, and the most authoritarian fist. In a way, this is true terrorism. There is nothing left to do for the women of T. A. except to shrill with enthusiasm in honor of the new era of freedom that they seem to perceive beyond the foggy horizon that our dark mountains inexorably obstruct. It is forbidden to call for a doctor (?), for a midwife, especially for a midwife (?), or a pharmacist (?). And, on top of this, one must welcome, according to our most hospitable tradition, our brave visitors who put on the airs of heroes and apostles, just as we would welcome the great saints of Islam one knows so well.

This evening, a colleague brought me news from the primary school inspector that all schools in the area have closed except for mine and three others. The regional educational authority made that decision. It is effective immediately.

I wonder if this is a wise idea. One can expect such a decision after the kidnapping of Dupuy. What is going to come of this? Was Dupuy kidnapped because he was a teacher? If that is the case, then I agree, the schools must be closed and people must be protected. Otherwise, it would have been better to wait. Then we would have found out why he disappeared. If Dupuy was careless enough to go beyond the bounds of his profession, then there were risks involved, and he was aware of this. So, it is simply Mr. Dupuy, a French citizen, who was arrested by the "enemy" and not the school principal. Why is it that this measure does not seem very wise to me? Simply because every school that is shut down will be under threat if it has not been condemned already.

### January 11

Speaking of schools, besides this threat, there is something that is even worse. This brutal response to an isolated act that the rebels believe to be fully justified is written with burning letters in the register of collective sanctions, of unjust repression dictated by both fear and mistrust that may be legitimate but also harmful. This is an unfortunate decision that exacerbates all the other blunders; an additional proof that from now on everybody has made the decision to use force in a merciless struggle that has finally obliterated any remaining pretense.

The day before yesterday, M. came to see me on behalf of the union.

—I have got 170,000 people behind me. They are asking that you look for a contact. I am ready to help you, if necessary. What we are interested in, what we would like to know is the position of the FLN toward public schools. You represent them. Find out if they share our ideal; up to now, we were sure, and this comforted us. Now, we are not so sure. Can they help remove this doubt? The SN will never stand politically against the FLN.[2] We do not dispute either their right or their duty to fight, but we would like them to assure us that they share our ideal. Then we will feel safe, and our duty in this country will seem to us greater and better than ever.

—Dear M.! You are right, we are apostles but, above all, we are men.

I have talked about this with a friend. He has a good head on his shoulders.

—What do you want to get mixed up in, he said to me. Can you be sure that Dupuy is innocent? Understand what I am saying, I know that teachers are good people. They teach our children, and we are thankful for this. You see, I felt that a weight had been lifted off my shoulders. Yes, I did, when I heard this morning that the school was closed and that the teachers in my village were moving away. Good-bye, that is what I was saying to them deep inside. Yes, good-bye and good riddance. Because these people will not be in danger anymore. I was afraid for them. Teachers are good people, that is for sure, but sometimes they take chances. Look at what has happened right here. The other day, the rebels were passing through. The principal knew it. No problem. He did not say a word. A good mark in his favor. But he started to speak individually with the older pupils: questions, answers, mysterious behavior. The kids talked about it afterward. The teacher wanted to know everything that had happened. Why was he so curious? Why does he want to busy himself with stuff that goes beyond his understanding? He is French, he is a patriot; maybe he wants to serve, make it hard for the enemies of France, provide information about what is going on in the village. He undoubtedly feels that this is his duty. Fine. The others, at that point, are trying to prevent him from fulfilling it. Do you understand what I am saying? Our mistrust of the French has no limit now because their bad faith is limitless. One can regret this state of things, but it cannot be changed. If the teacher cannot keep quiet, then it is better that he leave. Our children will lose one, maybe two, years of schooling. Eventually peace will be restored. And if they come back, we will welcome our teachers back with open arms.

At 11:00, I went into town: everybody found out on the morning news bulletin that Dupuy had been found safe and sound. I missed it. In any case, this is good news. I am relieved. In the end the rebels are not bloodthirsty, fanatical brutes.

This situation is worth commenting on, but I will not say anymore today.

I talked with a few buddies of mine. Now there are stories circulating around the villages in honor of the fellagha. T. relates with convincing fervor that they intervened in favor of a woman who was left in a sad state after her husband had repudiated her. Thamaouaqth.[3] They threatened the fellow, and he had to give his ex-wife her freedom back . . . Not far from Dellys, as the story goes, some terrorists stopped a jeep with a commander and his aide.

—Sir, we are members of the local resistance, but we are not going to kill you. Give us your machine gun.

—Here it is. I have also four clips for it. Take them.

—And there is a box of ammunition in the trunk, the aide added.

—Go ahead and take it.

—Thank you, sir. Have a good day . . .

There are several stories like this one that are making the rounds. In the future they will be worthy of becoming folk stories. This is how people create History.

### January 14

Dupuy has spoken with journalists and undoubtedly with the authorities. The newspapers are being rather quiet about the whole thing. However, it seems that they had their reasons to reproach my colleague, and that he has been accused of acting as an intelligence agent. It is lucky that he got out of trouble so easily. As for the school closing: three have been burned down in the area, and most likely more will end up the same way. It seems to me that the decision to close the schools was made too hastily, and that the school administration does not come off well in this situation. I feel that if the teachers had remained in their classrooms, that if they had stuck to pedagogy, they would have been left alone. Yet, it is also possible that it was better to shut the whole thing down for the common good. This avoids any temptation among our colleagues and protects innocent lives. You have to take things as they come.

What changes are going to occur now that we are being placed under military command? An extra turn of the screw, you can bet. It has already become obvious that the people we believed were safe are beginning to feel threatened. Yesterday, they searched Mr. I.'s house. Now he is in jail. Supposedly they found a list of contributions in favor of the rebels. They say that he turned over 450,000 francs to the police.

I. is a village policeman, which is the same as saying that

he is the village official snitch. Now he is double-dealing and has run out of luck. Maybe justice does prevail sooner or later. In any case, on the human side of things, I could excuse his behavior these days. He is just a poor devil without ideals or convictions. He was especially afraid of dying. Up to now, nobody has killed village policemen except the rebels. Now that he is safe, nothing else is going to bother him. If he does not like the diet they serve, he will surely loose some of his girth.

Yesterday, my colleagues wanted to hold a meeting to "energetically" ask for a displacement compensation for teachers in this area whose classrooms have been shut down. Their point of view is debatable, but I "energetically" refused to sign the motion.

I must write about two things that I have gotten wind of from colleagues.

1. Mr. S. has a married couple as his assistants. He owns a hunting gun. When the fellagha picked up weapons in his village, they did not ask him to hand it over, just as they did not ask the teachers in other areas to hand theirs over. There was something ludicrous about this. At a given time, the police would rush into a village with lists of gun owners residing there:

—Okay! Hand over your weapons.

After nightfall, the rebels would rush into another village.

—Okay! Hand over your weapons. In exchange for an "ALN" receipt.

The fellagha showed up at the home of this colleague. Then, a few days later, the police come calling. The police insist on getting his gun and invite his French assistant to go to the police station to get a submachine gun.

—These are our orders, the police explained.

The Kabyle colleague refused to hand over his gun. The French colleague refused to get the submachine gun.

2. My friend A.'s school is closed. He does not know where to go. He would like to continue teaching; he would like to live in the school, he has eight kids and does not feel threatened. He went down to T.-O. to see the inspector, accompanied by the village amin.[4] The inspector, who was in front of his office with some well-to-do people, said to them:

—Excuse me for a minute.

Indeed, a minute later, A. was out with the amin. The inspector basically told him the following:

—Do what you want. Stay if you wish. It is out of my hands.

According to A., the primary school inspector had lost interest in him because he considered him to be more or less an accomplice, as all of us natives are presumed to be.

To begin with, the inspector's expeditious way of seeing A. in his office was accompanied by a shrug in front of some well-to-do people. As if they had not already understood that the primary inspector was seeing a Kabyle, that this Kabyle was bothering him, and that he was not going to spend more than one minute with him.

**January 19**

Several schools have burned down during the last four days. I know of at least ten. They were beautiful schools with one or more classrooms, some with several classrooms. Two of the schools that were to remain open are now closed: the personnel are scared and have left, or they simply do not care and just want to go away for shameful, personal reasons. Before condemning them, I have to ask myself what I would have done in their place.

Yesterday, there must have been a major skirmish in the village of Michelet. The taxation office was attacked and the cash stolen. On several occasions, a helicopter flew overhead, most likely carrying some badly wounded fellow. All day long, an Air Force plane circled over the town. It was welcomed by mocking insults from school children who wanted me to witness their behavior. They laughed with glee when, at 4:00 P.M., from the balcony, we saw three ambulances advance slowly. They assumed that these were filled with corpses. "At this age, people have no pity."

Around 5:00 P.M., I, for one, saw about twenty GMC trucks and jeeps, either full or empty, returning from the fighting. The vehicles were covered with mud, and the soldiers looked tired and doleful. I saw tragic-looking faces wrapped in dirty linen, wiped-out soldiers who had collapsed on the laps of their comrades. I saw a speeding jeep drive by carrying, like a bird of prey, two miserable-looking, dirty Kabyles. One had a bandage around his head, a kind of rudimentary turban. My eyes met the gleaming eyes of the other, who was underfed and as thin as a rake. It looked like his black beard was devouring his angular face. Holding on tightly to the seat, he was cursing the entire universe.

I have some more information about what happened back home in Taourirt-Moussa. There were indeed quite a few dead.

They are sticking to fifty-seven as the number of dead. The people of Taourirt-Moussa loaded them on donkeys and deposited them on the roadside at Tagmount. They were able to count them. They are the first to admit that killing a few innocents from their home village in anger and burning down a few homes does not justify such a catastrophe. Who knows, had it been the French, they would have burned down everything and massacred everybody. Talk about objectivity!

**January 22**

Yes, there was a skirmish near Michelet. The following day, the newspapers paid tribute to the armed forces that killed one of the rebels, captured two others, and did not suffer any casualties. It is true that not all the readers saw the ambulances, the trucks, and the helicopters come by. In any case, it might be better not to say anything about what goes on, about those who die. There is nothing to be proud of in all this, neither for us nor for them.

Schools continue to burn down.

The older pupils are complaining about F.'s provocations while he complains of their arrogance. The older pupils do not like their teachers because they display not only the superiority of their knowledge but also the superiority of their race. The older pupils are more susceptible. Let us not forget that there are kids the same age as themselves in the underground.

I think that they are aware of a lot of things. Some may even attend clandestine meetings in their villages.

I found out that all the draftees who had to appear in front of the military authorities on the 14th have joined the underground. The resistance is getting organized. The resistance is strong because it has agreed to enroll young men in its ranks. This is an act that is going to be far reaching, but it also entails serious responsibilities. Whatever happens, the fellah is involved in the fighting from now on. Maybe he is not quite ready for a total rupture. He fervently hopes that the Republican Front that will soon be in power will bring with it this absolute panacea that will lift everybody's burden. But he also knows that there is no going back, and that he will not even want to be forgiven because he feels that there is nothing for which he should be forgiven.

**January 23**

All of us believe that the FLN is strong. It makes its presence known when it wants, where it wants, and always in an efficient manner. When all the poles fall at the same time over a distance of two miles, when trees, stone barricades, and trenches suddenly appear to cut off a road and stop car traffic, one has to wonder where this multitude that has spent time and effort has come from and which imperious finger it has obeyed. In the end, what intelligence has led this finger to be so quick and discreet in pulling off such a large operation in which everything was so meticulously coordinated.

Other isolated facts, insignificant ones so to speak, seem to indicate, however, that the French are more concerned, more careful about their lives. These facts seem to show that they have lost their enthusiasm. That is what happened with the amin of A. F., whom the local police detained for questioning past curfew and whom no one wants to host or to take home despite the mayor's request.

The same answer was given to the people of Ag.

—Find a solution yourselves. We do not have a car, and we cannot accompany you.

And do not forget what happened to the soldier on duty at the gate of Algiers. At 2:00 A.M., he is shoved to the ground and allows his determined assailant to take his weapon. The soldier gets back on his feet while the other placidly walks away, still turning around from time to time before disappearing around a corner.

When the soldiers are together and feel strong, they start shoving people around themselves, and at times they are insulting. Then they think that all of us are their enemies, and they are right to think so. Because nobody tries to approach them, except the street imps who run over to them when they come by in order to sell them a brioche, a loaf of bread, or a package of dates at twice the usual price; on the highway, when they speed by in their jeeps, they brush against us insolently, nearly running us over, and then drive off bursting with laughter; in the fields, they damage the huts and destroy the seedlings; in the villages, when they get the order to ransack, they do it with gusto. When we hear that many have been killed in an ambush, we are, of course, thinking about our people. However, we feel sorry for these naive young men, most of whom have blond hair, most of whom are good looking, and all of whom are absolute strangers to the disease from which we do not want to suffer anymore. Yes, we feel sorry for these poor young men and especially for their parents in Burgundy or Alsace. Good God, why did they come over here? Why do they die so stupidly?

### January 25

Yesterday, there was fighting in Azouza around 10:00 P.M.[5] Two soldiers (a sub-lieutenant and an NCO) were wounded. I hear that it happened around 2:00 A.M. At 9:00, a helicopter landed at the stadium. Everything was very hush-hush and resulted in all sorts of speculation. I heard gunfire during the night when I was dozing. We are right in the middle of the fighting.

### January 26

In Azouza, the rebels tangled with a French patrol right before it arrived at the school, at its doorstep. Reinforcements in the night. Two wounded soldiers. Each group stood its ground. Then, at 3:00 A.M., the rebels left, "carrying their wounded" as usual. These wounded may be nothing more than ghosts. It does not matter. At 5:00 A.M., the village is surrounded, and the searches begin. At first, they are going to burn down the house nearest the fight. The owner, a well-dressed Frenchman wearing a blue suit, has just arrived from France. Nothing scares him. He refuses to leave the house, stands ready to burn with his children, declares that he owns nothing else in the world but this house, which has cost him sweat, all the sweat in the world and considerable money in travel expenses. He offers to let the soldiers shoot him at close range in exchange for his house. They leave him alone. Elsewhere, men and women are meticulously inspected. They even use metal detectors even though all the weapons were confiscated over a month ago either by the fellagha or by the police. Still they search, they break, they break more things, they push people around, they slap, they yell insults, and then they go on to the next house.

Some trucks found on the road have been riddled with bullets. They usually shoot inside the cab, at the tires, at the engine, and they pour sand in the radiator, remove the spark plugs, and cut the electric wires. They also shoot at the cacti; they aim at the chimneys or at the windows. And they continue to search. Every single exit is guarded by a soldier with a submachine gun.

By the cemetery above the road, there is a flat area where people like to sit in the sun. Today, armed soldiers are warming themselves there. A path goes down the south side and separates this area from another that faces it. On top of it, someone is slowly putting up a small house. A man wearing blue overalls comes out. He is a carpenter who has come from the town to take measurements for woodwork. The soldiers question him; he shows his card to the nearest one.

—Okay, you can go.

Then the soldier gestures to another, who fires. The carpenter collapses on the ground. The soldiers kick him with their feet and send him rolling down the path . . .

A little further up, toward Fort-National, outside a village, a kid is picked up in his home and is taken away. He is twenty years old, but he does not look any bigger than the students in my classes. First, he gets into the police jeep with some others who have been arrested before him. Then, after an order is shouted out, he gets out and jumps into a military truck, where he sits on a bench seat among the French soldiers. He is as old as they are, but the young soldiers are burning with "the sacred fire within," and they are still pumped up from the fighting. The truck has two miles to go, two miles filled with turns and zigzags. At the fort's military infirmary, it is the corpse of the young Kabyle that is brought down first for an autopsy. In the evening, the carpenter's body is placed on the examination table; then the two cadavers are sent to Tizi-Ouzou. They will most likely be buried in some communal tomb reserved for dead rebels who were caught "with weapons in their hands" and who were fired upon "after the customary warnings."

More than ten suspects have been brought back from Azouza, interrogated in the barracks, and then released or detained. The village is in mourning; the people are shocked and silent. They have to be made to talk, they have to be pushed, they have to be asked questions. The preceding is their version of what happened. Is it entirely true? It is hard to believe. The best is to wait for other versions. Yet, all of this is horrible. *All of us* are living the same nightmare.

**January 29**

As for what happened in Azouza, the Kabyle version is more believable. Everybody agrees that the two victims are innocent, but no witness has come forward to say how, where, and when they were shot.

The village was surrounded at 9:00. The men were parked in the cemetery for an identity check. The houses were partly searched. It lasted until nightfall. Some people were arrested. The body of the carpenter was lying close by the cemetery from the very beginning. It was only the next day that the execution of the young man became official. He had been arrested and taken like the others, but separately. The next day, I saw two retired teachers, warming themselves in the sun while leaning against the post office wall. They seemed somewhat sardonic and disenchanted: they had just been let go. I also found out that the carpenter was carrying his veteran's card (eight years of service), that his father is a civil servant, and that his uncle spent his life as the bailiff of a mixed community. The newspapers are saying that the two rebels that were trying to escape were killed in Azouza. One of them could not be identified. The young one probably. Around here everybody knows him, and his parents are well aware that he was shot.

The truth, I am told, is that the military had prepared an ambush in Azouza to catch some fellagha chiefs who were reported to be on their way there. The ambush failed, two of their own were wounded, and maybe some died (?). They had to avenge this failure. The snitch still has to be punished. They will find out who he is eventually, or they may have some leads already. Then there will be yet another victim. Maybe an innocent one at that . . .

I have heard that the school in Tizi-Hibel has burned down. How sad for the school, how sad for the village, how sad for the kids of Tizi-Hibel. I could not sleep at all because of it. This was my school, my good old school where I learned to read. For twenty years it had waited for remodeling, and it seemed that it was going to have to wait for a long time. Its beautiful garden was lying fallow, its walls were dilapidated, and its wobbly tables worn down. The old teacher who was finishing his career there was losing his enthusiasm, and the lively intelligence and the thirsty minds of the children of our village were also lying fallow. We had no elected officials, nobody to take up our case, nobody to plead, to save the young ones of Tizi-Hibel. Then one day it happened, just like that. A busy construction site was set up in October, and work started moving quickly. The number of classrooms was doubled, partition walls were removed, a new building was put up, stairs were added. The construction progressed rapidly, and the school grew and took on a new appearance. Then it is finished. Everything is in working order. We waited twenty years! And this morning, the haulage contractor tells me:

—You know your school? Gone.

—What?

—Gone. It is over. They burned it down during the night.

—Burned it down? During the night? No, you are kidding?

—Nah, it is true. Along with all the stuff I brought in. Life! Sometimes . . .

A lump comes to my throat. I am angry at my people. I am angry at all those who did not know how to prevent this, who could not prevent it. Shame on all of us forever. Poor kids of Tizi. Your parents are not worthy of you.

In Tagmount-Azouz, they discover the bodies of Mouh Aït Ali and Boudjema Lhadj Kaci: sixty and sixty-two years old. Appalling. They must have paid for what happened in Taourirt-Moussa.

Last night (Friday to Saturday) we were awakened by gunshots from midnight on. At 6:00, you could still hear the mortar spit. The janitor comes in late and tells me that the immediate area around Fort-National has been overrun by military trucks. The soldiers stop and search everybody. They have surrounded Tablabalt (2 miles away). The pupils from the villages in that area are absent. At 8:00, the schoolchildren show each other a large black hole on the side of a new house in Tablabalt. You can see it from here. At 3:00, it seems to be over, and about forty trucks loaded with soldiers drive by. In one of these trucks, I saw a few young, pitiful-looking Kabyles. They are standing, bunched up together with their hands tied to the metallic frame that holds the truck canvass. In another truck, I saw go by the impassive Mouloud, my tall colleague, my schoolmate, my friend. He was standing alone, among seated soldiers holding submachine guns on their knees. He had his back turned to me, but seen from behind, he looked like a triumphant Roman emperor leading a tragic and sober parade that failed to make anyone smile. Those who saw him told me that he looked like a statue. The house with the gaping hole was his house. He had put his life savings into it.

Mr. L. tells me that the rebels had found refuge in Mouloud's house. They had spent the night there and were forced to move out after a violent encounter. Poor Mouloud. Is this really true? Even if it were true, I know that you are not a hostile person and that you are not bloodthirsty. How could you be a terrorist, Mouloud? I also found out that there were six victims, one of them a woman.

—You see, Mr. L. says to me, now we are living under military rule. It is serious business.

—I know, Mr. L., I know that it is serious business. Today more than ever.

**January 30**

This morning I got into an argument with some of my French colleagues. Over Mouloud, of course. L. B. tells me point blank, visibly pleased with himself:

—If anyone is going to pay, it is Mouloud.

—What has he done exactly?

—He shot at some French soldiers!

I immediately reminded him of what had happened a few weeks earlier when Dupuy was kidnapped. It moved me deeply. I felt a lot of sympathy for him. If there were some among the Kabyle teachers who were pleased that this occurred, they were thoughtful of their French colleagues and kept it to themselves, or maybe they were afraid. But at least, they did not display their feelings. While these . . . They are all happy and proud that Mouloud has been arrested. They are ready to eat him alive without waiting to find out exactly what he is accused of and how grave his crime is.

I read anger and hatred in their eyes. There they were, all four of them ready to contradict me, all four ready to insult me with their arrogance, all four of them ready to put me in that category that they despise, that they exploit, that they would massacre, and that they fear. A crazy fear. So I chose the most racist among them and in front of the pupils, I shouted at him:

—Mr. F., I have had it with you, I have had it up to here! I am as French as you are, and I should not have to remind you of this fact!

Shallow, narrow-minded Vichy follower, I am more French than you, and you are quite aware of it, however. Your rancorous remarks are motivated by your jealousy.

Six people died in Tablabalt. One woman in the bunch and three citizens, three innocent victims; the other two were fellagha. A battalion came to surround the village where the rebels had found refuge in some homes (Mouloud's, for instance). That is all that is known.

**February 1**

When I say that I am French, I give myself a label that each French person refuses me. I speak French, and I got my education in a French school. I have learned as much as the average Frenchman. What am I then, dear God? Is it possible that as long as there are labels, there is not one for me? Which one is mine?

Can somebody tell me what I am! Of course, they may want me to pretend that I am wearing a label because they pretend to believe in it. I am very sorry, but this is not enough.

**February 2**

I have received news from back home. Amar spent the night here, and we talked. Life is still possible over there. Yes, possible. A hellish life. He began talking, going back in time, one day at a time. When he got to the Aïd, he tried to go on because he had forgotten that I was there, with them. I interrupted him: I was happy. There are no more empty moments in my mind, and I am able to imagine what it is like without any difficulty.

—It is today, he said to me, or tomorrow, that they must pay the contributions. I will pay when I go back there. In your case, there is your old father.

—What contributions?

—Well, we pay five hundred francs per head, but only the men. So, in your case, you owe fifteen hundred: your father, your brother, and you. Rabah is in charge of collecting for the karouba.[6]

—Rabah! Why doesn't he mind his own business!

—He has to do it. The underground needs money to kick the French out. They need help.

—The underground is going to kick the French out? Is that what they say?

—Of course. Why else would they fight? They are determined, you know. Determined and strong.

—Glad to hear it, glad to hear it. And Rabah is one of them? Rabah is not an interesting fellow. How do you explain that?

—It is not about Rabah or what he thinks. They needed a representative for your neighborhood. They picked him and Ali.

—Ali, too.

—Yes, Ali, too. They are in contact with the foreigners. They meet at night. Orders are given for the village. They have to be obeyed, and that is the way it is. It is in everyone's interest, you understand? Kaci is in charge of our karouba.

—He is a crook.

—I know. He goes so far as to invite them to his home and give them shelter. Believe me, they behave correctly. In the village, we did not want Kaci to be the intermediary, but he volunteered. And now, they think he is doing a good job.

—Watch out, he is going to get the fellagha to do something stupid. He is a mean fellow.

—God is stronger than he is. If he tries to do bad, God will know how to punish him.

—Do you know what this money is used for?

—It is never wasted, you can be sure. For instance, we gave 500 francs the first time. You remember, it was used to rebuild the homes that burned down in Taourirt-Moussa. Well, since then, it has all been fixed. We have to pay every month. They put the money they take to good use.

—I am sure of that. And the school, why did they burn it? You were all there, and you let it burn down. Your poor children . . .

—First of all, we did not find out about it until the next day. But they did not do anything wrong.

—You are frightened.

—There is something else. It would have been occupied. Can you imagine our village with a garrison and soldiers with neither law nor faith. Think of our women . . .

—You rationalize everything in terms of the soldiers. Can't you all control your women?

—With the women of Tizi-Hibel, it is impossible. You should see how they behave with the fellagha who are good Kabyles and good Muslims. It is almost scandalous. When they meet one, they check them out impudently. It is a shame, I tell you. One of the fellagha even said:

—You people of Tizi-Hibel, the more we know you, the more we appreciate you, but your women! . . . Yes, your women are quite bold.

—This is what Tartuffe used to say.

—You see, and he is a Frenchman, isn't he? Is he one of your friends?

—Yes, I have heard of him. So now they like you?

—Like brothers, I tell you. They are good Muslims. When they gathered us at the press-house, the village elders were scared, but their leader was wonderful. He began by reciting from the Qur'an. A *fatiha* entirely done in Arabic.[7] You should have heard his pronunciation, his tone, and his zeal. You did not need to understand, it was that impressive. Really, you have to respect these people. Since then they have gotten rid of everything: snuff, cigarettes, and gambling. In any case, it is all forbidden by Islam. That is the way it is with them: Islam and nothing else. Are you a Muslim or not? Satan must be driven away from every place, from every heart. Let him find refuge somewhere else! Do you go to the coffeehouse? Empty your cup, speak with your friends, then return to your home. God has made you into a Muslim, and you wish to continue to ignore this fact? No, this will not be allowed. But, you know, we are happy, that is for sure. Now, even jokes seem out of place and irreverent. To tell you the truth, our hearts are no longer in it . . .

And so, the people of Tizi-Hibel, once the most villainous on the surface of the earth, have found their faith again; they are now paying the salary of a muezzin and frequent the mosque assiduously.[8] God is great! When he wants to gather his children, he does it just like this, with a sleight of hand: everybody has come back to the holy fold. Some come back from France for only this reason. As good Muslims, they want to be buried in the cemetery in Tizi-Hibel.[9] They were killed over there by pious and intransigent hands, one because he smoked, the other because he drank. Since they both were cousins, only one family is dishonored. To be specific, mine.

I tried to get more information about what happened in Taourirt-Moussa. He did not tell me anything that I did not already know, except for some more specific topographical details. Now, I see quite well where and how the various skirmishes took place. The soldiers, relying on the information from Moh Aït Ali and Boudjema El Hadj Kaci, the father of the assassinated driver, thought they were going to surprise the fellagha. But they fell into a trap and were massacred. In turn, those who came to avenge their brothers killed a young man whom I do not know and an old man whom I know well. A good old peasant of Taourirt-Moussa who never did wrong or got involved in politics, who knew nothing about anything and who could care less about France, Algeria, Cairo, or anything else. A poor fellow who lived hand to mouth, a tired old man with a heavy load of wood on his back who worked hard his entire life, and who was sought out and found by the bullets of a submachine gun down a steep footpath while he was returning to his village. A man used to arduous labor, a worn-down beast, this is how one must describe Amrane. No doubt his last breath was one of relief. They put a cartridge belt on him and placed a submachine gun near him, and then they categorically identified him: he was the terrorist leader for the area.

The people of Tizi-Hibel witnessed the whole spectacle from a distance. They listened to the submachine gun fire, and after the fighting, a few members of the maquis came to eat with our delegate. The only thing left was to find out the identity of the informer. It did not take long. Just about a week ago, they went to pick him up. He was tried, found guilty, and executed within an hour. Most likely, Moh Aït Ali was involved because the same fate befell him. He must have been terrified as no other human ever has been because it is impossible to imagine anyone more cowardly than he, even though he was a war veteran. Amar told me that the mail arrives on a regular basis, that it is taken down to Tizi-Ouzou every day, and that although the market in Béni-Douala is closed, the stores in the villages are well supplied; the bakeries are busy, life continues just the same as when I left it last September. In short, nothing has changed, and the villages live cut off from the official administrative organization just like in the old days. Except that now they are not worried about the *hakem* or the *doula*, the French justice that is always on everybody's mind and that is nothing more than the sharp, cold sword held by someone more powerful who simultaneously despises you and protects you.[10] Now we know that we are no longer protected, but we have our dignity back. That is why the locals willingly submit themselves to the mystique of the maquis members; why they are honestly beginning to rediscover exceptional virtues in the holy book of Islam and substantial competence in those who act in its name.

—Now, Amar says to me, justice is taken care of. The rebels settle problems between people, help solve disagreements, and determine punishments. They never make a mistake. They want a union in every village, as well as peace and brotherhood. You, as well educated as you are, if you ever listened and talked to them, you would be won over . . .

I have no doubt that I would be won over if I lived in Tizi-Hibel. I would have given them my total support, my admiration without any reservation. After all, I am a family man. On this particular point, I am not unaware of my heavy responsibilities. But, from a distance, I cannot help but remain cautious, especially because I am well educated and know a little history.

**February 3**

The socialist government that just came into office is instilling rage in the hearts of the other political leaders. A government ready to turn in its resignation. That is what they say. The newspapers fire a constant barrage of insults at it. Yesterday, there was a huge demonstration in Algiers to prevent the departure of Governor Soustelle. People were complaining on the radio. It was absolutely grandiose and terrifying. The speaker yelled between sentences and was happy to let us hear his yelling. This must have pleased the people living in the interior, those who could not participate in this show of strength, of determined will, of dominating brutality rejecting conciliation.

What was it all about anyway? It was a protest against the removal of a governor general and his replacement by a resident minister.[11] The governor was cheered as much as the minister was jeered. It so happens that Mr. Soustelle is a man of exceptional merit. It so happens that in his scrupulous honesty he looked for a solution to the Algerian problem and found one that was worthy of his heart, and his intelligence, and worthy of France as well. It was total integration, complete equality between the indigenous people and the French, the night of August 4.[12] There was no reticence. It also happens that the indigenous people are the ones who are rejecting this solution. They remain impassible in the face of the human torrent that, carried by insatiable frenzy, rushes toward the harbor. No, we are not heartless, but we are mute with fear. Anguish holds us motionless, gags our throats, and keeps our jaws tight. Is it really true that these French people want to "integrate" us? Come on! They do because, in reality, they know very well that it is impossible. Mr. Soustelle is a utopian: a year ago they were afraid of him. They would heave insults at him. Today they are doing the same with Catroux.[13] They needed a man with a iron fist. A valet but one with an iron fist. Not an idealist. They were furious. Then, they rapidly came to the conclusion that in a pinch a utopian could still do the job, and they rallied around Soustelle. Why do they take him away now?

Filled with worry and bitterness, we feel that the people who came out into the streets to demonstrate are shouting their anger at us. It is not Soustelle that they want to keep but their privileges, their wealth, and their slaves.

—Gentlemen, calm down. We know that you are the masters. Your shouts will not change our condition in any way, nor will they change yours. You are wasting your time, calm down.

—Gentlemen, you fear that Catroux likes us, and you reject our friends. You are right to reject our friends because they could not be your friends at the same time. But come on, do you know Catroux? He is one of yours, gentlemen. At worst, he will turn into a utopian. What is wrong with that?

We are filled with bitterness at the idea that all these

French people who came out into the streets to insult the government of the Republic are free men. Free in ways we will never be. We try to imagine, for one moment, one short moment, that instead of these French people, there were indigenous people in these same streets, going toward the same harbor and shouting with the same vehemence against any government of the same Republic, their fists in the air and spitting, under the eyes of compassionate policemen and members of the CRS, escorted by army motorcycles and tanks and preceded by the spahis.[14] And we thought further: what would have happened to us in that case? Is it really true that you can "integrate," Governor? Is it really true that we could have acted in this manner with impunity? Then why pretend that you are going to make us into what you do not want us to be?

I could say the same thing to Camus and to Roblès. I feel a lot of admiration for the first and brotherly affection for the other. But they are wrong to talk to us when we are waiting for generous hearts if there are any; they are wrong to talk to us when they cannot express their thoughts completely. It is a hundred times better that they remain quiet. Because, in the end, this country is indeed called Algeria and its inhabitants are called Algerians.[15] Why sidestep the evidence? Are you Algerians, my friends? You must stand with those who fight. Tell the French that this country does not belong to them, that they took it over by force, and that they intend to remain here by force. Anything else is a lie and in bad faith. Any other language is criminal because, for several months now, crimes have been committed in the name of the same lies; for several months innocents who had accepted these lies and asked for nothing more than to live within these lies have died. They have died. And these innocents are primarily indigenous people. The people who do nothing to escape their condition and who get shot so that others will remain silent. Maybe these terrorists will eventually quiet down. This will be the silence of death or despair. Again, power will regain its rights and deplore the hypocritical ills that justice has brought to the country. Power will be able to smirk as it pleases. It will be right to smirk: justice has always brought misfortune but has never eliminated power.

**February 7**

It has been snowing since the 2nd. The pupils in the lower grades stayed home. The electricity went out and came back on again only yesterday; there was no mail and no radio. But today

71

the newspapers arrived. *L'Echo* has a big headline that reads: "General Catroux resigns after the welcome given Mr. Guy Mollet in Algiers." This is followed by a smaller headline: "Violent incidents take place as Mr. Guy Mollet arrives in Algiers." "Under a shower of projectiles, the prime minister places a wreath at the war memorial only to see it immediately trampled by the crowd." Same large headlines for *Le Journal*: "Hostile reception in Algiers for President Guy Mollet." "A large crowd demonstrates for several hours from the main post office to the Summer Palace."

And so it is! Along with large pictures where one sees faces and more faces. One paper has nothing more than smiling faces and a caption that reads: "The crowd gathered under the balcony, and expressed its joy through endless applause when our newspaper informed it of General Catroux's resignation."

**February 9**

This morning someone discovered the body of Mr. A. across the highway at the entrance to the village of Azouza. He had been executed during the night. Mr. A. is a French citizen, a retired policeman, secretary of the Dar El Askri. Until recently, he continued to smoke and drink. Then, conspicuously, he stopped, most likely as a response to a stern warning. So why did this execution take place? Maybe they suspect that he reported the visit of rebel leaders in Azouza and, because of this, provoked the encounter of a fortnight ago during which many innocents and soldiers were killed . . . So here is the next victim, just as I expected.

**February 12**

The French press that reaches us is publishing detailed commentaries about the latest demonstrations in Algiers. It condemns or approves the attitude of the French in Algeria, the attitude of the prime minister, and is concerned about what the Muslims may be thinking. Everybody agrees that the situation is serious. Despite this, we all have the impression that Algiers has become a gigantic tower of Babel where a part of the population suddenly wakes up angry at another, which remains mute. It is difficult to know which group is more frightened. As for the newspaper articles, I think the most significant is the one by Mauriac in *L'Express*:

"But you, who are you? he writes to Mr. Guy Mollet. A stoic layman who does not budge when tomatoes are thrown at him? When it involves the head of the government, this courage leaves me cold, and that is not saying much. I admire somewhat Louis XVI, who on June 20, sporting a Phrygian bonnet, made it known through a soldier that his heart was not beating any faster. I like hearts that beat and, at certain times, beat furiously."

Farther on, he adds: "and outside, the other protagonist, a people of eight million men, observes and waits." [16]

I, for one, greatly admire Mr. Mauriac because he dares to say exactly what he thinks, what we all think. That is something that, as far as I know, no other Frenchman has dared to say: This people of eight million men is not French, and on its soil the French, who disagree with one another, are battling for the sole purpose of deciding the manner in which they are going to continue to impose their will upon it, to continue to live there, to continue to exploit and despise it, in the name of imperishable principles, in order to fulfill a highly civilizing mission. So this people observes and waits. It has not been doing this sanely for a long time. Yet it has been waiting for an eternity. It has always waited. You can bet we have been waiting for Mr. Mollet and that we have been waiting for Mr. Catroux. The general will not come. Mr. Mollet came. He was supposed to come in order to calm us down but instead he threatened us even though we asked him for nothing and we were careful not to insult him. His compatriots insulted him; he remained calm, and the good words that he promised us were then directed toward them. Then he got back on his plane, knowing quite well that we are used to waiting.

A fellow compatriot with only an elementary school education and who is filled with good peasant common sense said to me:

—You know history, don't you? Being pelted with tomatoes and other vegetables, that goes beyond being a regal welcome. A prime minister is more important than an adventurer or a plenipotentiary minister, right? So now, we can insult France? Another thing. If there had been young natives from the Casbah, from Belcourt, or Maison-Carrée instead of all these French people, what would the CRS, the police officers, or later France have done? Yes, what would France have done? Okay. Now, replace Guy Mollet with a Kabyle. I am going to tell you what the Kabyle would have done. It is quite simple. He would have gotten back on his plane without saying anything and he would have left the Algerians to fix up the mess by themselves . . . See what I mean?

Because I have some good peasant common sense myself, I winked maliciously with one eye and assured him that I knew exactly what he meant. It is basically the same thing that Mauriac was saying.

—Listen, I said to him. Let us pretend for a moment that you are a Frenchman from Algeria. Then, tell me in all honesty what you would have done?

—I do not have to pretend. I am a Kabyle. And when I go to France, they call me a bicot.[17]

**February 12**

Yet, it is necessary to put ourselves in the shoes of the French, even if they do not often put themselves in ours. In any case, these are equivocal sentences because, in the end, what we are reproaching them for is precisely that they are putting themselves in our shoes. They have taken over our land, all of it, they have left us with nothing, and they do not want to give anything back. To the point where they think it natural, logical, and human to them that a Frenchman be worth eight Arabs. This subtle exercise in arithmetic makes no sense to us.

Therefore, I must suppose that I have suddenly discovered that I am a pioneer Frenchman, with ancestors in Burgundy who settled on a small piece on land in Beni-Mered. I presume further that the descendant of these small-time settlers could do nothing more than become a lay elementary school teacher under the one and indivisible Third and Fourth Republics. My name is Durand.[18] I am a family man, and I have been on the job for twenty years. My thick, Algero-Burgundian skull is as tumultuous in this month of February 1956 as the *Plateau des Glières*.[19] My tormented heart goes through periods of enthusiasm and discouragement, hatred or fear. I do not know how all this is going to end. I know that I am in danger, as are other members of my family. And, like them, I will fight to defend myself . . .

**February 15**

Yes, I will fight because I have lived in this country and believe that it is my own. I have made a modest, stable life for myself here, a life that deserves respect. The tombs of my ancestors, of my parents, are here in Beni-Mered. I have done no harm to these Arabs who are rebelling, who are mad at me, who are going to slit my throat. All I do is ignore them—well, almost. Why are they now rising against me? All they had to do was get themselves a job, just like I did. They are unhappy, they are unhappy. Is it my fault, damn it? I agree that I have always been aloof with them and that, in my mind, I cannot get used to the idea that they are my equals. I have to admit this with total sincerity, and admit just as sincerely that, deep down, we settled here as winners, that consequently we are the race that rules, that must serve itself first. Why deny it? And, in all modesty, I never display this attitude, and generally we all have enough tact so that life is bearable for the Arabs, and we all deal with enough good faith to give to the best of them almost everything they deserve, especially the more obedient ones. But these people want everything. The country is theirs, they argue, and all that is left for us to do is get back on a boat or die. That is the state of things at the present time. So the conquest served no purpose? What right do they have to kick us out? . . .

### February 16

The Frenchman from Beni-Mered would have a lot of other things to say. It would certainly be right to say them. Just like P., the solicitor in Tizi-Ouzou, who argues that the rebels are wasting their time, given that Algeria has been occupied for over a century and that, in fact, there is a legal prescription because of the French civil code. All our pretensions are therefore unacceptable and illegal, according to P.

We must acknowledge, however, that the fellagha are quietly making fun of French legality and of the fact that the French call them outlaws. Outlaws or bandits. But this does not prevent these bandits from creating their own laws, executing them, and carrying out the punishment that they pronounce.

Yesterday, H., the photographer, was executed at his home. They came for him around 8:00 P.M. The meeting, I heard, took place in the mosque. He was heard, judged, and found guilty. He died the same way Mr. A. did. Perhaps he had made the same mistake.

What are we to think of all these poor people who have died? Most of them were old and had a family to take care of. All are "faithful servants of France." As such, they are entitled to a tear from the boss. One single tear. Just like the old dogs that are shot in their doghouses by their owners who, one fine day, run out of patience. They have decided to get rid of them, and right before they kill them, they manage to give them one last affectionate look. These people, of course, are not shot by their boss, but as long as they die for him, or because of him, it is as if he is the one who has sacrificed them. That is why they are entitled to a tear. Just one tear.

**February 17**

I have just had several conversations with French colleagues. It is more and more difficult to avoid talking about what is going on. As concerns H., one of them told me:

—It is strange, but he is not well regarded by the French. Yes, he is affable, polite, too polite even. What I mean is hypocritical. We thought that his sympathies were with the other side.

Another added:

—These people have their own reasons for doing what they did. If they killed him, it is because he did them a disservice. After all, they know what they are doing.

And I thought to myself:

—Yes, ladies and gentlemen, he must have done them a disservice, something that you profited from. But your eulogy is a bit short. Even if he did try and hide his preferences, he still could not gain your sympathy. Of course, he cheated. When one cheats on one's own, one must cheat openly, that is what you feel. French people from Algeria, we have spoiled you. It is going to be hard for us to make you understand the language of free men. And it is going to be even harder for us to speak with you as free men and not as "faithful servants."

**February 19**

It was only this morning that General Olié came for a visit. I did not go out to meet him and I do not know what happened during the ceremony. I can quite understand the fact that being seen with French officials, especially a general, can get people in trouble with the maquis. Still, not attending an official reception when one is a supervisor is a sign of cowardice. Of course, my case is different from all the others. One might think that I am attending as a member of the city council. Here again, why did I agree to resign under pressure? I did so because I felt like it: I had wanted to for a while? Then I should have resigned earlier. Who am I kidding: I am scared just like everyone else around here. No more, no less. Dialectic has never excused fear . . .

My colleagues got scared. Those who were French told me:

—Yes, we are willing to go. As long as there are some Muslims with us.

The Muslims told me:

—If you think that we are not in danger, let us all go, you in front. Well, after all, no. We will not go, that is all. You are a family man, and so are we.

The French added:

—Speaking of danger, you have to admit, we are in more danger than you. Because the day the fellagha decide to exterminate us, we will all be killed. As far as you are concerned, they will only slit the throats of informers.

I answered the French:

—Maybe you are right. In principle only. You see, up to now, we have not killed anyone except the mayor. But several of ours are killed each and every day. I am only talking about what is going on here. Ten Kabyles, one Frenchman. Here is the assessment. And then there is something else: the day when your soldiers decide to exterminate us, do you think that they will choose their victims? See our point of view?

We exchanged a sorry smile and started talking about something else.

There are rumors that H. the photographer and Mr. A. were both informers. Mr. A. was warned several times, and he even swore that he would come back into the fold. But he continued to provide information. He had a radio transmitter at home. They say he caused a great deal of damage.

As for H., he was very generous with the rebels. He thought that he had bought the right to live and to discreetly continue to do the things that had already earned him a license for a Moorish café. The outlaws saw things differently. A colleague told me that one evening a veiled woman was seen entering his home; it was supposedly one of Mouloud's former maids who, they say, had brought him information about a secret meeting of maquis leaders. She gave the information because she was mad at being fired, and H. did the same because that is what he did. Would not this make a good subject for a novel? But the many victims of this novel are not fictitious, like the good-natured photographer.

Speaking of Mr. A. and H., this is what is happening here: each time a Kabyle is killed, people talk a lot and their imagination goes into high gear. A day or two later, the victim is forgotten, and they wait for the next one.

—Well, they killed him, poor fellow. Yet, really, when you start thinking about it, right? I am not making any accusations but still, between us, you agree, he was a good man. How do you feel about this?

—Watch out, we do not know everything that is going on. Above all, we need to be quiet and hold our tongues. I have heard that . . .

—Really, I did not know. You know, I have heard things myself . . .

—You see.

We reach the same conclusions every time. Quickly. We live at a time when it is easy to die and when everyone is held responsible for their own death. While waiting to conquer the right to live as free men, we have the right to die as traitors.

**February 25**

The Aït-Atelli school burned down yesterday, and the day before the same thing happened to the school in Aït-Mimoun. Now that the snow has melted, there is a rising number of skirmishes and victims. An isolated farm was burned down in the Mitidja.[20] Its occupants were massacred and then burned. On the walls, someone wrote with the stem of a geranium: "Violence breeds violence." The journalist on duty concludes his report with a reference to the highly honorific gesture of a policeman who, before abandoning the farm, took care of the animals one last time.

—In spite of everything, let us not forget the animals, he said.

—Whose side is "violence" on? asks the journalist.

I myself am not at all surprised by the traditional gesture of the policeman. It is even a traditional and classical gesture that right away reminds me of General Hugo and his famous flask of rum. So this settles it, the act demonstrates his bravery.

In Azouza the day before yesterday, a patrol making its way through the village was attacked around 8:00 P.M. A mortally wounded lieutenant died a few hours later. He was due to be sent home at the end of the month. I am only reporting what is going on in the immediate area around Fort-National. What goes on here is about the same as what goes on elsewhere, at different times, or in different ways. It is true that "violence breeds violence." We live this cruel truth on a daily basis. It is the only truth that is left.

Yesterday morning, the French occupied Azouza again in order to check identifications. I have heard that every single man in the village had to come to the school, which is now occupied. They stood against a wall until noon, then they had to cut all the cacti around the houses, the leafy trees, and the bushes all around the village to remove any possible hiding place that might be used for an ambush.

During the checks, they shot "the rabbit," and he died this morning in the Tizi-Ouzou hospital.

"The rabbit" always claimed that his real name was "the lion," but it is only the young who called him that out of fear. As soon as he walked away, they changed their tune and shouted "Rabbit! Rabbit!" Then he would get angry but did not frighten anybody. It never lasted long, and "the rabbit" would display his usual smile. I cannot remember a time when I did not see him without his dumb-looking smile, and he most likely died smiling at the angels, the stupid angels of idiots because they could not prevent his death.

Yesterday, when I found out that he had been wounded, I burst out laughing. Now that I am trying to write about his death, my eyes are filled with tears. But I am quite aware that people will laugh every time they think about him.

"The rabbit" was a thin kind of fellow with a rounded back. His frayed, ample clothes were stained with sweat. He always had an old bag on his back, and he carried a crate filled with bottles or a block of ice. When he comes up from the "*caves du fort*" to bring his heavy load to the mess hall, he pretends not to see me, and his ruddy arms hide his red face and his bright red tarboosh.[21] All I can see is the tip of his nose and its crystal drop, which looks like a small ice cube. When he is finished with his chore, he comes back down with a smile on his face. As he walks by me and flashes his pearly white teeth, he brandishes a small loaf of bread. Each time he grunts a few syllables of a respectful greeting.

A true rabbit! Large eyes with a pinkish reflection, a pointed snout, a stupid or frightened look on his face, a voice that utters nothing but high-pitched or guttural sounds that surprised anyone who wants to understand him. He had this eternal smile that, although everyone knew better, expressed his joy at being alive, at living from one meal to the next, and at finding all of this quite hilarious and funny, so funny in fact that he wanted to thank the whole human race.

—Say, Rabbit, everything okay?
—Of course everything is okay.

—Say, Lion, everything okay?

—Couldn't be better. Thanks for your kindness! Thanks for calling me "Lion."

Poor old rabbit! I will be wasting my time if I wait for you to show up in front of my home. I will not see you anymore sweating under your blocks of ice in August or tottering in the snow with a box filled with wine bottles on your back in January. The soldiers in the mess hall will no longer be able to poke fun at you. So why did they shoot you, poor old rabbit? I heard that you tried to escape, when they lined all of you up against the wall. Although it is natural for a rabbit to try to be free, I know that this is not what you were trying to do.

But your simple mind did not quite grasp what was going on. You said to yourself: "I am their rabbit. They know me, they joke with me, they like me a little. Of course they like me. You know, the sergeant who runs the mess? Do you know what he calls me? "Lion," he does. I am not going to get behind schedule today. Do I have anything to do with these other people that they are frisking? After all, I am the Rabbit.

So, you left. And when they saw you leave, poor rabbit, they took you for a lion, and they decided to kill the lion. If this can be of any consolation to you, be aware that although you lived as a rabbit you died like a lion. Sleep in peace, my poor old friend!

**February 26**

I have been told that the French army descended upon the large village of Taourirt and that the home of the mayor pro tem was completely searched. That is all I know. But both he and his children are still under suspicion. The person who told me the news was scandalized because this gentleman is one hundred percent administrator and a knight in the order of the Legion of Honor. Everybody knows that. They also know that recently his children, while pretending to be submissive, have more or less been openly playing their progressive, federal, or nationalist hand, and that the oldest one has to be in contact with the maquis for whom he is the area spokesman. So, is it not reasonable that the French army would be somewhat interested in what goes on at the home of the mayor pro tem? The Kabyles would like to continue to fool the French with a lot of humility and without being disturbed. However, the French have been aware of the situation for quite a while. If they treat some of us kindly, it is due to some remnant of guilty naïveté, or it is because they still hope to bring back to those who might be well-intentioned but are also weak or unsure those who have always served them and have never questioned their superiority. In a way, we no longer understand the psychology of the French because we no longer speak the same language.

Up to this point, we were speaking the same language. Everything was fine. We were just as hypocritical as they were. Now, those in the maquis, our "legitimate interlocutors," are telling them how things really are. Fine, the French are responding to this crude language as best they can, but quite often they talk to us. We resent this because we have persuaded ourselves that they believe us even though we have been lying to them. We have to accept the following fact: They no longer believe us. They should themselves know once and for all that nobody either believes them or likes them. We act like good Kabyles, as we are supposed to, and they act like true French people. We can no longer anticipate their reactions, and they can no longer prevent ours; for we have stopped hypocritical dealings between ourselves. This is a mental divorce, a break that is going to be exacerbated even more by the fact that some live in hope and others live in despair, that the former aspire to a radiant ideal that they discover ecstatically and that fills them with enthusiasm, while the latter are forced to fight in accordance with a generous humanism that condemns the very principle of this struggle; a high and worthy morality that people yearn for and adopt, that they impose by force when necessary, and that was never imposed on them by force. All people except for the most backward, where this morality was introduced with a sword, where it was accepted against the will of the people who eventually adopted it to the point of rebelling today in order to claim their right to live according to this high and worthy morality, according to this generous humanism that they have been taught. . . And now the French master finds himself locked inside a circle that he has carefully closed. What prevents him from doing a good turn towards his disciple? It is because the disciple is, at the same time, a valet whose services are needed, darn it!

### March 1

Yesterday, *Le Journal d'Alger* carried a large and revealing headline: "Solemn Call from Prime Minister Mollet." Below, as large as the above headline: "Rebels, stop your attacks." Below this still: "Free elections will take place in three months." Poor France. Poor French people. I am not talking about those who live in Algeria nor those of current generations. No, I am talking about those who died for freedom, those who gave to their country the immortal principles that render France immortal as well.

So, according to you, gentlemen, do all these men who die on your side and on ours die only so that we can vote freely? That is what it is all about, right? The prime minister of the French Republic finally recognizes that we have never had the right to vote freely and now that we claim this right, they are sending soldiers to kill us. Is this how you apply the Great Principles of which you are so proud? Gentlemen of *Le Journal d'Alger*, do you know what a horrendous pleonasm you have spread across your front page? To vote freely? It is horrendous and tragic at the same time. Tragic for us. Tragic for you. Poor young Burgundians, Picards, Bretons, Alsatians who have died on Algerian soil to prevent the Algerians from "voting freely." Do you really know for whom you died?

As for us, it is clear that we owe these promised "free elections"—another fashionable term one does not hesitate to use—to the rebels' actions. It is just as clear that he who backs down from a stronger opponent does so reluctantly, and that when this force ceases to exist, he will be able to regain what has been lost. Finally, it is clear and logical that those who rebel, who fight and suffer, are not content with promises, and that their goal is to annihilate their enemy. The enemy who is not really France but who is also the enemy of France.

**March 6**

I have received news from back home through Ab. It is terrifying. The soldiers are ruthless; their actions have become acceptable, normal. The fellagha are ruthless; their actions have become acceptable, normal. For either of them, the readily designated enemy, the suspect to be threatened or manhandled, the accomplice to be shot, to be hit with a fine, or to be led to jail can be found in a Kabyle village. It sometimes happens that the soldiers and the fellagha meet. And of course each party views the encounters as heroic. Whatever the outcome of the fighting may be, one emerges from it bathed in glory.

The people in the villages are terrified. Their life is hell. At 6:00, Ab. explained to me, all doors are locked tight. They have ordered us to kill all the dogs because dogs bark when the patriots come by at night. They obviously ignore their duty as Kabyle dogs, which consists in being quiet and not signaling the whereabouts of the French who bivouac on the other side of the hill. It just so happens that at least one gun is needed to kill dozens of dogs. They took our guns away months ago. So the people had to hurl stones at the poor animals. Exactly like what happened during antiquity when traitors were stoned to death. A bunch of young men who had nothing better to do took care of the chore for a couple of bucks per dog. Ab. told me that this was not excessive. It is not easy to kill a dog. You work up a good sweat trying to kill one with pebbles or a cudgel.

— One morning, he added, I opened my door around 4:00. You know that my door overlooks the large kouba of the area where the ashes of our revered marabout are buried.[22] We see a multitude of blinking lights. My wife prostrates herself and calls upon us the benediction of the great marabout who appears himself in this manner in the early morning, as if to bring some ray of hope. I beg you, dispense with your skeptic smile. A few minutes later, about fifty military cars arrived in the village. It was for a search that lasted all day and during which our women got upset stomachs. This is really too sad. I have been a soldier myself. I would rather not say anything. My wife understood her mistake. When she looks at the kouba she makes a face that is, at times, filled with sadness and pity. The marabout is also suspect and powerless. Just like us.

About a month ago, the rebels kidnapped Ch. S. No one knows what has become of him, although it is not too hard to guess. Everybody was aware of his close ties with the rebels. People never imagined that his life might be at risk.

Also, S. Y. was machine-gunned. He was thought to be safe as well. He made it, and that is fortunate for him. Everything is so confusing. We would like to understand. Do we have to give this up? Must we spend our days in fear like hunted animals?

### March 7

Market day, as usual—last Wednesday it was banned— the main street is filled with busy and noisy villagers. No Europeans in the street. Nothing but compatriots. Perhaps it is the sunshine, or the possibility of shopping at one's leisure, but people seem more open and full of life, less worried or more determined. Maybe they also feel strong and big, really strong, like young adolescents who would be proud to be talked to like men for the first time. It is this kind of self-contentment that I seem to read in people's eyes. From now on, no one will be able to talk to these people as is if they were children. They would shrug their shoulders and crack you in the mouth. Can you blame them? Come on, let us face the facts and stop the killing. In the name of immortal principles.

**March 8**

I have learned that S. Y. was machine-gunned by mistake and that he has received an apology. If he had been killed, the apology would have been most likely presented to the parents. At the same time as the condolences.

On a personal note, today is my birthday. Nothing special. Happy, nonetheless, to have completed another year. Will there be any more? The M. C. is going to meet in a little while. Yesterday, someone brought a notification to attend the meeting signed by the f. f. assistant, who was sending me his best wishes at the same time. I returned it immediately with my refusal to attend the meeting and my best wishes. Behind the f. f. assistant there is a young captain who is a member of the SAS. He is the reason why I refused to attend. Here is a man who acts as a teacher and proposes to pacify us. The other day, he met an employee in the street. The employee was talking with his friends and forgot to greet him—maybe he did not him. The captain raced toward him to point out his rudeness. Then, while talking to him alone, he threatened to have his friends investigated. When he called a meeting with the councilors who had resigned, he did not fail to add that he would send the police after us if we did not show up. This is how he intends to pacify us. When the fellagha are not available, he starts by disciplining those who live around him. You cannot accuse him of wasting time.

As for those of us who have resigned under threat, we may consider returning to city hall if the threat is lifted. Or if, in his turn, the captain threatens us in the same manner. But in this case, we would still be able to select our master. And most likely, it would not be him.

**March 9**

The radio yesterday and the newspapers today are bringing terrifying news about the rebels' massacres of poor farmers near Palestro.[23] They were machine-gunned. Their farms were burned down because they were the enemy, and nothing more. Has the time for unbridled furor arrived? Can people who kill innocents in cold blood be called liberators? If so, have they considered for a moment that their "violence" will engender more "violence," will legitimize it, and will hasten its terrible manifestation? They know that the people are unarmed, bunched together in their villages, immensely vulnerable. Are they knowingly preparing for the massacre of "their brothers"? Even by admitting that they are bloodthirsty brutes—which in any case does not excuse them but, on the contrary, goes against them, against us, against the ideal that they claim to defend—they have to consider sparing us so as not to provoke repression. Unless liberation means something different for them than it does for us. We thought that they wanted to liberate the country along with its inhabitants. But maybe they feel that this generation of cowards that is proliferating in Algeria must first disappear, and that a truly free Algeria must be repopulated with new men who have not known the yoke of the secular invader. One can logically defend this point of view. Too logically, unfortunately. And, gradually, from suspicions to compromises and from compromises to betrayals, we will all be declared guilty and summarily executed in the end.

In any case, the news I get about the rebels' state of mind is not at all reassuring. Their prestige is eroding precisely because they want too much of it. Did someone not tell me back home that they are now behaving like masters? Like masters whose arrogance far surpasses that of the unseasoned and impulsive administrators or of the big shots we cannot forget. Because the hakem used a whip and the big shot screamed insults. But the rebels, they strangle, they hang victims from trees. O Villon![24] They cut throats, they shoot machine guns, they mutilate. They no longer tax themselves about the easy women who welcome them under the villagers' noses, give them shelter, give them information, complain to them, and somehow manage to inspire fear. In our humiliated villages, the whores make the laws. Despondency, amazement, and terror have replaced the naive enthusiasm of the early days. Pushed aside by the French soldiers, trampled by the fellagha, my compatriots implore in silence a god that despises them because they despise themselves. They hide themselves unarmed like women, and disgrace is upon them. I will never forget the grotesque sentences given out by the omnipotent judge who favored Dehbia and Kaltoum. And the sorry story of Ali Gu'idir.

People are hoping only for peace, regardless of the outcome of a fight that no longer interests them. Maybe they will have peace, the eternal peace they fear. They spend lots of time with their eyes raised toward the sky. That is the extent of heaven's promises.

## 1956

### Same day

Mouloud has been granted bail. Yesterday he came by in a taxi but did not stop. They could not hold anything against him. This does not surprise me. It is nevertheless surprising that the same union that was so prompt to show concern and alarm over Dupuy is the same union that acted as if Mouloud did not exist. It is true that the union mistrusts Mouloud and that the rebels mistrust Dupuy. The union is suspicious of Mouloud because he is Kabyle. Fine, let them think of all of us as suspects. What tops it all is that they are right to do so. Why be surprised, then? I would like to put the Gary Davises and all the citizens of the world, both the anarchists and the jokers, and all my good friends in my place. The whole lot of pacifists, the internationalists who despise themselves but have the right to love others. Because if we start being proud of ourselves, we are suddenly faced with people who have always been proud of themselves. And then it is no longer possible to think of oneself as evil. It is no longer possible to consider ourselves the equal of other men and to think about universal fraternity. Now, it is our duty to despise everyone else and, in that way, persuade ourselves that we are superior.

### March 10

Yesterday, there was an important demonstration of North African workers in Paris. Thousands were arrested. The French government is asserting, once more, that Algeria is French. Those opposed to the demonstration are saying that the motherland is in danger. The people of France have been given a solemn warning. As for the FLN, it is demanding Algerian independence and is prepared to organize a general insurrection throughout the country. There does not seem to be any room for conciliation. We may be about to live through some tragic days that will put an end to our perpetual anguish: those who fall will be at peace forever, and the survivors will no longer live in fear.

### March 11

It is impossible to excuse the members of the maquis for either their mistakes or their injustice. For the past hundred years, we have endured all of this and suffered the consequences of errors and injustice. So, gentlemen, why do you fight? If nothing is going to change, at least spare lives and let us be. When soldiers kill children, women, simpletons, innocents, it is neither new nor scandalous. You are neither French soldiers nor police officers. Do not consider yourselves powerful men or administrators. You have no right to do that. And if you insist on it, we will hate you. When the country begins to fear and detest you, you will no longer amount to anything. You will be nothing more than bandits, just as you are already called, or criminals who deserve to be hanged. And when they execute you, the country will breathe a sigh of relief.

Today is a beautiful Sunday. The French have gone to mass. Before noon, I walked by some of them along the main street. They were walking two by two. We exchanged discreet and rare greetings. We belong to different worlds. People no longer go to church as they once did. Last year, each Sunday was a celebration for them—men, women, young men, and young girls. They would come out looking happy, with shining eyes, and the superior and condescending look that they usually display to us. It was their church, their Sunday, the day when they accepted us with difficulty, whatever their feelings toward us might be. They offended us a bit, though, by pretending that they were not aware of what they were doing. Another feather in their cap that we instinctively resented. Today, they show a lot of nonchalance in going to church, as if they no longer enjoyed it or had grown skeptical. Now that we are paying more attention to them, they are less inclined to show off. Or, perhaps they consider the mass as a refined entertainment reserved for them alone, and they are turning away from it because they no longer want to be entertained. We have to admit as well that there are no more young girls or pretty ladies in Fort-National. All those that could leave are now far away. Others will surely follow. And it is enough to think about this, in the beginning, in order to allow the heart to move beyond it: little by little one forgets acquaintances, buddies, and old friends to whom one is linked by years of hypocrisy. One forgets people and things. One forgives one's own mistakes, but one forgives nothing to those who stay behind. One leaves without ever saying good-bye to others.

People in this frame of mind show the greatest indifference toward us. Planning to leave their own kind behind without regrets, people with whom they are more or less on nonspeaking terms, their indifference is objective, although mixed with sympathy. Deep down inside, I suspect that they feel that the rebels are right. Maybe in the spirit of Christian charity they want the rebels to win but, hopefully, after their departure.

## 1956

### March 12

I talked with Mouloud. He has been transferred here. He will have plenty of time to tell us what happened at his place, and I will have plenty of time to listen. The first thing he did was to praise the primary school inspector who came to see him in jail, the man who cried behind his thick glasses and whose throat was just as tight with emotion as Mouloud's so that they could not say one word to each other. Then the inspector went to get an attorney for him. Mouloud already had one. No matter, he took the second attorney. So the entire school district was worried about Mouloud's fate. So people did not forget him, and while he was suffering, men suffered in their hearts also. As for the union, M. told me, in plain terms, that the national secretary in Paris went to see the minister of war, which means that our susceptibility is satisfied, our mistrust is groundless, and our belligerence is unjust. So this is how a trench is dug, how hatred is fed, and how crimes can be justified. Misunderstanding, doubt, and lies continue to grow, leading toward our own undoing. Oh God, what can we do? Are there men here with names still worthy of saving our country? All the people who know or who feel that they are close to each other, as close and undivided as possible, who love each other as brothers, will their voices be heard ever again? Will they be trapped in one or the other of two molds that are separated by an abyss from which one can only escape as a traitor? Must one fall into this horrible, merciless abyss that continues to expand from one side to the other?

### March 13

The abyss! How could it not become wider when one knows what is going on in the places where they torture, at the PRG, behind the portal of the jail, at the police station, at the barracks, wherever one finds military or civilian authorities.[25] What bestial instinct and ferocious imagination do we all have within us that we act on to create the means to inflict pain. We cannot ignore this sad reality. Mouloud has met the poor fellow from back home whom I talked about at the beginning of this journal. He started by cutting down his neighbor's fig trees, and then he shot the village policeman in Béni-Douala. This guy no longer has testicles.

— He showed me his crumpled scrotum, Mouloud assured me. I felt it with my hands, there is nothing left inside. They burned it with electricity.

What I have reported is close to the truth. First, they stunned him with blows, and then he admitted to all the crimes in a logical progression: fig trees, poles, food runner for the rebels, criminal. He got nine years for the three indictments. For the crime, he is still waiting. Without illusion.

—What got me talking more than anything else is the spring, he said.

It is a tool that is introduced into the anus and that increases in size when they push on the spring. Then they pull it out brutally, and you feel your entrails tear.

—I could not take the spring, the simpleton concluded, as if to excuse himself.

The prisoners have made some unbelievable claims. Those that they have signed by hand would boggle the mind of even the most disillusioned person. A marabout is condemned to death because he lived in the lowlands. Egyptian pilots came into his home on several occasions after they had discreetly landed nearby to deliver weapons. The marabout got into the habit of distributing these weapons to his flock until the day came when he was discovered. Afterward he admitted to it and signed a statement. Most likely, while the agents were casually placing the instruments of torture in front of him, especially the famous spring. That was a lucky escape for the darn anus of the marabout.

### Same day

More information about the shots heard yesterday at noon. The rebels came to visit the tree nursery, and Edouard was almost burned alive inside his farm. He was able to escape at dusk with his sister and find refuge at the military post. Gasoline had been poured all around his house but it was not set on fire (?). The guard at the tree nursery was supposedly roughed up. Well, that was a serious warning. People living in the suburbs are very worried and no longer have any confidence in the army because it appears that the soldiers did not rush out to meet the fellagha when they heard the hail of bullets. This morning, however, they checked every ravine and all the bushes around the fort. Our French fellow citizens think that they are going to be massacred soon. Meanwhile, the Muslim population enjoys, as do the French, full military protection without fearing anything from the rebels. The French will tolerate this supreme injustice less and less. Being of sound mind, they will not be able to allow this ambiguous situation to persist too long. But if their way of thinking prevailed, what would be the fate of the Muslim population? In the surrounding countryside, the trees are starting to grow again, and the birds are singing once more. Men are living in anguish and expect to see nothing but dark days.

### March 14

Another market day. As usual, there are people everywhere. Around noon I took a quick walk around the town. People seemed tense, nervous, ready to commit any act of folly, anger, or stupidity. Throughout this crowd, I felt horror as if I was living a nightmare. A mysterious curse hung over us. I found myself in the middle of hell and the damned, with the bright Algerian sun shining above. Overwhelmed, I took refuge at home. I do not know where this feeling came from because this is the first time I have felt this suffering inside me. Maybe this is what fear is, a panic for which there is no specific justification or basis. The French, the Kabyle, the soldier, and the fellagha frighten me. I am afraid of myself. The French are inside me, and the Kabyle are inside me. I feel disgust for those who kill, not because they want to kill me, but because they have the backbone to kill. Then, on either side, one legitimizes the crime and justifies it. Thus, crimes are rendered necessary, like acts of faith or worthy deeds.

I have received a second request to attend the city council meeting. I am not going to answer this time. The captain will be furious. What a sorry attitude he has toward me, this captain! Has he figured out yet that I am afraid of him? At most he confirms what I suspect the French—at least those that know me—think of me. No, gentlemen, you are wrong. My pride is as strong as yours. What you can be convinced of is that I am as French as you are culturally speaking. But do not expect anything else. That would be impudent. I cannot disown your culture, but do not expect me to give up who I am, to accept your condescension, your racism, your anger, your hatred. Your lies. A century of lies.

### March 15

My first teachers were Kabyle like me. The one who left the strongest impression on me is still alive. A good man who liked the French a lot. Now he is eighty years old, and he no longer likes you. You turned him into a SFIO socialist, a free mason, and a French citizen who formally rejected his status as a Muslim.[26] When he decided to leave our village, some thirty years ago, he asked for an assignment nearby, "near the town and on the highway." He had the respect of his superiors and had very good evaluations. The post was given to a young French colleague who showed a lot of promise. My teacher already had ten years of service when this colleague was born. In response to his timid letter of complaint, and in order to console him for not having obtained the transfer he wanted, he was awarded the *palmes académiques*.[27] So he decided to wait, in the village, for his retirement, but he never wore the ribbon that he inadvertently solicited and that had been given to him as a compensation.

—All in all, he always maintained, I do not deserve this.

He taught me early on that France was my adoptive country and that, consequently, I was a little orphan to be looked after. This put in my heart a lot of humility and tender gratitude; and I liked France more than a French child. He explained to me the symbolical meaning of the three colors as well as the republican motto in which he believed with the candor of older children and with complete naïveté showing on his pleasant, round, and reddish face, which was always smiling. He talked to me about the emperor with the white beard who killed the Saracens and of Jeanne d'Arc, at whom he poked fun because of the voices she heard.[28] He felt a deep respect for the dazzling "sun king," but he liked the man from Béarn who was so good at "conning" the partisans of the Catholic church and who later died treacherously at the hand of a "fanatical white father."[29] My teacher had a knack for anecdotal facts and vague notions of history. He organized his storytelling without much malice and captured our interest wonderfully. In our minds, it was as if he could abolish time and distance, and the people about whom he would talk seemed to belong to our past. They had died, of course, but it seemed as if they were still around, very close. Not too different from the people of today. We made them our own to such an extent that all the other people about whom he talked, at times, seemed ridiculous and unpleasant to us. This included our own ancestors because we were slightly ashamed of them. We would excuse their ignorance and promise to redeem them by becoming "good French people." Our master split his admiration between Robespierre and the little Corsican who dominated the world.[30] He showed nothing but contempt for Dey Hussein, although his famous fan saved us from barbarism.[31] Finally, he swore by Jules Ferry and lived in constant fear of displeasing the primary school inspector.[32]

Yet, he was filled with subtlety and good sense. I suspect

him of having figured things out early on. But he was a fundamentally honest man and scrupulously followed the school programs that he was required to teach us both in letter and spirit. Yes, he figured things out very early on, yet he did not warn us about anything! When we started asking questions and seeking answers ourselves, an immense, internalized lie confronted us and posed an insurmountable barrier.

### March 18

The day before yesterday, General Olié, civil and military commander of greater Kabylia, visited the boys' school.[33] He arrived at 4:10 P.M. At 4:00 I was told that this visit was part of his program for the day. However, during the morning recess, the principal of the girls' school had talked about it with her assistants, and Mrs. L. B. had discussed it with her husband. He had relayed it to some of his colleagues, who all happened to be French, so that, when the general arrived, I happened to be the only one who was surprised by it and uncomfortable. A mean-spirited people might consider my attitude a petty one, caused by bad feelings. It is difficult to affirm this: the principal of the girls' school is the administrator's wife and, of course, is privy to the subprefect's secrets.[34] It was up to him to inform me. As a precaution, he could have demanded the utmost discretion on my part. He might have done so, if I had not been a Kabyle.

General Olié was very tactful and spoke about literature to me. My first impression was that he was a kind man, with an air of intelligence about him. It is really too bad that such a noble face belongs to the person in charge. He is the supreme executor of all decisions made in Paris by clever members of parliament whose inflamed logic is now playing, with criminal indifference, with the lives of the soldiers and residents of this country. When he gave my attentive, older students a profound look, I think I caught a glimpse of the immense pity that I myself was feeling for him at that very moment. On the other hand, the men who came with him acted like mastiffs or dull informers. All of them were upset at the consideration he showed me.

### Same Day

In response to a request by the government, some "Special Powers" for action in Algeria have been approved by a large majority in the National Assembly. Except for the extreme right clan—the Poujade movement[35]—everybody, communists included, is supporting the government's initiative to find a solution for Algeria. It appears that this solution will include a show of strength if the rebels do not lay down their arms. In other words, the rebels will be asked to admit defeat when, up to now, they have more than held their opponent in check. All this, while our neighbors to the east and to the west are hardening their positions and becoming more demanding, while Egypt and the Muslim world — if not the entire world — are condemning "colonialism" and preaching the fight for liberation. The French vote for "Special Powers" to show the world that they are unified. Their aim is to reconquer Algeria with military might and to pay the price that such an adventure demands with human lives.

It is extremely cruel that France should lose Algeria where it has done so much, given so much, to the point that the country has become part of France itself. But it is inhuman to massacre the indigenous people who know that Algeria belongs to them and that they have nothing in common with the French, nothing but this servile relationship that has been going on for a century. It is inhuman to send one's own children, descendants of free men, to die or to kill other children who themselves want to be free. Certainly, the loss of Algeria would be irreparable for France. Could France not get the Algerians to learn to like her?

### March 19

Today's newspaper is paying particular attention to the mountainous area of Beni Raten on top of which Fort-National is perched. The information provided by the press bearing the title "Important Operation" was announced last night over every radio station and proclaimed a victory. The news raised hopes because several dangerous bandits who had been a plague on the area were put out of circulation. Their death will restore peace and will calm the terrorized Muslim populations. Yes, this is what *Le Journal d'Alger* reports:

A large operation began on Saturday at the bottom of the Fort-National massif, between the main road from Algiers to Bougie. The military operation took place in the area of Tizi-Rached. It began in the village of Oussameur and spread to the village of Iraten. It was performed by the 27th Alpine Infantry Division and the 13th Regiment of Senegalese Infantrymen garrisoned at Fort-National, along with the cooperation of the gendarmerie brigades.

The goal was to destroy a terrorist group responsible for assassinations and several acts of sabotage.

After marching several miles at night, the armed forces encountered the rebels on several occasions in Belias (Ibehlal?), Ighil Ounechial (Oumechedal), and Ighil Hadj Ali (Tighilt El Hadj Ali).

A rebel sentry and eight other outlaws were killed, and one was wounded. Thirty-one suspects were apprehended, and weapons and ammunition were recovered. Five others were killed while trying to escape.

One member of the armed forces was badly wounded.

The main operation took place at the school in Tizi-Rached. It was carried out by three battalions made up of soldiers from the 27th AID and the 13th RSI and policemen.

In the quadrilateral area of Ighil El Hadj Ali, a group of about fifteen rebels was intercepted. Seeing that they were surrounded and with no way out, some tried to flee.

To prevent their escape, reconnaissance planes flying overhead fired a hail of bullets at them.

Nine rebels were killed. Six of those were identified as extremely dangerous. Twenty-one known and notorious rebels were arrested. Four suspects were remanded in custody.

Weapons, ammunition, military clothing were recovered.

As a friend explained it to me, about ten villages were surrounded at dawn on Saturday. Then, they proceeded with the usual identity checks. The men stood in line to be checked. The suspects were held separately. Their situation would be dealt with later . . .

In this particular case, the army may have gained its information from a young man in Azouza who recently found refuge in the barracks after being threatened by his friends in the maquis. A list was made, and several battalions were sent to the villages to arrest the Kabyles. There is no doubt that all those who were on the list were, in one way or another, cooperating with the rebels and responsible for some sabotage and attacks. But these people were not "troublemakers." To put it simply, they lived at home, did their daily chores, and spent their days without worry. In a way, their attitude was to wait and see. Seen from this angle, it is evident that the entire population is doing exactly the same, because the sympathy shown the rebels does not date from yesterday, and neither does the desire to help them if the opportunity arises. That is how things are. Nab the first one to show up and jail or kill him. No doubt about it, he is guilty.

From then on, one simple question can be asked: why do they hesitate in massacring everybody, in truly cleaning up the country, and, at the same time, in eradicating the problem posed by these "bandits"?

The information published by the press and broadcast by the radio bears a strange likeness to an official communiqué. Therefore, it is an official lie.

In Tizi-Rached, people are brought to the headquarters. They check their identity cards and read off their names.

—Is so and so your son?

—Yes.

—Where is he?

—Here, waiting in line.

His name is called. He is taken aside.

—Is so and so your brother?

—Yes.

—Call him.

He calls his brother. He is taken aside.

—Is so and so your son?

—Yes.

—Where is he?

—I don't know. He must be around.

They look for him. He has already taken off.

Once they have checked all the papers, they detain five people whom they intend to interrogate further at the station.

The next day, a Sunday morning, these five are found on the highway, near the village. Shot, mutilated, stripped, and robbed. They buried them next to each other in adjacent graves. Later, they will be honored as heroes. But today, the parents hold back their tears.

In Tighilt: a rebel "sentry" is shot. He was a well-known, cunning horse dealer who did not wait for the curfew to be over before going to town where he wanted to be the first to arrive. He was walking toward death. Of course, he should have stayed home. But the others?

Then they shot those who were on the list, just like in Tizi-Rached.

There were other victims in other villages. They brought back suspects at night in military trucks. By the end of the day, the fellagha had been completely driven out. A major victory for the armed forces!

It should be noted as well that the communiqué gives equal

credit for the victory to all those who took part in the fighting: the 27th AID, the 13th RSI, and the police. Nobody is forgotten. It is only fair. 8:00. I turn the knob on my radio: "Algiers, medium waves 306." I recognize the voice of Mr. Lacoste: "All of us, Europeans and Muslims, are united in the same desire for solidarity and social progress. Let us stand against the disease . . ." A plea in favor of the fight against cancer!

**March 22**

Yesterday, market day. As usual, a lot of people showed up. It was at its busiest at 11:30. Thousands of people were in town. It is difficult for those pressed for time to get through. Otherwise, there was nothing to do but to follow the waves of people going in one direction or another, toward either the Algiers gate or the gate of Djurdjura.[36] I had gone to city hall an hour earlier. My friends there seemed depressed, carrying on with their usual business, devoid of enthusiasm, tired and feverish at the same time, sitting down, then getting up for no reason, sometimes exchanging foolish, and senseless chatter. After some lukewarm handshakes, I left them to get back to my students and some excitement and life. We studied with interest a text of Mr. Duhamel protesting, with commendable force, those advances in mechanization that dull the mind: "Robots, that is what we risk becoming . . ." Just as I was finishing my lecture by agreeing with Mr. Duhamel, with the usual reservations, three shots rang out sharply in the center of town. It was about 11:30.

Through the large bay windows in the classroom we saw the crowd disperse, and a vague rumbling rose from the town. In order to see, the students spread out on the balcony, in the schoolyard, and all around the school. At the same time, people came and went at a manic pace. Submachine guns and automatic weapons started to spit toward the quarry and the village of El Hamman. At this very moment, I found out that Mr. B. had been shot as he came out of Mr. L.'s house on his way home. He took a few steps before falling dead in front of his house. The assassin disappeared immediately into the crowd. Soldiers rushed outside and began shooting at random. They had undoubtedly been ordered to shoot at bushes and ravines and to arrest suspects. Meanwhile, access to both gates of the city was forbidden to those on the outside as well as those on the inside. Around 1:00, the gunfire stopped. The searches and identity checks were completed around 3:00. The villagers left promptly for their homes, and the city was plunged into deathly silence, a silence heavy with threats, an oppressive silence that kills you little by little. The Kabyles and the French were not the only ones to avoid each other and simply turn their backs. The Kabyles were doing it to other Kabyles, and the French to other French. We were not afraid, but we were profoundly tired of looking at one another and talking about trivial matters. Everybody wanted to be alone, over there, quite isolated, totally removed from the others, filled with an overwhelming, passive anger, ready to refuse any explanations and to stop trying to understand, or even react. In families, this same incomprehension, this same refusal to speak, this supreme annoyance must have prevailed between husbands and wives.

I had to finish my day with my students. They studied in silence until 4:00. Mouloud came to visit, and I had to talk with him in the hallway. He said he had come to find refuge. He has been very careful since his arrest. It is obvious. He told me that, like many others, he was almost put in front of a firing squad but was saved because a general intervened. His hands were trembling feverishly. He had not yet recovered from the month he spent in jail. Like everybody else, he had come to the market to buy a few things. He will start his class here after Easter.

—If they come here, he said, I am teaching, okay? You will tell them that I am a teacher.

—Do not worry, my friend. You did not kill Mr. B. They are checking people's identifications, that is all. Just go home peacefully.

—Okay, okay, I will do that. But give me a chance to catch my breath a little, okay?

So while the students pretended to be working we started talking. His favorite subject: the jail. He had been arrested a second time. And put with political prisoners.

—Yes, I preferred to be among them. I rejected their special treatment, you know.

—Were there any leaders in the group?

—You bet, they had arrested a major leader, with weapons in hand. That was where he had to be. They are not afraid, those guys. They will take it to the limit. For the green flag![37] For Islam! Well, you can imagine: good Muslims, send the French back to the sea, etc. . . . Yes, I saw a leader. Fifty-two victims, my friend. He either cut their throats or shot them. All by himself. "We aim for the spine or other sensitive areas, he said to me. That way, if the guy survives, he is permanently neutralized."

I thought that Mr. B. had not survived and that now, his pitiful daughter must be at his side. It will not be long before she follows him. Mouloud continues:

—As for those who get their throats cut, the leader added, as if to show off, we do this to save bullets. And seeing that they are informers, we offer them in sacrifice, in memory of Abraham and to honor Mohammed.

—They are cruel.

—You bet, they are cruel. It is better not to have them as enemies.

—How can you do that?

—Yes, how can you do that? In any case, you, you are okay on the other side? Nothing will happen to you?

—That is hard to prove.

—That is exactly what I mean.

When Mouloud suddenly decided to leave, we forgot to shake hands.

When I went back inside my classroom, my students were minding their manners.

**March 26**

Thursday, around 3:00, the convoy carrying B. to the church and then to the cemetery makes its way sadly through a village devoid of Kabyles. The French are there, a small group of men, women, and children, wearing coats and capes and carrying umbrellas. A few cars, two jeeps, a military truck in lieu of a hearse—no flowers, no crowns—a half-dozen soldiers standing guard in front of the church. A fine rain drowned in mist is falling over all this. I wipe away the condensation that prevents me from watching them go by: my head is empty, my heart is empty. Just like all these poor people, just like other poor people who, from behind their windows, wipe away the condensation to see them go by.

I had been told, earlier, that despite the curfew on the night of the wake, someone had tried to burn down B. M.'s store across the street. Agent E., accompanied by a policeman and with the patrol looking on, poured out a bottle of gasoline in front of the door. The store owner, who was sleeping in the back of the store with his wife, woke up in time to avoid being burned alive. He shouted for help. Agent E., the policeman, and the patrol rushed to put the fire out.

He thanked them quite cordially, and then he returned to the back of his store where his wife was waiting for him. I have also been told that during one of the skirmishes the day before, a woman, a shepherd, and a cow had been wounded.

Everybody thinks that B. was shot in response to the executions that took place last week in Tizi-Rached and elsewhere. B. was no more a target than anyone else. He would go and spend hours in his field, less than a mile away from the village. So it would have been easy for someone to cut his throat there without being disturbed, to bury him, or make him disappear. Since they decided to kill him on a Wednesday, with a lot of people around, it was certainly meant as a vendetta and a warning as well.

It seems that the French, whose despair is limitless and who feel nothing but a quiet disdain for our victims, went to see the captain, the commander, and the subprefect to ask that soldiers shoot at the crowds. To their way of thinking, the scale of values that has been generally agreed upon since the 1945 massacres must be respected.[38] Therefore, one should not hesitate to kill a sufficient number of ignorant Kabyles to compensate for the loss of Mr. B., an officer in the reserves, a café owner, and a gunsmith to top it off.

The captain, the commander, and the subprefect supposedly responded by saying that things had changed considerably in the last ten years and that, in the end, nobody was forcing them to stay in Fort-National.

The subprefect is said to have added that if the day came when he could no longer keep order in this country, he would leave as well. As far as we are concerned, this answer, as sincere as it is futile, makes us happy.

The day of the burial, the French expressed their disenchantment at the fact that these poor funerals lacked glamour.

—If it were the mayor's assistant, they said to each other, things would have been done differently, and the general would have participated.

—And the prefect as well!

—Oh yes, the prefect.

Poor old L., who has not been able to get rid of cold sweats for the last six months, immediately imagined himself in Mr. B.'s place on the military truck, slowly and endlessly going down the winding roads covered with white sand that led to the cemetery. His parents, those brave settlers about whom he loves to talk, have been waiting there for him for decades. So L., the mayor, convinced that all the citizens of his village were bastards, started crying. They, on the other hand, thought that he was crying because of the death of poor old B. They calmed down quite quickly and forgave him his pretentiousness.

**March 27**

Last Friday, I went to Algiers. No problems during the trip there. I saw my brother and my friend Roblès. I spent the night at La Redoute. R.'s state of mind is practically the same state as mine. We have never been closer, and each of us is as sad and tired as the other. We exchanged a few painfully obvious comments, and then we said good-bye as if we were going to see each other again the next day. It was exactly the same with my brother.

When I returned the next day, I had to stop in Tizi-Ouzou for an hour where the usual identification checks were going on. A policeman had just been killed in the street, in plain view, in the middle of a large crowd. This crowd had been carefully screened. In the main street, a line of cars of all kinds and sizes was stretched out for nearly a mile. They brought the Kabyles in groups into the courtyard of the police station where they were bunched into geometrical formations, just as sheep are lined up on a market square. How many thousands were there? The policemen would search you, check your ID, review lists of suspects, and then either arrest you or let you go. Military trucks were constantly making the rounds, from the city to the police station, and from there to the jail. The Kabyles they were carrying on their wooden seats looked like indifferent travelers who have just paid the cost of their ride and whose conscience was now at peace.

**March 28**

My French colleagues have gone to Algiers together. They have an appointment with the chief education officer. They want to explain the situation to him and ask to be sent back to France immediately. Of course, they consulted each other secretly, and I was not supposed to know anything about it. One of them told me about it anyhow. I would have preferred not to be told anything. They are more demoralized than ever. Yet, nobody has ever threatened them. They could have kept a cool head, especially since the chief education officer is not prepared to meet their request. Their reasoning is simplistic, just as simplistic as their selfishness or pride. They no longer want to hear about maintaining the French Presence. They are finished with preaching and other such nonsense. If the secular order of things were restored, as well as all their rights and all of their privileges, they would indeed agree to stay and take advantage of the 33 percent. However, they seem to be saying that there is nothing else to hope for, that the rebels are strong and well organized, that the French nation is weak and corrupt. There is nothing left to do. All in all, they speak of France as if they were not French.

4:00 P.M.

The weather is awful. It is not raining, but the city is buried in haze and dust. The clouds rush in from the valley to the top of the fort, then from the crest toward the valley. It is impossible to see more than a couple of yards; then it clears up, and the haze envelops everything again. The wind screams sadly, growls with anger and threats; then the sun comes out again and smiles mockingly.

It has been just eight days since B. was shot. So today it was market day again. The many Kabyles who showed up at both gates of the city were given a short period of time to hurry up and complete their shopping. Then the patrols pushed them back, chased them out of the stores, the shops, the coffee shops, the stables, and forced them to leave without too much complaint, because as you know "we saw enough of them" last week. Around 10:00, the town was empty, gloomy, and the locals locked themselves indoors as a precaution.

9:00 P.M.

My French colleagues—men and women—and their children burst into my office. They are shaking and look pale. They mumble through an explanation about someone lifting a hatch in the ceiling at Mrs. J. B.'s: a terrorist had to be hiding in it, waiting for them to fall asleep before cutting their throats, or else, if he is no longer there, he must have left a time bomb. They refuse to go home and are asking me what to do.

It is hard for me to take this seriously, and I gently kid about this fellagha who seems to have come straight out of a detective novel. My wife feels just as I do. They try to convince me to check things out. I get up to go; but my wife, who is more level-headed, tries to hold me back.

When I reach the place, I find that access to the trap door is practically impossible from the outside. I really could not see why anyone would try to wriggle themselves acrobatically in there in order to murder a postal inspector, his schoolteacher wife, and their three children, when the city is overflowing with soldiers, policemen, administrators, and other officials. No, I really could not figure it out. However, there had been quite a lot a wind in the evening. Could it be that the trap door, which seemed relatively light, had been lifted up by the wind? I think that explains it.

We called the police and then went up to Mr. J. B.'s. He politely let me in first while L. B. stayed behind.

We were a group of reasonable people, courageous enough not to show our fear. Finally, what I had expected was confirmed. There was nothing in the attic, not even a small bomb or the tiniest fellagha. After congratulating each other over our exploit, everyone went home. My colleagues are completely terror-stricken. I feel pity for them and would like to be able to reassure them. However, when people feel persecuted, the only thing they recognize is a threat, the only thing they understand is danger, the only thing they imagine is a scene of carnage, and the only thing they think about is death. My poor colleagues, I cannot do anything to help you . . .

**March 29**

About an hour ago I went out to get some news, so I would have something to write about. It did not take long, and I went back to the school in a hurry.

In front of the Z. butcher shop, a young man from Aguemoun tried to disarm a soldier: he used his head to hit the soldier in the temple. So the soldier shouted for help, and the patrol showed up. They caught the young man and took him to the police station. The bleeding soldier had not moved, but the Kabyle was already long gone. The soldiers, long-faced and somber, patrol the street, submachine guns in hand. The Kabyles remain impassive and avoid looking at them. Yes, all this happened one hour ago. The young man must have been shot on the spot. On the human side of things, what will my brave colleagues of yesterday evening think of him? There is no doubt that they will rush to condemn him. As for me, I take my hat off to him.

**March 30**

I now have more specific information about what happened. Yesterday I was told about it by the mayor's assistant, so it is almost an official version. Some Kabyles who saw what went on say that it was nothing more than an exchange of blows.

Young Mansour, a former student, twenty years old, looks at a soldier. The soldier looks down on him and insults him. The Kabyle throws himself on him, punches him, butts him in the head. Other soldiers quickly arrive on the spot, grab the Kabyle, and take him away. Another young man who saw the whole epi-sode from the entrance to his shop is arrested for good measure.

In spite of Mr. L.'s quasi-official version, Mansour will not be executed. He will surely benefit from the leniency of the armed forces. At most, they will try to get information out of him by the usual method. But who can say when he will be re-leased? Because, in the end, as the newspapers are saying this morning, he is truly a daring terrorist.

Yesterday, during the night, around 10:30 P.M., the en-tire family was awakened by submachine gunfire. Soldiers were simply shooting at houses, and this morning, in the main street, I could see the traces of all those bullets on the facades. Then, I heard that they had searched somebody's home . . . hoping to discover a terrorist nest. This nest, which must truly exist, gives nightmares to honest people.

**March 31**

The young man from Aguemoun was "grilled" and then slowly made to denounce "suspects." Policemen wearing boots were jumping on his stomach. After he had been disfigured, he finally decided to talk. He was brought to his village where he pointed out his accomplices. A few, who had expected this to happen, had already taken off. Two others, who claimed not to have done anything, were arrested. One of them had just com-pleted his military service. He is back from the Aurès where he must have been fighting against the fellagha. When he ar-rived at the police station, he tried to escape. A burst of gunfire dropped him on the ground. They took him to the Fort-National infirmary, then to the hospital in Tizi. Badly wounded, that is all. Now, it is the same everywhere in Kabylia: on one side the rebels, on the other side their enemy. A merciless struggle has be-gun, an irreparable hatred has taken root inside peoples' hearts.

I am reading a few notes about the torture methods used by the Algerian police. I got this from a reliable witness, an in-telligent and idealistic young man who looks a bit weary and carries in his eyes the immense distress of those who suffer, of those who have stopped calling for help because they know they are wasting their time. However, they still have hope of finding justice by their deeds. He writes to me:

"During the first round of questioning, the police use a paternal tone—We will not hurt you but you have to tell us what you know . . .—Come on, do you think that we are going to buy that you know nothing?—Answer! And don't think that you can outsmart us. You know, many people, stronger and smarter than you, have gone down this road and they spat out everything they knew. What is on the hook over there? — An electric plug, next to it a blackjack and a rope. Over there, a bathtub. And this hole in the wall? Well! A guy we knocked off with a bullet . . . — Come on, man, no need to waste time. It is to your advantage to get it over with . . ."

Suddenly, when he least expects it, the brutal dance begins: four of the five policemen surround the poor guy. They slap him and kick him repeatedly with their fists and feet while hurling insults and vulgarities. When he is covered with blood and his clothes are torn, they take him back to his cell and move on to other prisoners.

During the second round of questioning, they use other means of torture.

1. The bathtub: this form of torture consists of plunging the prisoner's head into a basin filled with water soiled with urine and keeping him in that position until he blacks out. They subject the prisoner to this treatment eight to ten times a day. They also use hoses with a mask at the end, which they apply directly to the face. They only have to turn on the faucet . . . The torture is made worse by the sudden suffocation. As one continues to drink, the belly becomes excessively large. Add the cold cell and wet clothes to this torture. Since these sessions usually take place at night, the prisoner almost never sleeps.

2. Electricity: it is applied to the fingers and the ears. These sessions are multiplied according to the whim of the policemen. As soon as contact has been established, the electricity travels through the entire body. The brain is especially sensitive.

3. The bottle: an ordinary bottle, preferably with a broken neck. The prisoner is forced to sit on it and the policemen push down with all their strength on the shoulders of the poor fellow. The painful results of this torture last for months and months.

4. The rope: with a slipknot placed above the jaws, the prisoner is suspended for a moment, and left to dangle, with death clouding his eyes. They take him down when his tongue starts hanging out of his mouth or when he has turned completely blue. Sometimes, they suspend him by the feet and hit him with a flurry of punches. They frequently use the rope, they lash him with the blackjack, and they also hit the prisoner's soles, preferably with a pickaxe handle. The sole is a very sensitive and hidden part of the body . . .

There are endless ways to torture. In every police station and in the military camps, the policeman and the officer take all sorts of initiatives and think up all sorts of ways to improve techniques that cannot all be listed here because there are too many to mention. Those who have endured these treatments will never forget them because they are forever inscribed in their flesh.

### April 4

Yesterday, I saw old Mrs. S. and her sister, also elderly, enter city hall. They looked proud and somber with their powdered faces and black dresses. They were offering some furniture at a very low price, but nobody wanted to buy anything. Amara told me that they were moving back to France. He was interested in the mahogany desk of the late husband, the former city hall secretary, who was buried in Fort-National, where he had lived for many years with these two women. Amara really wanted it, but he had no money. He had bought Jojo's dining room set at a real low price the day before because Jojo wanted to get rid of it and leave the country as soon as possible. A. and Jojo both had tears in their eyes. A. wanted to pay Jojo more for it, whereas Jojo wanted to give it to A. as a gift. They immediately agreed on a price. Some separations are worse than death because they take even friendship with them and leave an atrocious void: nothingness. Soon, all that will be left in Fort-National are Kabyle families and soldiers. What will happen then?

### 6:00 P.M.

There was no market today. The people who came to buy a few things were forced out before noon. By noon, the town was empty. Armed soldiers everywhere. That is all. I went for a walk around 4:00. People look sad and avoid each other. Every time a Kabyle and a Frenchman cross paths, it is as if two enemies are meeting. One can read hatred on people's faces, the same hatred, the same mistrust. There are more of us; they have weapons, and they use them.

As expected, young Mansour was shot like a dog. From now, on it is quite clear that the police will shoot Kabyles like dogs. They are quite aware that Mansour is no more a rebel than anybody else in Aguemoun; they tortured him, and he gave them the names of some young men neither more nor less guilty than himself. One of them has already been shot because "he was fleeing." Yesterday morning, it was Mansour's turn to be shot because he himself "was fleeing." That is one less. That is what those brave policemen must have said, those policemen who never tremble in front of death. The death they bequeath so generously.[39]

I have been told that the military authorities had called in the leaders of Tizi-Rached and other Iraten villages to have them sign a declaration admitting that their children, who were killed by submachine gunfire during the recent sweeps, were carrying weapons when they died. In any case, everybody "knows" that they fell during combat, that they were surrounded, and so on, because when it happened the newspapers published a detailed communiqué that I reproduced in its entirety.

**April 6**

*Demain*, a socialist weekly dear to Guy Mollet, is publishing a report on the Tebessa massacres. There were hundreds of dead civilians and one thousand wounded because a single officer of the Legion had been shot. Last week, some people on their way back from Algiers saw villages burning along the crest line in the area of Haussonvillers. The maquis have distributed a pamphlet that gives more specific information about the police sweeps in the Palestro area. There are reports that napalm bombs were used and that settlers' families were massacred. After these massacres, which shame the rebels, first the French press and then the world press have indignantly raised issues of universal consciousness, which is always ready to cry for the innocents.

In Paris, in June of 1953, I spent one evening with a group of renowned writers. I remember the long faces, filled with despondency and anger when we heard the news from America that the Rosenbergs had just been put to death.[40] For a moment I felt that my illustrious colleagues wanted to showcase their own sensitivity. Then I felt guilty for feeling so little horror at this execution.

Now that everyday compatriots, acquaintances, and friends are dying, I see that I was right not to be troubled. No, death does not impress me. It is neither just nor unjust. It is death, and that is all. A man dies just like a day ends. And yesterday's assassin can be that nice policeman who usually talks with you and comes to shake your hands and joke once more. Until the day when you welcome him with a smile, and you empty the clip from your automatic in his stomach in a friendly manner. Then it is his turn to be buried, and nothing else is said about it.

Yesterday, a policeman enters a store to chase the customers out. He sees a kid holding a cloth that he likes.

—Give me six meters of this, he says to the owner. It is really nice. In ten minutes, I will be at the police station, and then you will have all the wives of the police squad here. They will not want to miss out on such fine cloth. You will see. He takes his time to pay, and as politely as possible, he empties the store of its customers: order received.

With a wink, the owner explains:

—This morning, he killed Mansour. He is in a real good mood because his boss is pleased with him. And the cloth, he paid one hundred francs more than the kid for it.

**April 8**

In a farm near Imaïnsrène, someone discovered the bodies of Yahiaoui and the crazy woman: their throats had been slashed. I heard from someone else that two other women from A.-A. have disappeared. Yahiaoui is a derelict and is always drunk. It would be a waste of time to expect anything good and honest from him. How could he possibly hurt the greater cause of the rebels? And the crazy woman? Up to now the rebels were aiming to right wrongs; now they are claiming to defend great principles.

Read a long article by Mr. Soustelle in which he continues his usual rhetorical argument about the Arab League, Egypt, and Pan-Islamism.[41] According to him, this is the real source of the problem, and the Algerian natives, face to face with France without outside interference, would have remained obedient like good little kids. That sounds obvious. The locals would have remained quiet, but they would not have changed their minds about the French, not until the day when some other group, other than the Arab League, the Pan-Islamist movement, or Egypt would encourage them to protest against their own fatigue brought on by enslavement. The article ends with a conclusion borrowed from Arabic wisdom: "When your son has grown up, treat him like your brother." While this is indeed a nice proverb, it leaves out the orphans.

**April 10**

Yesterday, the bus that carries the mail from Michelet was burned. I have no details. When I was in Algiers the day before, I heard of another sweep in Taourirt-Moussa. Several rebels and soldiers died. The hairdresser was also shot.

**April 11**

Some information about life in Kabyle villages: the maquis groups camp there on a regular basis. People are obliged to welcome them and offer them shelter. War is war. "Old woman, what are you doing, it is hot without doing that." It is not all that clear that the rebels speak in the manner imagined by Paul Déroulède.[42] Far from it.

As for the Michelet bus, one could see this as a threat against travelers, and many were again ready to insist on barbarity on the part of the rebels. Nothing of the sort happened. My information is that the rebels let everyone leave as considerately as possible. Then, they took the bags and set the bus on fire.

The people from the villages around Michelet are no longer able to come to the center for supplies. A pass is required to come in and to get out. The goods taken out have to be weighed. Michelet, I have heard, is sad and lifeless. Sadder than Fort-National. There is nothing like that here. Except that, now and then, nonresidents are expelled from the stores as well as the town.

### April 13

Nowadays, and this has been going on for a while, it is customary to use local labor to repair the damage caused by sabotage. The troops arrive at the village, call out men, go after others, and make lists. Everybody has to work. Forced labor, in the proper sense of the term, and all that is associated with it: poking, insults, threats, and fatigue. It may be possible to justify the principle, but not the method. Because the old, the sick, and the weak are not spared . . . The result is that the army is spreading terror throughout villages. This is splendid pacification!

I have heard that the policemen who often go to Tablabalt held an inquest the other day about the woman who was shot by one of their own last January. They are asking the village leaders if, by any chance, anybody could give a description of the rebel who shot her. No, they could not; nor could they testify that this rebel was a policeman. The woman is dead and buried. That is all they know. Even so, the compassionate authorities are going to get busy and prepare a file, so her widower can receive a pension. He really earned it by hiding behind his wife.

It is with the same "innocence," the other day, that some policemen of the PRG came to gather information about the carpenter who was shot in Azouza. They were looking for the assassins—an investigation against "persons unknown." The attendant of the justice of the peace is said to have replied[43]:

—Go to the army barracks, there you will find the people you are looking for. Everything is a joke to this guy!

## 1956

### April 18

The newspapers bring me sad news. Mr. H. was shot yesterday in front of his house as he was getting out of his car with his seven-year-old child. Mr. H. is more French than the French and, I believe, married to a French woman of the respectable bourgeoisie. He was intelligent and had an excellent reputation as an attorney. I do not know how he stands with regard to current events, but I know that he was in favor of integration. He told me so when he came for a visit last December. During our conversation, I got the feeling that he knew what he wanted out of life, but was unsure if he would be successful. He left my office with lowered shoulders, as if he were already overwhelmed, out of commission. I made him understand that not only do I no longer believe that integration is a solution but that there is no one among us who could unite us—be heard by both groups—and that, in the end, it is best for us to be quiet. Was he a victim of mere verbal carelessness? Or of even graver carelessness? All one can do is guess because, once again, one is forced to admit that an intelligent man is not executed without a reason. What is this kind of reasoning worth in these times we are living? I do not know.

On the other side, things are just as bleak, so to speak.

Boudi told me that his brother, who was arrested in Taourirt a few days ago, has not been found yet. Some people saw him entering Fort-National in a jeep and being taken to the police station. His parents asked to see him. They were rudely turned away and told that the police did not know the individual, and that, in any case, he was not there. Good God, where is he then? It was only two weeks ago that he was released. This time, it has to be a kidnapping.

### April 20

No, it is not a kidnapping. Arrested and interned, that is all.

### May 10

Ascension—Aïd. End of the Ramadan. Nothing special has happened during the last twenty days. By this I mean that each night the radio station and each morning the press bring us details about the skirmishes, attacks, and sabotages while my compatriots peddle other details about police sweeps, arrests, executions, and vexations. Nothing special: men fall day and night, and those who remain gradually familiarize themselves with a situation that is no longer new, that in the end will seem normal, and in which everyone will attempt to make life as pleasant as possible. Those who stay behind are sick of being frightened.

Relations between the French and the Kabyles have never been as frank or cordial. Our behavior toward each other comes from the heart, and it is a pleasure to note. We have both been relieved of the heavy burden that was choking us: the burden of our common hypocrisy, which is as old as our common history. From now on we look each other in the eyes, and we say without bragging or bitterness:

—Sir, we are not on the same side. Your servant, Sir!

We belong to two different worlds, and we are equally happy to confirm this at every possible occasion, in plain language. We must take advantage of this while all of us are still armed. What will happen to us or to them tomorrow? Those we no longer encounter, those who went somewhere else and shook the dust off their shoes without carrying away any regrets or leaving any memories. They are no longer here, and it is as if they had never been here. As we slowly recover from our recent anguish, it seems that we have lost the ability to be moved or to feel pity. We are gradually becoming insensitive, just like those who, privileged by fate, become luckily immune to contagions, while providing devoted care to others who suffer from them. We may very well be spared from the epidemic, but we will not be grateful.

The newspapers now mention secret talks and meetings that are taking place in Spain, Morocco, Cairo, and even here. An important Muslim politician and others no less important have joined the ranks of the FLN. While troops are being mobilized in France, there is still hope of an upcoming settlement. We welcome this news with great calm and dignity, but this is only out of weariness.

### May 11

Aïd. Market day. Many people are here to buy meat. Larbi arrives from back home at 10:00. We talked for a long time. Right away I asked him for more details about the police sweeps in Tizi-Hibel last April 28.

Young Guermah is summoned by the police in Béni-Douala for some truck business in Algiers, or a collision, or something else. He goes there and answers questions. One thing leads to another, they manage to pump him for information, and he makes a confession. Yes, he is a terrorist like many others.

He gives names. All the young men from Tizi-Hibel and A.-F. are on the list. The mounted police, policemen, and the army come to arrest anybody they can find. Many have escaped into the countryside and have not returned. Some have fled to Algiers or Paris. The village has lost almost all of its young men. Some thirty have been arrested. All have been tortured as humans have never been tortured before. This news along with an immense terror spread throughout the tribe. People are living in anticipation of another police sweep, and able-bodied men no longer dare to sleep at home. They leave at sunset. Twenty of the thirty suspects have cracked. They have given details about everything from the first contacts with the maquis to the last ditch dug with their teams. Mohamad Amar, the cell leader, was subjected to the most savage tortures. It is a miracle that he survived because he is over fifty; he has suffered from tuberculosis, and we know that he is physically weak due to a pneumothorax. From 1945 to 1950, he was an active member of the Communist Party and was even its candidate for the Regional Council. He could not take the blows, and even though his companions have forgiven him, they are surprised that he could not resist. No, they are not upset with him, but they feel sorry for him. The fact that all the others have spoken is not surprising when you get an accurate idea of the ruthless manner in which the "client" is questioned.[44] What is surprising is that insignificant or simple-minded boys were able to take these blows without saying a word. There were ten out of the thirty, and they were the ones whom no one would have trusted. "What do you expect," admits Larabi, "they are like donkeys. A donkey is a stupid animal, but it is also hard-headed. Everybody knows it."

— So, did they let them go?

— Of course. They did nothing! One of them did not even open his mouth as long as the dance went on. The others repeated ceaselessly: "Me, sir, I did nothing." Then, they took away all those who talked. Now they are in jail. They will retract their statements because I have heard that they no longer hit people in that jail.

What is surprising in all this is that Guermah should have spoken immediately. Some suspect he did it spontaneously because that morning, before answering the summons, he told the djemaâ that if the police ever held him in Béni-Douala, he would empty the whole village at once.[45] He succeeded in doing so. Some also suspect that the Guermahs had been making plans for awhile. They had decided to build and dig foundations. It so happens that, from this moment on, the road between Béni-Douala and Tizi-Hibel has been impassable every night. Perhaps this is to prevent them, and especially them, from getting their materials through. They have come to the conclusion that the village people are especially mad at them, given that they paid more ransom money than anybody else. So, to put an end to this, they decided to hit hard, even if it meant getting one of their own involved and tortured. This hypothesis explains the threats uttered by the young man.

Then, we talked about the informers in the army's service in Béni-Douala.

—There are two of them, L. told me: one is a drunk from Tizi-Hibel known as Ravachol.[46] He is arrested after a fight with another drunk, and the maquis order him to pay a fine of 500 francs. He refuses to pay so they order him to pay double. He does not refuse, but instead, he goes up to Béni-Douala to seek asylum from the police. They give him a military outfit, and he struts around in a jeep when he serves as a guide during police sweeps. He chooses to start with his own village. Now that his anger has abated, he discreetly informs the Kabyles of up-coming military raids. All of this, seen from a distance, is rather childish and almost comical. When, for instance, he enters a house for a search and afterward reassures the women and jokes pleasantly—the men are always parked outside in such circum-stances—he helps himself to whatever he likes. He is known to like 5000 franc notes in particular and to have stuffed a pillow full of them.

His partner in crime, the other informer, is from Icheriden.

—He has already been executed, L. told me.

—Tough luck, that will teach him to be an informer.

—Wait. Yes, he was executed but not killed. Let me explain. The maquis found out where he was and cornered him. He was with another guy, condemned just like him. The maquis fired their guns at them. They both fell with buckshot in their temples. They were taken into a bushy area and covered with ferns. Half an hour later, the guy got up, his temple grazed by the bul-lets. He had scratches from thorns almost everywhere else. His clothes were torn and dirty. That is it. So he immediately went to Béni-Douala to seek asylum from the police. They gave him a military outfit, and now he struts about in a jeep during police sweeps. He is, however, a false guide. He spies on the military as much as he can and informs the population. The rebels have forgiven him, but they still do not trust him completely. With him, you never know. He has just been ordered by the maquis to leave Béni-Douala and return to his village.[47] He has obeyed this order.

—He also looks like a donkey? I said to him.

—No, he was lucky. The cartridge was not correctly prepared. Any hunter will confirm this: when the buckshot and the powder are mixed inside the case, it is not much more powerful than small pebbles you would throw. It cannot kill anything.

**May 15**

Lately the attitude of the policemen and the soldiers has changed noticeably. Their anger has reached a fever pitch. I hear that people are shot almost anywhere, that they feel they are in enemy country, and that the only efficient form of justice is a quick justice. What is the life of a Muslim worth? For the time being, it is worth a burst of a submachine gun, but you cannot be certain that they will not lower this exchange rate. Those who survive will find out very soon.

Yesterday, four people from Icheriden and one from Aguemoun were shot in cold blood. I have heard that beforehand they are forced to wear a military outfit. Later they can be honorably listed among enemy losses, as armed rebels who have been shot.

**May 20**

Among the four who were gunned down was a seventy-five-year-old elder who was disfigured by the shot before he died. Three of these unfortunate people are guilty of helping the rebels. This is how it happened. A city hall secretary (a retired military) asks for a 1000 franc bribe from a father who was registering a birth. This is mentioned to the administrator, who informs the police. The police interrogate the secretary, who denounces and accuses the plaintiff. At the same time, he accuses two other people, including the elder who made the mistake of saving his life.

—I owe him my life, he says. The rebels put a knife to my throat. He pulled me out of their claws by guaranteeing my good behavior. He saved my life, but he is the terrorist leader in the village. An important leader.

So first they tortured the elder and then shot him. The fourth victim is from somewhere outside the village. He had been in jail. They brought him along with the others just so they could deal with him. All four were shot in front of an embankment, under the Ichiriden monument. The policemen of 1956 undoubtedly shot them as an homage to the valorous conquerors of 1857 because they consider themselves their direct descendants.

Yesterday, however, not too far from the same monument, some patriots executed a policeman from Michelet. I learned that the rest of the day was nothing but police sweeps, arrests of suspects, or worse. That is all I know for now.

**May 21**

According to the newspaper, the policeman was only wounded.

A student tells me that during the night the army encircled T.-A. and that, around 2:00 A.M., the two sons of the mayor's assistant were executed. They had been considered suspects for quite a while.

I no longer dare to go out for news. We are all suspects.

The police avoid me—those who know me—the soldiers look at us sideways. The few civilians around keep their distance and act haughtily toward the Kabyles. Now they are conspicuously armed when they go out, and each of us can almost see the revolvers that swell their back pockets. The other day, G., who was trying to walk steadily alongside the main street followed by whiffs of anisette, pulled out his weapon more than once while staring at Kabyles. Each time, he was content to squeeze the butt and then put the revolver back in his pocket, having laboriously groped his large bottom to find his pant's pocket.

Almost all of my French colleagues are now certain to leave. They are happy about it. Once away from here, they will be able to breathe. I understand them quite well. However, I fear that, after the long months of communal life without problems and almost without confrontation, we are separating without regrets. We greet each other with total indifference. This is where both groups stand.

**May 27**

The villagers of A.-A. and T. were encircled Sunday night, just a week ago. The soldiers arrived at the square in front of city hall around 10:00 P.M. and went down to the village around 1:00 A.M. The executions (two in T. and one in A.-A.) took place at dawn. The officer had a list. He had someone point out the suspects' homes. Most of them had fled. Those who were found were jerked violently from their beds, then shot—undoubtedly after a classic interrogation.

Around 8:00, the same officer tells the village leader, Dj., that the soldiers had shot two suspects who were trying to flee. The officer was asking him to come to identify the bodies. They were those of his own children, and only this morning at Dj.'s home, this same officer had enjoyed the cup of coffee you offer out of hospitality to any stranger who comes by. Dj. knew that his children had been pulled out of bed. He also knew that they were suspects. He had accepted that they had been arrested, jailed, and condemned. Yet, he had thought that they were in the hands of the law, and this had reassured him. However, both of them ended up in ditches on the side of the road, riddled by bullets and barely recognizable.

Both were buried inside the mosque, in a communal tomb next to each other, as if in the womb of the same mother.

At precisely the same time that the two brothers were discovered, the people of Aguemoun were removing the body of their marabout from the tall grasses that cover the brush. According to policeman J., this marabout had not answered his warnings and had attempted to flee. The marabout's wife knows quite well that they came to get her husband around 2:00 A.M., and that she heard a burst of submachine gun fire two hours later.

The next day, the newspapers reported a skirmish with a small band of rebels close to Fort-National. Three rebels were killed, but there were no losses among the soldiers. This must have pleased the "honest" people.

I came back from Algiers with Djidj the day before these assassinations. Before reaching Tizi-Ouzou, we were checked six times. From the turns in the road shaded by eucalyptus trees extending from Haussonvillers toward Camp-du-Maréchal, one could see three villages that were burning on the Bou Segza-Sidi Ali Bou Nab. Old and young Kabyle women and children were waiting on the side of the road with shapeless bundles at their feet. They have evacuated the population over there in order to fight a real war. The spring sky cannot dispel the sadness from these drab images.

**May 28**

The police adjutant has told me that they have evacuated the citizens from Michelet. I got more specific information from the policeman and other witnesses. Recently, there was a police sweep after an attack. They lined up all the men against a wall, with their arms raised, and had them offer their backs to the submachine guns. In the meantime, the soldiers were everywhere:

in homes and in stores, they pillaged, destroyed, and ransacked the town. In the streets, you could see pieces of cloth with goods spread on top and mixed into unbelievable combinations, oil and gasoline leaking. Doors had been smashed in, locks had been shot at, and blinds twisted. . . The desolation of war, the waste caused by an attack of raving madness.

The newspapers are publishing long commentaries about the massacre of seventeen young Parisians at the hand of some rebels in the Palestro area. The poor kids who were caught in a trap by a Kabyle guide were shot by surprise. Then, so it would seem, the people of the village went after the bodies in a rage and mutilated them. This is the other side of a grotesque medal that we are minting with the flesh of innocent people in order to safeguard the right of the strongest. The newspapers, however, are only talking about one side of this medal, in fact, while purposely ignoring the most hideous side. The other side? This is what is said about Palestro. (See clipping.)[48]

**May 31**

Yesterday evening, around 7:30, H. Ahmed was shot at his home, half a mile from town. We had just passed each other and shaken hands. I found out about the whole thing at 6:00 A.M. as I was leaving for Algiers. So I am postponing my trip, but it is not to mourn the dead or to go to the funeral or even to meditate over the vanity of life. No, it is simply because everything seems ludicrous to me, and this trip in particular. Whether I stay or go to Algiers, what is the difference? I might as well stay. I wanted to go see my brother, knowing that the police swept his neighborhood. I wanted to see Roblès and find out how it feels to be in Algiers. I wanted to get some information about the student strike before deciding what to do about my daughter's schooling. Why bother? Why bother? Here, all the students in middle school are on strike. They tell me that the school is empty in Tizi-Ouzou. It must be the same everywhere else. However, L'Echo d'Alger is announcing that the strike is in effect only in the universities and that absenteeism is low in secondary schools.[49] People think that it is a joke, and since the Echo is the source, that nobody should be surprised. The truth is that the older students are intent on continuing the strike, and some, as I understand it, have already joined the maquis.

Yesterday, my French colleagues were jubilant over the so-called failure of the strike. H. came to speak to me in a sardonic tone, as if I were responsible in some way and as if this failure were in some fashion mine. This really upset me. As far as my colleagues are concerned, it is clear that this strike is somehow my doing and that, if I had my way, the kids would return to school just to please me. Of course! These kids come to the front gate each time they see me there.

—Sir, can we take our things?

—Sir, will I be able to take the BEPC exam? [50]

—Sir, have you sent out our files?

The SAS captain told me in a joking manner that he wanted to shut down the middle school, but the sub-prefect had prevented him from doing so. I answered that the school was indeed closed and that, in theory, it was possible to close without changing anything about the situation. I also could have told him that it was not a captain's duty to shut down or open a school. However, he brags everywhere he goes that he has damaged my reputation. In effect, he is bragging about his impotence. He fears nothing, and he will certainly go far.

To get back to H.-A., the person who brought me the news this morning was not at all impressed.

—They are just settling the score, he said to me. They riddled him with bullets just like they did to Dj.'s sons.

—So you think he did it? I said.

—You bet. The maquis do nothing lightly and are sure that it is him. So he paid. Everybody is satisfied. It is dangerous to play one side against the other.

—Yes, it is bad news, I replied.

June 10

A few days ago, I found out about the deaths of Si Chérif and G. Saïd, both from my home town. The maquis hanged them. These executions are to show the people of Tizi-Hibel that the maquis know the names of those whose denunciations precipitated the brutal police sweep I talked about earlier, the arrest of some thirty young men, the panic in the village, and the fear in people's hearts.

It is difficult to condemn or approve the dispensers of justice. It is just as difficult to expect a kind of infallibility that is not within man's scope. The heart bleeds, however, when it witnesses this kind of spectacle: today's executioner inescapably becomes tomorrow's victim, and this, in turn, will call for another executioner.

June 12

My students are all refusing to take their exams. They are

on strike. For some of them, this is a minor problem, and the strike is an alibi that will allow them to claim later on that they have acquired the level of competence expected for that grade. For the others, other possibilities are conceivable, or at least other exam sessions. What about the candidates for the National Exam who have reached the age limit? In general, I believe that they are happy about the strike because it proves that they are behaving properly, that their heart is with the maquis, that, like everyone else, they dream of freedom, independence, and Islam. Among the Kabyles, there is a sustained enthusiasm, an essential stubbornness, an absolute belief in a better future. The thought of dying for this kind of future no longer frightens anybody. Everyone accepts this idea with the certainty that the sacrifice made by those who die will ensure the happiness of future generations. People also think that it is time to avenge our ancestors who, a century ago, were ruthlessly crushed by a well-armed conqueror who was desperate for colonies. So the young, beardless French soldiers appear as nothing less than the successors of the first Zouave soldiers, while the young Kabyles that are facing them want nothing more than to avenge the first moudjahiddins.[51] A century of living together has been deliberately forgotten. A metallic, ice-cold bridge has been thrown over a century of Franco-Algerian history. This bridge is similar to the Sirat that leads to the resting place of the chosen; it is as fragile as a rope, as sharp as a sword, and it is gradually being stained with the dark blood of the sinners. A blade on fire stands poised over this century; it is stained with the blood of men: that of the fighters and the victims. In the end, it will form a bloody line of retribution across a useless page.

### June 13

Yes, there is a feeling of great enthusiasm and determination. Everyone claims to be more patriotic than his neighbor or his comrade-in-arms. Everyone feels that he is able to give lessons, to be a leader. Everyone is worthy of command and obeys while waiting for a better appointment. This thirst for military stripes enhances warlike virtues, helps everyone commit injustices that diminish the villagers today and that will exhaust them tomorrow. The brutal executions, the arbitrary ransoms, the arrogance of a brand-new, narrow-minded, and scornful authority will, little by little, look like a yoke that will become more unbearable than the one from which we claim to be breaking free. All this cannot last long and will act against the tyrants' apprentices once we figure out that we are allowing ourselves to be led by men with neither scruples nor education. They are bandits who should go back to jail, not leaders or guides for a people suffering and thirsty for dignity, ready to die in order to gain men's respect.

In many places, people have already reached that stage. They wonder where this adventure will take them. They wait and are perplexed. While they wait, savings disappear and revenues diminish. Businesses are failing and dying, and poverty is settling in. The young flee to France. The villages are emptying out quickly. In certain areas, there is a sense of real panic, of a run-for-your-life situation, of a deliverance. Afterward, the maquis can always speak of treason, of shameful fleeing, of resignation. To feel at ease, the oppressed have no other refuge than the home of the oppressor. If the oppressor is smart, he will take my word as a spontaneous compliment. Indeed, it should enable him not to regain those illusory privileges whose loss he regrets but rather to hold firmly onto those ties of friendship that remain intact despite a century of lies and disdain.

**June 21**

On Saturday the 16th, they inform me of General Olié's visit. The general has decided to visit the school. This time, he wants to see me. During his previous visit, he had indicated his desire to get to know me better. So his visit is set for Tuesday. I am waiting with a certain amount of anxiety. What does he want to tell me? How will I answer?

Monday the 18th. Phone call from Algiers. I have been invited by the regional academy to take part in the plenary session to discuss the results of the BEPC. So, I have a providential way out to avoid my face-to-face visit with the civil and military commander. I am a bit afraid of him because he is extremely intelligent and has a far too flattering opinion of me. Fear of deceiving him? A little. As well as some distrust. Why? Why is he interested in me? He honors me too much. On the other hand, if I avoid him, I am sure to really annoy him, and this would be an unforgivable faux pas. Okay, I will stay.

The education inspector arrives with two colleagues at 7:00 "to give the CAP" to a candidate who has already passed it![52] He seems surprised when I tell him of the general's visit and decides to wait for him . . . At 3:30 P.M., the cortege stops on the square in front of city hall. The captain had assured me that there would be no classroom visits or meetings with teachers;

in short, there was not going to be an official reception. I had taken advantage of this to not put up any flags and banners. I did not really want to do it anyway. Now that I was at the gate with the education inspector and a few colleagues, all I had to do was wait for a sign to go to city hall for this historic meeting.

But no. General Olié sees us and comes over immediately. We welcome him in front of the entrance. He is followed by his aides, just as when I welcomed him a few months ago. His aides, thinking that he wants to see me alone, let us get ahead, and we are alone when we go down to the two middle school classrooms where, by chance, elementary level students and their teachers are working on a lesson. We go inside both classrooms, sit in on the lessons, and then return to the main entrance where my colleagues, the education inspector, and the general's cortege are waiting. And that was it.

## June 22

That was it, except that he wanted to know how my writing was coming along and whether my next book had been accepted for publication. When I offered to let him read the manuscript, he seemed surprised and thanked me for the show of confidence that I had made to him. He looked at me for a long time, as if he were trying to read my thoughts and see if I, in turn, could read his. Did we understand each other? I think so. A few minutes later, when I was alone with the education inspector, he said to me: "Why don't you give the general your manuscript? He is a good man, and you see that he only wants to know you better." And the education inspector, because he wanted to be at the center of attention, offered to take the manuscript to him . . . It is quite obvious: the general must have mentioned my offer. So what he was most interested in was knowing what I write about. This is what I was able to read in his eyes. It was a request and, at the same time, almost a prayer and a solemn warning.

"You see," he seemed to be telling me, "you write, and that is very good. Do not condemn us, you above all. We have educated you; we have given you a formidable weapon. We want your gratitude. Of course, we are not asking you to compromise yourself—you are a family man. All we ask is that you plug your ears and close your eyes, nothing more. The thought, the cruel thought, that you might be keeping track of everything is unbearable. This would be the greatest of crimes, be sure of that. Think of the gravity of such behavior. I can be reassured, you are an honest man, a man with a heart. You would not do anything against us, and we even hope that you might do something for France, the country that has so totally accepted you."

Did I read you correctly, General? Then, I have said almost all there is to say about your quick visit, and your even shorter meeting.

## June 23

We need to know if the patriots are fighting for a just cause, because, in the end, an honest man, a man with a heart—I am willing to consider myself as such, all modesty put aside—cannot remain indifferent to the cruel drama that is developing, amplifying, and threatening to carry us all away like an infernal whirlpool. If this cause is just, what can one expect from a lucid man? What else can one expect except participation in the fighting, an enthusiastic and complete endorsement of a better ideal, and the sacrifice of one's life for the happiness of others. An honest man, a man with a heart, must neither be quiet nor refuse to hear. The whole question is to find out why the patriots are fighting, what they want, what is being denied them, what causes dozens of innocent French or Arab victims to fall daily, men who have no reason to hate or kill each other but who hate and kill each other anyway. The whole question is to find out . . .

While I quibble over this in the relative solitude of my office, skirmishes are taking place almost everywhere, planes hum overhead, tanks speed noisily toward villages, the authorities are secretly collaborating, military personnel are holding meetings, informers are providing information, the ruthless maquis are cutting throats and hanging people based on the flimsiest of evidence, the soldier fires his automatic weapon at random, and the frightened population understands a little more each day that the French are the only ones responsible for their misfortune.

## June 24

Yesterday, I asked H. to discreetly deliver a copy of my *Jours de Kabylie* to the subprefecture with a dedication to General Olié.[53] The subprefect will make sure it reaches the general. He approves this discretion, feels that I cannot be too careful, and that, whatever my current attitude is, all of them understand me. "Mr. F. is a man of the future. We trust him." So I understood the general's intentions correctly. This is very flattering for me. I also believe that I am granted the same esteem and the same confidence in the other camp as well. I am maintaining my balance on a very tight, thin rope. This week, for example, I have most likely given the maquis the feeling that I am leaning toward the French side. They realize, however, that in my situation I cannot avoid official receptions. They do not always understand why the French assign me so much importance. So they wonder if I am not seeking some important position in some hated government branch, which is currently hounded from every side and, at the same time, tries to compromise both the timid and the ambitious. How to answer these questions?

I have heard that Mr. H. has been killed for having accepted a subprefecture. It turns out that Soustelle has as much esteem for me as he did for H. (Journal, etc.). But Lacoste left me alone whereas H. was called in by the Resident Minister.

The only thing I have to do to reestablish a precarious equilibrium is to decline the next official invitation. But this is not the only reason. To put it in simple terms: I refuse to side with the oppressors. I prefer to suffer with my compatriots rather than to watch them suffer; this is not the time to die as a traitor simply because you might die as a victim.

**June 26**

Guelmi, who has just returned from my village, tells me how Saïd G. was executed. He was called out at 9:00 P.M. The family had gathered for dinner.

—Come out, someone shouts to him, we need you.

—You can see me when it is broad daylight. It is too late to go out now.

—Come out, or we will break the door down.

—Break it down. I am not coming out.

The door starts to give way under their blows. He opens. They grab him and drag him away. The women try to get in the way, beg, lament, show their babies, implore their pity, invoke several saints. He is taken away nonetheless. The procession of women and children follow them in dark and sunken streets. They go through the village with muffled growls, sobs, hiccups, and moaning. Saïd, like a disjointed puppet, no longer resists. At the edge of the village, the fierce executioners turn toward the women, threaten to kill everyone, promise that Saïd will come back, and order them to go home. For a moment, not one of them move. From the bottom of the hill, they hear Saïd shout with a strange, almost unreal voice:

—By the bread and by the salt that you have eaten in my home, do not kill me.

Those where his last words, words that left him and rose

swiftly toward the women. Later, his last breath would do the same.

They hung him from a fig tree behind the bakery.

— The next day, Guelmi concluded, he went home, feet first. They had kept their promise.

## July 1

Last Thursday, I went to Algiers. The same insecurity reigns there as does here. The same stifling atmosphere. People have the same worried and scared look. There, however, one is lost in the crowd. One does not really get the feeling of being targeted. It is possible to find a place where one can meet friends with whom one can speak openly. It is possible to find a place where one can smoke a cigarette in peace while discreetly drinking an aperitif. A week earlier, there were a few days when assassinations took place in some streets following the execution of two outlaws. Then things calmed down. Obviously, whatever the citizens of Algiers may think, it is easier to breathe there than in Kabylia.

In Fort-National, things are still bearable. But what about the villages in the countryside where the Kabyles live among themselves? What a hell, my God! At night, people hole up without light, sound, or conversation. They will break down your door, brutalize you, and take you away. If, on the other hand, you are a "suspect," some dark evening, they will call on you, take you out, and strangle you. When the soldiers cannot find anything out of order, these patriots find a pack of cigarettes on you and impose a fine. When you decide to leave for France to work or find shelter, the French refuse to let you through, or the rebels refuse to let you go. If you want to sell a piece of land in order to feed your children, you are warned against seeing a notary, so the buyer refuses to buy, and you keep your land. If you have a disagreement with your neighbor, do not think for one moment you will find disinterested judges or lawyers. Your cause will be heard, and the new doctors of law will split the difference of opinion without any room for discussion. Alexander cut the Gordian knot, and others cut the throat of informers.

I still have not seen my new house in Tizi-Hibel, but I can imagine what it looks like. It has been a year since I last went home. My wife, who lacks my imagination, and my children, who want to go on vacation, are dying to go see our new home. So we will go see our new home. At my risk and peril, of course.

Those who cannot do without a cigarette or snuff come

up with crafty ruses to appease their passion. The mason's un-skilled laborer on a nearby construction site goes to a corner, unties his shoe, removes his sock, and finds a small bag between two toes. He opens it feverishly. He removes a small pinch of snuff that he avidly places under his tongue, and then he quickly puts his sock and shoe back on and picks up his shovel.

His mouth is shut tight. Do not speak to him. Wait until he spits out the pinch of snuff. His lips are tight together; he presses down with his tongue on the pinch of snuff, which has a bite to it, invigorates him, and relaxes him. It helps him enjoy his work.

### July 4

For the last few days, the word has been circulating that tomorrow, July 5, all activity will stop for the whole day, as a sign of mourning, to commemorate the "sad anniversary" of the French landing in 1830.[54] The workers will strike, and it will be forbidden for people to go out, perhaps even into the streets. Blood may be spilled, and victims may fall. It is hot, people are overexcited, and the tension will surely rise: it is supposed to be hot tomorrow. What will happen here? What will happen in Algiers and in other large cities? What will be the reaction of the soldiers who have camped in large numbers in Kabyle villages? What will happen, in particular, in my own village, where sol-diers behave like conquerors, full of self-importance and with-out self-control when they see villages that look dead and sleepy homes from which nobody ventures? What will happen when the soldiers will have spent an entire day in this hostile silence of the Kabyles, who will be holed up inside their homes? What will happen when the natural world, exhausted by its own beauty, is overcome by the sun and its verdant green withered by the onset of a burning summer?

### July 5

5:00 P.M. The town is empty. That is all. It has been empty all day long. From my window, I have not seen more than a half-dozen civilians. I mean that two or three passed by and then re-turned. Mr. Perrin with his kid, young J. L., and P. at the city hall window, then my colleague M., also at the window. I say window on purpose. The houses are blind or one-eyed. People have shut themselves up and closed their window blinds. Some have cautiously opened the blinds of one window. One only. Or a half. Everything is sweating terror. I am one of those who have opened up. At noon, we have to close again, as if we had received an emphatic command. Now we open a blind or a window halfway.

It seems that we all face the same danger, whether we are French or Kabyle. For once we understand each other in our desire to stay home in silence, sadness, and fear. I almost forgot to write that I saw F., my colleague who never goes out, and who may have resolved to be seen outside today in order to give us all a lesson in intransigent and stubborn patriotism. He seemed tense and arrogant. He was moving forward in fits and starts, his chest held high, tripping over imaginary fellagha who were not at all impressed by his aggressive manners since he was reluctant to revel in this act; he sweated fear like all of us.

Since this morning, military trucks and jeeps have passed by. Up until noon, reconnaissance troops armed to the hilt have patrolled through the streets of the village. But this is neither more nor less than usual. However, the soldiers have respected both the silence of the civilians and the sleepiness of the houses. It is only now that I hear them calling out to each other as they please. I see a few civilians who venture out on their balconies, wearing pants and undershirts. Maybe the village is about to wake up from its long nap.

## July 6

Nothing else happened yesterday. That pleases me. In the evening, someone officially admitted on the radio that "the so-called insurrectionary strike started by would-be nationalist organizations was a total failure." The commentary added that, thanks to police control and the arrest of the organizing leaders in Algiers, there were no attacks, and freedom was respected. In sum, the call for a strike was only partially answered in Algeria. I do not know what happened elsewhere, but in Fort-National we all have a precise idea of this failure.

Once again, there is explicit proof that the rebellion has a united front, that the population toes the line and is happy to do so. If nostalgia for the old days still exists among some, it is a shameful feeling that people not only do not express but also try to suppress within themselves, sincerely, as one tries to suppress remorse or to forget a mistake. What everyone fears right now is not appearing patriotic enough or getting a "lesson" in civics from a neighbor. Nobody wants to get lessons, and everybody claims to be giving them.

## July 12

Four days ago, there was another police sweep back home.

I still do not have precise information beyond this newspaper clipping, which mentions thirty dead rebels.[55] Another newspaper mentions only three. This is not a typo. The truth must lie in the middle. What is more, it is not rebels but village people who are listed as dead. They brought them out to be shot and had the bodies identified by people from other villages before telling them either that these villagers had been found there murdered by rebels or that they had tried to flee when they were called out of their homes. After that, a different communiqué was written by the press. Eventually I will get some information, at least concerning the number of the victims. For the rest, my compatriots have as much imagination as the soldiers.

Yesterday, at 1:30 P.M., as I was about to start my nap, a policeman was killed in front of L.'s place. It was on the exact same spot as Mr. B. last April. This victim was a man from France who had arrived in Fort-National two weeks ago. A victim like all the others. I do not think that there was any particular reason to reproach him. He was a policeman, that was enough. He was killed because the conditions were right for killing.

The opportunity was good, and the terrorist was able to escape, just as the one who killed Mr. B. escaped by disappearing into the market-day crowd. It was also market day yesterday.

This time, however, things took place in a different manner. I mean the reprisal. This time it entailed more than simple identification checks. Much more. First, there were bursts of gunfire throughout the town that must have caused damage. They reported one casualty and several wounded. Just like that, firing at random. Then the town was sealed off while military vehicles sped off quickly in all directions to round up those who were trying to go back to their villages. Once they were sure that nobody was left behind, a few clips were fired into the countryside just to put their minds at ease. Meanwhile, the town was overflowing with Kabyles as if it were the day of an official reception or some trumped up elections. The only difference was that people did not look happy.

### July 13

The long line of people who had been at the market started moving like a procession around 2:00. The street was congested with them. They were moving forward with their arms in the air behind their donkeys on which they had hastily placed their purchases or whatever they had not been able to sell. There were also herds of sheep and a few bulls and cows. Once in the square, the people abandoned their animals and continued walking, their arms in the air. Once the animals were on their own, under the surveillance of totally indifferent soldiers, they started to drop their loads and scattered; tomatoes, fruits, and meats fell off the *chouaris* and were trampled in the dust under the animals' hooves and the soldiers' boots.[56] One old man had the time to remove his turban quickly and use it to tie his cow to a tree. Donkeys were braying on a slope, nervous and biting each other. Then they went down the slope, only to fall and get up again, leaving their load in a jumble on the ground. A young donkey, made wild by the heat, mounts another and, for over an hour, manages to capture the interest of the soldier in charge of keeping an eye on the area. While the soldier could testify that the animal was not successful in his attempts, he did not see anything else for that whole hour . . . The endless line of people with hands in the air walked toward the Algiers gate in this ridiculous fashion. The old men moved like crabs and looked pitiful. The young looked ashamed and submissive. The whole group resembled a pathetic herd that the policemen shoved, hit, and insulted. Those who held baskets or bags and thought that they could get away with raising only one arm quickly found out they could not: they had to raise both arms and forget their purchases. As a result, along the way the road and the sidewalks were strewn with food. Some more or less naturalized French civilians distinguished themselves by their rudeness and showed great zeal at the expense of the Kabyles. They must be the ones involved in counterterrorism. Certain types of individuals, who are usually afraid and remain hidden, suddenly reveal their secret thoughts and display very clear opinions at such unique opportunities. The most eager of all was the local tax collector, newly arrived from France, a so-called foreigner, an expert at "French Presence."[57] E., the policeman, also played an important part by leading the search teams in the homes of all his creditors, his wife's friends, and also those who helped him out by humiliating him a little. Since E. is thin-skinned, he needs a lot of things for which he humbly asks the Kabyles, and the Kabyles, generous as they are, let him have them.

## July 16

The entire male population ended up in an area above the police station, hands in the air. They were then led to the Fodder Lot for identity checks, which took at least four hours. In the meantime, military and police patrols scoured the town and carried out minute inspections. No, brutal inspections! In homes without men. I saw all of those from the street below who were picked up at home pass by in front of the school. They had to go as they were found: bare-headed, in shirt sleeves, or wearing house slippers. They were honest merchants, respectable civil servants, and school children. My students passed under my window, their arms raised ridiculously in the air as if to give an illusory benediction or to beg without much hope for a pity that has been refused them in advance. In the homes, the police searches were brutal. They manhandled children, insulted women, and broke down any door that was not opened quickly enough.

## July 18

Around 6:00, they began to release those they suspected the least: first I saw the kids running back to wherever they had left their belongings or their animals and then the men, distraught, hurried, and febrile. They had to hurry to recover their stuff so they could leave as quickly as possible, run home, where they had to arrive before curfew, and avoid being shot at on the way: some live about six miles away, and they had one hour to get home. While panicked people with tormented faces were running around and children had tears in their eyes, the patrols continued to search in those homes that had not been visited until then. It was at that moment that G., a policeman, accompanied by three soldiers, came to see me. They entered my office, and G. apologized in a mocking way. They had come to search the teachers of indigenous origin, that is, M. and myself. Nothing was said about Mrs. J., a Frenchwoman from Ajaccio, a teacher without degrees who has been tenured for a year.[58] I handled things well and even joked with the soldiers about the shrewdness of using weapon detectors. The next day, I wrote a letter to the academic inspector. But, after thinking about it, I decided not to send it. It reads as follows:

Dear Inspector,
I take this opportunity to bring to your attention the fact that the captain, a special delegate to the community, has requisitioned a classroom in the boys' school and remodeled it into a refectory, for the benefit of the police. This classroom should be returned to our use by September 25.

Further, following the assassination of a policeman last Wednesday, a search patrol came to the school to inspect the lodgings occupied by teachers of indigenous origin. This included my lodging as well as that of Mr. Menouer. The same thing happened to Mr. Ouar and Mr. Aït Meng, who lived outside the schoolgrounds. Mr. O. was taken away for an identity check with his hands up, but he did not have to endure any kind of brutality. The search of the school was performed properly, but some policemen forced a classroom door and broke a lock.

Yes, after thinking about it, I did not send this letter. The captain who "heard" of this incident came to apologize. He was almost glad it had happened because, as he said, "now the rebels no longer suspect you of being on our side."

No doubt. On the contrary, Captain, it is you who suspects that I am not on your side. This does not prevent me from sleeping at night.

### July 19

Yesterday, there was an attack against two tribal soldiers in Michelet. Other tribal soldiers killed in cold blood those who had been at the location of the attack. I heard that they killed an old meat cutter and his son near the animal that they were butchering for their customers. Today's newspapers announce that "the author of this attack and his four accomplices have been killed." The number stated by the press is exact. Nothing more. The commentaries are believable. Long live pacification.

### July 27

For the last ten days, rumors have been circulating that we were on the verge of a cease-fire, especially during the Brioni Conference held jointly by Tito, Nehru, and Nasser. Some Algerians have gone to Yugoslavia. Yet, nothing seems to be happening. There has been no decrease in the frequency of skirmishes, attacks, and police sweeps.

Somebody else has been killed in Fort-National on the construction site of the new police station: a foreman from Spain, shot by a terrorist. The same day that Patrocinio was assassinated in Michelet.

Yesterday, I saw Si Lhacen from Tagrag. The soldiers have killed H. M. and a young boy I do not know. This happened after the July 5 strike, on a Saturday. The soldiers arrived there at 7:00, gathered the men at the local council house for an identity check, took H. M. and the other one aside, and then gave orders for everyone to go home and lock their doors.

—Today, you will be on strike, just like Thursday. We will shoot all those who stick their necks out.

—We went home and prudently locked ourselves in, Si Lhacen said. It was their answer to our attitude of two days before. I have to tell you that on the day of the strike, nobody stepped outside. We had complied with the patriots' orders. All that was left was to heed the soldiers' orders. That is the way the game has to be played: you have to please both parties. But, in all honesty, I have to admit that if we were happy to please the maquis, we did what the soldiers wanted for fear of being shot.

Anyway, we shut ourselves in, and the village falls back into the slumber from which it had been awakened by the first rays of the sun right before the soldiers' arrival. Around 7:30, we hear some submachine gunfire, and we ask God to protect our souls. Then a long silence falls heavily over our small village at the same time as the heat becomes overbearing. You have been to Tagrag. In July, it is an oven, and we bake in our clay huts. Wearing a gandoura, I am bare footed and bare headed, crouched in front of my closed door. Around 11:00 we hear the heavy tread of patrols marching over the pavement and crunching the loose stones that are hardly in short supply around here. They bang on the doors, which remain closed: wives hold back their husbands, who try to get up, and children cling tightly onto their fathers, whom they feel are being threatened. You see, at that moment, each family is isolated, alone with its fear and bad conscience. We feel both guilty and cowardly. The enemy is in our village. We know that the enemy's selections are arbitrary. Our lives depend on chance and above all, we think, on the sturdiness of our doors. I look at my door with the utmost gratitude. It would be hard for them to break it down. And yet, they almost have. I do not know where I found the courage to open it. No, it was not courage. It was more like annoyance: I had had enough of seeing the door shake. They grabbed me as soon as I opened it.

—Please let me get dressed.

—Come on, hurry up.

I put on my old slippers and my burnoose, and they take me away, a submachine gun pointed at my back, which is shivering and dripping with sweat.

I cross the village with the policemen. They explain to me that I am not going to die but that I must follow them to the mosque, inside the cemetery, to identify the rebel who had been shot that morning while we were locked in our homes. They needed another compatriot to testify as well. I wanted to stop at the first door in front of me.

—No, they said, we know the person we want.

They pointed to the house of the secretary—the one who was hanged by the maquis.

—Here, knock on this door. The secretary's son will come with you.

I had a hard time getting him outside. He was pale with fear.

At the cemetery we identified the bodies of our poor cousins. They had been shot at 7:30 and, since then, had remained in the sun in pools of dark, muddy blood with dozens of large green flies hovering above.

—Here are the rebels that the soldiers shot. Do you recognize them?

—Yes, we do. They are our cousins, but they are not rebels.

—We are not interested in that. Family names, first names . . . sign the report. Now, you have one hour to bury them. Go get all the help you need. In one hour, they must be underground and you must be back home. Anybody who is late will be shot. In one hour, there should be nobody left outside. Understood?

We buried the two poor fellows in their clothes, without washing them, without prayers or ceremonies. We had the time to empty their pockets and retrieve watches, identity cards, and wallets. The women and children were not allowed to come and see the bodies.

### July 29

A young girl was shot by a terrorist in Tizi-Mokrane. I heard that she had a bad reputation. A young man coldly emptied his revolver into her lower abdomen. Then other young men came and carried her by the arms and legs to go bury her. A children's game, in a way, without significance or consequence. The scene did not last long. They had to find something else to do, find a new game, like talking about the upcoming liberation, the greatness of Islam, or the sense of honor that must govern everyone's actions. It was especially important not to suppose that these particular young men had all been, more or less and each in his turn, the lovers of this girl of easy virtue.

### July 30

B. tells me that the girl was known and tolerated but that they reproached her for spending time with the soldiers garrisoned at the school. She went to see them and they fear that she was bold enough to bring others with her and to start giving information . . . Of course. She had been warned on several occasions, and finally the patriots executed her.

Yesterday, operations took place on the north mountain (Affensou-Tizi-Rached). Trucks were parked above the school in the evening. The soldiers seemed tired. Today's newspaper is reporting a victory without further details.

**August 2**

The Kabyles understood from the start and quite astutely the importance of the Suez Canal for world navigation. Since Nasser has just nationalized the canal, and newspapers devote long columns to it, and radio stations discuss it during each of their programs, they tell me the following:

—This is a shortcut that saves French, English, American, and other ships thousands of miles. Egypt holds the legitimate passage rights. All the others have to do is to go through and say thank you . . . after having paid. This is the language of an independent state. We understand the colonialists' arguments: they have dug and built at their own expense. But who dug and built? Neither Mr. Lesseps nor the banker, but the Egyptian worker.[59] It is the same with Algeria. They keep telling us about all their beautiful accomplishments. In the end, it is Arab labor. Yes, sir. It is Arab labor so despised by the arrogant employer who finds shelter under his helmet and, with his hands in his pockets, keeps an eye on everyone. Nasser told them what he thought about western democracies.

—Gentlemen, leave me alone. Go ahead and massacre dirt poor Algerians with your modern weapons, your planes, your NATO divisions. Go on, go on with your big principles, go look around the Aurès Mountains or Kabylia. This canal is mine.

It boggles the mind to hear such comments coming from these people. When I think that I could never interest my students in the Suez Canal or the Panama Canal or in the stock market! One should never teach history to those who look decisively toward the future, children and people who are suffering.

**September 9**

Vacation in Tizi-Hibel from August 6 to September 6. The children really wanted to go there to see our brand new house and also to verify that we had a real home. I was a bit apprehensive about venturing out into the countryside, handing myself over to the fellagha and the soldiers and throwing myself into the lion's den. On the other hand, I was eager to live close to the maquis, to get better acquainted with them, and at the same time to remove all my doubts—those that concern me and those that make me want to revolt. I wanted to know, once and for all, what dangers were threatening me. I wanted to form my own personal opinion about the mind-set of the liberators. I have returned with my doubts, but I have left my illusions and my candor behind. I discovered much suffering and little enthusiasm, much injustice and little devotion, and cruelty, egoism, ambition, arrogance, and stupidity: a people that is used to being beaten, that continues to take it, but is tired, very tired and on the edge of despair. My people from back home inspire pity, and I am ashamed that I have peace of mind. What follows is a series of events that I witnessed and that may help to explain my overall dismay. But from the start, you must renounce any formal condemnations and look for the source of evil. There are only victims; there are only guilty people; there are only dispensers of justice. At any time, you could be one or the other. There is no other alternative.

In the welcome that I received, I sensed surprise at times, at other times understanding, but always a certain wariness. The first evening, in the council house, everybody listened to me when I spoke. I felt as if I had to exaggerate my grievances against the French in Fort-National, if only to emphasize that I was being persecuted just like everyone body else.

—I need to do that, I thought. I will earn their sympathy.

Big mistake. They do not care. They know what is going on. They know precisely that I have nothing to fear from the French. In any case, I could not have matched what they had to tell about reprisals, vexations, and threats. So they told me everything, as if they were trying to convert me, to make me share their anger, their hopes, their certainties—all of their feelings. And those feelings were shared by everyone without exception—by my parents, my friends, my enemies; there was a consensus and I had to think, act, and speak like everybody else. There were several times when I had to express my anger, my hope, and my certainty; and all of it bore a direct resemblance to what they had felt. Once again, I was back home. They allowed me to share in the inner life of the village. I could enter into a group, a category, a clan that was hostile to the neighbors, a clan that either fights to defeat the rival or holds back and waits. Such a clan plans its vendetta or its treason, directs its propaganda prudently, consolidates its attack plans, or prepares its defense while continuing to proclaim, during its many meetings, the sacred and compulsory union that not only makes the village into one block but all of its men into one single man. I shared in the threats that weighed on everyone, but I was not risking anything in particular. For the maquis, I was a submissive "civilian," as subject to compulsory labor and as docile as any other. For the French soldier who sees in each of us a deceitful fellagha, I was the new face of just one more fellagha in Tizi-Hibel. Even if my self-esteem had to suffer from the disdainful anonymity in which these brave fighters put me, at least I was allowed to spend a quiet vacation in a location where brute force, cruelty, and poverty reign. When I saw the soldiers and the maquis arrive, I had nothing to do with either of them.

When soldiers drove by in their trucks, they would flip us off or sometimes sketch out a salute that immediately turned into an obscene gesture when no one responded. When they arrived on foot and proceeded toward the djemaâ, we would run away as fast as possible, and they had an empty village to cross.

When the maquis were due to arrive, the village lookouts would discreetly empty the streets beforehand and then bring them into the village, again deserted. We would call them "brothers," and we were happy to welcome them as brothers. Happy and worried, especially when the person in charge had imposed these people on us and had gently ordered us to give them shelter. I saw some of these poor fellows show off because they had been given this honor: not only did they show off for a whole day, but they were more patriotic than the most enthusiastic rebels. They prepared a good meal, did as much as they could, hid their temper from everyone, and, in the end, felt as if they had passed a dangerous test: after all, they had made an important contribution to liberate their country from a century of slavery: they had given shelter to fighters.

In reference to forced housing, some suspect that the person in charge is quietly favoring his karouba and his friends. He always sends our "guests" to the same area. But try to find the courage to mention this to him, especially since he has publicly explained that he is always guided in his choice by tactical factors, rather than egotistical or distasteful motives. So it becomes a question of strategy rather than personality. There is nothing left to do but bow eagerly because we are good patriots.

I found out that Sebtah was shot and killed by the military.

I sat on the bench where young Ghersi sat when he was killed by a bullet from the army. It came from the building where the nuns live. At Madène's invitation, I went down to Taourirt-Moussa. I went back to my old school and saw the garden and my classroom. This is where, in 1951, I wrote in my own handwriting "the Kabyle schoolboy" on the back blackboard. My colleague was kind enough to keep it as a souvenir. I did see a lot of disturbing things: burned houses, orphans, widows, places that had been discreetly marked, a sort of testimonial to the blood that was shed there. Will I ever be able to write down all that I have learned? Yes. Will I ever be able to say all that I have felt and all that I have promised myself that I would say? Where would I find the necessary patience to do all of this? How will I sort out my conflicting feelings without forgetting about the victims themselves or the cruel God or the human beast? Why not forget all of this just as the dead are already forgotten? Yes, forgotten, buried under other dead who call for still more dead, as if they were in a hurry to be forgotten in their turn.

As for Sebtah, his sister-in-law explained to me that, in a way, he deserved to be shot by submachine guns. He was a hoodlum, hard to deal with, and disliked by everyone. As soon as he became a liaison officer, he started insulting and threatening anyone he did not like.

—Yes, cousin, a hard-headed man he was. Ask your father about the things he would say to him. He would enrage that poor old man with comments like: "And your kids, we will get rid of them, and you will croak in misery. And we will drag you out by your feet. . ." He did not even treat his own brother well. Believe me. He went so far as to insult the maquis, and they had to give him a good thrashing to bring him back under control. No, he was not an easy fellow. You know, that was his fate . . . They tell me that he died ready to utter another insult. So we have a *moudjahid* in the family. Now they are writing songs about Sebtah. It comforts his mother. In any case, she gets six thousand francs. So everything is fine.

I listened to the cousin's endless chatting, and I had to admire the steadfast philosophy of the people back home who refuse to discuss fate, even when this fate is blind and takes on the human form of a young soldier in a modern army who has come to our home to defend the values of that eminent civilization that Sebtah and his friends were undermining.

It was Moubarek who offered more important information about my cousin's death. I listened to him as he told his story for the hundredth time. He feels that, as long as he lives, he has to tell it. It is as if he now has nothing else to do in this absurd world where our lives have no more value or meaning than those of wild beasts in the eyes of well-equipped hunters.

—I was on my way to Béni-Douala to get a postal order. On the way, near the old oak trees that you know, some soldiers on duty ask for my papers and then order me to walk. We head into some empty fields and down a narrow path toward a brand new building. Once there, I discover two bodies on an earth embankment. The soldiers position me in front of them. Since I was not close enough to the bodies, they push me forward. I stumble. They push me again so I move forward. Okay. Stop. I have my back to the soldiers. There is a body by my right foot and one by my left foot. I say to myself that there is enough room for me in the middle. I decide, however, to fall on the body on the right. It is larger. I fold my burnoose over my arm, and I pull my wallet out of my pocket. I cannot think of anything except for falling on top of that large body. I keep saying to myself: "Thump. Right there over the large one. Thump." I turn halfway around and hand my wallet to the officer.

—Eh! What?

—For my children. My pension booklet is in it.

Instead of taking the wallet, he slaps me hard across the face. I falter and start falling over the larger body. But he holds me up. My cheek is burning, and there is a constant ringing in my ear. Ashamed, I look with compliance as if to humbly ask him to be forgiven for my conduct.

—Stand up. What do you think, you old goat? We are not here to kill you. Look at those bodies. The fellagha are the ones who kill. Not the soldiers. Get it? Look at them. This is the work of the fellagha.

That was when I figured out that they were not going to kill me; so I straightened up completely and looked at them candidly. They started to laugh. And I must say that I laughed with them. From that point on, everything was all right.

—See these two guys. Look at them carefully and tell us if they are from your village.

It was a formality. I had to identify Sebtah and then go with them by jeep to Béni-Douala to sign a paper in which I stated that I had found two bodies and alerted the military who followed me back to where I had found them.

With one stroke of a pen, Moubarek signed something and returned to the village bearing the sad news. When my cousins went to see the captain of the SAS to ask for permission to take the body, he agreed and explained that Sebtah and his friend had been freed the preceding evening and must have been shot by some rebels who were passing through. The Kabyles from Béni-Douala who saw them driving in a military jeep around 6:00 can always accuse the soldiers in question, and Moubarek can always explain to his compatriots that he signed a false statement. Only the official report matters; it alone will allow Mother Sebtah to receive a no less official pension. She will then regret that her hardheaded son died with an insult on his lips, without being quite aware of the crimes of which he was accused.

### September 29

I have to finish writing the impressions that I have brought back from my village. They are already part of another world, seeing as how other days, other events, and other deaths have followed . . . Spent two days in Algiers. Saw L. I. A. and my friend E. R.; read and heard comments about the Farès declaration in *Le Monde*.[60] No, Farès does not want to be like Ben-Arafa. Good for him. The Muslim students of Algeria are going on a total, endless strike. If the Kabyles are in despair in their villages, so are the French in Algiers. The winds of panic blow everywhere. People approach friends and acquaintances with a certain indifference—without any hypocrisy—while acting openly confrontational. Each person says what he thinks of the other, and it is exactly what his neighbor thinks of him: in other words, nothing. People are not thinking of anything. No more friends, buddies, or compatriots. We are brothers or individuals who all look alike and who are united by similar feelings of doubt, fear, and discouragement. Everything is falling apart, and what remains are thousands of puppets who tremble at the thought of being destroyed.

The day before yesterday, someone shot at the amin of Ikh, here in Fort-National at 7:00. He was slightly wounded. No one went out of the way to help him. Yesterday, someone shot at a captain. After shooting the terrorist, who could not escape, the soldiers patrolled all day long, put the Kabyles in a holding pen, and searched everything. A minor civil servant told me:

— You see what the French do when they are concerned: they check everything under the sky, kill a suspect, and jail the rest. The suspect may really be guilty, so why don't they stop there?

When the amin was wounded, they did not do a thing. Basically the French would like to see us exterminate ourselves. We are stupid. We should understand.

I am sure it took that civil servant a while to figure that one out.

### September 30

The pamphlet for the student strike is circulating.[61] Threatening telegrams are reaching city hall: parents and teachers are both being threatened. The lists of students who are required to attend school are now printed in advance.

### October 6

So far, we have had from 28 to 65 students (22 of whom are French), out of the more than 500 that we had expected. The requisitions, prayers, and threats were unsuccessful. The situation is the same everywhere or almost the same. Everybody is following the FLN to the letter, and one cannot truthfully say that it is only fear or patriotism that is driving this blind obedience. I say blind, because this student strike is truly harmful. How can we deny it? It is just as harmful as the other excesses of which I have heard. Brutality reigns, weighs on us, and makes us suffer physically. Paradoxically, perhaps, it will win us over, and we will gladly accept it in our hearts. Apparently there is no way to put a stop to our pain except through brutality, which goes head to head with another form of brutality. Mr. Lacoste calls this "the force of pacification."

There are more and more stupid and atrocious attacks in the cities. Innocents are cut to shreds. But what innocents? Who is really innocent? The dozens of peaceful European customers in a bar? The dozens of Arabs lying all over the highway around a bus torn to pieces? Terrorism, counterterrorism, terror, horror, death, blood, shouts of despair, shouts of atrocious suffering, and death rattles. Nothing more. Peace.

In this Kabyle village, thoughtless young men tell you about the death of fat Hocine.

—You know, that guy, he is really heavy. We tried to hang him. He took the olive tree branch to the ground with him. It looked as if the entire tree was going to fall. No, it was just him. He rolled down to the ravine like a bag of manure. We finished him off by hitting him with shovels because he did not die when he fell. His head exploded with the very first blow, just like a watermelon . . . We threw some dirt over him. When we got back to the village, the maquis members were eating bread and grilled calf liver. My friend did not want to eat and turned up his nose in disgust.

In a city of the Mitidja where I traveled in a dream, S. stuck to the facts when he told me his story:

—They came for me at my home around midnight. The soldiers, the DST, who else? [62] They had to break down three doors to get to me in my bed. They took me away. No, I did not say anything. I knew I was done for, and I did not say a word. So they started beating me up. I had a big advantage, I was thin. The first blows almost knocked me out, so the rest was of little interest to me. Afterward? Anything you can imagine. They ripped my poor rags to shreds: they sliced pieces of flesh from my body, pierced me with their bayonets, broke my ribs and my arms and legs, cut my throat according to the Muslim ritual as we perform it back home, riddled me with bullets, stamped their feet both with fear and joy, and I just let them do it. I let them do it after a certain point. After a relatively short point. That is the advantage of being thin. And as I looked at them from a distance, I felt both amused and triumphant, out of their reach, free, and happy. It is a good thing they did not notice.

With contempt, they abandoned me under a bridge, several miles from town. The next day, in full daylight, they went back to my home to arrest me as a suspect. They had most likely forgotten that they had taken me away the day before. Nevertheless, I had to be found under the bridge, my father had to identify me, which, believe me, was not easy. Yet, in the end, when my father flatly declared that the feet on the cadaver could be only those of his son, they were able to complete the inquest with the conclusions that you know and that the press reported: It was a FLN leader killed by the rival MNA faction. My family was left alone. As for me, I continue to secretly chuckle about all this. Because, you see, I would not want them to hear me.

### October 8

Back home, the situation is the same as when I left a month ago. Salem told me yesterday that the maquis are constantly around and that they are ready to fight in the villages, whatever the consequences might be for the noncombatant— which really means the entire population. The local rebel administration set up by the maquis is almost always made up of former malcontents and "hard heads," and old scores are quickly settled in the name of the resistance and the fight for freedom. People are somewhat surprised: for some, it is the unexpected access to a position of leadership that gives them a better feeling about themselves, makes them conscious of their unsuspected worth, as well as the temptation to abuse their powers somewhat; others who are forced to be quiet and to obey, who are used to the capriciousness of fate, await peacefully for the wheel to turn again to bring them back to the place from which they fell. For the majority, it is a question of getting used to a new order, of accepting new advice and saluting the new masters. However, the majority is in complete disarray; it continues to make mistakes and errors. It alone pays a heavy toll.

### October 14

Women have learned from experience not to speak rashly. The cost of a hasty comment is quite costly for poor women. A severe or questionable statement, a word one should not have said, or one interjection, and the woman has to pay a fine.

—So, you are not very pleased, are you? So those who fight and die do not deserve your silent gratitude? Five thousand, or we will strangle you. A piece of rope, old woman. Get it?

She does understand, but she moans, resists, implores, and ends up coughing up the five thousand while promising to keep her mouth shut from now on.

Yamina, on her way to the spring, stumbles on a rock and curses the times. Her big toe is bloody. A patriot appears in front of her, grabs her by the throat, and gives her a lesson:

—What was that? You curse against the year 1956, the year of our victorious struggle, of your liberation, you tramp! You swear instead the act of rejoicing! Five thousand francs. Bring it to Kaci . . . I will go there tonight. Watch out, I know who you are.

One fine day, Fatima sees soldiers at the entrance to the village.

—Good day to you, she says. She expresses "Good day" in French and "to you" in Kabyle. A fellagha grabs her.

—Old hag, can't you speak Kabyle?

—Good day to you, my children. God help you, protect you and . . . This time she says the whole thing in correct Kabyle.

—That is enough. Ten thousand francs.

—I thought you were French soldiers.

—Twenty thousand! In this case, a patriot looks aside, spits on the ground, and goes on his way. You, you deserve the rope. Twenty thousand. Bring them to Kaci's. And may Satan take you away!

## 1956

I met Belkacem and Hocine when I taught in their school. Hocine was hanged. Why? Belkacem went to live in a military camp with his entire family after a fight during which he was beaten up. He told the French military all he knew about the rebels' activities in his village. A sweep of the place was unsuccessful. However, a few days later Belkacem disappeared mysteriously: he is no longer in the camp; he is no longer in his village. The last I heard, his wife and children are back home. The patriots executed Hocine's sister-in-law because she spoke ill of them and Belkacem's sister because she cried over his death. They both had children.

### October 17

Last week, there was a major battle in Port-Gueydon. The radio is announcing that more than one hundred rebels in uniform have been killed. Both the air force and the navy took part in the fighting. From another source, I hear that the Kabylia maquis members have almost all made their way toward the battle site, leaving the villages and the population in peace, at least for a few days.

In the newspaper *L'Espoir*, I found this story, which seems to be related to this episode:

Three Kabyles (Zaïdat, Achiche and Yazouren) considered to be trustworthy servants were charged with forming clandestine groups of some fifteen to twenty men identical to those of the ALN. With the help of volunteer officers, commissioned and non-commissioned, these armed groups were to work, in "official clandestinity," toward the liquidation of the ALN in the Kabylia department that has been a test area.

After his departure, Mr. Soustelle, the author of this project, informed Mr. Lacoste of this 'important undertaking'. . . The three servants, however, in agreement with the people in charge in the FLN, switched sides and joined the maquis with twenty-two submachine guns, six Garand guns, two hundred sixty-four carbines and their servers.

They are reporting that the Port-Gueydon expedition was a punitive expedition.

Who got punished in the end? Probably the disarmed population of the villages.

Is this really the kind of action they are counting on to restore the people's trust? Or are the people in charge simply trying to smother the revolt, to silence a people so as to proclaim—in the eyes of the French and other nations—that Algeria has been pacified and that the Algerian problem does not exist? To persist in this lie does not hurt "truth"; it hurts only people: it tears hearts, it kills bodies, and spreads hatred and madness.

### October 22

Last Thursday (the 18th), Yaker was killed near Tamazirt. He leaves five children behind. He thought he was safe because he had given pledges to the maquis. God only knows what pledges! He was the secretary of the mixed community for the last ten years and knew everyone. At one time, he was very powerful, feared, and respected by the Kabyles and enjoyed the trust of the hakems. He was playing the administrative game to the utmost, and his tragic death was not unexpected. Last year, he left his office suddenly to go to France and returned shortly thereafter. After that, it seemed that he had settled his misunderstanding with the maquis, and it has even been rumored that he gave information to the resistance.

Not too long ago, he told me that the new hakem did not trust him and that they were trying to give him a hard time. I advised him to put up with this trouble rather than risk the ones that might come from his compatriots.

Another day, when we were talking about the school secretary who had been hanged and whom he knew well, he told me that he was not only saddened but surprised about what had happened.

—Yes, I am surprised that Si Chérif, smart as he was, let himself get caught . . .

And so it was: Yaker was just as smart. He got caught nonetheless.

People suspect that he had revealed the name of several snitches. In turn, another snitch mentioned his name: it is a vicious circle in which, sooner or later, imbeciles get caught because they do not understand. The same thing happens to wise guys who think they have figured things out. Poor Yaker, even if he deserved his fate, how can you not be moved by the sight of this brood of children waiting all night long for a daddy who does not return, hoping against hope that he spent the night in his office, at a friend's house, anywhere. Anywhere except the police station, which is very close to their house, where the police are waiting for an official doctor to come to do a hatchet job of an autopsy on his body early in the morning.

## 1956

### October 28

Last Monday (the 22nd), at 9:00 P.M., a plane landed in Maison-Blanche.[63] In it were five FLN leaders on their way to Tunis, where they were to attend a reception for the sultan of Morocco and take part in the conference in which the Sultan and Bourguiba were going to participate. The plane was flown by a French crew working for the Moroccan state. The crew received orders to fly to Algiers, and the DST captured the leaders of the rebellion.

French public opinion has not concealed its joy or the importance of this capture. The abduction is viewed as a great victory, as though it were the prelude to the final victory. What final victory? The smothering of the revolt, the death of the rebellion, the rebirth of Franco-Algerian friendship, confidence, and peace? Why not fraternity! In other words, once these scums, these scruffy individuals who are the cause of evil, are in jail, this evil will immediately cease to exist; the Arabs will no longer be discontented, and the profiteers will stop shaking.

Kabyles of good faith have really tried to put themselves in the place of the French, who are rejoicing at this sweep, who are rejoicing even when they hesitate to admit it; no one has understood anything. No, we do not see how this constitutes a victory or a remedy, but we can easily understand how this has put an end to trust and hope at the same time. It is quite clear that we are being treated as a colonized people, that is to say, as inferior beings who, quite naturally, are not entitled to any benefits of international law. We see that none of the rules of honor can be invoked in our favor, nor the respect of promises, nor simple human respect. In our case, the only efficient arguments remain force and tyranny. The only goal is to make us better, to free us from our psychological complexes, our eccentricities, and to make Frenchmen of us, conscious Frenchmen whose desire to remain fanatical Arabs is inflexible and persistent.

It is obvious that the French are adamantly defending their rights to Algeria. They have acquired these rights by force, and they are intent in maintaining them by force. In our eyes, just as in theirs, force alone will legitimize them. Nobody has ignored this reasoning since Pascal.[64] It is hypocritical of both of us to want to argue over this matter. Nobody wants to discuss anything unless it is to convince their opponent of their strength and to win a battle without fighting. We already know that this fighting is not fair and that we are weaker. So perhaps it is others who need to be convinced, and maybe it is others who need to be held back so they will not interfere in this business, so they let the French reestablish a French peace and allow the Arabs to become submissive again while being ashamed of the dead . . .

There is a strike today in Fort-National, just like last July. I did not see anybody in the streets all day. Nobody? Well, no Kabyles. The French went to mass as usual, but did not linger. The soldiers did the same. I heard the call for a strike on radio Cairo: it appealed to all Arab countries to observe the strike "as a sign of mourning for martyred Algeria." Good job, Mr. Lacoste!

**October 29**

Reaction: the town is closed to the populations of Beni-Raten. The only ones allowed to enter are the civil servants, employees, and clerks (for the Europeans). All the stores are closed. Mr. L.'s business is open, and so are a few bakeries, the pharmacy, the butcher shop, and Ch. and H.'s vegetable stands, so that the population inside the ramparts can buy staples. They have not distributed the mail, but we are listening to the radio. The town is silent, as if dead, but the main street is clean and attractive. I walked it alone from one end to another with narcissistic pleasure. I looked like a shipwrecked person happy to have escaped a collective drowning. I then encountered other survivors, and we joked innocently.

A soft, but agonizing sun seemed to be telling us:

—Take advantage of the last few good days. The town belongs to you only. Enjoy it while you can.

At one point, I started wondering if I were really in Fort-National, in Kabylia, or in Hungary where thousands of dead had just fallen.[65] Or was I in the Middle East, in Morocco, in Tunisia, or somewhere in one of these many countries where they kill and murder so abruptly? I felt a certain amount of pride in being right in the middle of the fighting—on the front line— while others are obliged to sulk in an obscure yet peaceful corner, far from the holy places where you feel alive and take advantage of the situation. Finally, I wondered where this obscure yet peaceful corner was hidden, and I had to conclude that, in all reality, it does not exist. The world was feeling its own vitality and taking advantage of it. Men had discovered their destinies and the fact that, if they killed one another and died, it was only in order to be happy, because there is no other reason to fight.

Yes, happiness in this world or in the next, and quickly. This is the twentieth century, damn it!

### October 31

I hear that things are getting better in Hungary (15,000 dead) but are getting worse in Egypt, which the French and English air force bombed this morning. Yesterday, Israel attacked Egypt.

The town looks just as empty as before. We live in the strictest of privacy, and yet it feels as though we are in a tiny Kabyle village, a place where people know if the neighbor has diarrhea or if he is going to eat hard flatbread.

Tomorrow is November 1st. There will be another strike.[66] But we have been on strike since the other day. We have been forced to remain on strike, and so, this time, we cannot even brag about starting a new strike.

### November 2

It was calm all day yesterday. Until noon, I had not seen anyone in the street. Then, there was a small gathering on the square: the captain, the administrator, the secretary, and two or three shop owners. These shop owners were among those who were detained yesterday, who were not allowed to go home, and were therefore forced to open. What is going to happen? Around 2:00, I find out that some store doors are forced open, and crates of vegetables are being taken out into the street. However, there is nobody to sell them and nobody to buy them. H., my neighbor, who has been locked inside his store since yesterday, is not concerned. It all ended in a flat and lugubrious calm. In the evening, the radio tells us that the strike was a total failure in Algeria and, at the same time, gives us details about the raids by Anglo-French planes in Egypt, the Hungarian Revolution, and the reactions in America and around the world.

Today, the city comes back to life, the stores reopen their doors, the Kabyles arrive in droves. They look hurried and concerned. There are rumors of many arrests in the villages. People are also talking about the reported death of Mohamoudi, which they do not believe really took place, especially considering that it was announced by the Algiers' newspapers.

Today, the city comes back to life and starts a new year. What can we expect from it? More suffering and death? More uncertainty, anguish, and terror? More misfortune?

It has been a year since I started writing down my feelings. God knows that I did not lack material, but I was short on desire, taste, and drive. I did not write down everything, of course. Only guide posts, so that later, if my life is long, I will still be able to feel the sad memories of the dark years, of the gloomy days.

Do I need to conclude now in order to bring this year to a close? Unfortunately, nothing can be concluded, and nothing can be erased besides the columns of days on a pocket calendar. Here again, however, one calendar follows another with fresh columns that one wants to cross out all at once; days that will have to be nibbled away with the lives of people and will require tears and blood to disappear one after the other. Everything goes on. And, in a similar way, I will most likely continue to keep my writing in my notebooks. Here, there is no one but myself with my despair, my powerlessness, and my irresponsibility; here, there will be no one but myself with my fear and my revolt, my egoism, my peace of mind, and my guilt. But how many others like myself are living in this drama; living like witnesses, sullen yet lucky, relying on chance to keep the torment away. Each one of us is guilty for the sole reason that we belong to a category, a race, a people. You fear that someone will make you pay with your life for your place in the world, pay for the color of your skin. You fear that someone will attack you only because nobody has done it yet. You wonder why you are doing nothing when you are almost certain that there is nothing you can do. You cannot even feel sincerely sorry for the victims, nor can you pity them in the dark with the secret and clandestine joy of the survivor. You are ashamed of your uselessness, you are jealous of the torturer, you are jealous of the victims. You admit that you are not worth much, and yet it may not prevent you from falling. You think that the future will be better for everybody, that independence — or at least equality — will ensure that your children lead a respectable and happy life; but you cannot guarantee anything for them beyond the next minute. In the meantime, they stand around you and seem to ask if you are not thinking about abandoning them and leaving by yourself, just like that, without warning anyone. Sometimes you start asking yourself about the value of words, words that no longer make any sense. What is liberty, or dignity, or independence? Where is the truth, where is the lie, where is the solution? More often, you are very tired, no longer able to think of anything, or to feel the weight that is crushing you, or to simply say: This will come to an end. It is already over for some: those who have died and have left this place and who, from afar, undoubtedly think of us at times without any sympathy at all when evoking our memory in the imperfect tense of the indicative conjugation.

Last year in school I had colleagues named Albert or Max or Fernand or Renée. This year I am left with Mohand, Mouloud, or Ali. In a way, the team is more homogenous. (All we are lacking is students.) The others have left feeling belligerent, and belligerence is the feeling we maintain here. The split between us took place in one instant, as if we were tired of seeing each other. This separation was a deliverance for everyone.

Therein lies the gulf between us. What we feel one for the other is most definitely not indifference.

Many faces have disappeared from Fort-National. Faces that we liked and faces that we detested, but faces that were part of the scenery. Now the scenery is different: it is of no interest to us, and we walk by without seeing the Europeans, this world apart that no longer has anything in common with ours. We know that, in their eyes, we are plagued with all kinds of flaws. They know, just as well, that in our eyes they have lost all the qualities that we thought they possessed and that they assumed they had.

As for our relatives who are not around anymore, our feelings for them amount to no more than a diffuse affection shared by the stones of our houses, the trees in our fields, our crests, and our valleys. This Kabylia is so poor and so wild. We have become part of it, we feel pity for it, and at the same time, we feel pity for its children: those who were tortured by the police, those whose throats were cut by the maquis, and all the others who are still alive and weighed down by threats.

I receive letters from Roblès on a regular basis. At a time when a sense of camaraderie and friendship is failing me, his has remained fraternal and strong. Roblès is more than just a friend or a Frenchman. I cannot connect him to any motherland because he is from everywhere, and that is exactly where I come from, poor friend. I think you have to be pitied even more than me and that the confusion you feel as a non-Muslim Algerian is more moving than mine.[67] Let us wait—to use your favorite words when you find yourself in an awkward situation.

**November 5**

The international situation is very confused. In the Middle East, Israel has pushed back Nasser's troops and now occupies the Sinai. The Anglo-French troops have landed in Port-Saïd in order to take over the canal. This triple aggression has aroused the UN's disapproval, and solemn warnings have become part of speeches, votes, and prayers. On the other hand, the Hungarian insurrection that had triumphed over the regime and wanted to break away suddenly from communism and Russia has provoked the anger of the Russians, who have returned to Budapest to crush the revolt. There is a second wave of indignation in the Western world: especially France, America, and England, where speeches are followed by declarations, where insults fill newspapers, where the standard of ridiculed liberty is held up high, where one proclaims the Rights of Man, where one shouts one's furor and horror at the Russians' monstrous attitude to the point of totally forgetting what is going on in the Middle East and, even more completely, what is going on in Algeria. Although, to tell the truth, there is no possible comparison to be made between, on the one hand, the martyrdom of the Hungarians or the well-known savagery of the Cossacks and, on the other hand, the elimination of rebel banditry and the pacifying action of the French army in Algeria. Of course, I am not saying a word about Nasser, because everybody knows that he cannot be trusted, and they detest his arrogance. No, in reality, the Arabs have nothing in common with the Hungarians, nor the Cossacks with the free world.

Three of the five unfortunate young men arrested in Taourirt-Moussa on November 2 were executed yesterday morning. This took place in the countryside near the village of Aït-M. Afterward, the police went to see the local Kabyles to tell them that the army had shot a few rebels and that they could go look for them and bury them. After searching through the bushes and ravines, the Kabyles eventually found the bodies. They were identified and buried, and the families in Taourirt-Moussa were informed. These families thought that their children were still at the police station, still being subjected to cruel interrogation. All of a sudden, they have been reassured. It is over; the kids will not be tortured anymore.

When I turned the knob on my radio set a few moments ago, they were talking about the indignant emotion of the prime minister, or rather, about his offended indignation: they were still talking about Hungary.

**November 8**

Since midnight yesterday, all hostilities have come to an

end in Egypt after a Russian ultimatum. Eisenhower has been reelected in America. The *Canard enchaîné* is such a witty newspaper. This week it is publishing some nice cartoons and nice parallels. Very funny.

Another world war is taking shape on the horizon, and the UN is trying to fend it off.

**November 9**

Heard on the radio: a caption for a cartoon published in India: Boulganin and Kruschev: "Our hands are covered with blood.— Yes, they are. Let us go wash them in the canal." Fine. What about Algeria in all this? Algeria has been forgotten! . . . Because I spend so much time thinking about those who are falling around me, I probably tend to place a greater price on the life of a Kabyle than on that of a Frenchman, an Egyptian, a Hungarian, or a Russian. . .

I am no longer young. That is a fact. Okay. I realize with some trepidation that I had to wait until I was old to understand that force is always right. Pascal is wrong when he says that the failure to strengthen justice has led men to justify force. Men did not justify force; they made it into a deity, and it does not require any of their justification. When one meets force, one humbly uncovers oneself, one gets on one's knees, and one begins to adore it. That is, if it has not already crushed you, and if you have been given the time to humble yourself.

**November 4**

It is 11:00, and I can still hear the military band at the end of town.[68] The military review has just taken place on the square in front of the city hall, right under our windows. No Kabyle participated, although all dignitaries and all employees had been individually invited. My friend Larabi peered at the whole scene with his one eye from behind the windows of his office. He was living an intense quasi-Cornelian drama, caught between unreasoned fear and the equally unreasonable desire to enhance this solemn occasion by his presence.[69] There was a group of Kabyles at the door quietly observing the events. If need be, there would be among them a faithful observer in charge of informing the maquis. In a moment, he would go tell them: "No Kabyle took part. The employees remained behind the windows; the other civil servants and dignitaries stayed at home. Maybe they wanted to . . . but they did not attend. They were afraid."

From that standpoint, he would be right to talk like that. But the truth, I think, lies beyond this. This occasion, just like a mass, or one of the meetings in the parish hall for a weekly movie, had the distinct characteristic of being French—and uniquely French at that. A Kabyle would have been out of place, and this ostensible nonparticipation is like a small, pleasant act of vengeance for us, an act of courage that fills us with pride and, for a day, gives us back some of our dignity. We are quite aware that, up to that point, we had been attending "their celebrations" to fill up the place, to bring in some life, as second-class guests or benevolent admirers who were supposed to applaud while keeping their distance. Now, this is out of the question. What they do is of no interest to us, but they pretend not to believe this and multiply the opportunities for inviting us. Today, once more, it was at their expense.

The day before yesterday, Larabi came to tell me that he was preparing nearly one hundred invitations.—"Each one of you will get his own, he assured me. This time, you will have to come, okay! The wind has turned toward unity. I believe that it is going to be over soon with the Russians, the Americans, the Arabs, the Hindus, and the Hungarians . . ." Almost like a Russian salad. I answered that, as far as I was concerned, nothing good would come out of this salad and that, in all likelihood, the Kabyles in Fort-National would not attend the ceremony. My analysis was so correct that Larabi himself stayed put behind his window.

I must add that he did in fact invite all of my colleagues. Except for the primary school teachers and one European colleague, who, acting like a good patriot, joined his own people fifteen minutes before the officials arrived. So you have to conclude that this invitation was more a means of intimidation. Did they suspect that we did not want to attend? Perhaps. Yet, it is a major blunder to forget the most interested one among us.

Larabi and his masters are certainly wrong. The wind has not turned toward unity. As long as they continue to shoot Kabyles, search their homes, deprive them of mail and food, spread fear and hatred, as long as they maintain these methods, nobody will attend their ceremonies. And even if they did change, nobody would attend as long as the panting shadow of the victims and the menacing shadow of the maquis continue to hover over us.

## November 12

A. B. A. is back from his home. He is completely astounded by what he has heard. Three villages have been bombed and set on fire. The men have been taken away, and the women and children wander aimlessly through the douars seeking asylum. The soldiers have spread death, terror, and destruction. Here are three villages that have been emptied, destroyed, and erased from all maps, oh Oradour![70] A. B. A. tells me that in Meckrek the men were brought out of their homes and penned. They let loose five police dogs that attacked five men at random, made them fall, bit them, and dragged them in the mud. Those were the ones fate has picked: the men were made to stand up again and were shot on the spot in front of their companions so that they would not forget. Then the trucks were filled with what men were left—healthy or not, young or old. The women and children were thrown out, and the village was set on fire.

The same operation was carried out in Tigounesseft and Zaguernant. I have heard that today the target is a nearby douar.

G. has returned from my village. There has been another police sweep there following a denunciation. Thirteen compatriots have been arrested, but the others had enough time to escape. What is left of my village now?

Rabah, who had been arrested on November 1st, is in Béni-Douala. One of his eyes has been punctured. The day of his arrest, he had been knocked unconscious by the butt of a rifle and taken away, near death, in a jeep. They interrogated him afterward. He is old and weak. Will he ever get over this?

A. B. A. is indeed right. He has good reasons to be astounded. That is the way we feel, but we have got to keep on living. Our conscience is stirred up, yet we keep silent. Of course, these are crimes that should be denounced. To whom? To the Hungarians, perhaps. To the weak people of the universe who suffer and die so the strong get stronger. To those who are exterminated for the greater glory of mighty nations. To those who fight to live on in a world that wants to negate them. All of them could hear us; and they would raise an uproar along with us; one that would rise into the sky and would shake the divine throne.

### November 13

I saw the SAS captain and immediately spoke with him about the situation. He is not very happy with the contacts he has had during the last few months. He admits that it has not been possible to reestablish confidence in town. A failure, after all. He is clearly disappointed by this and told me that he had been ordered to change strategy: "It is going to be very hard, and I will not be able to do anything for the population. You heard what happened at Ogdal; now it is the turn of the Ouadhias;[71] tomorrow it will be here. It is going to be like this throughout the department [district]." Ogdal? It is the douar B. A. talked to me about yesterday. Today's paper mentions it in passing: a short paragraph like so many others. Good God, what is going to happen? Is the era of hypocrisy about to be replaced by the era of hysteria? The captain seemed to imply it could not be any other way.

"In the douar of Ogdal (CM of the Djurdjura), an operation was able to engage a rebel group entrenched inside a cave. Six rebels were killed. A military rifle, two hunting rifles, and two automatic guns were recovered. There were no friendly loses."

### November 19

I believe that the captain's predictions are about to come true. Today, one town was sealed off. It would seem that a major part of Kabylia has been declared a forbidden zone. Only the civil servants, employees, and business owners are allowed in. The dominating presence in the streets is that of soldiers wearing green fatigues. About ten minutes ago, I saw a dozen go by, with large black or fawn dogs on leashes. Dogs that have been trained to fight and are ready to jump at a Kabyle.

The people from my village who were arrested last week are almost all in Béni-Douala while the military waits for evidence of the blows they received to disappear, or for the decision to finish them off. Faci Rabah has been tied to a pole since his arrest; but the others are free—in a barren, concrete room. Four have been released, including Dehmous Saïd, who has returned to the village near death because, unlike the others, he could not take the bottle, the electricity, and the blows. The whole village is under house arrest. Families are tightening their belts, and everything is rationed. They are just waiting for the arrest of those who the informer must inevitably denounce. We also wait for our area to suffer the fate of the Ouadhias and of Ouacif. A. B. has told me that the story of a Ouacif group that had come from the Oran area to visit their village. When they went to T.-O. to ask for a pass from the prefect, he stated that he was not aware of any monstrous police sweeps. Maybe he really does not know what is going on? Just like the terrorist who leaves a bomb in an overloaded bus and does not really "know" how the bomb explodes and how many people are killed . . .

Since the Hungarian affair, I have been reading motions, letters, and appeals in favor of the poor Hungarian people everywhere. And I think that these honest people who are so scandalized and that those sensitive souls who are so torn could have done the same thing for Algeria. They did not. I tell myself that in all these texts that the press publishes, each time the word *Hungary* is used, it could be replaced—without exaggeration—with the word *Algeria*, and yet it never is. Is it because the world that sees us suffer is not convinced that we are humans? It is true that we are only Muslims. That may be our unforgivable crime. That is a question I would like to discuss with Sartre or Camus or Mauriac. Why? Yes, why?

### November 21

We are living in peaceful and silent isolation. No more traffic on the streets. No vehicles pass by except for jeeps or military trucks. Bus service to Algiers has been interrupted. Since the maquis have banned the reading of Algerian newspapers and the bus from Algiers cannot bring the other forbidden newspapers, we would not get any news if it were not for the radio. You need a pass to leave or enter the town. We are all here, however, and we are not unhappy . . . They say that those who live in the villages are living even more difficult times: mail and postal money orders are not delivered, and the most basic provisions cannot reach them. Nothing that can be eaten is leaving town. They are talking about providing the villages with officially controlled supplies and weighing everything. I have also heard that all the men will be transferred to the villages and that they will only be allowed outside their homes to get fresh air for a few hours each day. There is talk about limiting food, freedom, and, in some cases, about shortening lives. The only outcome that is shown as possible is "the rallying" of the masses. I doubt whether the people who are putting up with all this humiliation will submit to that one.

### November 22

On the contrary, I feel that they are resisting more and more, and that one day they will call for a general massacre. This day may come, and they are not afraid of it. What now seems inconceivable is peace, the peaceful or friendly cohabitation with those who more and more present the image of implacable enemies. Or maybe it is necessary that the tragic generation of those who fought so ruthlessly against each other be totally eliminated or disappear. No, I do not see how the Algerians and the French will be able to feel esteem for each other or even tolerate one another.

## 1956

### November 25

My colleagues who are used to going to their home villages on Sundays were not able to leave town. Those that have passes are only free to circulate from 8:00 to 11:30 in the morning and from 4:30 to 6:00 in the evening. Outside these hours, one must stay home.

The population does not seem to be suffering too much from these restrictions. People are no longer eager to take walks or travel. I also think that the villages are reasonably supplied and that those who can no longer receive postal money orders can get credit and help from their families and friends. This is part of our culture; and it is obvious that the French are avoiding—as much as possible—inhuman and revolting measures. It seems that the authorities are taking into account not only the opinion of those who are subjected to these measures but also the opinion of those who are directly in charge of carrying them out. All of this could create a climate of understanding, and among us, exhaustion would set in along with the desire to have things finally resolved. Unfortunately, those in charge are slowing this elan down, stamping it out as soon as it becomes obvious. They are adamant in not wanting things to improve without their participation because, obviously, that would work against them. If one were to allow the soldier and the Kabyle to stand face to face, far from their respective military machines, I think that the Kabyle and the soldier would shake olives from the olive trees with rods and hunt wild boars in total peace.

### November 27

Saw old Ammour Mehand from Ikhlidjen, amin, c.m., who has lived in Fort-National in the back of his store since last October. One evening around 7:00, someone shot at him. I talked about this when it happened. Neither the French nor the Kabyles showed much concern about it. I did not see him again until just yesterday. He extended his hand toward me in a supplicating way:

—Are you all right? I said to him.

—Yes, thanks. Eh, what do my friends think, those that know me, those I know, those that I trust and hold in esteem? . . .

—I am glad you made it . . .

—Oh thanks. They know where the shot came from.

—Who are you talking about?

—The French. It was a soldier who shot at me in the dark. Someone saw him from the café, on the other side. How could it be one of ours, I ask you? Me, I have not done a thing. I am a Muslim.

He left, quite unhappy, certain I would not believe one word he had said. I ran into one of my buddies right after that.

—What did he tell you?

—Oh! First I told him that I was happy for him.

—Well, I did not tell him anything: what a scoundrel! Nobody has said anything to him. He thinks that you are naive. The proof is that he avoids everybody else, and when he goes out, he disappears like a thief.

### November 29

The maquis respond to these restrictive measures in the following way: they tear up the passes that are hard to obtain; they finish emptying the town in which people of the villages were carefully allowed to filter in; in a way, they "finish" the work of the police and the army. In the near future, those from Beni Raten will lose the habit of coming to Fort-National, the habit and the taste for it, and when the doors are opened wide again to welcome them, nobody will show up at the door . . . The day before yesterday, Lamara, the big guy, was executed. This had been expected for a long time; but people thought that he had calmed down and was minding his business. Who knows, maybe he decided to change all that.

Each time a traitor or so-called traitor is executed, anguish seizes the survivors. Nobody is sure of anything anymore. People are really terrified. Terrified of the soldiers, terrified of the outlaws. It is a terror that hovers mysteriously and inexplicably. Nerves are on edge.

I have received a copy of J. Soustelle's book.[72] I find it difficult to write to him. What would I say? Mr. Soustelle is an intelligent man, but he is mistaken. Mr. Soustelle is generous, but he does not tell the truth. Was he duped after all? Is he deliberately trying to dupe people? How can I tell what I think when his book cheapens our suffering, our tears, and our blood?

### December 2

Our captain has lost one of his men, along with his weapon and equipment: it is assumed that he left during the night to join the maquis, also taking with him some secret papers he was able to find: there were names listed on those papers, especially that of the big guy who was executed twenty-four hours after the disappearance of the native policeman. If this is true, I know some people must be having trouble sleeping.

A. B., who has returned from his place, tells me that the Kabyles are starting to get hungry in the villages: nothing is getting in. It is cold and it is snowing. How long can they last?

People are expecting a settlement in the French and foreign political milieux. Mr. Mollet is expected to make a speech, but he has been postponing it, first day after day, then week after week. Reasonable Kabyles with whom I have talked think that it is hard to come up with an agreement; there will not be a settlement at all because it would be nothing more than treason. Nobody wants to betray the dead; and the dead fell for freedom. We might as well die as they did rather than to say, at a later date, that they have died in vain. This is what I was told, without either boastfulness or enthusiasm, just a sad evidence of an unavoidable period we have to go through, with clenched teeth while recommending our souls to God.

### December 7

We are short of food: no bread, vegetables, or meat. People are fighting over canned goods. The blockade was lifted the day before yesterday and put back in place a half hour later. Outside the city, the maquis have torn up all the passes. Then letters were sent to all the employees, all the civil servants who worked in the town, telling them to immediately stop coming to work. Yesterday, everything was closed. Not one Kabyle came to the office. Policemen patrolled in the evening and delivered requisition orders that will not be followed. Our mail is not being delivered. Among all the civil servants, only the teachers did not receive the letters from the maquis. So, in the meantime, they work with the hope that such letters have not been written and that they will be left alone.

The little village of Imaïnsrène was "checked out" yesterday. From here we could see the men dressed in white assembled at the entrance to the village, near the cemetery. It lasted all day. There was a lot of military traffic all day long. A chopper flew over the town the entire morning. It was a dead town, a town deserted by its civilians, who were holed up at home. The bus traffic between Michelet and Algiers through Fort-National has started up again. I am told that everywhere else the situation is normal and that we owe this very special attention to the captain, who is also the acting mayor and the prefect. In any case, I do not think that this is going to help the case for pacification.

### December 8

The Arab employees have held an open-air meeting to discuss the situation. They decided to ask for an audience with the subprefect to respectfully indicate to him that the "civil servants" will not be able to return to work if the restrictive measures are not lifted. My colleagues delegated me to represent the teachers, and everybody chose me as the spokesman. In front of the acting administrator, I dressed up my speech with vague and respectful formulas, but the transaction was still made quite clear. I spoke for five minutes. The acting administrator spoke for an hour. He was speaking directly to me as if I was giving him the opportunity to say everything that was on his mind and he was taking advantage of it. As for me, I was quite pleased with the turn our meeting was taking, and I listened the best I could. Mr. Dessanti is a young, well-educated man. He is open-minded and expresses himself with ease. He spoke with much warmth and precision.

—Gentlemen, he said to us, if you think that the measures that bear heavily upon you were initiated here, you are wrong. Mr. Guy Mollet himself is aware of the situation. Do you want to know why these measures were taken? It is quite simple: we are in the center of the rebellion. No other area has seen as many acts of cruel terrorism committed in its midst. These restrictions were mandated right after the atrocious, inhuman, and cowardly assassination of Lieutenant Jacote of the Ouadhias. The cowardly bandits attacked a defenseless man, a valorous man who was there to spread good will to help the Kabyles. And these bandits, who do not dare to face you when they strike, who shoot at you from behind and then flee, kill, according to statistics, four Muslims for every European. These are the people who intimidate you, these assholes without honor . . . I belong to the extreme left, and I agreed to come here only on the condition that I could work according to my principles and my ideals. Ideals of fraternity and justice. There are a few civilians who are trying to accomplish their mission in Fort-National, and you cannot disgust or discourage us . . . We could also leave and let the army do what it wants. We could put the army in charge of everything, and then you would hear no other voice but that of the military, that is, the voice of the canon . . . I know that the Muslims are intelligent people and that the Kabyles, in particular, are inclined to compromise. Well, the time for "compromise" has passed, believe me, because we are going to be intransigent, and we will hit hard. You are free to declare yourselves our enemies. I will be frank with you: leave and you will get nothing else from us but our bullets. Otherwise, stand with us. It is the FLN that gave us this model of how to proceed. Consider the case of X, who was shot; he, also, wanted to compromise. We knew that he was courting the rebels while we kept on paying him a salary and feeding his children. This did not sit well with the FLN. They killed him because they do not like double play. Neither do we. From now on, we will not allow it. So you have to choose. The restrictions will be lifted for those who stand with us, and they will lack nothing. They will become like us, exactly like us. Together with them, we will build this new Algeria that we all long for. The others are our enemies. They are headed for ruin and condemned to death. You have the requisitions, and I can, if you wish, send the police to look for you and place you under arrest. You can be sure that those who do not respond to the call, those who refuse to work, will be immediately fired and considered rebels . . .

We left the city hall totally aware of the intentions of the authorities and all a bit shaken. We decided to meet again at 5:00 to decide once and for all what we should do.

At 4:30, I explained to my teaching colleagues what the exact situation was. I also told them that the Fort-National "civil servants" seemed to be in a state of disarray and needed good advice and a good idea. I added that they were waiting for this idea to come from the teachers. After having discussed the matter, my colleagues asked me to suggest that the FLN be contacted to ask that the strike be extended to cover all the employees of the district.

Around 6:00, new meeting at the Hamiti place. They were waiting for me to speak. I had to speak, give them the advice of the teachers. They all rallied around the idea: we have decided to return to work while waiting for (1) the answer from the FLN and (2) the arrival of the new subprefect from whom we will seek an audience as soon as possible.

Then we went to see the captain to request an audience and to inform him of our temporary return to work. He did not hide his satisfaction, and we talked with him until 7:00.

He told us in particular that he had made sure there would be no trouble for some compatriots. In some cases he even saved the lives of those he thought were interesting and momentarily lost. He told us of his disappointment and lassitude at the lack of comprehension or awareness of those he administered. He regretted not to have been able to fraternize more with people "like" us and assured us that he is filled with bitterness as he gets ready to leave. We also regretted that we, like the captain, were powerless toys in the hands of a blind fate. We left each other with this reasonable wish: that better days come for all of us, days of unambiguous reconciliation rather than frightful submission to a brutal force that rage is about to unleash . . .

A little while ago, a policeman brought the pamphlet that summarizes, just by chance, what we heard yesterday. It is clear, neat, and precise: either you are French or you die.[73]

### December 11

Today there is a pedagogical meeting in Tizi-Ouzou. There were about one hundred teachers from Kabylia who either were able or wanted to attend. I have been told that the situation in Tizi-Rached is just as difficult as in Fort-National. The same is true for other areas. My colleagues from Tizi-Ouzou told me that all the men in the village have been packed into a shed for the last five days. Night and day, and it is cold. The women and children are allowed to bring food to the prisoners—whatever food they want and whenever they want it. It does not bother the soldiers to snap at the kids or shove them aside when they do not get out of the way. A colleague was there for forty-eight hours before the inspector got him out. Every day they pick out a Kabyle from the group and shoot him a few steps from the shed. This morning, it was a native policeman who had the audacity to bring coffee to the prisoners; yesterday, it was a twenty-four-year-old man.

In Tamazirt, my friend K. suffered the same fate as the colleague in Tizi-R. They put him in a shed for three days although he was a school principal (six classrooms), a knight in the order of the Legion of Honor, and the former president of the center.

On the way from Fort-National to Tizi-Ouzou, and on the way back from Tizi-Ouzou to Fort-National, we went through six police checks. The highways are completely deserted, and the villages seem dead. In Tizi-Ouzou, life moves at a very slow pace. There is hardly any activity, almost like at Fort-National a month ago. There, at least, it is possible to get food. It feels like December 1940, after the defeat.

### December 12

The "civil servants" of Fort-National are hiding in their offices. Nobody mentions the word *strike* anymore. However, the captain knows exactly what happened. He knows that certain people were asked to talk with the FLN to get orders. He knows that so and so, who left Fort-National with passes, will not return any time soon—to avoid being arrested. He already knows who the leaders are in this business, or he will eventually find out. He also told me that one of the supervisors—one of the most intransigent—came to him to apologize for being part of the delegation that I led. If the "civil servants" make a move, he has his hit-list of leaders ready, those whom Zizi (the informer) will point out.

### December 13

Yesterday, I talked with poor Mr. L. His employees left him a week ago, and when I came in, he burst into tears, like a helpless, old woman who has just lost her lifelong spouse.

—You know, Mr. F., who would have thought that Boussad would leave me? Oh! Yes, they wrote to him as well. They did not want to let me have him. Why? Tell me why they did that?

The tears continued to flow down his large face, ridiculously creased with fat. He was leaning against shelves; like a gigantic mollusk, his flabby mass towered over me. He was crying like a child.

The fellaghas did this to him. They are not letting the employees enter the town. They have torn up the passes. They do not give a second thought to Mr. L.; he is not any trouble, he has never acted against them. He gave them money and expected to be treated with respect, but no one respects him.

—Mr. L., do not be mad at them. They took certain measures without thinking about particular cases. Your own people should have thought about you and not abandoned you . . .

—You know the French do not like me. I have given thirty-five years of my life to this community. Not one single reward. Did you see how they got rid of me last year? Thirty-five years. A kick in the butt.

—Yeah, and what a butt! I thought to myself.

—Not the slightest reward.

They could, at least, have awarded him the Legion of Honor (which, I understand, his sexual preferences would prevent him from ever receiving).

Poor Mr. L., he could never separate himself from either his business or Fort-National. Fort-National, where he was born and where he will most likely die alone; die of old age, just like his house, which is slowly falling apart; die of the inertia and boredom accumulated over decades; die of sorrow at the departure of the most tyrannical of all valets; die in the midst of a general indifference; die with little fear of that meaningless death he has dreaded for sixty years!

### December 15

Serdjine, from Taourirt-Moussa, came to see me in my office. He became infamous in August after he gave the army the names of some people from his home and told them everything he knew about the maquis . . . Everyone body thought he was dead or had been killed by the soldiers for some reason or another. I told him all that. He told me that it was a strategy of the SAS captain from Beni-Douala, who wanted to keep his family from being mistreated. He added that the fellagha had already executed his poor sister. He did not have the courage to look me straight in the eye, but on his way out, he kissed me, and I think that he felt like crying. "That is what life is like," he said several times. Then: "You know, these are mad dogs that bite the hands that feed them." "Be careful, over there, it is hell. Here you are in paradise. Good for you." "Our merciful God decides our destiny; there is nothing we can do ourselves. Okay, my wife and children and I found refuge with the army; there are eight of us. He knows, if I am wrong." The He in question is "Our merciful God." The mad dogs are the fellagha. Belkacem looks younger and has put on weight. His children have probably gained weight as well. "Listen, Belkacem," I said to him at the end of our conversation, "you are a reasonable man; be careful. I beg of you, make sure that what you say does not come back to hurt you. There is one God, and he judges us, you know that."

— "Yes, I know," he answered.

### December 22

There are rumors circulating that rationing is going to be lifted. People will be allowed to move about freely, and businesses will reopen and replenish their empty shelves. This means that we will be able to go outside the walls of Fort-National, to buy bread at the baker's. Yesterday and today we got some good white bread, as many vegetables as we wanted, and a slice of steak.

This has been going on for more than a month. Maybe the villagers got hungry, but they remained calm. Had they been asked to demonstrate their allegiance to France publicly? Had they been pacified? It does not seem that way. These measures have been rescinded by the same administration that mandated them. That is all. But it did not help alleviate the resentment.

It facilitated getting rid of a few suspects, jailing a few more, upsetting everybody, and showing the Kabyles that they do not have a good conscience and that it is futile for them to even try to find a solution where there is none. As for us, we now have a good conscience, we are sure that we are right, and we are ready to pay a heavy price for such a privilege: the same price that we are asked to pay every day. Because unanimity costs: on the one hand, it requires the life of the patriots and, on the other, that of the traitors; sooner or later, you are put into one of these categories. Is it always the appropriate category? In the end, it is of little consequence for the one who dies.

### December 25

Yesterday, Monday, there were a lot of Kabyles around. The gates were opened wide, and people dashed into Fort-National with sly smiles on their faces. They made a lot of purchases while assuring others that, during the period of rationing, they had not lacked anything. Young B. told me that, among the maquis, everyone's morale is better than ever, and that they are turning away volunteers and preparing for a liberation parade that will take place soon. He also told me that they feel much disdain for the "civilians" that we are, and that, when the time comes, we, "the spineless" or "the slaves," will have to throw ourselves at the feet of them, the saviors . . . The total number of deaths for the area is estimated at fewer than twenty. Four were liquidated by the FLN as traitors, and the others were shot by French soldiers. However, there were a lot more victims in the Ouadhias, so I have heard.

The radio stations are announcing an upsurge of acts of terrorism in urban areas. Today, their commentaries are pessimistic. French journalists are complaining about the lack of understanding that France encounters almost everywhere in the world (America, India), and fear that they are facing nearly general hostility in the UN.

It also seems that a selling fever has taken over French and Jewish property owners in Algiers, and that Muslims with cash in hand can buy anything they want.

### December 29

Two days ago, I took my wife to a radiologist at 107 Michelet street, in Algiers. Yesterday, Mr. Froger was shot in front of his residence at 108 Michelet Street.[74] Mr. Froger was buried earlier today. A funeral procession of 20,000 people followed his casket from the high end of Michelet Street to Saint-

Eugène. Algiers radio modestly reports that serious confrontations have taken place at Government Square: five terrorists killed, twenty cars burned out, and several stores vandalized. Radio-Luxembourg provided more information, especially about the importance of the procession and the comportment of its participants. You could hear the bells of Sacré-Coeur and the funeral song. Then, outside, the great clamor of the *Marseillaise* soon transformed into a tremendous cry of anger. You could detect insult in this cry, and this was impressive. Finally, the procession was followed to Cheval Square, and in the Arab district, violence broke out, engulfing those brought there by chance.[75] It was no longer impressive, but terrifying. From the moment I turned the radio on, I had enough time to imagine the square, the Arab district filled with Muslims who, being more or less clothed in rags, were more or less considered suspect, and who, being more or less dark-skinned, were viewed as more or less unpleasant, and these suspicious and unpleasant Arabs fleeing in front of well-behaved, correct, well-dressed young people who were nonetheless indignant at the cowardly attacks, the odious crimes of a fanatic mob. They were so indignant that instead of seeing brown they saw red. It was as if in their eyes each Arab had been transformed into a gigantic red fez, and it was necessary to tear up all these red hats in a rage. So they buried poor Mr. Froger quickly, and the riot that his funeral was expected to start was avoided that evening. Poor Mr. Froger, last year, was held responsible for the fighting on February 6, the tomato fights in front of—and maybe on the head of—Mr. Guy Mollet. This year, it almost happened again. Because of him. But this time, as far as we are concerned, we paid too much. Poor Mr. Froger, may your God take your soul. Ours would not want it.

I made a note of my visit to Algiers the day before, because I could have waited two days. And since the attack took place exactly where my taxi had stopped, I could have arrived just as the funeral procession was getting started and could have gotten stuck there with my wife and children . . .

A few days ago, A. A.—another bigwig, although this one is a Muslim—was attacked at the Franco-Muslim Center and suffered serious head injuries. The affair was quickly and very discreetly contained. Nevertheless, a few minutes after the aggression a "terrorist" was shot. This discretion might be explained by the fact that the person in question rejected any talk about rebellion, yet continually talked about the tricolor flag—

under the folds of which he claimed to live and wanted to die. His excessive and unchanging zeal had become inefficient. If he were to die now, it would be between two white hospital sheets, and nice ones at that. If he were to survive, he will talk about the flag again and continue to be wary of terrorists.

In the end, nobody takes his untimely remarks seriously. He did not deserve the general ire and indignation that automatically start following the death of a truly "great patriot." I do not know if this official candor will provide food for thought to those of our big shots who might be tempted to display this kind of patriotism that, until 1954, allowed them to represent and defend us and that they renounced in a moment of panic. As for impartial observers, it is clear that they must retire and stay inside their apartments. They must do this solely to avoid death and to prevent some passing "terrorist" from getting killed for their sake.

### December 31

Today, people speak of the execution of five "traitors." Three in Taourirt-Moussa, one in About and poor L. Amer from Aït-Mimoun, a friend of Omar's whom I know well. I was far from expecting such an end for him.

I do not know how guilty or how innocent all these people —as well as dozens of others—are. Almost everywhere in Kabylia the situation has begun to deteriorate, all of a sudden. After a difficult month of severe rationing, people were cold and hungry; they became frightened and discouraged. So they probably started contacting the SAS and the army in order to sell information, to get their own people thrown in jail, or to kill their own. Perhaps the maquis were also forced to carry out a "necessary cleaning." There will come a time when the army and the maquis will compete to see who can be the most brutal and cruel; for the former, it will be in the name of a system that it is desperately trying to defend, and for the latter, in the name of a freedom that is difficult to conquer. The victims of these implacable angers endure them with surprise and panic because they are finally conscious of being caught in a hellish whirlpool from which the most tentative attempt to escape seems utopian.

# 19**57**

January 6, 1957

For the last few days there has been a considerable influx of people from the mountains in search of supplies. Trucks from Algiers are coming in with impressive quantities of semolina, cereals, sugar, and coffee. Everything has sold out within a half day, and the trucks return to Algiers. The district is under military control, and it is difficult, if not impossible, to leave it. The iron grip around Fort-National was loosened a little, but now it has been tightened around the tribes. Tribe dwellers come from almost everywhere, from Michelet, from Azazga, from back home, and they cart away everything they can find on the backs of animals, by taxi, by van, or on their own backs. They supply the stores in the villages in preparation for the bad days everyone expects; people buy and buy and pay cash—whereas in the post offices, money orders are piling up because of orders not to distribute them. The receipts in Fort-National alone total almost 100 million.

It is obvious that the proverbial Kabyle solidarity that is being put to the test is functioning flawlessly. The Kabyles have never felt so united, so homogeneous, and so invincible. This is an attitude of which any mountain dweller can be proud, and with good reason. But it is also highly educational for the attentive observer who suffers vicariously with suffering men, and who seeks to see clearly in a world where cruelty and stupidity are competing for first place. Why do they not allow these people to be who they are, exactly who they are, especially when they will never change? Why were they cornered into finding friends in places where they never dreamed of finding any? Why have they been made into enemies, when one day they will have to be won over at any price? A result that has already been achieved.

When one mixes with the crowds overrunning the stores,

one can feel the ancestral, acerbic soul of the old Berber ancestors being reborn. At the same time, a rancor that will never disappear is taking root deep within my heart. Yes, this is the only result.

### January 8

My colleague B., who has returned from his hometown, has brought me information about what is going on there. He is in the habit of exaggerating. However, in spite of his exaggerations, we cannot dispute the truth about the atrocious crimes and systematic rapes that have taken place in the Ouadhias. Soldiers were free to defile, kill, and burn. The maquis, for their part, found it necessary to overwhelm and terrorize the population in order to prevent them from rallying around the French. It is as if the fellagha and the French soldiers were competing to see who could be more cruel. The French aim to dominate ruins, while the fellagha intend to free the ruins from this domination. Whatever the outcome of this fight may be, it will not be easy to rebuild.

Bedd. told me that after the death of Lieutenant Jacote, they raided the douar. The first village was literally emptied of its inhabitants. In the other villages, they picked up all the men. The men were locked up together for fifteen days. About eighty of them were shot, a few at a time, every evening. The tombs had been prepared ahead of time. On top of this, after fifteen days it was noticed more than one hundred other men had disappeared. The guess is that they were locked inside gourbis filled with straw and burned.[1] Not one gourbi or straw stack is left in the fields. The women remained in their homes in the villages. They were ordered to leave their front doors open and to stay alone, one in each room. The douar was thus transformed into a populous BMC, and they let loose companies of young Alpine chasseurs or other legionnaires. One hundred and fifty young girls were able to find refuge at the convent of the Soeurs Blanches or among the Pères Blancs[2] . . . No trace can be found of any of the others.

These are typical practices during wartime. They are familiar to the Germans and the Russians, for instance, when they invade enemy countries. One would like to be able to ask Guy Mollet if the French, who committed such acts among the Kabyles, continue to consider them patriots or if, after suffering such affronts, the Kabyles will agree to remain French subjects or French citizens. One would like to be able to remind Guy Mollet that the Kabyles, still ignorant and barbaric enough that they can be accused of fanaticism, have kept the memory of ancient customs, and that, in these circumstances, they remember the following: their ancestors used to fight frequently. When one of them could not defend his honor—when he knew he would lose or was about to lose—he would sacrifice his wife and his daughters to prevent them from being raped, and then he would die at a great cost to his enemies. What will the Ouadhias do? They will not cut the throats of their dishonored daughters. Certainly not . . . What will they do? They will wait. However, all those who have knowledge of this same situation share their shame and their anger. They feel the same way because they are neither Germans, nor Russians, nor French. Because these primitives, these barbarians, these fanatics have not evolved enough to accept the idea that anyone can rape their women with impunity. They consider this the worst of crimes because, since the beginning, as Kabyles, their mores, their laws, their reason for being—everything is based on this taboo, this sacrosanct respect that mandates the protection of women. It is quite doubtful that such a brutal intrusion against outdated mores, which aims to put a backward people in tune with the modern world, is going to help bring about the sense of human brotherhood that Mr. Guy Mollet dreams of and that Mr. Lacoste is trying to achieve. One could add that if either of these socialists were a native of the Ouadhias, they would see the Algerian problem from a different angle. From its true angle, perhaps.

### January 10

Yesterday, there was a thirty-five-minute broadcast of Guy Mollet's declaration of intent. We had been expecting this declaration for the last few days, and then they postponed it until the day before the opening of the UN debate. It was finally delivered yesterday, and the whole world was able to hear it at the same time as ourselves. As I was listening, I had reactions, specific ones. I wanted to comment, refute here, and agree there. But why bother? The French prime minister promises the Muslims of Algeria what they have always hoped for in vain. Then he promises the French in Algeria what they have always had and now fear losing. Yet, as the prime minister can offer us only what he would take from them, his declaration of intent becomes, as I see it, nothing more than the blinding light from a gigantic soap bubble.

## 1957

### January 11

Visit with the subprefect to receive information about schooling (report to the regional education authority). During our conversation, I had the opportunity to ask him for more details about what happened in the Ouadhias. He did not want to give me any, just as I did not want to tell him how we felt about the declaration of intent. He did, however, describe the death of Lieutenant Jacote and admitted that the soldiers had shot all the suspects who were on their lists. How many? He does not know. I told him that numbers were coming up in our conversations, that we always tend to remember the highest numbers, and that, in every instance, it was better, if possible, to bring things back to their just proportions. In the end, he did not want to give me any numbers.

One thing I had the courage to tell him is that the circumstances of this death, as horrible as they were, did not excuse what followed. He explained to me that they considered the douar collectively responsible for what had happened because, in fact, the entire douar knew about it. The ambush had been openly prepared. Every person had been an accomplice in Jacote's death, which is even more cowardly since this man had never hurt anyone. He had managed to win people's esteem and confidence, he always traveled without a weapon or escort, and, on that particular day, he was alone with his wife. He had been married for a month: "Do I have to tell you that the very people who invited them to have coffee knew what was coming, and that the purpose of the invitation was to give the killers more time to get ready . . ."

When the news arrived that Lieutenant Jacote had been killed and his wife wounded, obviously everybody could understand the anger, the rage that overtook the military camp. The retaliation was brutal, blind, and savage. All of that can be understood. What cannot be understood is why it is called pacification. Maybe the maquis attack the peaceful officers of the SAS in order to remove any ambiguity. Is the government not deliberately sacrificing these young officers by having them play such a thankless part? As for the unknown fellagha in the villages who are just as peace loving, their error is to remain there and not figure out where else they could go. Their loyalty to their land and the ancestral gourbi is an involuntary and useless act of heroism that will be dismissed by other men, the same as their fear and death.

## 1957

### January 12

Today there is a meeting of Muslim fathers at the office of the justice of the peace. We have been ordered—for fear of threats that are specifically detailed and distressing—to send our children to school as of Monday (day after tomorrow). I was a bit proud of my part as Maître Jacques.[3] Monday I will have to report the absence of the children, my own first. I do not see, though, how the schoolchildren who live inside the walls of Fort-National can avoid being taken to school. In any case, I feel the student strike is a tragic stupidity. So much the better for them if we are forced to send them to school.

I was able to read the entire special issue of *El Moudjahid*.[4] I was sorry to find that it uses the pompously idiotic style of a certain regional weekly. In these thirty pages there is a lot of faith and selflessness, a lot of demagogy, pretentiousness, and some naïveté and concern as well. If this is the best the FLN has to offer, I am certain that they are pulling strings for some fat bourgeois, a few politicians cowering mysteriously in their "courageous" silence, while waiting to scramble for the spoils. Poor mountain people, poor students, poor young men, your enemies of tomorrow will be worse than those of yesterday.

### January 14

The mother superior of the mission of the Soeurs Blanches came to see me. She has brought news from my hometown. Things are difficult but not any worse than I had imagined. She visited the Ouadhias as well. B. told the truth about the dead, the rapes, etc.

### January 16

I have been sick since yesterday. A bad flu, and yet this entire time that I have spent in bed—with fever, headaches, pain on my side, sneezing, and painful cough—this whole time I have never stopped thinking: it is true, it is true, it is true . . .

Sophisticated people who claim to be giving the world moral lessons shoot dozens of innocents to death without blinking. Delicate and scrupulous people coldly assassinate their own kind.

Civilized men who enjoy every kind of happiness and opportunity, all of life's advantages, massacre and rape an indigent people who for centuries has been burdened by the same inexplicable curse.

Men who have everything come to destroy men who have nothing.

169

## 1957

Can words express the horror that grips us?

Will such crimes remain unpunished forever? If the Algerians are the cursed people of the century, all that remains for them is to die as one and the sooner the better. But we must die standing up and must curse the executioner.

I learned this morning of the death of Hamoudi T. He died fighting, and these days one cannot wish for a better death. He escaped from the police station last August after having knocked out, it seems, S. He had just been arrested inside his store. Since then he has been able to join the maquis to fight and die in combat. Honor to him! The police would not have waited long to kill him if he had remained quietly in their midst. I heard at the same time that fighting, skirmishes, and ambushes have cost a lot of blood both to members of the maquis and to French soldiers. Dead and more dead. And when it is all over, the only thing left to do will be to fraternize again, after having returned to the womb of the bittersweet motherland. There are those who are hoping for precisely this.

The UN conference on the Algerian question will open in a week.[5] Here in Algeria, an insurrectionary strike—one that the French are trying to quell—will start simultaneously. We understand the sacred character of this strike. The Algerians must proclaim their suffering and anger to a world that hesitates to believe them. Those sickly sweet and hypocritical voices that will protest their innocence and will overwhelm us with imaginary kindness—fanatical and ungrateful that we are—must be drowned out by our shouts, the shouts of those who are skinned alive, the shouts of those who are afraid, and the groans of those who are dying. The best possible scenario would be if all of our dead crossed the Atlantic so their sinister laughter might be heard at the tribune of the UN, behind the Parisian sirens who already flatter themselves with having seduced Uncle Sam.

In a week, in a month, there will more information on this subject. Is it not time to conclude? This is where these notes about troubled times will stop. Troubled, somber, tragic, every adjective that comes to mind. Troubled for me, however, because I still cannot see clearly. For the past two years, I have been observing, writing down objectively, ready to like or hate, to explain and to give everything, ready to understand and determined to explain. Now I understand. There is no need to go any further. I can die today, be killed by a firing squad tomorrow: I know that I belong to a proud, great people who will remain so, I know that we have shaken off a century of sleep, that from now on nothing will plunge us back in this sleep again, that we are ready to go forward, to grasp in our turn the flame that people fight over. And I know that we will keep it for a long time. It would not amaze me that this romantic finale appears somewhat childish and surprising coming from a pacifist like me who despises all displays of patriotism. I will simply say that this is not a prophecy but a wish. Further, I wish my people—my country—all the happiness of which it was deprived and all the glory it is capable of achieving; when I have witnessed its blossoming, its joy and pride, I will be able to despise my patriotism just as I despise other examples of patriotisms. Just as Mr. Mollet, a disciple of Marx, detests his own, in the name of which he massacres Algerians in a brotherly manner.

**January 22**

I hear of the deaths of Hached Moh. Ouamer, back home, and Rezki, here—one after the other.

The first was abducted at night from the bed he was sleeping in with his wife. The maquis entered his bedroom and gave him time to get dressed. Gullmi told me all of this.

—Hurry up, they were saying to him, you can argue with our leader. He is waiting for you up there.

—Okay, okay, I will get dressed carefully.

—Why dress carefully? Come on, hurry up!

—No, you see, I do not like cold weather and I am sick. It is freezing outside. Give me my thick hat, my wife.

He was trying to make things last a few seconds more. But one of the maquis, irritated by his chattering, grabbed him roughly and put a rope around his body. From that moment on, his wife said later, he did not open his mouth. He remained prostrated, incapable of understanding what was really happening to him. Then they took him away while advising his wife and his sister—who had gotten up to see her brother—to keep quiet. This took place two days ago, on Sunday night. Yesterday, around 7:00, the army came to sweep the village. The soldiers came into Hached's house. A lieutenant who knows him well asked after him and was surprised not to find him in the village. The women were trembling like leaves, trying hard not to say a word, feeling like saying something, fearing to do so, and, finally, assuring the lieutenant that Hached had gone to Algiers, the day before, for personal business. They resisted the temptation to complain, thus avoiding troubles for the village and the rope for themselves.

It is only this morning that I heard about the death of my old colleague, Rezki, from Taourirt-Moussa. The maquis grabbed him as he was returning from a distant field with his wife and children where they had picked olives. Most likely he was shot, and then his body was left in the countryside. This morning, the people from Taourirt-Moussa will go look for his body so he can be buried discreetly.

### January 24

I just ran into Rezki's son, who is also my student. I put my hand on his head, and he started to cry. "You are a man," I said to him, "and so is your brother. Do not cry." Then I left in a hurry. Djebbar, the assistant I have often mentioned in my notes, who is a cousin of this colleague, caught up with me to tell me that the maquis rarely make a mistake and that it is better not to get mixed up in matters that are none of our business. So this is what we have come to. The common idea is that the killers are always right to kill, and the dead are wrong to be dead. I fear the intransigent patriotism of each person is confused with collective cowardliness, and this destroys within us both the feeling of justice, which was not all that strong to start with, and our very sharp sense of curiosity. One becomes blind, deaf, and mute so that the "good cause" can triumph and the carcass can be saved.

### Same day

Young Rezki came to see me in my office. He told me that his father had been killed by former students whom he recognized. They were people from the village who were masked, but he recognized them anyway. One of them even lowered the scarf that hid his face: he was pale because he had just missed his old teacher. Rezki took off for the fields, and the others followed him. Soon the son and the mother lost sight of both the runaway and his pursuers. They went up to the village shouting and alerted the army. The body was found forty-eight hours later in a stream: he had a bullet in his forehead and several in his back.

I let the young man talk. They now reproach his father with spending too much time with the military. I understand that he is also suspected of having been an informant. Maybe the maquis have proof. The kid claims that there are also other things, village gossip about old grudges and jealousies. Do the maquis consider a man's life so cheap they can condemn him just like that? Can any member of the maquis, even a bandit, take it upon himself to kill someone merely because he does not like that person? All this is sad. When young Rezki had finished speaking, he got up and left without saying good-bye; and I watched him leave without a word. He looked like a robot.

I am one of these complicated people who learned a lot of useless things in school. These useless things make me, as well as others like me, physically ill, and all of us together become strangers in our own land. All of us together? There may be only a handful of us. For the others, nothing is complicated. The problem to be solved only has two results: one must live or die. To live by killing in order to conquer. To die after having killed to allow others to conquer, and if we all happen to die without having conquered, our collective death shall still be a victory. Those who shoot their brothers or cut their throats or hang them actually have this feeling of having conquered, and this comforts them. It has become fashionable not to pity "the traitors" and to condemn their souls to the devil when one hears of their death, to heap their soul with retroactive hatred that, according to some people, makes you look good but may not prevent ending your own life in the same ignominious manner. Now, there is among us much capacity for fear, that very same capacity that used to apply to pity.

**January 26**

I have just found out about the death of my friend Madène. He was arrested at home last Saturday and taken to Béni-Douala, where, after questioning, he is rumored to have been executed in an atrocious manner: he is said to have stepped on a mine. Nekili told me that his body had been brought back in a sack, so riddled with bullets that his arms and head had been severed.

**January 27**

It is horrible. I have lost my taste for living since yesterday. Today, there were rumors that the strike would start tomorrow. People rushed around like ants to make their last, hasty purchases. Starting at 2:00, the town began to empty. Starting tomorrow, we are going to have to lock ourselves in. The army is certain to react. What is going to happen?

**January 31**

The primary education inspector wants a report on the strike, and I am responding to him today. Here is my report:

To answer your memorandum #57/G regarding the school situation at our own institution since last Monday, I am honored to confirm that service was provided normally on Monday evening, all day Tuesday and on Wednesday evening.

Monday morning, the Muslim teachers just like the students did not report to school, and I had to send home four European students who were waiting at the gate.

Monday afternoon, the police escorted the teachers in; they were requisitioned and went to their classrooms: there were a dozen European students.

Tuesday, all the European students were present (twenty-two) as well as seven students of Muslim origin.

Wednesday morning, the same number of teachers was present, but those teachers who had been escorted to the school limited themselves to keeping an eye on the students.

Wednesday evening, each teacher returned to his classroom and worked normally.

An administrative report relating the facts and nothing else. These facts, however, have been written with sorrow in our hearts, and we are living a horrible week that seems not to end. Monday morning, the town was dead and sad. But soon the French showed themselves outside, encouraged by the police and the soldiers who traversed the streets with the kind of resolute walk reserved for the day when there is going to be some rough stuff. Rough stuff? All the doors, all the store blinds were pushed in. As far as the Kabyles are concerned, there is no doubt that the soldiers and the policemen took part in the plunder. One of my colleagues reported to me that some of my younger students went inside various places to steal. A few minutes later in class, no wonder I felt like I was wasting my time trying to explain the classical niceties of *Andromaque* to them.[6] All this could make me doubt the value of my teaching. But is this all that I have with which to reproach myself?

In the evening there was a large procession of compatriots who were being brought back from the villages, namely the owners of the stores who will remain here like prisoners behind their counters.

Tuesday, then, there were a few Kabyles in the streets, in particular, a few of those who had been brought back the day before and were forced to go out, either to answer a summons or to do some necessary shopping. Then, more Kabyles were brought back, and the town was repopulated. Colleagues would arrive morning and night escorted by policemen dressed in black and armed with submachine guns, who appeared to be in a hurry, but who still behaved courteously. All this took place under the gleeful and mocking eyes of our younger and older students. These colleagues would take their meager number of students inside ice-cold classrooms. They had the sad faces of people whose dignity had been offended, and they worked half-heartedly, even forgetting to maintain such discipline that the small number of students could not, in any case, disturb too much. But, of course, these colleagues are unhappy! It is because, from the very first day, we were made to sign a requisition order; it is because this strike, which everyone considered sacred and indisputable, was one we were in the process of breaking; it is because the FLN is notorious for not being amused when its orders are not respected; finally, it is because a half-dozen primary school teachers have already been executed by the so-called FLN for various reasons, and nobody wants to feel sorry for these unfortunate colleagues because they are traitors. Okay. We will refuse to answer the requisition order, and we will ask that those sanctions provided by law be applied to us with leniency. As far as I am concerned, I have a stoic attitude about all this because, in principle and in fact, I do not have to teach.

Wednesday morning, the teachers agree to leave their home only after the usual warnings. At school, they refused to work, but they helped me supervise the students. The teachers had showed up properly and warmly dressed, ready to go to jail. We had all stayed up all night. I know that my wife pretended to sleep. She woke me up rather early, as if I were going to be visited by an education inspector, and started her chores before the children woke up. They wanted to be part of the excitement as well. At 8:00, I was dressed, and I left a house swarming with worry and curiosity. To pass the time and calm their nerves, the kids started to squabble openly and cry to their hearts' content because my wife, insensitive from the beginning, was looking at them without seeing them and listening without hearing. They noticed what was going on right away, those crafty kids.

Around 11:30, a few moments before the end of class, Mr. D., who replaces the subprefect, showed up at the school accompanied by the captain. He wanted to ask for explanations and particularly to explain a few things to us. First we had a little chat; then my colleagues had to be assembled to hear him speak.

—Gentlemen, he started, this is the first time I have come inside your school, and I am sorry this had to be under such sad circumstances. You have a very nice school here. In the small town where I was born, what am I saying, in my village, yes, an insignificant little village, we do not have such a nice school. Far from it. (*Your village is far from being as important as the subprefecture currently under your authority, I thought to myself*). And yet, we have provided France with great men, government ministers, and congressmen. No, we do not have a school like this. So, gentlemen, I would like to ask you a question: why do you refuse to work? You are civil servants, you have been on strike. We have provided you with an escort. For one day, then two days, you refuse to follow the police. Then you follow them, but you do not work. You have received requisition orders, and you refuse to answer them. You are disobeying the law. You are singling yourselves out, and in a lamentable way, because you are the only ones, along with the postal workers, who are refusing to return to work. Everywhere else everybody has gone back to work.

—Sir, we are scared.

—This is an argument that I will not accept. Do you know what the cost of disobeying the law is? Talk to a Kabyle attorney since you no longer trust us. You are French civil servants, and you are paid French currency, but you no longer respect France. You no longer fear France, but you are struck dumb with admiration for the vulgar assassin who hides and shoots from behind. You respect these people despite the fact that they are cowards. Yes, the rebels are cowards, and they will not chase France away. France will remain here because this is France. You will never have your independence because you do not deserve it. Your rebels are abject people, they sweat duplicity and lies, they are slimy and repugnant, and we despise them. We like people like Mr. F. and admire their merit, but the rebels, not at all, gentlemen! We are a civilized people, a refined and idealistic people, an enlightened and just people, and we are not going to be held up to ridicule by barbarians. There is somebody behind Mr. Fer. who pressures him, and we know who it is. I am asking you a question; speak, I am listening. This is between us; nothing of what is said here will be repeated. There is a leader, an agitator, among you. If he is a real man, why does he not speak, why does he not open his mouth to answer . . . Speak, you are men . . . No, you are cowards; you, too, are sweating with fear.

What kind of educators do I have in front of me? Cowards who are not ashamed to be led to their teaching jobs by policemen with submachine guns. What will your teaching be worth from now on? No, that is too shameful! It is grotesque. The Algerian elite! Oh, you can be proud of your elite! Algeria is counting on you to become a country? I feel sorry for her. Do not think for a moment that we are going to allow it and that you will continue to graze on the money of France without working. Gentlemen, I find your reasoning stupid; you are thinking: we are going to twiddle our thumbs, and at the end of the month, the money will fall in our pockets just like that. Yes, you are sheep, and all you know to do is graze. But now it is over. Speak. It is ten minutes until noon. You have ten minutes left to reach a decision . . .

Okay. So you do not want to answer me?

—We cannot, some voices whisper.

—Let me tell you that there are six thousand civil servants who are looking for appointments. We do not need you. We are going to fire you, and you can go to your Fort-National FLN organization, whose leaders you know, and where you are members, I know it. Yes, you all belong to it. There was a meal, on Saturday, at the notary cadi's place.[7] But the notary cadi is lower than zero, a slug, a mollusk, a coward. Yesterday he came to the subprefecture. He was there for two hours. He figured it out. It is over for the notary cadi. As for you, leave, join the maquis if you are men. Because there, at least, there are men. Leave, and we will go looking for you in the djebel [mountain], and we will find you because we are stronger and more courageous. Goodness is sometimes confused with stupidity. We will no longer be stupid. There was once a valuable man here named Laburthe. Because of you, he was bowled over. Now he is in deep shit because he believed in you. He thought you were interesting. Here is a man who could have ended like Igame. He was bowled over, I tell you. Look at Mendès-France.[8] He is loathed by the people of France because everybody has figured out that he is a defeatist. The people of France want to keep Algeria. Keep Algeria, even without the Kabyles. Do you think that we have waged a war? No, we have not, but we will. Two cannons aimed at each village. That is all. And the village ceases to exist. I am not here to sacrifice my promotion. I am here for France. I am here for the France that you want to hold up to ridicule. It is my turn to sit on the legality that you are mocking. You will go back to work, and you will work correctly. Otherwise, you will be immediately dismissed and arrested. For those among you who are hardheaded, I will accept no further responsibility. We have special powers. We are going to use them, of that you can be sure. Good day.

The subprefect left. He was scandalized by our faces, "slimy and sweating with fear and cowardliness," after having conspicuously shaken the hand of the director, who did not have the courage not to extend his own.

He did not have the courage because, before seeing all the teachers assembled in a classroom, the subprefect said something like this to the director:

—Mr. Director, I am here to bring the compliments of Mr. Vignon, the prefect. Your school is the bastion of Kabyle resistance. The teachers in Fort-National are the only ones, along with the postal workers, who refuse to work.[9] Do you know that you are held responsible for everything that goes on in your school? Maybe it is unfair, but you are the person we know. You are a family man, and I understand that you have seven children. Think about your children, and go get your colleagues . . .

After the departure of the subprefect, the captain came back to join us in the classroom. Some of my colleagues were able to exchange a few disillusioned words with him. He wanted "to soften the impact of the blows a little," but he was wasting his time. The blows had penetrated deep inside our flesh, which will remain bruised forever.

At 1:30, everybody was in the school yard, ready to go back to work without further problems. We could not find anything to say to each other; we were all trying to express some pity, some fondness, but each of us felt that we needed for ourselves the futile comfort we were trying to provide to one another.

Today, we have a day off to reflect on what happened yesterday. But at 3:00, the captain came unexpectedly into my office and winked at me maliciously, as if he were looking for an accomplice. There was also some insolence in his wink, along with triumph, victory, and cruelty . . .

**February 10**

It has been six days since I last wrote in this notebook, and getting started again this Sunday is like torture. I know, however, that I will not be bothered. How to get started? What do I start with? There is so much to say that everything is muddled up in my mind, and it is possible that what is essential will refuse to come out and will continue to stifle me. Yesterday, the new prefect met with "the administrative personnel." We belong to his "personnel" now. You could not make a face or refuse to pay him your respect. We already are submissive, pacified, and strengthened. Some colleagues have assured me that they have heard on the radio that Fort-National is a normal town where school attendance has remained 100 percent. It is true that we have seventy-five students out of five hundred. All those from the center have been coming to school regularly since the strikes. I have already had two meetings with the subprefect. He talked to me about the devil and God, the good fire that would continue to burn (God knows what), and the bad fire that will put itself out. He told me that the mistakes made by the teachers are a significant factor in the context of all that is happening, because it is the young troublemakers, our former students, who are throwing grenades at people's faces. He told me that once this is all over—soon—there will be a need for people like me to rebuild what has been destroyed, that is, the good old institutions that have obtained such "marvelous" results. Then the subprefect left to go back to his subprefecture.

For the past week, the captain must have been thinking that I am some kind of local warrant officer in charge of transmitting peremptory orders. When I tell him that my colleagues can discuss or refuse, he answers that, in that case, he will break their backs or smash their faces in.

For the past week, mail has been coming in erratically. Even though my letters are insolently opened, they are, however, hastily resealed.

For the past week, people are towing the line, looking like beaten dogs. They laugh without any concern in front of their devastated stores; they come to work on time and welcome people with an affable smile. The teachers are just as punctual as the others, putting all their hearts into improving their teaching methods, discussing pedagogical ideas, and calling on each other with a distrustful air that instills deference.

For the past week, we have been made to understand that we are living inside a walled area and that we are, so to speak, prisoners.

As I have said, the captain burst into my office around 3:00 P.M. on January 31:

—You have got to get your colleagues together right now. They *must* sign a document for me. Here is the one signed by the postal workers: "I promise upon my honor to return to work as of the 31st." Name, date, and signature. I gave the postal workers ten minutes. I am giving you an hour. I want these papers before 4:00 P.M. I am taking them to the subprefect, and there will be no sanctions. I will be able to talk in your favor.

—What if they refuse?

—If they refuse, I will smash their faces in. Listen, it is for their own good. If they refuse, they will immediately be arrested. Don't you see, it is serious. They *have* to agree. Give me this weapon for protecting you; otherwise, too bad for you. Quick, call them together. I will be waiting for you.

I gathered my colleagues, and we wrote our declarations "upon our honor," while admitting with some bitterness that the word *honor* in our mouths and at the tips of our pens seemed ridiculous from that point on.

The captain was waiting for me in his office, at city hall, and I got there after the assessor, who had come with a lowered head to perform, as we had, his act of submission with whatever honor he had left.

While talking to the captain, I learned that they had set their sights on one of our colleagues from the trade union in particular and on the notary cadi who had had the unfortunate idea to invite us to lunch one day. That day, according to the reports of the informers, had become the one directly preceding the strike, and the friendly meal had become a highly subversive meeting during which the security of the state had been placed in peril. Some of us, quite simply, might be executed.

While I was attempting to convince the captain of our innocence, or at least of the uselessness of a banquet as a setting to foment a plot, a young civilian came in, shook our hands, and casually began using the informal form of address with the captain.

—Hello, Mr. F. he said to me.

I thought that he was an officer on leave or an agent from the Sûreté.[10]

The young man immediately jumped into the conversation, and before long he was the only one speaking because I was so surprised by what he said. As for the captain, he did not say a word but smiled maliciously and, it seemed to me, went on being domineering. The thought that this man had come in on purpose occurred to me immediately. Now, however, I am not so sure.

He was a young man who said what he thought and was

almost likable, free in his demeanor and even freer in what he said. He had the darker face of the people from the south of France, but he did not speak like them. He looked as though his face had been cut with large strokes of a pair of scissors by a clumsy craftsman who had let the different contours of his face stick out—his nose, his cheekbones, and his chin. He had a large mouth and sharp black eyes that constantly came to the aid of the words he used and made his thoughts more precise. He had a mouth and eyes that disallow any misunderstanding.

—Isn't the cadi the 'éminence grise' of the FLN? Like Mr. F.

—He is no threat, the captain underlined. A coward, that is all. We have destroyed him, psychologically speaking.

—The cadi is bitter, I said. He could not withstand certain types of police harassment. You should have intervened, captain.

At that point, the young man flew into a rage.

—I cannot follow your reasoning anymore, Mr. F. The military receives orders; they carry them out. This means that a second-class soldier can kick you in the ass. The fact that you draw a stipend from the Editions du Seuil changes nothing about that.[11] I find the people who rebel against our discipline and punctually follow that of the FLN amusing. You have to make a decision. That is it, we no longer allow passivity. You have to resist the rebels, whether you like it or not. When I was sent here, you see, I was glad. I liked the Kabyles. Well, I have been living among them for seven months now. I do not know any more cowardly people on the face of the earth. Under these conditions, you know what I do? I kick people in the ass. That you can be sure of, and I do not hold back. Yes, I wanted to become friendly with these people, to get to know them better. When that is not possible, however, there is still another way to get acquainted with them. It is through informers that we achieve this goal. That way, we get to know all of you. And let me assure your that we will stay in Kabylia, if necessary, even without Kabyles. You will have to admit, that is not hard to do.

—Of course, it is not difficult, but it is not reasonable either.

—Listen fellow, it is no longer a question of reasoning or judging or applying the law. All it is about is destroying—destroying all that is bad, all that is in the way.

"You built a house with your savings—French money, by the way—well, we will destroy your new house. Who is preventing you from rebuilding it if you wish? By the way, you have a nice school and a nice apartment. One bomb! You and yours are blown up. Instead of your school, there will be a nicer one. Besides, there is no reason to blow it up: someone shoots and you fall. Accidental death. A simple little report. Your friends will always be able to miss you."

—Of course, there comes a time when a man no longer argues.

—Indeed, yes! First he reestablishes peace . . .

While he was sending all these threats my way, his eyes would light up and dance in his head. He looked like he was hallucinating, and my calm and passive demeanor seemed to drive him out of his mind. Perhaps he took my amused smile as irony, and he was right to do that. I refused to take him seriously. I exchanged a few words with the captain regarding the school situation; then I got up to leave the room. At that point, the young man was silent. He seemed exhausted, like an attorney who has just finished an impassioned plea for the defense. I read some melancholy in the look that he lifted toward me when I extended my hand to him. All is not lost, I thought, as I was leaving; the monster still has some humanity in him.

When I asked about the name of this man, I was dumbstruck to learn that I had just dealt with Mr. Achard, the administrator of the Ouadhias, the one who had ordered dozens of executions, rapes, and tortures in that unfortunate douar. At that moment, I understood that his threats were probably not made in vain.

As of February 1st, we have all gone back to work. They refused to give us an escort. Our children were automatically sent back to school. Every morning, the police come by to pick up the list of those absent, and severe warnings are sent to the parents. The people of the center no longer resist. The children have to learn; the stores have to be opened in rotation; the grey card must be returned and the car towed away, the Moorish cafés must be closed.[12] Orders must be received and executed. That is how it is.

The other day, the captain calls me in to inform me that in accordance with his promise, no severe sanction will be taken against us. However, one of my colleagues is in quite a bit of trouble. It is no longer the trade unionist; it is someone else. Maybe it is both him and me (I am imagining this). The captain let me know that the information concerning this colleague comes from three different sources and all were in agreement: he was alleged to be someone high up in the FLN. The captain told me that he had a team of informers in his pocket, that in the reports he received he knew how to make allowance for whims, lies, and personal hatred in particular, and that there was practically no chance of a mistake, for he struck only when he was totally certain.

I said nothing because I did not want to alarm my colleagues. But I advised them to go out as little as possible, not to speak with anybody, and to wait with a cool head for this horrible nightmare to end. In any case, the town—which the people of the countryside bring life to each morning when they are allowed to enter for their small purchases—is horribly empty in the afternoon. A dead city for inert bodies. A dead town among the desolate scenery of a dry, severe, and frigid end of winter.

**February 17**

Yesterday, I went back to Algiers, where I spent the day with Roblès. On the way there, I traveled in the van of my neighbor, H. We stopped in Hussein Dey to see the people from Taourirt. There were two "refugees" who had fled from there for fear of being arrested. They had very low morale and were constantly obsessed with death; they came to me with tears in their eyes. I saw Dj.'s son with them. He was crying also because his father was assassinated a day earlier. He was there because, in his turn, he was going to be assassinated by the maquis. In Hussein Dey, they are reunited, victims of either the maquis or the French. They have become closer because of their common anguish. They are dazed by the same terror, crying the same powerless, useless, and almost ridiculous tears that carry no more weight or meaning than the tears caused by a raw onion. Old Dj. has already lost two of his sons at the hands of the soldiers. They were "suspects." Okay. Everybody misses them and speaks well of them. But their memory was not enough to save their father, who was clearly "on the administration side," assistant to the mayor and more. Sure, they were waiting for him around 5:00 Tuesday night as he was returning to the village. The bus was stopped, two passengers were forced out—Old Dj. and someone else. They were shot on the spot. That is it . . .

Algiers looked sad when I saw it again, just as I had imagined. Guarded, motorized, militarized Algiers, as it used to be described; but I was lucky not to have seen anything else. In any case, I did not go out unless I needed to.

I gave Roblès a notebook dealing with the first two weeks of this month and particularly with our strike, and with Mr. D.,

Mr. T., Mr. A.—an amusing two-week spell one would never want to live through again. We talked until midnight, and yesterday I came back by bus. Yes, I arrived safe and sound in Fort-National after a painful trip that lasted five hours. God is great, nothing happened.

The bus went on its way this morning. Less than a mile from Fort-National, the maquis stopped it. They shot I. The news reached me about an hour after it happened.

Yesterday in Algiers I found out that Dahlab was abducted a month ago back home, at the same time as Hached. While the latter was released, poor Dahlab has not been seen since.

**February 18**

My wife was sick all night long. This is because of I. and his children, whom she saw as they passed by going to school. He left a bunch of them behind, the poor fellow. He had just gotten out of prison a few months ago, after having served a long sentence. Everybody thought he was connected to the maquis. He himself did nothing to stop the rumors, acting rather carelessly and frequently traveling to Tizi-Ouzou, each time letting people know that he was going there to make contact. Few were surprised to hear of his death. For many, however, all these murders are losing the original impact. One wonders if all those who have fallen were really traitors. Doubt and apathy invade people's conscience a little bit at a time, and despair gives way to anger. If this continues, everyone will accuse themselves of treason, and all the united traitors will rebel against the killers, who, in turn, will die in a cruel manner. Death will seem less and less fearsome, and survivors will consider it as nothing more than a natural event waiting fatefully for you at a street corner, an accident that, from this point on, cannot be outsmarted. Then all those who have the most to lose by cooperating with the French will work even harder, and they will agree to play the part they had refused to play earlier: they will again become faithful servants and will wait quietly at home for street "accidents" to stop.

Roblès talked about all these attacks in front of me: for him, they are despicable and unacceptable. He feels that the perpetrators are not entitled to any pity.[13] He is just back from Paris, where he has spent a lot of time with Camus. Camus refuses to admit that Algeria could become independent and that he would be forced to show a foreign passport each time he returned—he, who is Algerian and nothing else. He believes the FLN is fascist and that placing the future of his country in the hands of this organization is absolutely unthinkable.[14] I understand quite well what each man is saying, but I would like them to understand me as well. I would like them to understand those of us who are so close to them and so different at the same time. I would like them to put themselves in our place. Those who told me what they really thought last week, who told me that I was not French. Those who are in charge of French sovereignty in this country have treated me as an enemy since the beginning of these events. Yet, while treating me as an enemy, they would like me to act as a good French patriot; not even that: they would like me to serve them just as I am, for no other reason than gratitude for the fact that France has made a teacher, a school administrator, and a writer out of me; for the fact that France pays me a large salary that enables me to raise a large family. In simple terms, I am asked to repay a debt as if everything I do does not deserve a salary, as if this school had been built for my pleasure and filled with students to entertain me, as if my "teaching" were a generous gift that costs me only the pain of extending my hand to take it, as if this writer's talent with which I am a little infatuated were another gift, involuntary this time, but no less generous, one quite obviously destined to defend the cause of France at the expense of my own people, who may be wrong but who die and suffer under the scorn and indifference of civilized countries. Quite simply, I am asked to die as a traitor in return for which I will have paid my debt.

I said all of this to Roblès, who found nothing to answer in return, who was as sad as I was, and who admits what the others refuse to admit. I would like to tell Camus that he is as Algerian as I am, and that all Algerians are proud of him. I would add, though, that it was not so long ago that an Algerian Muslim had to show a passport to go to France. It is true that the Algerian Muslim has never considered himself to be a Frenchman. He has no such illusions.

**February 20**

B., who has returned from his home, has learned that in one village, there are forty-nine dead. Struck with panic, the inhabitants had fled from their homes and were running in all directions. The soldiers killed them like rabbits. He admitted that it was a local "terrorist" who had started the shooting— one criminal act that had provoked a brutal reaction.

At Béni-Yenni, Aït-Frah, Tamazirt, and my own village, there are sweeps because of denunciations. The army is using members of the maquis who have surrendered. And these men who are no doubt terrified of their punishment are revealing hiding places that they have used, pointing out homes where they were welcome, and denouncing compatriots who gave them shelter. The soldiers remove the weapons from the hiding places, burn the homes that were used for asylum, arrest the Kabyles who had been compromised, and execute the more zealous ones. I suppose this is a correct way of applying the laws of war, but we must not expect anything from people who have been treated so harshly. The victims of so much cruelty, the witnesses of so much suffering can forget tragic times, forget the soldiers, and forget the French, just as a person who has been hung forgets the rope—that is, by no longer seeing it.

Thousands of other victims, those who have more or less fallen as traitors will not be forgotten either. For the moment, each of these victims is leaving relatives in a state of repressed sorrow that they are ashamed to show and afraid to express. The day will come when people are no longer afraid. Then, every-thing will have to be accounted for, accusations will be levied, and perhaps it will be right to do so. Also, whenever possible, people will avenge themselves and hold their heads high . . . God knows what will happen, God knows when the Kabyle will be able to return to his peaceful existence and his precarious happi-ness, God knows when he will be able to evaluate the rebellion in a beneficial way. For the time being, the villages are dead. The fields are empty, and in the spring that is being reborn, it is misfortune that blooms before the plants, and, under a pure sky where a dazzling sun shines, our children, our women, and our old folks wait, with frozen hearts, for the return of truly beauti-ful days. Entire days without seeing a soldier again, entire weeks when nobody will come to rape, fire a submachine gun, or burn. They wait petrified by terror because they fear that, for them, these days and these weeks are coming too late, because months of hope and impatience ended with a few speeches, far from here, at the end of the world where it is hard to hear their voices, far from here, where illustrious men, aided by idle chatter, can remove suffering and distribute happiness. It so happens, how-ever, that these long discussions did not remove suffering and did not bring us happiness. All they said to us was "Wait," "You have to wait."

And when you tell a dead man to wait, he responds: "I

have an eternity to do that." But the person who is still alive? For him, it is very simple. He only has to die, him too.

**February 24**

In Aït-Frah, five people were shot. At random. Only one tried to escape and then to defend himself before being killed. It appears that the guy did that to protect others who were trying to escape.

Seven people were killed in Tamazirt. A young man who had been arrested and held in the camp was shot while he was running after a ball that someone had kicked and that he had been ordered to retrieve. Attempted escape!

During the sweeps, the soldiers bring back chickens or rabbits, old smoky baskets, rustic canes, burnooses or carpets, Berber-style jewelry. Above all, they prefer bank notes, which they are quite skillful at finding.

**March 1**

This week, we were visited by the prefect Vignon. This happened on the square. He had come to officially install the new subprefect. We were "invited" to attend the ceremony, accompanied by our students so it would look more crowded. All the other civil servants were there, including the chaouch, the local carpenter, and maybe even the cook.[15] No other Kabyle, however. First the captain spoke, then the subprefect, and, finally, the prefect. All this has left me with an uneasy feeling. I had never seen the prefect, but he seemed sympathetic and intelligent. He certainly is a man of merit; and I was ashamed for him, for myself, for the men who kill, and for those who die. Yet, I returned to the school feeling a little more comfortable, somewhat freed from this shame because, I told myself, I sense that, in their hearts, these men did not approve; that they were distraught, desperate, and excessively sad, just like me; that all of us had been crushed by the same blind force; that what we or they were responsible for had considerably diminished or been reduced to zero; that the only ones you can hate are those who show off, justify themselves, or make threats. There may be circumstances when the victim and the torturer suddenly lose their individual attributes, come closer together, become one, and feel the same pain and the same helplessness in a brotherly manner.

The day before yesterday, the guard posts were attacked in the middle of the afternoon. At the same time, a convoy was stopped a few miles away, near Taourirt . . .

1957

### March 2

Nothing specific about this so-called skirmish. On the other hand, several people are dead in Azouza. The soldiers shot randomly at people. There are wounded in Aguemoun. This morning, a dead man who had been killed at 10:00 P.M. was lying on the road to Aït-Atelli. What business did he have being there? Was he taken out of prison for an execution? Such was the case for an Azouza fellow whom several people saw when the police brought him back to the village yesterday morning. People thought that the reason for the escort was to check on or to use information that he had given them ... At noon, a policeman went to city hall to report his death and to specify that he had died during a shootout.

At Béni-Yenni, they succeeded in forming a delegation. At night, the maquis showed up. They grabbed the delegates to hang them. One of them opened fire and alerted the military guard, which came to the rescue. Now he has found refuge there.

I have been told of several rebel surrenders in several locations. These rebels, once reassured about their fate, change their gear and become guides.

I had the pleasure of hearing of Mr. Achard's departure.[16]

### March 3

It has been eight days now since brave old Belkebir was abducted. What did he do? What did they do to all these others who were grabbed right after the strike? There are about ten of them around here. And yet the orders of the FLN are followed. And yet everybody agrees that the French are unhappy, disappointed, troubled; that the French fly into rages and then jail or kill. Everybody has decided to poke fun at the French, to make them into enemies so as not to die as traitors. Yet people continue just the same to die as traitors, to die shamefully so that the "pure ones" are allowed the illusion that they are really pure, so that cowards might learn to fight, so that the future heroes of the Algerian nation might recapture without weakness our common dignity that has been for so long ridiculed, and to ensure forever and indiscriminately the happiness of all the widows and orphans.

In the meantime, in the villages, people are getting tired of this. Money is demanded of them, they do not know where to get it, they have to provide shelter for the maquis members and feed them good meals, they have to cease all contact with the French and still manage not to lack anything. All of them have to become outlaws and obey—albeit blindly—only the outlaws. Those in charge of villages arouse both fear and admiration. They are well dressed, large, fat, and arrogant. They have already taken power. They are already independent. Yet there are all the others who are dying of hunger, terror, and suppressed anger. One of these days, it is going to get tough for the independents.

### March 4

I found out what was going on back home after Guel's father came to visit him. Today, Guel went there himself and has returned. He is distraught. His wife told him that during the last sweep, four days ago, the soldiers were not embarrassed to fondle the girls. At night, when they come to inspect the homes of those who have fled to sleep in the fields, they do not find the suspects, of course, but they find their wives and their sisters. And sometimes you can hear the women scream. The captain insists that the village must rally. He must have noticed that the best way to achieve that goal is to have the soldiers rape the women. This "method" was successfully used in the Ouadhias.

We expect that it is going to be used in our area. Before this happens, Guel wants, if possible, to bring his wife here so she can be protected. All one can do is approve and feel sorry for those that will not be able to flee . . . or at least for their husbands!

—Here, I told him, is an infallible way of emancipating women. This time they will figure out what the cost of rebelling is, and of only pretending, with a wink, to kick the French out of Algeria.

One also wonders why the maquis pick this particular time to move away from our village and go elsewhere to demand lamb roasts and wool carpets from other villages. I do not mean to say that sweeps should be prevented and that tanks should be stopped, but why is it not possible for these small patrols who go on their excessively impudent and disgraceful night visits to meet another patrol of "battle-ready patriots" who could have a little talk with them? Guel had the same idea, and many others from back home have thought the same because they have really had enough.

### March 5

The captain went down to Taourirt. He gathered the population that has just been given a third guard post, positioned at the mosque.

—I am happy, the captain said, that you asked for a third guard post.[17] This shows me that you are with us and that you want our protection. In any case, it is your right, and we will protect you against those who are killing you. You are with us, not only because you have asked for the third guard post, but you did not hesitate to offer your mosque and its minaret as a watchtower. Very well, this makes me happy, you understand!

"Now I am going to ask you for something else. We are going to create a djemaâ, and you will select the members.[18] Good. Who are they? Let them step forward . . ."

"I see. Perhaps you prefer that I select them myself. Oh, this will be easy. I will write names on pieces of paper, and we will choose them at random. That way, everything will be on the up and up, right? . . ."

The captain went on speaking in the same tone of voice suspended in the most anguished silence. Nobody asked for this third post; nobody wants to be selected; nobody wants to be hanged or have his throat slit. Béni-Yenni is not far from Taourirt. The maquis are located between the two villages and are quietly waiting for the captain to select their victims.

### March 6

We were all waiting impatiently for Guy Mollet's return from America: he was supposed to take care of the "Algerian question" after his return from America; but it appears that an essential question must be resolved by the Chambers first: the decision has to be made whether to increase the price of milk by a few pennies or not. In reference to Algeria, let us wait and see.

### March 16

I went to city hall and was told of the upcoming inauguration of the new room that will house the school dining hall. They are getting ready to go pick up kids in the villages, and they expect normal schooling within the next few days. The opening of the hall will have the look of a rally—discreet yet significant.

I found the captain filled with optimism: the Kabyles are tired of the rebels; the Kabyles were returning in droves. It is quite obvious at city hall where everybody was asking for official documents or for work. My friend L. looked modestly triumphant, and all the faces looked openly around, eager to copy the radiant face of their boss.

I was told that the harkis were formed in Tamazirt, and that people were armed.[19] The first desertion will be chastised so as to prevent others from finding the need to leave. All things point to the fact that soon it will be possible to announce the pacification of Tamazirt. This will bring about a series of acts of pacification. Then confidence will return a little at a time with the help of collaboration and nice weather. With the spring and the drought.

In the meantime, in Paris problems are piling up, and the House will discuss them all week in order to try to find a solution. Mr. Mollet refuses to be voted out of office over a few pennies for milk. His entire political approach is being discussed. Of course, Algeria will be taken care of afterward. Once more. And once more, nothing will be decided.

It seems that now, in contacting us, the French have made our well-known fatalism theirs, and they rely on the mektoub for the resolution of the big question, the only question: keeping or losing Algeria.[20] While the Muslims rely on the mektoub to safeguard or take away their lives . . .

*Le Figaro Littéraire* published a very long article telling of the arrest, torture, and death of Pierre Brossolette, hero of the Résistance.[21] I received this newspaper at the same time as the daily, which reports the death of Mehidi, an arrested FLN leader who had just "committed suicide" in his cell . . .

*L'Express* is publishing the first comments of Servan-Schreiber.[22] It is fantastic. But censorship will bring down its implacable claw on the daily. That is to be expected.

The secretary for a (new) teachers' trade union writes about the strike in its bulletin:

The teachers seemed immune from any kind of shortcomings. Yet, that January 28, some deserted the school, forgetting the teachings received from attentive and caring teachers, forgetting their duty to pass on this teaching to the children put into their care.

Ignoring this magnificent mission, they abandoned their post without a word, without even having the courage to say whether their actions were motivated by fear or conviction.

If we might express to them what we feel in such circumstances, we will say that those who trampled on their duty must silently accept the consequences of their behavior . . .

He is talking to us and he seems to say: "Good grief, you have to be courageous, darn it. You are traitors, aren't you? Well, then, say it out loud and without anyone telling you to do so."

Dear Sir, you are forgetting that traitors are also cowards. You have to take them as they are . . . and continue to fatten them, because, if left alone, they would be thin, very thin. This is precisely why they are traitors. They regret it as much as you do—the fact that they cowards. Believe me, there is nothing they can do about it.

### March 18

Exactly a week ago, Mazari's kid was shot in Azouza. It was on Sunday, during the night, very near the spot where his father was killed last year. His father was innocent; he was in the wrong place at the wrong time, and he was accidently killed. The son was in his last year of study and preparing the first-level exit certificate. All of us took an interest in him, in order to try and alleviate his suffering: he ate free at the school dining hall; he got his diploma. Just a good fourteen year-old kid. The soldiers shot him a week ago. I do not know why. Those who saw him said that he was unrecognizable and that he probably was tortured before he died. Maybe he was tortured to death, simply finished off because someone had gone too far . . . Young Mazari is with his father now, but his mother was left behind to suffer.

I hear that another of my students from Taourirt-Moussa, now grown up, was wounded and caught with weapons in hand: he was a member of the maquis. He was one of my best students, frank and tenacious. What drove him to join the maquis? What will happen to him now? Poor Manser, you, too, will stop suffering soon, but you will need all your courage. Clench your teeth, Manser, and your fists as well, just like you did when you were in school, my young one. And God bless you.

People are being tortured at the police station in Fort-National just like everywhere else. Those who get out talk about blows, electricity, the bathtub, and the rest. Those who do not get out get out all the same, and one day they are found near their village, riddled with bullets.

### March 21

They are hastily preparing for the inauguration of an unfinished school dining hall. Since Monday, a substantial meal has been served to about a hundred kids who are picked up in the villages by trucks every morning. These kids are returning to school with the carelessness of innocents. They are happy to be eating well and tease their teacher with all their heart. The inauguration will take place in three days in the presence of a general, the subprefect, and the colonel. I will have to welcome them and compliment them in public. We will take advantage of the situation to decorate the school.

The day before yesterday, the captain called me in for a "serious discussion." First, some instructions for the ceremony, then optimistic news about the mass rallying of the population, and, finally, his intention to install a twenty-foot pole in the school yard from which we will solemnly raise the flag. This is to be done in the presence of the kids, with religious silence so that we teach them to respect the flag. This operation will take place on a regular basis once a week.

I simply indicated to him that such a decision seemed too important for me to make, that it was the prerogative of the education inspector to give me instructions, and that, therefore, the captain should get in touch with him. That is where our conversation ended; but yesterday evening I saw the mast with a worker at each end. The captain was absent from city hall so I asked that the subprefect see me.

The subprefect, in front of whom I evoked ridiculous memories (1941–42), found little amusement in the initiative and promised me to intervene. Upon my return to the school, the pole was up. Five small flags were floating at the top. This morning, the flags are still floating, but the students will not be back until tomorrow, Friday.

**March 22**

10:00. There are no students . . .

**March 28**

A dramatic week. Last Friday, the students did not show up. That evening, I met the captain at city hall. He was returning from a "fruitful" operation. He was happy, a little bit off kilter, like someone who has just completed a difficult exam. His explanation went like this:

—This morning, I went to pick up the kids. There was nobody. The fellagha had come by the day before and had forbidden school attendance. They may even have taken some kids away and ordered the others to remain hidden. I did not insist. I knew where the fellagha were from, so we went to find them in their lair—around Maouia and El Misser. Results of this operation: fifty dead, including a leader; weapons recovered; the Icherriden gang annihilated. I am happy. We will have peace.

In front of me, he phones in the results of the operation to the commandant. I was led to understand that there was no loss on the side of the "forces of law and order."

—It is not over, he added. Tomorrow we will go at it again, and I will be gone the rest of the day.

—Is the reception still on?

—More than ever. You will welcome two generals and the subprefect. We will have an inauguration for the dining hall. As for the students, we can always find some.

Saturday, it seemed as if all the soldiers were gone from the town. Some Kabyles who had come from El Misser said that they did not suffer too much from the sweep a day earlier, but that something must have happened in Maouia. Helicopters have been repeatedly passing overhead with stretchers. The city is dead by 7:00 but comes back to life at 10:00, and from our bed, we can hear the humming of the engines and the noise of the returning soldiers.

Sunday, the helicopters continue to fly overhead. The radio reports one hundred and thirty-seven dead in two days, including an important leader, and mentions five wounded and one dead on the French side.[23] The Kabyles in Fort-National anxiously await the news from a different source.

Monday. The reception took place with only our students, those from the center. There were not many of them. The generals appeared to be straightforward and courteous. Their behavior was open and friendly toward me, and they seemed satisfied by the neutral welcome I provided them. Like myself, the generals did not want to discuss anything that did not concern the school.

The Kabyles who had been invited to attend did not show up. The small celebration, with far too much decoration, looked as provocative as possible the day after a deadly operation.

This evening, I learned that the maquis' account of the fight was completely different from the report on the radio . . .

**April 1**

In the newspaper of the 30th, there is a detailed report on the generals' visit. Larabi let his heart speak. He mentioned the radiant sun, the snowy peaks of the Djurdjura, the return of hope and unshakable confidence. Then he proclaimed his joy at seeing Kabyles massacred, at hearing proud military music, and at admiring the martial gait of the soldiers. As for the school, he makes us say kind things that we never said and feel other things that we cannot feel. Finally, he revealed that despite those present, some notables had prudently remained at home.[24]

The secretary and his boss surprised us with their spectacular rallying. A worthless informer testifies to our loyalty to the "good" cause and provides us with the conspicuous service of guaranteeing our treason. Thank you, my dear fellow. We will not fall in your trap, and all the lyricism of all the secretaries will not pacify anyone . . . This will be nothing more than another provocation.

In the same newspaper, the sad epilogue of arbitrary arrests continues. It deals with the murder of our old village policeman from Béni-Douala. Two people condemned to death. Undoubtedly, two innocents . . .

I learned also that Mazari's kid had a brother-in-law: the one who, last summer, killed an officer in Fort-National and was shot on the spot. So the Mazari widow has lost her husband, her son, and her son-in-law. A novel. A sad novel.

The gentleman who told me last February, "We will keep Kabylia, without the Kabyles if necessary," is quite right. The country is emptying out. All of those who can leave are doing so. They flee the forbidden zone, the infernal zone of death, the torture, the rationing, the hunger, the humiliations, the lies, the informing, and also the rope of pointless hope, the blind carelessness and irrational heroism. No, it is going to be quite difficult to keep Kabylia without the Kabyles.

**April 2**

Read in *Le Monde,* dated March 30, a stylishly written article showing great insight into the Algerian drama.[25] The article is entitled: "For an open dialogue on the Algerian problem." It was written by J. A.[26] In brief, Mr. A. sums up, in noble words that the best of the French writers would envy, the recent remarks made by the FLN delegates during a moving press conference in Tunis. Very well. Let those who have assumed the overwhelming responsibility of our rebellion and who have accepted the suffering, torture, all the crimes and deaths, and all the horrors as the unavoidable cost of a liberation—let them appeal. This is the equivalent of a true renaissance for the Algerian people, an unexpected advance without which life hereafter would be impossible for any man worth calling a man. Well, let them appeal to French opinion, to the whole universe, and let them ask these other human beings to acknowledge them as such. Such an appeal would have to be moving. Why does Mr. A. feel it is necessary to follow in their footsteps? Does he really believe that his siren song, together with the concert of all the voices, has particular virtues and is the ultimate recourse for us? If he truly believes it, he deserves the eternal gratitude of all Algerian people, who find, during their darkest hours, the best of their prodigal sons. Yet, with a little Christian humility, he might have been reluctant to assume such a great role. It so happens that the prodigal son was sincere, and Mr. A. is not Kabyle. Everything that makes us Kabyles he has totally rejected. He asked for everything from France, and France gave it to him. In the first place, the virtuosity of mind that takes the place of nobility of soul and modestly veils inadmissible ambitions, insane dreams, and shameful calculations. Mr. A. is a skeptical Pharisee who is trying to play an important role. He suddenly discovers it in the bloody tragedy that has been tearing us apart for the last three years. It is the part of a brilliant mourner who does not console the victim and certainly nauseates the executioner. Of course, I am not saying that France is the executioner, but the system is. And it is precisely this system, not France, that has served this gentleman, just as it has served myself and many others, by the way. So, a sense of decency consists in being quiet; courage consists in fighting openly, in rejoining Abbas, for instance, in giving up everything one has gained to rejoin the people, the fighting, and to say, "Here I am among you, my hands are clean, my pockets are empty, I am the prodigal son, ready to serve my country."

One discovers among the young Kabyles an attitude, a logic, some simplistic yet significant reactions that I am tempted to compare with some more subtle behavior.

The village terrorist approaches the maquis leader from the area and says:

—I would like to join the maquis. I am ready to kill somebody. Pick a victim.

—No, the other answers, you are fine right where you are. We do not need you in the maquis.

—Yes, you need me, the terrorist insists. I am tired of living in the village, without weapons, always on the lookout, always fearing a sweep. I must leave.

—No, you will not leave. Do you think that we do not know what the "civilians" do? You have done nothing to support our cause. And now all of you want to leave to join us and share in the benefits for very little work. No, now it is over, we have won. No reason to share in the profits. We have freed you; we will be your leaders. Stay where you are. We know who you are, and you are not worth much. Just continue to give us shelter and keep on the lookout. If you are arrested or killed during a sweep, you will have gotten what you deserve.

This harsh frankness slows down juvenile enthusiasm and dissipates naive illusions. However, nobody waited for anyone at all before starting a project for the future and setting a goal. These are no longer "castles built in Spain," but "palaces of Revolt."

### April 4

I have been thinking that it may be time that I ask myself a few questions. Unfortunately, I have been doing nothing but that for months. I say, "What is it all about?" and I know quite well what it is about. However, I stick to ideas, and I refuse to face facts. The Algerians are fighting to get rid of privileges, and the French kill us so it will not happen. No, in reality, we cannot look any further.

Maybe we can after all. There is something else. Under my window, shovels are making crunching noises against the sand and the concrete. The Kabyle workers are mixing mortar to construct a building; the French architect drew the plans for the building; the Italian contractor and the Spanish foreman are in charge of a large construction site where a building will be raised. The Kabyle workers are mixing the concrete and wasting time: they have a good time, get busy when someone looks at them, then lounge around some more and take a break. There are ten of them, and they hardly do more work than one person. At night, in their village, they will welcome members of the maquis and will help them the best they can. At the end of the week, they will go get their pay: there will be ten of them getting paid enough for twenty, and in the communal accounting, their pay will equal forty. At city hall, the captain, as special delegate and his secretary, who specializes in acrobatic moves, waste paper writing reports and requesting aid. At headquarters, they waste the funds and distribute aid.

In the countryside and in the towns, lives are squandered, and men's blood is wasted. In the mountain villages, the military waste their ammunition on insignificant beings who are asking for nothing more than to die.

There is still something else, although nobody knows for sure what it is. There is this frenzy for waste, for quick destruction, and this desire to rebuild even faster. That is not all, however. The French say to us: "We have done you a lot of harm. Come on, you know we are right, my children." And we answer:

"Indeed, this remains to be seen. Keep on giving, dear torturers of our heart." A quiet fear has taken root inside us, a fear that is a form of courage, a definitive hatred that no longer needs to be flaunted. Among the French, it is the cruel deception of no longer being able to like us that often becomes a blind rage, paid for by those who are most vulnerable as well as those who are true innocents. That is the most monstrous of wastes, the only incurable one, the one that destroys love.

Now, can one claim that this love did not exist, that there was nothing else but privilege? There was something that was very hard to define but that made peaceful coexistence possible. We had the unshakable hope of improving our situation little by little, of confidently making our way toward a delusional equality. The French had this quasi-fraternal condescension that consisted in tolerating us, in graciously letting us play second fiddle while asking us to understand them and, in a way, to help them maintain their preeminence. In that respect, we agreed to help them, while thinking to ourselves that all we needed was patience, that the day would come when everybody would find their proper place. Then the cards had to be put on the table . . . Now that they have been dealt, why should we want to return to a bygone era, since there are no more dupes on either side? Why all this waste, why all these speeches?

No matter how much I think about this, I have to yield to the facts.

**April 12**

This morning, around 8:00, the captain addressed the population: he was riding in his jeep, and his voice, amplified by a loudspeaker, woke up the bourgeois who were sleeping in after spending the night awake because the sad Ramadan has fallen upon us since the beginning of the month. The loudspeaker said: "All men aged fourteen and older are invited to gather at the city hall square for an important message . . ." or "Everybody without exception as of . . ." and finally: "Those who are not on the square by 9:30 will be considered suspects." I remembered that when my children went out at night two days ago, they found a bundle of FLN leaflets in front of the school. Directed at French draftees, blacks, Algerians of French origin, they had been left all over town . . .

We got up to clean the house a little before the search. The town was sealed off, and there were sentinels in front of each building; the search began around 9:30. Our turn came at 1:00.

Overall, we were treated correctly. I do not believe that they found any leaflets or a duplicating machine.

In the afternoon, they made us listen to a never-ending harangue in Kabyle through the same loudspeaker. I am told that the guy who was haranguing us is a former member of the maquis who surrendered a few months ago and who has done as much damage to his compatriots as he could. This man, and a few others, are customarily paraded around during the sweeps. Each time they arrive in a village, they point out those who provided them with shelter when they were in the maquis, those who collected money, and those who helped the rebels. Those who are pointed out like this are automatically arrested, and more often than not, they are shot without any trial. If helping the rebels is a criminal act deserving death, if it is the law of war, nothing must be said against it. Except that, in this case, all the Kabyles would have to be picked up and executed. If no one has the right to execute them, it will be necessary to hide all these crimes, to deny them, and to find other explanations. In any case, one does not need much imagination to do that.

I am told that I know the man in charge of the post in Azouza. His name is Gourmand (?) and he has been living in Fort-National for the last three or four months. He is as thin as a rake and looks half-dead; he often came to the film showings I used to organize at the rural club. He used to go to church frequently. I remember that he always smelled of wine. He is the one who killed one of my students. The other night, he went to break down the door of an old colleague to have him beaten by his men. Then he got another old man outside, after having beaten his daughter-in-law. She did not want to say where her husband was. The old man was shot on the street, and the soldiers refused to let him be buried until the village children went back to school. He remained there for two days. When people were finally allowed to bury him, his body was badly decomposed.

His son has a high school diploma. He had been arrested a month earlier. One of his school friends was in Tizi-Ouzou while working as an officer in the intelligence branch. His friend came from Tizi-Ouzou by helicopter, got him out of jail, and helped him make his way to France. So the sergeant knew where the boy was. He did not need to beat up the wife or to kill the father. Maybe the sergeant was a bit drunk.

In Tighilt, a Kabyle was killed during a sweep: "He was

trying to flee," they said. His brother, who had been denounced by the member of the maquis on duty, has been arrested. He is being taken to the camp in Tizi-R. In that camp, they usually shoot the most conspicuous guests. So they shot the brother. Now there are fourteen orphans. The father went to the camp to claim his son's body. He has not returned.

In any case, justice on the other side is just as swift. All that is needed are a few oral testimonies that are verified when possible, and the sentence is administered. It may happen that the sins of the condemned do not merit death; even so, this does not prevent death. It may be that the person in question has been very helpful up to this point. This is not taken into account. That was the case, a few days ago, for a well-known person in Bou Smahel who had his throat cut at the same time and on the same spot as his son. Others who, not long ago, did heinous stuff are forgotten and keep quiet. The larger the sum, the better they are forgotten: they "redeemed" themselves, it is presumed. The term is indeed adequate.

Finally, they are settling old scores and feuds and making it look like a maquis operation. In general, the rich who made people sweat under their hats for a living are now sweating with fear. People remember that the rich treated them unscrupulously, that the father practiced usury, and that the son was not serious. When people like that fall, their former victims rejoice, as do the jealous. We are witnessing all kinds of purges. This one could have every appearance of a swift form of justice, which the vague justice of men sometimes likes to claim as its own.

### April 16

This morning somebody discovered the body of the amin from Aguemoun on the side of the highway, one hundred yards from the city. He had been executed by soldiers during the night . . . A. explained to me that the amin was considered a francophile. That was always the impression that he had given me. However, as a village leader, he was most likely intimately involved with events around here. Maybe he collected funds or he welcomed the maquis members into his home. He had been arrested during the latest sweep. After they interrogated him for a week, they released him during the investigation, and he returned to his village, in wretched shape. He thought it was all over. Yesterday, the army came to pick him up. He dragged himself all the way to Fort-National, and during the night, he was taken outside the city on the road that leads back to his village. That is exactly where some passersby found him this morning.

I have been told that the specially delegated captain was surprised and affected by this death. He called Captain Croizat, who told him that he had received orders and could not furnish any further explanations. I know young Captain Croizat very well. He is a nice and intelligent man. He is the father of five very young children.[27] I know his wife also. I have heard that he is in charge of executions in this area. The amin from Aguemoun was fifty-three years old.

I saw a young man from Azouza walk by in military dress: a recently recruited terrorist. The people from Azouza are expecting a catastrophe, because the army executes those its informers denounce, even when the magistrate has released them.

Besides the one in Aguemoun, there were three other executions at Ighil Ou.

At noon, I saw some soldiers, at the Djurdjura gate, checking bags filled with provisions. One of them, without ceremony, took a carton of eggs from a basket belonging to an old man, and the old man left, happy to have gotten off so lightly.

During this sad fasting period of 1957, here is what it is like in Kabylia: there are the maquis on the one hand, and on the other, there is the army. Between the two, there is the population, which gets beaten up. Just like a punching ball between two boxers. The army severely rations, sweeps, destroys, and kills. The rebels force themselves on the population, demanding lodging and protection. They also ransom and kill. Healthy men flee, go to jail, or join the maquis when they can escape death. The children, the women, and the old ones stay behind as punching bags.

### April 19

In any case, the bag is well aware of the blows it receives, and I have the feeling that it accepts those that come from one side somewhat more gracefully. The day before last, in Azouza, the military guard stops and searches a truck from near here; the famous sergeant handles the driver roughly, pokes him with his bayonet, cuts his shirt and jacket with a knife, and threatens him with the worst kinds of torture. Then he orders him to turn his truck around. The fellow turns around to complete the maneuver, comes back straight at him as fast as he can, and stops five hundred yards farther. When the soldiers arrive, running, at the truck, the driver has disappeared. So they burn the truck down and return to their post. As for the young man, it is not difficult to guess where he is now. I should specify that last year in his village, Imaïnsrène, the fellagha had neatly slit the throat of his mother, who was a little crazy. He did not hold it against them very much.

And so it is in a multitude of cases. Nobody grieves those who die as traitors, and nobody wants to be subjected to the same fate. Not out of cowardliness, but because everybody is a tried and true patriot, deeply patriotic, and because the divorce with the French is an absolutely conscious one. I have been told the story of this fellow from back home who refused to accompany members of the maquis being put on trial.

— You will give your side of the story, he was told, and if you have not done anything wrong, you will come back.

— Never, he answered. I do not know what you are reproaching me with, but I will not come with you. Suppose that you condemn me and kill me; how will I introduce myself to God: as a traitor? At my age? Me, who has always considered it an honor to be killed at the hands of the French. No, I will not follow you: that would be admitting that I did something wrong. Kill me right away, if you wish; merciful God will judge, but I will not be put on trial by you. Kill me or let me go.

Apparently, they let him go.

When, in one family, there are, simultaneously, victims of both the soldiers and of the maquis, it is useless to say which ones people cry over and venerate. Maybe one day, they will be considered in the same light, and both will be seen as heroes of the liberation. I have sent my condolences to the brother of a victim of the rebels. He was not upset at all.

— You know, he said to me, it is our turn now. You know my brother, right? But war is blind, however, and each of us pays his tribute. Life is not worth much anymore. What matters is to live as a man, because, one way or the other, we must die.[28]

B. was arrested during a sweep. At least I know that he has not committed any criminal offense: he would have bragged about it to me. I have always advised him to keep quiet and to focus on his studies. He is a smart and emotional young man. Very susceptible. It would be a shame to humiliate him and turn him into a rebel.

1957

**April 21**

B. was let go. He just had to take a few slaps in the face. He does not want to go back to school, but things are not good for him in his village. This short training period did him some good, however.

**April 28**

Easter holiday. Ramadan. Sad, rainy days. Patrols traverse the town nonchalantly, and some fathers from the villages hurriedly finish up shopping for meager supplies that they may not be allowed to take back home with them. I have hardly been out for the past few days.

A newspaper from Morocco (P. D. I.) is attacking me violently for my last book. I answered as best I could, and I wonder if my answer will be published.

Another newspaper filled with official propaganda, probably written by the army's psychological unit, praises the book on their second page and declares, blithely, that I do honor to Algeria. What honor? What Algeria? According to all appearances, the psychological service is determined not to leave me alone.

Yesterday, I saw a goumier distribute like a leaflet this newspaper that speaks of me, and the confused Kabyles received it with the same revulsion that they generally show when they receive other such tracts.[29] They are right to be careful, of course. They are used to it.

This morning, a goumier slid a tract from the captain under my door. In it we are advised to rejoice secretly during the Aïd, which occurs—the day after tomorrow—even if we pretend to be deeply saddened sons to please the "bandit" rebels.

The authors of this subtle tract claim that they can read our hearts in depth and empathize with this poor population that is terrorized by the FLN and amorously coveted by the army. This is proved by the fact that, these days, people can go out and get twenty pounds of semolina instead of the normal ten pounds. Indeed, it is time to celebrate without getting caught and to revel behind closed doors.

**April 29**

A little while ago, we met an old man from Tighilt in front of O's.

—Are you okay? we said to him.

—No, not really, he answered. Then he began to speak in a

calm voice. He was wonderful. The words came out of his mouth in a distinct and clear manner. No passion and no beating about the bush. Oh my God, what simplicity, what nobility. When he left, my friends explained to me that he was the father of two children recently executed by the army who had left fourteen orphans behind. So the soldiers had let him go.

— No, something is wrong: the day before yesterday, I was in the bus. We got stopped in Tamaz. Everybody had to step out. Houamdi was taken aside, then they let us go. H. remained behind: he is still there. It is one of the guys who was recruited who pointed him out. You know the one. He is from our village. My God, I was afraid. He could have pointed his finger toward me. He had reasons to. Last year, his father sold me a mortgaged field. I sued him and won. And last year I beat up their shepherd when he let his herd damage my young fig trees. Yes, I beat him up. And I won my suit. That young recruit could have avenged himself using the army, and I was afraid.

Houamdi should tell them:

Me, I am an honest man, leave me alone. Don't listen to this traitor. He has been fighting against you for two years, while I spend my time getting bread to feed my children. Now you are giving credibility to a traitor, and you want to kill an honest man. No, this is not good. Tell me, gentlemen, against whom are you waging a war? You say that it is not against peaceful people. Did you catch me with weapons in my hands? Then let me go?" That is what he should have told them. However, the behavior of the French boggles the mind. It looks as though they want to kill us all, clean up the country, and save only those who will join the French after having shot at them. It is not easy to shoot, though. Someone who is not used to shooting, who has remained peacefully at home to cultivate his field, how do you expect him to start shooting from one day to the next? It is not that easy at all to kill a human being, a son of Adam, who looks straight at you and knows that you are going to kill him. Well, there are people who get used to doing that, you know. I admire them. But when they are recruited, those are the ones who must be killed, and not us. If for no other reason than because they have given death; they are ready to receive it. They should not be tolerated one single moment: they are no longer fighters, they are bandits.

So why do the French not do away with them? Maybe it is

because they are bandits, like them. You only have to understand what the life of a person is worth to them. Do you know that they shoot in the fields at random, just like that? When someone complains, they say: "Do not try to run away. When someone runs away, that means he is scared, and when someone is scared, he is guilty." That is the childish reasoning upon which the life of a Kabyle depends, a Kabyle who is a son of Adam like another human being. Brutes, I tell you. There is nothing human left in them. So we are no more afraid of them than we are of wolves.

—No, young men, I am not okay. I am not okay, but do not worry: if there is suffering, there is no dishonor . . .

### April 30

Yesterday evening around 6:00, a young man from Taourirt—on his way to Fort-National to work in a bakery—was killed by a policeman at the construction site near the Djurdjura gate. Some people from Taourirt had just passed him a few moments earlier. He was harmless and had the appearance of a child. He looked about fifteen. I used to see him selling newspapers in the streets. He was neither a rebel nor a terrorist. The Kabyles who live across the street from the police station told me that a policeman called out and told the lad to follow him. He took the young man to the ramparts, at the foot of a fig tree, where he fired a burst of his submachine gun and disfigured the man hideously. Then he dragged the fellow onto the road. That is where the people from Taourirt found him this morning. They immediately returned to their village to bury him on the last day of Ramadan.

Among the policemen at the post, there is one in particular who is a hothead. He continuously beats and threatens the Kabyles. People assume he is the assassin. They also say that the captain is quite upset about his methods, and the Kabyles are hoping that this hothead will be transferred somewhere else . . .

### May 6

I am back from Algiers, where I spent three days. I saw some people from back home at the hotel. What a tragedy! They have become unrecognizable: gaunt, weak, silent, and wretched. The desolation one can read on their faces is only a pale reflection of the sufferings they have to endure back there. The soldiers strike, steal, torture, and kill. The son of Si Chérif was shot down below the convent of the sisters. He did not die but was badly wounded. He had been taken as a suspect to Béni-Douala;

after the classic questioning, he was dressed in a military tunic and given a gun. Then he was brought back to Tizi-Hibel by jeep. Once there, he was told to leave, and then he was shot.

They mention places that I know in Béni-Douala: a store, or the workshop of a blacksmith on which soldiers have put idyllic placards: "Villa of Dreams," or "Villa of Pleasure," or "Sweet Confessions": these are the places where people are tortured.

In T.-H. the other day, a lieutenant gathers the population to select leaders. Nobody wants to be one, nobody wants to speak. So he says to them: "We are still going to vote: those who are for us, stay; the others can leave. For me, this will be a sign, and that is all that I am asking you to do." Nobody moves.

—Come on, make up your minds. Those who are against France, please have the courage to stand up.

So Hocine, the village idiot, gets up.

—Lieutenant, for me, these kinds of things, they go right by me. I have to go to my field. Is that okay?

—Go on, fellow.

This causes a veritable stampede; they all get up and follow the idiot. Everybody wanted to go work in the fields. The lieutenant was left all to himself.

He had enough good taste to laugh and to shout at them: "Come on, can't you leave me at least one for France!"

In Tagmount, where the post is located, the soldiers of this same lieutenant threw a grenade in the courtyard of a dwelling: they wounded an old woman, a young girl, and a goat—or something that looked like a goat.

In T.-H., the rebels came to take up a new collection and bled dry an already destitute population. They abducted two old men, including the colorful Moktar. They have given full powers to the "Canard," who is the most mischievous of all sons of bitches and who tyrannizes honest people. They all complain about the "Canard" and would be capable of eating his flesh raw, on the condition that someone turn him into a cadaver first. In the meantime, they put up with him, like cowards.

**May 7**

I found out about Moulouda's abduction in Aguemoun. He is our street sweeper. The poor fellow is simpleminded and harmless. He is no more capable of reason than my youngest child—who is three years old—he has got a large mouth, and he is both friendly and ugly in a funny sort of way. At noon, another street sweeper showed up to take our trash can, and my wife had tears in her eyes. Oh well! Moulouda no longer exists, just like the days that pass by.

**May 9**

Yesterday, it was VE Day and therefore a holiday. The day before, I had received a letter from the captain, who imperatively ordered us to attend the military parade with the children at city hall square. So we went, but the chore was humiliating for my colleagues, and they showed their reluctance the best they could, calmly leaving their students with me before they went to stand under a locust tree, behind a car. I went back to the school in a very bad mood and locked myself in until morning.

This morning, at the home of Lug., I heard some dismal news: the small village of Aït Saidh (also known as Zegane) near Tamazirt experienced some terrifying events yesterday morning. Around 5:00 A.M., a patrol encountered some rebels who had spent the night in the village. Fighting. Two blacks and one policeman are killed. The maquis pulled back. The Tamazirt post is alerted, and all the other blacks assemble and begin a bloodbath in the small hamlet. Nineteen men are killed in cold blood, at home, in their beds or in their small courtyards. Madame Pernin said that the only ones left there are the women, and that a teacher was saved, thanks to a policeman in whose arms he found refuge. He is a colleague who had gone there to attend the funeral of his father and his brother.

The women, Madame Pernin added, were all outside, moaning and wringing their hands on the national highway. Those driving on the road could see them, but the travelers and the Kabyles had to watch out. The blacks were attacking everybody. They stopped the bus that came down around 8:00 to manhandle and bludgeon the passengers. The driver was hospitalized in Tizi-Ouzou. Another driver replaced him to continue the service: he, himself, was beaten up that evening as he arrived from Algiers.

The final account of this catastrophe is not yet known. However, today's newspapers are reporting that "nineteen rebels were killed in the area of Tizi-Ouzou." [30]

I have been told that soldiers from the Fort-National garrison have gone to disarm the blacks.

**May 10**

*L'Echo d'Alger* reports that twenty-six rather than nineteen rebels were killed to the east of Fort-National. I have been told that this number includes an old colleague who retired seven years ago. Perhaps this concerns another dark series of events, in another village in this region.

As for the other colleague, he was forced to go to school when there were no students there and while the bodies of his father and brother were lying in his family home. I have been told that the army is refusing to let bodies be buried as long as students have not returned to school.

Regarding school attendance, it seems that the authorities have decided to act with the utmost firmness and to use the harshest means necessary in order to have students in classes. People do not understand these tougher measures just one and a half months before the beginning of vacation, while most of the Kabyle schools have burned down. There are only four left in the area (including ours). Here, each time the children are brought back, we have to keep an eye on the doors and the city, and we are certain that the students will not return the following day. Today, there is nobody except those who live inside the ramparts. There will most likely be a blockade of the city center: nobody will be allowed in from the villages. In any case, we will suffer from this as much as they will.

### May 12

I found out that my brother-in-law, Amar, was executed by some soldiers last Tuesday, May 7.[31] He was seventy years old. He had been a member of the village djemaâ, and it is possible that he was asked to assume certain functions in a new djemaâ and that he refused. I do not believe that he could have committed other crimes . . .

Larabi's son was telling me again yesterday that the blacks in Tamazirt bludgeoned the bus passengers and that someone else had died in Aït Saidh (or Zegane) because of them. The women are wandering on the national highway, crying with despair and anger. There is not one single man alive in the village. People from other villages came to bury the dead after the soldiers finally allowed them to do it (Thursday evening or Friday). In Azouza, there are no longer enough men for the funerals: the local women have to perform that chore.

The bus has not been going up to Tizi-Ouzou since last Wednesday. That day, the travelers were forced off the bus. Then the passengers were forced to lie down on the road, and the blacks began hitting them with shoes and hacking at them with knives. They also made the travelers crawl and knocked their heads against rocks; then the blacks grabbed the passengers by their arms and legs and threw them into sharply graded fields or against hedges. They stabbed the driver in the buttocks. After the ordeal, he had to drive standing up all the way to Tizi-Ouzou, where he arrived exhausted and was then taken to the hospital. The school principal, the wife of the administrator, found one of her clerks among the torture victims. She was able to free him and take him with her.

Earlier, I was standing in front of the radio, listening to the news. I was listening with half an ear while thinking about my brother-in-law. The speaker was describing the splendors of the Farnese Palace in Rome, where President Coty was welcoming President Gronchi for an equally lavish dinner.[32] He was describing the immense hall with its gigantic frescoes depicting the mythological love affairs of Greek gods, as well as the well-matched and sumptuous colors of the table decorations, the dishes from Sèvres and those made of gold brought in from the Elysée Palace, the violets from Parma, the roses from I do not know where, the menu in the purest tradition of French gastronomy, with old vintages, chickens from Bresse, and, finally, the brocaded, gleaming, radiant guests, the swishing dresses and indirect lighting.[33] I was vaguely listening to all this while thinking about my brother-in-law, who was over seventy years old, who was crippled and like a skeleton, who was poor and honest. He was so poor, in fact, that he could not flee Tizi-Hibel, like all the others who went to Algiers, far from the submachine guns of the lieutenant of the SAS. All the others who are also poor, gaunt, and scrawny—as I saw them last week—all the others who are unhappy and pitiful, yet lucky because they have temporarily escaped the submachine gun bullets.

I told myself they are trying to destroy us ruthlessly in order to smother our rebellion, to keep Algeria—and especially the Sahara. I said to myself that a president of the French Republic—secular, democratic, etc.—would never have gone to see the pope if Algeria did not have to be kept at all cost. Perhaps, because the pope does not want us to be destroyed, one must go out of one's way to explain to him, in his presence, that it is of vital necessity for the Western world and for Christianity, and that, in any case, this is none of his business, and consequently, he has to keep his Christians under control.

If the colonialists could reach this merciful God, they would not hesitate for an instant. They would go see this merciful God to explain their viewpoint to him without worrying about his advice, in any case. Because they do not need advice, they only need to explain: they would even take time to explain things to the devil.

## May 19

According to information from back home, my brother-in-law was shot in the fields. The day before, the lieutenant had asked for him and some other old men that they wanted to force to organize a municipality; he had gone to hide in the fields. The lieutenant knew that all the suspects would flee at the sight of soldiers, so he decided to look for them in haystacks and ravines. Then the next day they scoured the entire countryside, and seventeen runaways were shot. That evening, the bodies were gathered and returned to each village. Two of them came to our village: a young man of twenty-three and my seventy-year-old brother-in-law. The person who told me all this added that, if the old one had stayed at home, they would not have shot him. It is obvious. Everyone knows that you cannot get much protection from a case of "ifs."

A few days ago, D., the administrator, had someone tell me that he wanted to talk with me discreetly about the young man who was killed by a policeman at the Djurdjura gate. We met in a street in the evening, and he gave me a few details about the assassination. He is offended and he would like me to circulate a motion to be sent to the prefect. After having thought about it, I have concluded that this motion is useless. In any case, nobody would sign it because this death was only one among thousands of others, because the subprefect who knew of this episode had shut his eyes and plugged his ears. As for the prefect, he will be discreet or will discreetly penalize some policeman, because the administrator, as I hear it, wants to use this motion to carry out a personal vendetta against the police. I got the little piece of paper glued above from his secretary, who gave me some details and who hopes, as much as his boss, that we would cautiously raise our voices to be heard in Tizi-Ouzou "without alerting the press, however." On this piece of paper there is the precise date of the death and the family name and first name of the young man, as well as the date and place of his birth.[34]

## May 26

Sunday. Last Wednesday, the Mollet government resigned after an unfavorable vote on new taxes. You do not have to be a politician to understand quite well what happened: the Right brought down Mollet because he is asking for money. Well, he needs money so that he can "pacify Algeria" and protect the notion of "French honor" on which the Right is so dependent. In short, they are forcing a man from the Left to do the dirty work and refusing to foot the bill. Ah, the poor fellow and the poor Left!

Soldiers recently shot the amin of Azouza after torturing him. He was a "fund-raiser" but also a disabled veteran, an "administrator." Now, he is nothing. There is a well-established rule: you systematically kill all the "suspects." In the army's hands this is a trump card. You just follow the directions of the rebels who surrender, those who are pampered and who spit complacently. This is undoubtedly why raids from now on are carried out in the countryside. Villages are spared. Soldiers wander around in nature firing at anyone. The latest raid, just below our village, resulted in another six mortalities last week. My God, who are they?

**May 27**

Ali Chekkal was killed yesterday in Paris just as he was leaving the Colombes stadium with some officials, including the president of the Republic. The final match of the French Soccer Cup had just finished. They arrested the terrorist at the scene. He did not try to escape, and the police had to protect him from the crowd.

**May 30**

Yesterday a patrol was attacked right outside Fort-National. We witnessed "the war," in the words of my youngest, who was greatly amused by the crackle of machine guns and other automatic weapons. We saw the ambulance pass by on its way to the infirmary and then a small car. That lasted about twenty minutes. It was almost 6:00 P.M. when it started. Then the landscape was engulfed in fog, and a dismal rain began to fall on the wounded or dead. Today, I was told by a French source that a sergeant had been wounded and by a Kabyle source that the entire patrol had been wiped out, that the ambulance was full, and that it had made several trips. I saw it go back down one time and then go up but not down again. Where is the truth? And why must it be truth? At any rate, it is hardly pleasant.

The radio is announcing that the rebels have slaughtered all 302 men from a village in Mélouza who wanted to ask the troops for protection. Officials claim that "this nameless massacre" stirred up considerable emotion. There is indeed reason for alarm, yet the news broke yesterday, and today's papers gave it only a small space among all the other communiqués. Yesterday, people thought that some rival gangs were settling the score. So they shrugged their shoulders while rubbing their hands with glee. Now that they have another version today, they are crying brutality. Yet today, like yesterday, the dead themselves have not changed.

### June 3

Alas! All the newspapers are talking about the Mélouza massacres. Horrible photos are splashed across front pages, and world opinion, now vigilant, is beginning to express anger and disapproval. A disgrace! A disgrace, a stupid act whereby an entire nation is condemned, and its people shamelessly reveal their inhumanity. From now on, what name can those who promised accountability evoke in order to be able to speak? Who will be able to believe them? On the other hand, who will pause before believing other crimes, all the crimes that we did not fail or will not fail to charge them with? While there might be a psychological or political explanation, it would not have anything to do with human nature or conduct. In any case, the victims' blood needs no explanation. There is no justification that will dry the children's tears or blot out the unspeakable horror that that hellish night fixes forever in the haggard eyes of those women.

### June 10

The massacres of Mélouza! They are still getting plenty of ink. President Coty spoke to the civilized world, which, apparently after hearing his voice, is calling us barbarians. The FLN appealed to the pope, accused the "armed forces" of genocide, and made a list of collective crimes that included Mélouza. The pope refused to believe them. The major newspapers, both French and foreign, all agree that French soldiers have played no part in this.

Just a few days later, three bombs exploded at rush hour in three of the main thoroughfares in Algiers: ten dead, a hundred wounded. Innocent victims—French and Arab.

During the same week there was a skirmish in Kabylia near Michelet, near Fort-National: one hundred and twenty-five rebels dead.

So this is war, and it is horrible. But there is nothing more to say. Nothing to say because when you state that, on one side, there are one hundred and twenty-five dead and on the other, a few dead and wounded, we know what this means. We know what the death or impending death of these thousands of rebels means, and we say nothing because there is nothing to say. This is because a dead man can no longer speak, and the man who lives fears that he will die if he speaks even though he realizes that, one day or another, it will be his turn to die. It has been decided that we should all be killed as long as we persist in our demand for independence. Unfortunately, the very idea of independence has become our only reason to live. We are, perhaps, wrong to have allowed this crazy idea to become so imbedded within us. But tearing it out is no longer an option, for the heart where it has taken root would be torn out as well. So they might as well kill us right away.

Those who criticize us for not screaming in horror and not denouncing our own crimes—and who do not hesitate to denounce their own—have it made. They stand in noble triumph over our cowardly silence. But they think that we are not listening attentively to them, that all we hear is the thunder of their protests. In truth, they are mistaken. We hear them loud and clear.

—We are real bastards, they tell us, we torture and kill you so that we can stay in your home and keep your riches, while leaving you to your filth. Yes, we are SOBs, and this must stop. We know that Algeria is ours and that you will keep your filth forever—so why should we kill you? Come on, answer us, admit that we are bastards.

In response, we say to them:

—Gentlemen, for us, it matters very little whether you are this or that. And, while we are at it, let us say that we are bastards, just like you. That is not the point. What matters is knowing whether or not we are at home, whether or not you are in our home, and if you want to leave us the fuck alone.

There you are Mr. Mauriac. As for our congenital barbarity, hereditary and all, it is a question of washing your dirty linen or being hit with a stick, a question that Madame Sganarelle answered with humor a long time ago.[35]

Everything else is nothing but casuistry, tragic hypocrisy.

**June 13**

A bomb exploded at the Casino de la Corniche Sunday, June 9th: ten dead, about a hundred wounded. On the 10th and 11th, there were violent demonstrations. Six dead and about twenty wounded, all Muslims. Poor Kessous's appeal is trivial, as tenuous as a hair in soup. A soup made bitter by discontent and blood. For a long time, already, each one of us thought he was right. So much so that there is no room left for discussion, only fighting and destruction. More and more there seems to be no way out except death. But between the appearance of serenity and this inescapable and brutal evidence, there is a steady accumulation—from all of us on both sides—of egotism, foolish hope, childish pretense, and hopelessly blind faith. The wake-up call will be very difficult for the survivors. As for the others, they and their noble illusions will be dead. Afterward, all this will not have been in vain, because the harrowing passage will have been facilitated for them. We can only pity those who see, know, and die needlessly, without having appeased anger or served ambitions. For there are no longer any innocent people on either side, do you not agree?

## June 18

Around 10:00, we heard a detonation, and from the classroom, the students (in the seventh grade) could see men beating each other with chairs on the glassed terrace of the hotel. Then a car went by on its way to the infirmary. We found out that the captain had just been the target of a grenade attack. There were about six wounded, but the captain had not been touched. The army and the police began to scour the city, rounding up the native population and assembling them in the square outside city hall. The construction site facing city hall was vacated in a flash. A policeman from above called over to one worker who had stayed behind. Other policemen explained that he was a European and he was left alone. Patrols and vehicles came and went in all directions. Then we saw the Red Cross ambulance ascend and approach the Algiers gate. It was transporting the seriously wounded to Tizi-Ouzou.

Toward noon, I saw high-ranking officers (a commander and a colonel) arrive at the square. A former fellagha began to harangue the crowd gathered there. He positioned himself in a jeep near the mess hall and started talking into a loudspeaker. I thought I heard that the aggressor had been shot and that, among the wounded, there were some seriously injured kids. The former fellagha was urging the shopkeepers to be careful; advising them not to offer the terrorists any refuge; and condemning the criminal acts of those who had not hesitated to cause the death of innocent people. Finally, they had the corpse pass by on a small donkey led by a Kabyle, pushed by another, and ridden by a third—who clasped the body as if it were an unmanageable load. On seeing the cadaver's feet, I turned away. At that time or later, I do not remember any more, a soldier was filming the crowd from all angles. Toward 12:30 everybody had been released to go get something to eat. What exactly had happened?

**July 2**

I am leaving Fort-National soon to go settle in more peaceful surroundings in Algiers. At least that is what I hope. On June 22, I visited my new school and quickly returned to attend the ceremonies celebrating the centennial of the fall of Souk el Arba on June 24, 1857.[36] The captain had been preparing for this event for months. Every house in the city had been quickly whitewashed, the alleys cleaned, the embankments weeded. In front of the school, just opposite my windows, they cut a few meters of the inelegant embankment and threw up a thick wall, upon which they built a wood plank platform covered with miniature cement tiles. On top of this they installed a model of a monument made of very thin laths and bright white plaster. It was a cardboard ornament for a sham ceremony, since the grenade attack had stripped away the gravity of a patriotic display that everyone, aside from the captain, would gladly have missed. In fact, we were missing the Resident Minister, the prefect, and the public. What remained was a parade on the square with a hundred of our pupils as spectators, a bunch of real flowers placed at the foot of a false monument, and a handshake with the general. The maquis have ordered the Kabyles to flee the city. The captain gave his agents the order to confiscate identity cards in order to prevent local residents from leaving. But, by and large, the city has never been as gloomy and deserted as on that Centennial day.

From that day on, we teachers could consider the school year over and our troubles bad memories. We were free until October—free to hide, to escape, not to respond to official invitations, not to attend ceremonies; free to go on strike and to sleep late. Until October, we will most likely forget, and each of us may perhaps realize his own insignificance by verifying that this lapse had absolutely no impact on the daily lives of the people who, in our absence, continue to plot, to fear, to suffer or die. We may find that just being temporarily out of the loop is as ridiculous an advantage as being at the back of a line, when you are waiting for an ordeal to which everyone in the line must submit.

### July 31

Here I am in Algiers, living with my family on the outskirts of the big city in a very populated Muslim neighborhood where poverty exists alongside opulence; corrugated shacks next to beautiful bourgeois villas. I left a sad region where there are only old men, women, and children.

Since the grenade attack at Fort-National, the Kabyles are forbidden to circulate wearing their burnooses. In the morning they arrive in ridiculous processions. They seem embarrassed, as if losing the burnooses were tantamount to losing their virility, their manliness. Bah! They will adjust and, by winter, will buy—if they have the means—coats or raincoats. What wouldn't they do if it were demanded of them? At this time, beatings, insults, humiliations no longer have any impact, and there is nothing but death that can affect them with any real certainty. From this point on, killing them is the only way to hurt them; and every single one of them is waiting for it.

Before leaving, I found out that there had been a major skirmish back home at Tizi-Hibel. The rebels and soldiers fought all day long in the fields, and my compatriots, who were there farming, were forced to flee toward Tizi-Ouzou or Algiers. In Algiers, they met up at the "Bar Maritime" where, as fate would have it, a terrorist threw a bomb at them because they were drinking alcohol.

The soldiers arrested my brother-in-law, Chabane Maou-dji, in his field and made him transport bodies on a donkey that did not belong to him. That evening they let him go, but they took the donkey with them to Béni-Douala. The next day, my brother-in-law and the animal's owner went before the captain to demand restitution. The captain returned the donkey to its owner, but he detained my brother-in-law and had him shot. When his older brother went to find out about him, he was told that he had escaped. Mohand would have believed the soldiers if he had not recognized his brother's shoes lying in a corner. Chabane has left him with a half-dozen orphans. But he takes comfort in the thought that he himself is not yet dead, that their house has not been destroyed like so many others in the vicinity, and that, although the battle has cost the soldiers almost fifty men, the maquis lost only four. These figures are, of course, un-reliable—just like everything reported by transient fighters.

In recent days, the newspapers have reported contacts be-tween the government and the FLN during the International Congress of the CISL, which was held in Tunis.[37] A Tunisian law-yer, on a mission for Ben Bella, was arrested and had his brief-case confiscated when he got off a plane at Orly. Officials have flatly denied any contacts. Denial as well by the FLN, which is expressing suspicion, and rightfully so.

In Tunis, Bourguiba has officially proclaimed the Republic and had himself elected president.[38] In Algiers, bombs are ex-ploding almost everywhere and every day. In the courts, judges are continuously finding survivors of torture guilty. In France, Muslims are killing other Muslims. Good God, when is this all going to end?

**August 8**

It has been fifteen days since I left Kabylia. I have no idea what is happening there. But there is probably nothing happen-ing of which I am not already aware. In short, this vacation has brought nothing new, and everyone is waiting apprehensively for the next session at the United Nations. Those Muslims who are the most realistic are completely aware that the UN will not be able to dictate its will to France and that France will not ac-cept being given orders. Yet they are hoping for an agreement. The other Muslims—those who are neither realists, nor ideal-ists, nor politicians—are simply wretched and would like it all to end. They want peace restored so that they can start living again, even if nothing is ever changed. They tell themselves that in the old days, life was still possible. Now life has become dif-ficult. It is death that is possible, that can strike you in any form and any place. What can we win by revolting?

People will be careful not to speak in these terms, but you can read it on their faces; it determines their behavior. You would not have to push them too far before they quit believ-ing, quit being afraid and ashamed. You would not have to push them too far to turn them into defeated men prone to any plati-tude and ready to deny anything. If this is the objective of pacifi-cation, it is not far from completion. There will soon be a people with crooked spines who, unlike the parachutists and other sol-diers involved in pacification, will be waiting passively for the stick, their anger suppressed and their dreams lost. Then the

French soldiers of the twentieth century will be able to claim that they reconquered Algeria just as their ancestors did in the nineteenth. What is important is to know if this new conquest will also last a century.

**August 14**

A skirmish, extremely lethal for the maquis, occurred at Bouzegza. According to the press, it followed and was meant to avenge the battle or ambush that cost the French soldiers 25 men. An official communiqué reports 128 dead prisoners—without counting—versus 11 soldiers dead and a few wounded. In Algiers, the people responsible for the bombings at the end of July and the beginning of August were apprehended and arrested, and their terrorist organization was dismantled. They have made us a promise that Algiers will soon be completely peaceful.

After drawing up an austerity plan to straighten out the financial situation (a plan hailed by the press), the president of the Council, B. M., and the ministers are hastily preparing a *loi-cadre* for Algeria.[39] They intend to introduce it to the UN soon after Mr. Pineau submits it to the Americas (Latin America included).[40] They are also announcing the more or less imminent visit by the prime minister, which will be followed, sometime later, by a visit by Mr. René Coty.

I read two brochures on Algeria by R. Aron and J. Soustelle.[41] Controversy. The first uses data on hand to prove that Algeria is not a profitable venture for France and that it would be better, after weighing the entire situation, to let the Algerians be . . . Who could ask for anything better; and we are screaming it to whoever wants to hear it, up to the last, agonizing gasp. The second brochure offers proof that Algeria is France; and that the Algerians are French people. For this reason, it would be not only the greatest act of cowardice to abandon them but also an obvious sign that France is in decline. In 1939, Mr. Paul Reynaud said, "We will win because we are the strongest." Now Mr. Soustelle is saying, "We will stay because we are the strongest." Can I, in all sincerity, hope that the future that proved Mr. Reynaud wrong will prove Mr. Soustelle right? After all the suffering endured by the Algerian people, this simply cannot be possible. If I wanted this, I would deserve to be hanged. We are at the point where only despair taunts us. Even if we were to suffer more after finally gaining our independence, even if we had to endure oppression by self-serving or fanatical people, we are truly at the end of our rope, ready to throw ourselves into the arms of a tyrant, provided that he also be the liberator.

News from back home: soldiers are going into the fields, exploring the underbrush and ravines, then setting fire to everything. The olive plantations are scorched, and the olive trees are burning like torches, along with the fig trees and other fruit-bearing trees. What is happening is exactly what happened centuries ago when the Vandals came and set fire to the Roman plantations. This proves that the face of war is always the same; men have the same instincts. However, it seems that back home it is not about war but pacification.

I found out that Mr. Ameziane was killed after being tortured for an entire week: he died without saying a word. F. Saïd was arrested while working in his fields. As soon as Dehmous Idir arrived in Algiers from France, he heard about what was going on in the mountains and immediately bought a ticket for Paris. For him, Algiers was too close to the infernal mountains.

We cannot say that Algiers is a paradise. Life is possible here, as long as you stay at home. Just across from the school, I watch patrols who stand at the intersection and meticulously search all the brown-skinned men who pass by, all the brown-skinned women veiled in white accompanying them, and all the old cars that they are driving. I do not think that we can dispute these searches, which are intended to prevent accidents and the death of innocent people. But I also observe the soldier's movements, which are, to a great extent, protective. Such is the signal he gives to a beautiful car carrying beautiful women accompanying gentlemen who, though not always handsome, are always non-Muslim. This beautiful car slows down imperceptibly; then it starts forward again with a short acceleration, like a coquette who flashes you a friendly smile and accepts a compliment that is obviously owed her. So my heart sinks; and I tell myself that, in any case, these men who watch everybody and who claim that we are to be their compatriots, could, if they wanted to save appearances, humor us and our "sensitive" natures by pretending to stop everybody and inspect every car. But I am very concerned that the diplomas of indestructible brotherhood are, from this point on, only directed at the foreign observer and that among ourselves, the era of hypocrisy has ended in order to make way for a time of violence and hatred. To terrify, destroy and propagate as much hatred as possible. This is the only tie that still binds us. To me, this seems obvious today in spite of the undeniable fatigue that pushes people to comply mindlessly. At times, such fatigue accounts for the smiles on people's faces—smiles that I periodically intercept, smiles that are directed at the French, who interpret them as friendly smiles. In reality, these are the grimacing smiles of a conquered people.

**August 21**

Ziram came to let me know that they shot three men whom I know well at Taourirt-Moussa: Ouerdane R. (sixty years old), Leklou Ahmed, and a mehloul [a local native]. I got news from back home about the deaths of a dozen others who belonged to various villages of the tribe. Some people who came for questioning at Béni-Douala were released, only to be machine-gunned halfway home by a patrol that was waiting for them. A pretty picture for a communiqué.

It seems that they are in the process of coldly eliminating everybody who is still in their prime. The only ones spared are the spies, who fall—sooner or later—into the nets of the ALN and those old people who are strictly harmless. They are cleaning house. The day when there is no one left in Kabylia, the rebellion will fizzle out by itself just like the fire that Sévigné describes.[42] The method is excellent, and its success certain, for it is false to assume that the survivors will resent the French forever. Everything will be forgotten, even the dead. The people I meet from home seem like trapped animals who, nonetheless, continue—among themselves—to envy each other, to trick each other, to set ridiculous traps for one another, to begrudge and detest one another. In the beginning, those who had suffered deaths in their families were able to take a certain pride in it and boast about their heroes. Now every family is familiar with death, torture victims, prisoners, and traitors, and there is no longer any pride or shame in it. People are also starting to look at the French objectively, to recognize their courage or intelligence as well as their cowardliness or duplicity. The French, oddly enough, have become closer to the natives as men; and both groups have become friendly again with the jackals, hyenas, and wild boars living among the maquis. It is all happening as if all the maquis had become a jungle with their own fauna and their own laws. Those who cannot survive in the jungle flee at full speed and then die.

In Algiers, on the other hand, you get the impression that you are living in an organized society. There are two clans: the police and the suspects. The military police station themselves at every intersection to check on suspects. They walk along the major roads to keep an eye on suspects. They position themselves at the entrances of buildings and in front of public transport in order to frisk suspects. Armed and powerful, the police inspire great fear in the suspects. They use their force frequently and, at times, their weapons. A criticism has been leveled at the ALN for steering their sinister activities toward the anticolonial struggle by recruiting the guys in the middle. They have substituted real gangsters, paratroopers, and others for the guys in the middle who wanted peace with their compatriots.

They steal outright and indiscriminately. B. told me the sad story about a shopkeeper on rue de la Lyre who was robbed of 90,000 francs. He went to a superior officer to file a complaint and recovered his money. The story should have ended there. But, one evening, the paratroopers came back to get him when he was closing. They took the money and killed the old guy.

My neighbor, the butcher, must have known about this incident.[43] Last Saturday, he had a visit from a soldier he knew who usually stationed himself in front of his door. The soldier came in and calmly emptied the till. The weekly receipts totaled 127,000 francs. The private was clever. He had thought it through. The butcher did not interfere. Perhaps he was thinking about how he might recoup his losses from future clients.

I am told as well that they are breaking into stores and helping themselves. They are robbing babies and women, and every time specific cases were cited.

The European civilian belongs to one or the other category only if he has brown skin or wears the uniform of the territorial guards. As the case may be, he either beats someone or takes a beating himself. But he generally floats between the two, becoming more nervous and confused.

I received a communist leaflet, the first in more than a year. Bravo! These people act clandestinely, like fish in water, whereas the average mortal would suffocate. They sing the praises of their heroes but do not mourn them excessively. They fully embrace the independence movement and, for the time being, omit any topic that might breed dissent. That can wait until later! In my opinion it is clear, first of all, that they are absolutely sincere; secondly, they are supported by the French Communist Party and Russia, not all that self-evident. Reading the leaflet, you have the impression that Russia hopes to introduce communism, first in Algeria, and then to expand into AFN (French Black Africa) and beyond. In other words, they will defeat the Eisenhower doctrine from here just as they are attempting to do in Syria and Egypt; thirdly, it appears that the FLN is looking decisively toward Moscow, that the warning given by F. Abbas to the United States is surfacing a little late, and that our leader has already "kissed the snake." I would like to know what he thinks of the "snake." But I am afraid that the result will be different from the one on which he is banking. The American counteroffensive could disrupt any plan: all it would take is for the sultan to release the Algerians because he fears the communist bogeyman. Then Bourguiba would become reticent, and finally, France, which would insist on its role as the advance guard, would have the support of the West in warding off the Bolshevik threat. The Algerians could do nothing at that point except beg for mercy. I wanted to talk about survivors, and there I go, off into the world of lofty politics like an astrologer who lets himself fall into a well.

**August 27**

Manser and Medjeber Areski were among the people executed at Béni-Douala.[44] Last week the newspapers reported a large operation back home. There were forty rebels killed. The Muslims are saying that in Bouzegza, the armed forces fought at night against each other by mistake . . . The fight supposedly cost them hundreds of men . . . However, in Algiers, every time there is a nest of terrorists, it is discovered and destroyed. Those arrested and tortured spill everything they know. The snitches are kept busy, and the man in the street worries about his future while playing both sides. I read of the harrowing incidents that have happened to my former collaborator, Khris. *Le Journal d'Alger* is very hard on him.

**August 30**

Received some propaganda about the Mélouza massacres. It contains excerpts from the foreign press condemning this horrendous crime, condemning barbarism, fanaticism, and the savagery of those who committed it. Those responsible? Who, precisely are we talking about? The foreign press is basing its coverage on the news published by French agencies. But nobody has the courage to admit to this crime. This refusal to accept responsibility proves that man has hardly changed, that he is a wolf to other men, ruthless, ready to conquer, inflict pain, and exercise his power—provided that he himself remains sheltered and unafraid. When man stops being fearful, he goes back to his basic nature—which is to be fierce, greedy, and insatiable. The weaker his victim is, the more he enjoys his power to annihilate this victim. Satisfied with his own strength and using it to dominate the weak, he believes he is fulfilling his destiny as a strong man to the fullest extent. So there it is: twentieth-century men set free from their skepticism and anguish. They live and they feel alive. They are no longer spectators but men of action who want to built a new world. They are clearing the terrain, sweeping away the debris, and sacrificing countless victims on that altar. This new world will be beautiful, solid, and stable. Gentlemen of the FLN, gentlemen of the Fourth Republic, do you think that a drop of your blood is really worth anything more than a drop of anyone else's blood—blood that, because of you, is being shed on the scorched soil of Algeria? Do you truly believe that, with your dirty hands, you are going to build the better future that you are promising us in your hysterical speeches? You, who have manufactured our misfortune, do you think that you will not also share in it? What is this force that bruises and crushes people over and against this other force that appears and disappears? The Russians have just tested their intercontinental ballistic missile, which scientists call the "perfect weapon. "Two days later, the Americans launched their own missile. Also a perfect weapon. There is nothing left to do but vaporize the planet.

## September 3

But no, poor Medjeber Rezki was not killed. Tortured, yes. Unrecognizable, of course. But quite alive and completely surprised to be so. So surprised that he has lost his mind. It is like I am telling you: he is deranged. He came to the Hôtel du Rhône, where my brother saw him and chatted with him.

—Well, gee, it is you, Mr. Feraoun, it is really you standing there in front of me and I in front of you. Look me in the eyes. I have always been convinced of two things. Two things. And of these two things, it is either one or the other. There is life and there is death, and between the two there is a wall. All right, you are either alive or you are dead, right? It is over for a corpse. He is over there on the other side. There is nothing left for him to do here. He is where he belongs. As for myself, you can see that I am here . . . Explain it to me, please. Explain it to those people. Give us your thoughts, plain and simple. Good God, it is perfectly easy . . .

## 1957

Medjeber never stopped. They advised my brother not to talk with him because, since his arrival from the countryside, he had done nothing but chew on the same arguments over and over. He was incapable of discussing any other subject except when there was not anyone left to listen. He would just keep on talking in order to convince himself.

The people of Taourirt-Moussa buried a body that could have passed for his. It was the body of a boy from Ighil Bouzerou. Three days later, Medjeber, barely recovered from the torture, is released by the military. He returns home, but at Taourirt, they greet him coldly — and this eventually drives him crazy. The first people he meets when he enters the village are seized by terror. They stand there for a good minute before running into their houses, locking their doors, and commending their souls to God. All this takes place in broad daylight, and the dead Medjeber looks exactly like the living Medjeber. You can imagine the scene: the village, all the houses lined up on the main street from one end to the other. Then, people rushing to get home, the doors slamming one by one. And as the wretch approaches, there is a holy terror that dissolves houses as it radiates outward, like a thick fog. Finally, his confusion at scaring his own family, his wife and children, who continue to weep.

I think that there were reasonable men who in any case did finally get a grip on themselves. But this unexpected reception, after all the horrendous suffering, perhaps created a certain apprehension, and after the fact, the village did not know how to get completely over this apprehension in order to bring him back fully into the fold without any hesitation. It was as if something definitive and incurable had made him a suspect who had to be kept separate. All of this must have boggled his mind. He was sent to Algiers to help his mental problems and to allow some time for public credulity to let go of the ghost.

### September 14

I hear there was a big sweep at Fort-National. They picked up nearly every shopkeeper and artisan in the city — about thirty of them. The operation took place while Larabi was in France. Rumor has it that he went away on purpose after he and the captain had organized the whole thing . . .

Mohand came to see me and confirmed his brother's disappearance. Up to this point, he had been able to escape the questioning at Béni-Douala, but not the insults, scuffles, and beatings during the raids at Tizi. My own father was beaten by paratroopers: he could not even get out of bed to go to the holding pen. "Besides," added Mohand, "the others did not treat your father well either; they did not hit him, but they forced him to put them up. It was the 'Canard' who set the whole thing up out of jealousy. Yes, he is jealous of you." Thanks, dear Canard.

The people of Taourirt are often present at the torture sessions that take place at school. The soldiers cook up all sorts of sophisticated methods to make the Kabyles talk: they make them drink gasoline, they tear off their nails, hang them by their feet, insert objects up their rectums, put straw in their mouths, tie, hit, cut, and burn them. But electric shock is the worst. Apparently, everybody heard the agonizing cries of Méziane when he was being tortured this way. It lasted quite awhile; then the cries got weaker and, gradually, faded into an anguished murmur. Then the soldiers sent someone to get a bottle of water for him to drink. After that, they killed him. For one entire day and night, the terrified village remained silent. Yet everyone kept hearing Méziane's disembodied, cunning voice, tirelessly repeating a mocking and pathetic cry, the same cry that, at the height of his pain, he had directed toward his father, the author of his miserable days: Hey Dad! Hey Dad! Hey Dad! . . .

**September 26**
The beginning of the term is almost here. Everything is in full swing at the academy. Lots of confusion, lots of chaos, they say. Taking advantage of recent events, certain people have managed to get unexpected promotions, whereas others will be leaving empty-handed. I ran into some French instructors who gave me a condescending welcome. They are, once again, happy to be alive. They acknowledge the mess that has been made but stand ready to roll up their sleeves to repair, to reorganize, and to rediscover life's pleasures. This contagious optimism is directly drawn from the newspapers, which offer daily spreads concerning a variety of items: the outcome of a large-scale operation, the name of a famous terrorist leader who has been arrested or killed, an important change in the *loi-cadre* project, which tends towards minimal reforms. In essence, they want to safeguard the status quo of those earlier times that cost us so many lives.

**October 21**
I witnessed the stampede at school. It took me three weeks to form the classes, identify returning students, and make a list of the new students I will be recruiting tomorrow. For the past three weeks people have been invading my office, the cor-

ridors, the classrooms, pushing the children forward, getting themselves kicked out, coming back in to try to put the teachers off guard and try their patience in order to secure a place to which they have no right—all this so that I sign certificates that give them access to benefits . . . I think this is the reason for all of this uproar. To collect, they have to present a card verifying their child's enrollment at school. That is the only thing on their minds when they ask me to sign while promising to keep the child at home. They want the money, and if worse comes to worse, they will do without school. This is typical for the poor people living in the shantytowns. But the others earnestly wish to go to school, and they rush over here. It has been seventeen months since the strike started and two years since the first schools were torched. The strike was officially lifted and will eventually be nothing more than a bad memory. The older boys have returned to the high schools to get their diplomas. I can imagine their state of mind, their disillusionment, their despair. What kind of motivation will these kids have left? Who will they believe tomorrow? They are the vanquished who have barely fought. Oh, I know very well they will be welcomed back. That in itself, will be a cruel punishment and a well-deserved lesson, because if they came back and found the professors petulant and their classmates wary, they would also remember why they left and feel justified at having done so. No, they will receive a warm welcome because the professors and students will hardly be capable of doing otherwise. For they are as miserable as the deserters.

What about the course of study that I created, loved, and abandoned? Am I a deserter as well? Is the course going to be given new life? Yes, of course, and so much the better.

The end of the student strike is very important: the country is tired of bloodshed. Soon the dead, all the innocent dead, will revolt, cry out for mercy, and demand the end of the war. Those who rushed headlong into it believed they were doing the right thing. Now their "religion" has shown its true colors. They sought happiness but incurred one loss after the other. They fought for freedom but encountered death, torture, prison. Clearly, this adventure has been a disaster: they played and lost. This is obvious to them now, and there are some who are keeping a low profile, hoping they will be forgotten. They are experiencing the morbid joy of having been let off, unlike their father or their brother or their son who died in vain in an unfair fight. They are like the survivors of a shipwreck who miraculously escape drowning. They are like those who flee a horrible catastrophe and pinch themselves, unable to believe their good luck. It is truly difficult to trust completely in such luck because it is not yet over, and everything could start up again. Almost any little thing would suffice to put us on the road to death. Death circulates day and night, blinder than ever and as scornful as possible. She who is satisfied with an old woman, with the old woman's grandson, with the old woman's goat. She who lingers over Raviche, the brave Raviche who is no more wicked or shrewd than Candide, no more rebellious than the best of the settlers, no more aware than the wisest of children.[45] He had come to see me here in Algiers. He was happy to live peacefully in a village filled with fear. He was happy to meet patrols with kind soldiers who smiled, and just as happy to meet groups of rebels who were pensive, formal, and brotherly. Showing no anger toward either side, he obeyed both. He came to see me the 1st of October. On the 3rd, Raviche was machine-gunned in his field while climbing out of a haystack. He was all smiles when he left me, all shriveled up under his empty crate, the same crate in which he had brought delicious Kabyle grapes to me here in Algiers. He did not suspect that he was moving toward death; that death, blinder than ever, utterly scornful, would surprise him in his field as he climbed out of a haystack.

### November 9

Why was his daughter mute? That story is more tragic than a fabliau, infinitely sad, fraught with all of our sufferings, misfortunes and crimes.[46]

The girl fell on her head from the dome of our fountain, lost consciousness, went into a coma. Her father had just been arrested, brought to Béni-Douala, and tortured to death. Both he and his daughter were in comas at the same time. The mother, in a state of terror, gave birth to a second daughter and then lost consciousness as well. The entire family is near death.

The army decided to save the girl. She was transported by helicopter in the arms of a soldier whose orders were to remain absolutely still throughout the flight. Imagine the amount of patience and concentration that everyone, especially the soldier and the doctor, needed to save the girl. They saved her, all right, because they had to save her. They had to save her while letting her father die because she was innocent and he was a terrorist. You can bet that they knew who each of them were. They saved the girl but she remained mute.

I saw her leave the hospital to return home: she will be able to smile at her mother but unable to speak to her. The first thing that she will do if she ever recovers her speech will be to demand to see her father. And then she will curse the people who gave her so much care while they beat her father to death.

### November 13

The day before yesterday there was a big demonstration in which many Muslims participated. Mr. Lacoste was able to talk about the trust that would be restored by peace and prosperity on the horizon. The only problem, however, was that the Muslims present had been hauled down there by force in trucks. All in all, it was a spontaneous demonstration, as called for, with radio coverage and television screens. But it appears that the television screens were quite revealing. Damn! The laws of optics have nothing in common with Lacoste's laws.

I was amazed to find out that Mokrane had been assassinated in France by the FLN or the MNA or whatever Algerian patriot, national liberator, or avenger of our race, etc., etc. Oh, the bastards! Even if they were to execute all the Kabyle Mokranes, the Kabyles would still be capable of hunting down an honest man among themselves. How will we ever forget such crimes? Clearly, the killers are seeking an independence that is different from the one taken from them; that is, the independence that would allow them to kill with impunity. The native people of Algeria—yesterday humiliated, today tortured and tracked down—will proceed directly toward slavery, the worst kind of slavery, a slavery that they have never known. My curse on the executioners of the people! The hatred that they sow daily will sprout as rapidly as the proverbial seeds of Kabyle turnips.

### December 17

I should perhaps note down a few significant events that have attracted attention this term: artificial satellites, the West's panic at the Russian success and the American failure in space (Sputniks and Grapefruit), and now the NATO conference, currently taking place in Paris. General Eisenhower fell ill at the conference and was still quite sick during the sultan of Morroco's recent visit to America. Finally, speaking of the sultan, there is also the reception he gave to Bourguiba and their mutual offer of friendly aid to Algeria.

Even though the Algerian question was discussed this year, like last, at the UN, we did not have any strikes, feverish expectations, deceptions, or anger; rather, there was a sense of fatigue, almost indifference. Both the French Algerians and the natives read their newspapers and ponder their ideas of reproach, hatred, and tolerance for one another for lack of something better. The French are still hanging back, not yet claiming victory. The Algerians still have faith in their liberators. Both feel that it will not be much longer until things fall into place. It is easy to foresee that both will change their tune since one eventually pays for one's sins. In every area, the mess has been extraordinary.

### December 25

I was given the book of a paratrooper, who writes: "We have pacified Tazalt."[47] I am confounded by the young man's ignorance. He is the only one who believes his behavior is pacifying. But whenever the paratrooper decides to squeeze information out of someone, or simply to have someone provide him with it in exchange for being taken into his confidence—or for other reasons—that someone ends up with his throat slit. Prior to the incident, the victim knows exactly what is waiting for him, and the paratrooper shares in his certainty. As soon as the deed is done, he notes it with some regret, and without any hesitation, he invites another Arab to take the same straight and narrow path inevitably leading him toward the razor-sharp knife of this super modern "Damocles."[48] One has the impression that the mighty paratrooper is playing the role of a little soldier who cares nothing for his playmates as they await the arrival of a different Santa Claus who has pledged to bring them all new toys.

The bad part about all of this is that the Frenchman can no longer understand the Arab, that is, if he ever did understand him. Whereas all of the former's actions are inspired by the most chauvinistic, anachronistic, and, I grant you, noble patriotism, he calmly demands that the Arab surrender himself, that he "love France"—a very popular expression today—that he get his throat slit by his own brothers for the tricolor flag. In return, the Arab is entitled to pity, to the same pity that the Prince of Condé had for the cook Vatel, but with this difference: today's Frenchman does not bear the slightest resemblance to Condé.[49] Unlike the prince, who slighted death, the SAS officer disregards the deaths of all those Arabs who fall because of him, for him, or by his own hand. Whereas Condé risked his own life in combat, this officer risks the lives of others. Yet there is still a resemblance: Condé believed that his own life was worth the lives of all others combined, and the young French officer believes that his life is worth the lives of all Arabs combined.

The paratrooper's naive testimonial is prefaced with a maxim by Father de Foucauld.[50] It is addressed directly to Arabs and is preceded by a virile statement by this hero of modern times, Saint-Exupéry.[51] The maxim obviously pertains to the French.

There are no solutions in life; there are forces underway. We have to shape them, and the solutions will come. (*Saint-Exupéry*)

When I entered religious life, I thought that my recommendations would primarily concern kindness and humility: with time, I see that what is most often missing is dignity and pride. (*Père de Foucauld*)

It does seem that the reverend's words are addressed to the Arabs but, good God, why does this young French paratrooper reappropriate them for the benefit of his own kind? Why does he not understand that Arabs can have their dignity, their pride, and even the trappings of a patriotism that they draw up from the very depths of their souls. This sentiment, which the paratrooper encounters at times in "savages," proceeds, in his opinion, directly from the most intolerant fanaticism and leads to a xenophobia completely devoid of moral values. On the one side, the one that already has so much, more needs to be added, he feels. Why would one think there would be the slightest trace of noble feelings for the other side? It is futile for the lieutenant to keep looking. He will not discover anything, and he will tell you that, plain and simple.

Now that we have established this with absolute certainty, there is nothing left to do except follow the young man and observe him as he executes his lofty mission—a mission for which he has cheerfully reenlisted—by relying constantly on the chief's opinion before saluting him and mimicking his astonishment at the last line of the book: "So, Tazalt, was it a dream?"

I had already encountered another SAS officer a long time ago who, acting on the same prejudice, wanted to deny us everything. This particular wretch would talk every chance he got about his exploits in the French Resistance in an effort to persuade us that our situation was not the same. Of course, our situation is not the same as that of someone who acts like the ss of the Gestapo. But for his listeners? Maybe they knew that they were imbeciles. They knew it, accepted it, and were willing to have it repeated. This is why they did not join the maquis.

When one is provoked by such an odious display of power, glory, and heroism, one takes to liking one's hardships, one pardons one's ignorance, one finds excuses for being a coward, and one prefers the worst hardships and pain rather than submit to a senseless arrogance that demands nothing less than the faithfulness of dogs and brings nothing more than humiliating caresses.

Good God, if there is nothing else that the rebels have managed to pound into the Arabs' heads, it is a sense of honor and human dignity. Besides, the Arabs have always had it, but no one believed it; and even they were beginning to doubt it. The rebels came straight out and said:

—Listen to us, brothers. You are men, and that is certain. Quit doubting it. The time has come for you to let other men know it so they will believe you when it is their turn. Rise up.

So the Arabs rose up to fight while hanging onto a slight hope of survival. That is it. Why do they want to make them "savages," "salopards," or "assassins"? [52] Sure they are, just like everyone else.

Besides, the paratroopers' opinion of the fellagha is no different from the fellagha's opinion of the paratroopers. And I imagine that if a rebel had kept a journal and had it published, he would lump us all together just as much as a paratrooper does because of his ignorance and his naïveté.

Both the rebel and the paratrooper make the mistake of believing that they are defending a just cause, killing for a just cause, and, yet, unjustly risking death. Strengthened by their rights—and, in the eventuality of this wrongful death that cowers behind a bush—they become cruel like trapped animals and try to prevent their own deaths by suppressing the lives of others. The people who are truly responsible for this have prudently removed themselves. They are the ones who have made the monstrous blunder for which thousands of innocent people are now paying. Some sly opportunists thought that it was enough to raise a little finger in order to destroy the powers that be, to topple odious regimes, and to replace them with their own; other sly opportunists thought that it was sufficient to silence the howling pack and that the government could not be shaken. It is unfortunate that the people who are safe and firmly in command have not yet changed their minds. They do not see any reason for doing so.

**December 29**

In truth, we cannot even use the term *error*. *Tragic illusion* is more appropriate. The Arabs are correct in thinking that Algeria belongs to them exclusively; the French are correct when they claim that Algeria and all of her resources belong to France. It is the age-old story of the oyster and the plaintiffs, one that eventually works itself out to the disadvantage to all parties involved. There is one unique feature: in spite of what anyone fears, there will not be anything left for the judge.[53]

As we approach the new year, the situation seems worse than ever. Poverty, which has already taken hold in the countryside, has now reached the cities, where low salaries and unemployment have suddenly precipitated an unexpected rise in prices.

Now that they have stopped recording murders and attacks on invariably innocent victims, it seems that ordinary life has again become tenable. This is especially true since police harassment—random yet supremely humiliating because it is always aimed at Muslims—has also been discontinued. Even so, the general state of mind has not changed: people are settled in their own clan next to an arsenal of hatred over which they carefully watch. They are convinced of their own rights and are simply waiting for public sanction. Then they discover for themselves a treasury of friendship, and they generously spend it on their adversary kneeling before them. Each person tolerates the other because, in the end, each one is confident that he will win, and that his victory alone will be enough to ensure everyone's happiness, first and foremost his own.

It is useful to note that those French people who are most inclined to imagine a possible future in which the Muslim has his rightful place show more discouragement than enthusiasm. This is because they thoroughly understand that in a poor, overpopulated, and underdeveloped country, it would be futile for a person of an already privileged status to hope for a better one. Everything leads them to fear that the situation, on the contrary, will be reviewed and that the future, overall, will hold nothing but bitter surprises. A sense of hopelessness binds them to those who blindly cling to the status quo and refuse, a priori, to question it. These people view life as a fight without mercy. It is a battle that they accept with dignity, while sending others to fight or die for them, to die for eternal France, the mother they share. In contrast, the Muslims' dreams for the future are more promising, if not more plausible. Yet here, too, we can separate those who think, the intellectuals so to speak, from those who no longer think.

The latter, who are by far the most numerous, want nothing more than to find happiness. Once the French have left, everything will be easy, and no one will want for anything. They are all convinced that they are active participants in their struggle for liberation, simply because they are present and are humiliated on a daily basis. They belong to a massive movement called Muslim Algeria, an ailing movement, covered with pus and blood, a movement longing for a miraculous cure. These people are at least sincere and deserve attention. Yet, once again, interest will be focused on the others: the brutes, the shameless, scheming intellectuals who continue to hedge their bets. If France remains, she will have to use these intellectuals—those who have not burned their bridges. In the event that France leaves, they will rush to scorn her. If worse comes to worse, they will be able to satisfy themselves by playing secondary roles while waiting to prove that they have always been of good faith and that, as good patriots, they have understood the need to be prudent for the greater good of the new Algeria. This will be the time to demonstrate their abilities to all comers. It is likely that the future has some disappointment in store for them as well, for there are indeed schemers who, being even more vicious and audacious, have bet a bit more money on one side of the scale. Enough to make it lean slightly—without risking their necks too much—because they are quite certain that they will be needed right away. So these pals will make it their business to coldly eliminate the timid.

Finally, there are the people who overbid like M. or S.: bastards who could hang themselves from the large strings they pull. Let us not even mention they have forgotten their roots; but they insult France, who has done everything for them—and this to our detriment—because not only did she adopt them immediately but she gave them her own image, which they blacken. This is certainly enough to sicken even the enemies of France. And it is thus that these double-dealing traitors end up betraying each other, astounding the world by revealing their hypocritical faces. They were believed to be more adroit, if not more honest.

So as the year comes to an end, the problem remains unsolved, and we are left with inordinate hope and great fatigue. Will time gradually heal our wounds and subdue our passions? Or will the impassioned and wounded gradually disappear so that, in the end, the problem also disappears and is therefore no longer posed? It all basically comes down to the same thing. There is already one thing for sure. Positions have not varied; the general state of mind remains the same. The natives are waiting for the French to leave, and the French are automatically killing anyone who wants them out. Who will be the first to give way? That is the problem.

# 19**58**

January 12, 1958

Ak. came to see me bearing bad news from Kabylia: deadly skirmishes for the French in the riverbed just below our area. The village of Takrat, already empty for three months, was razed to the ground. Other villages of the Iraten were evacuated by order of the military or the rebels. Every day dozens of suspects are shot, and sometimes the victims are people who just happen to be there. At Adini, they arrested eight men pointed out by a turncoat. Only four managed to get back to headquarters. From my window, I saw Mouloud, the driver of a Girard bus burned by the rebels, go by in a jeep, two paratroopers on either side. A week later, he was taken to the Villa Sesini for questioning.

A few preliminary signals seem to indicate that terrorism in the city is being reorganized: attacks are recurring in various places, and there has been a proliferation of neighborhood in- spections and massive arrests. Every day the radio reports wide- spread fighting, violent encounters, bloody hand-to-hand fight- ing, "important rebel bands."

In France, the Gaillard cabinet is more preoccupied by the economic crisis and constitutional reform than by the plight of Algeria and, especially, that of Algerians. The official stance is that pacification has recorded some significant results and that, in order to pursue it, France must tighten its belt, borrow money, mortgage Algeria itself to an impartial lender, while dangling it like a carrot before this infant Europe, whose own birth was indeed laborious.

At the international level, the events in Algeria do not make much more noise than the annoying buzz of a fly. What counts most in this arena is proclaiming peaceful intentions in the name of its large population, which is extremely conscious of the dangers of an impending atomic, astral, apocalyptic war. Conscious but highly organized any way.

## 1958

### January 17

I read A.'s article in *Le Monde*.[1] There is nothing more Jesuit than the heartbreak that he simulates, nothing more false than this inferiority complex that he dares to spread out lengthwise in columns. Here is a gentleman who has denied everything to the Kabyle. He is gallicized to the tips of his fingernails, received everywhere without reticence, admired and listened to in the literary circles of Paris. Editor-in-chief at the national broadcasting system, he is now rediscovering his roots quite unexpectedly—namely that he is a bicot who has been intimidated, an inferior man who can neither be assimilated nor integrated. If it is not modesty, I do not know what it is. A fabric of clichés that reeks of treason!

I also read the pamphlet *Lettres de rappelés* in which they asked some soldiers who had been discharged to give their opinion on Algeria, the Algerians, and pacification.[2] Poor soldiers and poor letters! Why do we need their opinion? Yes, in a way, I understand. To read it is to realize that the French will never be able to consider the Algerian Muslims as their equals. Like us, they know that Algeria is not France but, rather, the property of France, a very profitable property that must not be let go. This reading reveals that the only problem is the very presence of Muslims. You could call it a hitch. So what is to be done? If only they could get it in their heads that these good chaps—or nasty, as the case may be—are simply men; but complete men, as respectable and intelligent as any others. No, they do not want to entertain this idea because it does not fit the psychological profile of the army of pacification.

### January 25

I heard about Ak.'s arrest. The day before yesterday, at midnight, they went to his house, woke him up, and brought him back to the famous villa nearby. His brother says that they are accusing him of harboring people at his house, including a much sought after terrorist. I am aware that he has been providing shelter for as many of his relatives and friends as possible, so there is nothing surprising about the validity of the charge. Nothing surprising about poor Ak. taking risks for these people. How could he not do so? How can he be defended now? I mean, what kind of arguments can be used?

This is where the tragedy for the people of this country lies: two clans fighting to the death, while calling for the participation of Algerians who happen to belong to one or another clan, at least by birth. It is normal for the person at fault to wait for the help of his family and friends. But does not "help" imply that you are asking someone from the opposing clan to be your accomplice, to close his eyes, and to betray his own? Is this not tantamount to calling upon his generous and noble heart after you made a point of hurting him? There are no simple solutions to this kind of problem. It may be resolved when each individual candidly makes up his mind either to live as a Frenchman or die as an Arab. To choose the first is to risk dying as a traitor. The second option offers a remote possibility of survival and entry into Mohammed's paradise, where our fortunate neighbors have preceded us.

**January 30**

Salah reassured me that as a result of Ou.'s intervention, his brother will not be tortured but questioned routinely and, perhaps, let go. We will see. I hope that he did not do anything indiscreet.

I had a visit today from the young Ramd. He brought news about the violent clash that just happened at Aït Frah. There were many civilian casualties as well. One of the wounded, who was truly overcome by either panic or remorse, went to the army to ask for protection and began to blurt out everything he knew. So, thanks to him, they were able to find a cache containing documents, including a notebook with a list of everyone who had paid in and how much. Captain T. was elated to discover my name on the list and did not waste any time spreading it around Fort-National. However, the sum that he claims I paid is incorrect. I am ready to explain to him, if the occasion presents itself, exactly how things transpired. But, before I do that, I prefer that he tell me exactly what his buddies were coerced into paying, and what costs he is covering for those who are very close to him, and whom he protects, the better to use them.

I believe that this is the source of his resentment: he was not able to use me, and not only did I get clear of him, but he now has a strong sense that I do not want to depend on him. He is also aware that I have been my own man for a long time, and that I do not desire anything, except to see the end of this dreadful nightmare, bloodshed, and devastation. He is quite aware that I could either adjust to Algerian independence or choose to be French. But this decision is mine to make, and I will do so candidly in spite of all those captains or other cutthroats. I have made the choice, and it is nobody else's business.

What matters most for me and my children is peace, and the end of poverty, suffering, and crime. Above all, let there be an end to the grief of innocent people, an end to the blind hatred that lashes out at them. What matters is being able to live a decent life. Such a life would ensure that no one tramples on the dignity of their neighbor, that a man who seizes an inordinate amount of power no longer believes that he is your master. This man, your fellow man, would no longer be tempted to dispose of your life as he already disposed of your honor, to insult you, to bring you down to his level where he could get at your throat. My dear Mr. T., you are not worth much, and your head is where we should be looking for lice. Let us suppose for a minute that I want to get involved in the struggle and do so against you. Is this not the only way that I can fight you? You know that I am not involved, and yet you want me to join your side? Why would I join you and follow your orders? Is your cause just? Is your mind superior? Even if it were, why would I judge myself according to your standards rather than my own?

I can assure you that my peers quit asking themselves such questions a long time ago. With crushed spirits, they are waiting for peace of mind; they are waiting until it is their turn to "pay." You and your peers are keeping track. Who will be the first to present the bill? It is still anybody's game.

**February 9**

Ak. is in the hospital. He stayed three days at the villa and will probably spend three weeks or even three months in the hospital. Since no visitors are allowed, it is safe to say that he will go to prison when he leaves the hospital. What exactly are the charges against him? He must have gotten caught up in a chain of events: informing, torture, confessions . . . They told me that he supposedly tried to kill himself. Poor Ak. He does not really mean any harm. It is his kindness, especially his naïveté, that bothers me. I am angry at myself because I cannot help him.

The day before yesterday I had a visit from Captain Sau, who is a lot like "T."—but with more substance and more candor. We have been in contact since I began running a pedagogical organization that offers classes in a tent in a shantytown. He created the program and uses students as teachers. We quit talking about professional or administrative matters and moved onto politics. I found out that the prefect is looking for important Muslims for the Algiers municipal delegation. The captain told me that he put me down as number one on the list. He added that it was the least he could do.

Obviously, I knew that I deserved a place on this list, even first place. As far as this goes, I would rather be on the city of Algiers list than on the Fort-National list, where they would have undoubtedly considered it excessive to give me first place. This is vindication for all of Mr. T.'s attacks on my self-esteem.

As for accepting it, that is something else. This morning I discussed it much more openly with Mr. Christofini, an administrator. I am really not too sure about what role I would play in this kind of commission. My place is neither there nor anywhere else. I do not agree with any of the things that are going on: crime, torture, massacres, attacks, extortion, poverty, fear, shame, death. This is exactly what they are preparing to build on. I must either be the laborer or the builder's apprentice. It is better to be part of it and to build from the mortar of death. That way your conscience is clear.

Although I have nothing to say against this *loi-cadre*, I have even less to say for it. Nevertheless, people must accept it; certainly those who believe in paradise and who, while waiting to go, are living in hell. People will not give up paradise, and all the *loi-cadres* of the world have not the foggiest notion about it.

**March 3**

In addition to the *loi-cadre* vote, February has been a month marked by serious incidents on the border between Algeria and Tunisia, so serious, in fact, that nobody is talking about the *loi-cadre* — or at least — nobody believes in it any more. Constitutional reform "is at a dead end." The events on the border seem to have blocked everything else. First, there was the bombing of Sakiet, a small Tunisian village with an FLN training camp.[3] There were hundreds of civilian casualties, including women and children. Tunisia confined to their barracks the French troops stationed on Tunisian territory, demanded the evacuation of Bizerte, and filed a complaint with the Security Council. The army carrying out the operation is under the wing of the French government. The international press is, by and large, denouncing the scandal. The United States and Great Britain are offering their good offices, which have been accepted. The U.S. sent to Paris, via London and then Tunis, Mr. Murphy, whom the Algerians know quite well. For the moment, this is where things stand — perfectly ruined. Once again, they are declaring an impasse. The French media are beginning to question the idea of pacification, recalling, once again, mistakes that were made in Indochina. They are becoming increasingly pessimistic about the future of French Africa at a time when American lenders are enforcing a strict audit of France's treasury department. People are looking openly to de Gaulle, whose long silhouette outlines the horizon. It is as if this fabled pilot is the only one capable of saving this ship in distress.

Everything is happening on center stage and in broad daylight. But let us not forget about the events taking place offstage, in dark labyrinths and deep tunnels where you see nothing, hear nothing, where terror's powerful pincers grab you by the throat, and where that desperate, superhuman cry that might save your soul while you offer up your body is pulled back into your gut. With both soul and body destroyed, you return to that nothingness you should have never left. It is almost two years since the people from back home dove into a similar kind of deep tunnel. With no more hope than people condemned by the apocalypse, they sink deeper and deeper every day.

During a bloody battle, the soldiers brought back the bodies of about thirty rebels, which the people of Tizi must have thrown, at night, into a large trench they had dug in a hurry. They say that the dead included three or four people from the village—Kaci's brother Hocine and the famous "Canard" who, after living through the last few months of power and excitement, will sleep peacefully. At Taourirt, young women brought up cadavers from the ravines in order to give them a decent burial. Ak.'s brother Ramdane was killed at Taza, and we assume that Ak., who was arrested, tortured, and hospitalized, eventually got out—only to be taken God knows where. I heard that the community at Béni-Raten is literally starving. The families who left the douar had to return, at least the women and old people, in order to enable the roving rebels to find food and lodging. The maquis, now better armed and more numerous, are still enforcing the harsh punishment of hanging and cutting throats. The soldiers of pacification are hitting harder and harder, with less and less discrimination and pity. The clearest result of all this is, I believe, planting a definitive hatred for the French in the hearts of the Kabyles. These French refuse to realize this and seem to forget the evil they sow at the very moment when, after finishing one strike, they are already preparing to deal other blows.

## 1958

### April 1

It has been a month since I last opened this notebook in which, for three years, I have made a practice of writing about my anxiety or my confusion, my pain and my anger. In truth, I believe that I have said and rehashed absolutely everything about the subject. What good does it do to repeat and reframe the same matters one more time? What else has happened during this past month of war except what could have happened during other months? I am overwhelmed, and I live here as though in another world; far away from our tiny villages whose echoes no longer reach me; far from the nearby Muslim city from which I am totally estranged; far from the European city where both lethargy and agitation are rampant due to the onset of a calm that everyone thinks is deceptive and full of nasty surprises— tears and mourning—and lastly, far from the state of political turmoil in which making deals, lying, and madness seem to be the normal expression of man's nobility.

Since they arrested Ak.—now in a camp and out of danger —I have not had any contact with my family. Friends no longer think about friends. Perhaps they are accusing one another, mutually and secretly, of being cowards or traitors. What do I know?

E. Roblès comes over to chat with me whenever he can get away. For his part, he no longer sees anyone, and despite his rather optimistic disposition, he is as discouraged as I am.

This evening we took a walk around Algiers. By chance, we ran into Camus, who seemed happy to see me and whom I may perhaps see again. I enjoy talking with him well enough, and I think he feels the same.

### April 3

Titi sent me some news from back home. If you can call it news. It is all stuff that I know. There are no young people left in the village. The men and women who have stayed on live in a perpetual state of terror that has become bearable. The men have taken on a haggard look, one they will have until the end of their days. They have lost, my sister told me, all their arrogance as well as their superiority complex regarding women. They flaunt their weak and cowardly side so unconsciously that they give the impression of being relieved, even pleased, about their condition. Everyone has gotten used to speaking softly, holding a finger to their lips. As a general rule, it is expedient, acceptable, and advisable to marvel at "our brothers' " exploits. You must never doubt their invincible courage, nor the cowardliness of French soldiers who fall to the ground like chestnuts when the northerly winds blow across our region. Given this situation, you must trust no one, because words misunderstood are oftentimes words misinterpreted. You can never foresee the problems that might follow. Once and for all, you must convince yourself that "the brothers" are powerful, infallible, and rigid, and as inflexible as the law of retaliation for a pound of flesh. Can anyone assure you that the soldier who calls you over, the officer who questions you, or the SAS captain is not in collusion with them? My poor sister, who has been deeply affected by it all, lowers her voice, asks if anyone outside can hear her, calms down, and gets up the courage to speak ill of someone. Once she lashes out, just try to stop this barrage of words, suddenly accelerating like a rebellious, chaotic, and continuous cry, like an abscess that bursts, like a somber sky that suddenly purges itself in a blaze of anger.

Everybody knows that "the brothers" are not infallible nor courageous nor heroic. Everyone also recognizes that they are sadists and hypocrites. They can only offer death, and yet everything must be given to them; they continuously extort, appropriate, and destroy; they never quit preaching about religion, prohibiting everything that they normally prohibit, and whatever else it might please them to prohibit. We have no choice but to call them "brothers" and worship them like gods. But when one of them becomes deceitful and begins to denounce his hosts, we must waste no time forgetting this false brother. We must not, however, begrudge the others nor quibble over his support. We need everyone's support. At the moment, women are tending to the wounded, carrying them on their backs when there is an air-raid warning, burying the dead, collecting money, and standing guard. Since the rebels started mobilizing women, the soldiers are beginning to arrest and torture them.

Perhaps a new world is being constructed out of ruins, a world where women will be wearing pants, literally and figuratively, a world where what remains of the old traditions that adhere to the inviolability of women, both literally and figuratively, will be viewed as a nuisance and swept away.

This constitutes a form of brilliant revenge for all those peaceful attempts at emancipation that were generally resisted and not at all helpful for the unfortunate woman on the road to liberty. Tomorrow, the women of Algeria will no longer have any reason to envy other women, except, perhaps, education.

But in the interim, women must participate in the unfair fights, torture, suffering, and mourning that wretches have been piling on the country. These same wretches are the ones who want to pay such a high price for an illusory and problematical happiness. They are the ones who hold the reins of government and yet refuse to consider any sensible solutions. They are the privileged who are not willing to let go of their privileges, the ambitious who want to scale mountains of cadavers and who would be ready to pay for their wonderful paradise with the incomparable hell of others.

It sometimes happens that some poor fellow's nerves suddenly snap, and as he becomes submerged in a state of lucid madness, he begins to talk and talk and talk. At the djemaâ, in the cafés—everywhere—he says exactly what he thinks about "his brothers." The people watching him become alarmed and feel sorry for him. They know that it is futile to try and stop him. If they enjoy listening to him, it is because, in a sense, he reads his words from their hearts. He talks, they listen to him and then, in a gloomy state, return to their homes, while he goes off to talk somewhere else. No, it will not last long. One fine morning, he disappears. God has his soul now. One week, a fortnight, one month later, they find him in the bush, disfigured, half eaten by jackals or hanging from a tree, his eyes gouged out, an ironic grin on his face. At the djemaâ they sneer, saying that he deserved his rope. The leader of the terrorists courteously provides the details of the lynching. Then they denounce his great sins and place him among the ranks of traitors whose deaths are the sole means of erasing the village's shame.

Who would have said one day that Mohand Ouamer, seventy-five years old, and "Dangereux," thirty years old, would be heroes? And there are surely others from all over the place who knew the risk and calmly accepted it.

The sheer number of individual dramas and obscure, gratuitous murders not only provokes a clear rejection of violence but also confirms human dignity. Those accused of treason who die as traitors are neither worse nor better than the heroes. The traitors have no more liking for the soldier, the Frenchman, or France than the heroes. This is because our cup, now filled to overflowing with humiliation, has been filled indiscriminately by the caravans of "masters" who passed through. And the nameless terrors that have settled into our hearts are inspired by the same wild beast whose persistent cruelty can take, turn upon turn, one face and then another.

Harmless boys who are forced into the maquis—which is equivalent to being forced into suicide—suffer an equally stupid death. They start off by standing guard; then, through no choice of their own, they start acting like terrorists. They start fighting, commit a blunder, and begin to run away from the soldiers; they live in the fields near the village; in the end they become guilty of civil disobedience, of being downright outlaws. And so one day the ALN, in a spirit of benevolence, hands them an old gun, with the obvious intention of having it recovered one day by French soldiers who will include one more armed and dead fellagha on their tally sheet. These kids are ripe to kill themselves, having experienced the unspeakable terror of a hunted animal.

### April 11

Camus came yesterday. We spent two hours just talking very openly. I felt immediately as comfortable with him as I do with E. Roblès. With the same brotherly warmth, he pokes fun at mannerisms. His position on events is exactly as I thought it would be—incredibly human. He feels tremendous pity for those who are suffering. But he also knows that pity or love is impotent, completely powerless to overcome the evil that kills, that destroys, and that would like to wipe everything out and create a new world where the timid and the skeptical are banished along with all cowardly enemies of the New or the Old Truth rehabilitated by submachine guns, contempt, and hatred.

### April 18

A few minutes after Camus left, a horrible drama unfolded at the home of my friend, E. R. My poor friend, his poor kid.[4] This drama had nothing to do with current events, but isn't everything related to current events these days? It seems that even the serene skies of Algeria have become more troubled, the elements more capricious. The trepidation and anxiety besieging the rural population have now reached the cities, where everyone fears for the future. As all efforts lead them toward a government crisis, the French see an inevitable foreign intervention appearing on the horizon. This will put an end to their insufferable pride, crimes, and atrocities. The final hour seems genuinely to be approaching and promises much blood and destruction. After this moment, what will the future hold?

I received Henri Alleg's pamphlet.[5] This young man should be congratulated. Nothing he writes is fabricated. Everyone is aware of the torture sessions. What would be interesting to know would be his reactions as well as others'. Real heroes, worthy of admiration! Lads of this caliber will be able to rebuild the world and, first and foremost, "build a new Algeria."

**April 23**

I saw young B., who is getting ready to leave school to join the fight. He came to ask my advice and, above all, to proudly announce his departure. I told him that I was against violence, even the fellagha's violence, and that I would be heartbroken to see one of my former students who was aware of my feelings on the subject being callous enough to kill. At that point, I did not want to delve into the problem, so I talked to him as I would my own son.

He also admitted his disappointment and disillusion with the attitude of certain members of the maquis who indulge in all sorts of unacceptable and excessive behavior in the villages. He believes that it is time to restore some sense of order. It is evident that the boy has a deep understanding of the situation. Even so, he has not yet understood that all participants in the struggle are men and that our men are, for the most part, uneducated . . .

I also saw Mrs. F., who still feels nostalgic for Fort-National and will not allow herself to forget the happiness of the past. She informed me that there had been little change in the situation in Kabylia, except for the worse. "The split is getting deeper and deeper; the Muslim employees are leaving the government offices in droves; the people are no longer getting any supplies; dozens upon dozens of men are dying every day for one reason or another . . ." But the idea of living somewhere besides this country does not even occur to her. "We will end up getting quite used to insecurity." Now there is a real Algerian woman for you, or I do not know what I am talking about! Mrs. F. personifies quite well the gambler used to winning who one day, on the contrary, begins to lose and yet continues to play because it is his destiny. So why would all the French in Algeria not accept defeat, albeit a momentary one? Because we have been speculating in vain for a hundred years. If only they could accept it, all the horror would stop in an instant. I can predict for the French of Algeria that not much time would pass before they were victorious again because, in the last analysis, these people are skilled. This, above all, will count on the day they face our "uncultured" masses.

Lastly, I saw the journalist C. R., who just returned from Tunisia, where he was received by Bourguiba. I asked him for an update on the Tunisians' economical and social situation. He told me that the crisis, which the press had magnified to an extreme, was barely perceptible. Bourguiba does not bear any resemblance to a dictator. The Tunisians seem happier—their demeanor, that is—than they have ever been since the Protectorate. As for the "fellagha" who supposedly have the country in hand, it is Mr. R.'s impression that they have been eclipsed and are being as cautious as possible. He did not see one of them in uniform, not even near the border.

**May 13**

The lengthy crisis in the government regarding the succession of the Gaillard cabinet has finally provoked a rebellion among the French in Algeria, and the army has seized power in Algiers. Today, a huge demonstration took place from 1:00 on. At 6:30 P.M., protesters began occupying the GG.[6] Most of my French colleagues ignored the order for a general strike put forth by a Vigilance Committee (comité de Vigilance). I was moved by their gesture. Those who did not come, all of them women, were able to phone up and use the excuse that public transportation had been shut down. My children had trouble getting back at 1:00; so they spent the afternoon at home. All the shops in town are closed.

**May 14**

Revolution is in the air: people have barricaded their homes; protesters are moving along the large thoroughfares of the city; stores are closed. The radio is talking about a Committee of Public Safety (comité de Salut public), which has taken over everything, has occupied the GG and is controlling broadcasting. The newspapers are publishing large-scale photos and close-ups. It appears that none of this is directed at the Muslim population, which fears the worst. The notorious committee is demanding compliance.

Evening: Radio Luxembourg is claiming that Paris is still in control of the situation and that the generals are following orders—call it a delegation of power. In Paris, Lacoste says that he is washing his hands of the matter. The new rebels are being judged harshly by the international community. The general impression is that nothing good will come of this situation for France and the Republic. In Algiers, Massu has been appointed to take charge. In Paris, it is de Gaulle, and in the meantime, the Left "is trying to save democracy."

The whole thing was set off by the national homage paid to three military prisoners of the FLN, condemned to death by the FLN. For France, this constituted a "cowardly assassination by cutthroats in complicity with Bourguiba." Once the dead had been honored, we had to shout aloud that we did not want anything to do with a government that was going to sell out and prepare a diplomatic "Dien Bien Phu." The protesters waited until Pflimlin had been voted in. Then they created their own Committee of Public Safety in order to demand the dismissal of this defeatist government. The committee must have had inside information in order to decide that Pflimlin was getting ready to abandon them.

In essence, the Algerian war will be a very hard blow for France and perhaps a mortal blow to the Republic. Afterward, this same misfortune will provide an effective remedy for Algeria and its people. For is it not fairly common that the patient finds relief only by the very remedies that kill him? Have we come to this?

**May 18**

Mr. Soustelle arrived in Algiers yesterday afternoon. The reason: more demonstrations. The forum, the GG, and the main thoroughfares of Algiers have been jammed with people for four days. The Muslims are being pampered and coddled, especially the protesters. I saw some dregs from the Maison-Carrée or somewhere else pass by, while a bunch of idlers cheered them on. Cars decked out in flags honked their horns in a frenzy: "French Algeria! French Algeria!" The general euphoria is bordering on hysteria. This is truly a Franco-Muslim community, in a state of hysteria. But, behind this mob, one less impressive than is generally assumed, there is another mixed group that people refuse to take seriously, another silent group that remains perfectly calm and that is delighted with this masquerade. Truly, this revolution cannot be taken seriously. It would be a mistake for those in Paris to give up, unless, as usual, this is part of a predetermined agenda.

The way things stand, all Algerians would accept any radical remedy that might rid the country of its misery, any real solution to this problem which has yet to be solved. This would include those Algerians who persist in shouting out their bogus satisfaction while rigidly clinging to an arrogance that is now irrelevant.

**August 15**

For three months, France has been calling for de Gaulle to take over. A new constitution has been written up and will be voted on in a referendum on September 28. In general terms, the Executive Branch is going to monopolize the wheels of the "public machine," a sine qua non for national recovery. Another equally necessary condition of the same reform process is the definitive annexation of Algeria and the Sahara. It was not that long ago that people did not talk about the Sahara, since it was implicitly part of Algeria. Now there is Algeria, there is the Sahara, and there is also "Algeria and the Sahara."

Good God, knowing that "miracle men" do exist, why have they waited so long to summon de Gaulle? Why has there been so much blood spilled, so much suffering, so many tears? So, there you have it: suddenly, a big revolution erupts in Algeria and in France. A new regime moves in, denounces the old "system" of government, claims to be victorious and capable of solving everything, and finally begins by declaring that everything is over—the revolt, the FLN, and France's departure from Algeria. This has all happened without anyone knowing exactly how—the sole reason being that people decided that it could not be otherwise. Algerian nationalism? It does not exist any more. Integration? It is already in place. So you are French, old man, nothing else. Quit bothering us. That is it.

The FLN does not want this referendum and has started a wave of terrorism in France. This is impressive and specifically designed to be so. Moreover, it goes hand in hand with a ruthless squaring of accounts.

The campaign for the new constitution is now open. It seems that the "yes" vote is heavily slated to win. As for the fate of Algeria, this constitution gives rise to diverse interpretations, and, as usual, people will choose the one that satisfies their desires. My God, when is all this going to end? I am quite concerned that this atmosphere of fear, suspicion, insecurity, and anxiety will eventually become the common fate of future generations, who will become inured to living in a constant state of alarm. Perhaps this will encompass the entire human race; a normal situation; a return to the vulnerability of the "cave men," and beyond this, the diabolical consciousness and science of men at the height of progress. Or better yet, the indomitable mushroom, which will destroy our planet as well as any we might inhabit.

All of this distances me from both my smaller, immediate worries and the voting offices at Clos Salembier or anywhere else. What made me think about all this are the explosions that are lighting up a good part of the world: Iraq, Iran, Lebanon, Cyprus, China . . . I can imagine the alchemists of the planet—bearded, dressed in black, delivering pedantic speeches about peace and hope while slyly preparing to vaporize us and themselves as well.

### September 16

Yesterday in Paris there was an assassination attempt on Mr. Soustelle. The electoral campaign that says "yes" to de Gaulle is now open and seems to be progressing peacefully. Unable to create a coalition, the "no" voters are clearly in the minority. The "yes" voters, who get on just as poorly, are interpreting the ambiguities in the constitution to fit their needs. In Algeria, the constitution means integration for some and independence for others. The FLN and the PC have called for people to abstain from voting and are threatening anyone who plans on helping the "colonialist's referendum."[7] Several black African countries have decided to opt for freedom, and prominent journalists are generally asserting that the colonialist era is indeed over. The French are beginning to accept the idea of losing their colonies. To get this far has required countless lives and rivers of blood. In France, FLN terrorism is conspicuously on the rise in spite of extremely harsh, protective, and repressive measures whose use is unprecedented in democratic countries. When the French have to contend with death, torture, and camps on their own soil, they may perhaps understand that Algerians are, to be sure, savage assassins but without a doubt are patriots as well. When this day comes, perhaps the Mediterranean will no longer flow through France the way the Seine flows through Paris. The Algerians will see that it is not enough to have their own country or to be recognized as independent in order to enter the paradise of their dreams. Surely, many of them will be surprised one day to find that they miss their hell. But, in the end, each person's dignity will be saved. And this is what matters most.

### September 20

The FLN government is being formed in Cairo. Today's

papers identify those involved. *Le Monde* has published slightly ironic biographies of the ministers. In general, this coverage is considered an embarrassing response to the next referendum, which is being contested in advance by the FLN and all of the Arab states. The "yes" campaign is now in full swing; and all of the great supporters of integration—or rather the status quo—are succeeding one another in Algeria like "grand puppets" on a vast stage. It is enough to read the speech given by Bidault yesterday in Algiers to be convinced that the French have absolutely no intention of changing. I am wondering if the army is not, after all, the biggest dupe in this whole sad affair that began on the 13th of May. Once de Gaulle has the immense approval he is calling for, will he know how to bring the reactionaries to their senses, or will he be content to refuse the independence that Algerians have been seeking and dying for each day with fierce simplicity? They may say what they want about pacification—the Muslims who supported it will be the first to disown it. Even if there were some sincere people in this group—undoubtedly there would be many—pay no mind to them; they would follow the reactionaries and settle in France. I think that this country would give them the same welcome as its own children. It might be possible, then, that these thousands and thousands of ties that have been forged during the century between individuals of both races would work for the communities. Death, bitterness, and hatred would then be forgotten; and this would result in a true reconciliation between two peoples who have shared a long and intricate past. In the same way that one refuses to be duped, wisdom will reject integration and grant independence in order to defeat all the follies, rectify all the mistakes, erase all the crimes. De Gaulle is a wise man. That is what I think.

**September 27**

This evening, some paratroopers and village policemen came to search the premises. They opened all the closets, inspected stoves, cabinets, every nook and cranny. It lasted an hour and a half. Then I turned in all the keys to the school, which will be occupied until tomorrow evening. I managed to state that it was more common to speak to the son of the concierge (a pied-noir) since he had more authority than I did. They were especially intent on discovering some spot they imagined I wanted to conceal. So I remained cool and refused to accompany them.

In Algiers the CPS [Committee of Public Safety] is bracing itself, getting ready to seize power in the event that de Gaulle refuses integration. The provisional Algerian government, on the other hand, is consolidating its structure, gaining recognition from a number of countries, and offering to negotiate independence with France.

Several journalists are already traveling all around Algeria to report on the election process. Everyone agrees that the voting will take place in normal fashion, without fraud or obvious pressure. The problem is that all the Muslims are so afraid their vote will not be anonymous that they apparently will all vote "yes." I am not convinced that their fears are not justified. Besides, this is not a fear, an obscure, deep and irrational terror, the most basic survival instinct. This is our common condition. We are all Algerian Muslim civilians, all candidates awaiting redemption through independence. We have all paid a great price for having the impudence to hope, and all we have left is the desire to live.

**September 28, 4:00 P.M.**

Since this morning there has been a continuous parade of men and women filing by on their way to vote "yes." It does not seem that a "no" vote is even an option. There has been absolutely no constraint, and monitoring has slackened off since the inspection commissions, village policemen, and other paratroopers discovered the sheeplike docility of the pathetic Muslim electorate. The "no" votes are deep purple with very light blue envelopes; but you have to fold the ballot to slip it in. If you go about it right, you can vote "no," and the commission will not see a thing. Those supervising the polls are cordial, yet cynical. They know that you are voting yes so they presumptuously lift the corner of the envelope, take it from your hands, and slip it into the ballot-box. Without wasting any time, they give the correct ballot, rather than the other, back to you. Since the client agrees with the cashier, everything goes as well as possible in spite of some pushing and pulling. It was the same scenario when I went to vote at the Arcades, the same easygoing manner, the same boredom. The leaders' sense of enjoyment was the same — serious and subdued. The client's psychological attitude appeared to be the following: "Everybody is voting yes, so why should I sacrifice myself by voting no?" What sacrifice? Once again, everybody is convinced that he is being specifically monitored, that they are trying to find out how he voted, just him, so that he can be reprimanded without delay. This is exactly what I was thinking about yesterday: everyone was panic-stricken.

Those who might have the presence of mind to take advantage of the bedlam and vote no—if it is in their hearts—are indeed rare. It remains to be seen if the control commission will notice any of this.

9:00 PM. I must point out that the commission will eventually understand the exuberant joy of the non-Muslim population. This has to be said in the typically passive tone—whether imposed or not—of the Muslim voter. I am talking about a real and profound joy, an equally moving and demonstrative joy that the non-Muslims experience in relation to the Muslims. Even the most humble and sensitive of Muslims—that is, the women—have been truly won over by this sincere friendship, these affectionate looks, these tender and fawning gestures enveloping them. There is no hypocrisy on either side, but a real sense of brotherhood; built on trickery and lies, and protected by machine-guns pointed in every direction. In an hour, the polls will be closed. At first terrified and then mystified, Algeria will be done voting. Perhaps, at the very least, something good will come out of this "historical day." If nothing else, shouldn't this be the end of pointless killing?

**September 29**

People seem sad and quiet. There is no longer any activity in the little square, and very few people are in the streets. It is as if this purely Arab neighborhood were immersed in a state of mourning. Pedestrians slip away to burrow in at home. I think they are feeling guilty about what they did yesterday. I talked to some people who told me with a straight face that they felt intimidated and that their viewpoint had not changed. They are die-hard Muslims, meaning nationalists. Maybe it is remorse, or possibly the desire to put on a show, that makes them talk. Too late, poor folks, the radio is exultant, and so are the newspapers. You made a choice; you voted, and "voted well."

**October 2**

I found out that, on the eve of the elections, some soldiers killed three fellows at Tizi-Hibel. Yet, the next day, everybody from my region voted.

Here, I suspect that people are, above all, tired of war and ready to accept almost anything, provided there is peace. I am talking about the Muslims. Motivated by their success, the non-Muslims can manage for quite a while longer. They no longer doubt victory.

Larabi, another source, has informed me of Captain T.'s

departure from Fort-National and the kidnapping of Kaci A.[8] This last bit of news has deeply saddened me. But finding out that an individual who has done a lot of damage is leaving has helped to make up for it.

**November 1**

Yesterday, at about 7:00 P.M., I had a phone call from my colleague Bekri.

—Hello! Is it really you?—Yes?—I want to see you. I have not seen you in a hundred years.—But I saw you.—Where?— In Algiers. Not long ago.—Listen, can we see you?—Without binoculars.—I will not be alone.—Ah, who will be with you? —Azem Ouali, for instance.—Good, come over.—Aren't you afraid?—No!—Wait . . . *A whispered discussion, then consent.*— So, you cannot come, naturally.—Naturally!—Don't you have a car?—No, I do not have a car.—Listen . . . *A whispered discussion.*—By the way?—Yes.—Okay, we will come up. We will be at your house in a quarter to a half hour.—I am waiting for you in my office.

At 8:00 P.M., Bekri came over, a captain by his side.

—Do not be afraid. We did not come to arrest you.

—Come in, gentlemen.

—Captain Citerne, from Agouni-Gueghrane. Please excuse us, Mr. Azem was not able to accompany us. It concerns security. Do you understand?

—Yes, I understand. Let us go into my office. What can I do for you?

I already knew what was going on. Why was Bekri trying to intimidate me? In any case, I do not give a damn about his Captain Citerne. A charming captain, at any rate. Good-looking kid, very relaxed, direct, simple. He seems to me to be a bit of a braggart. First, he says that he knows the Kabyles better than they know themselves, to the point where he is now more Kabyle than F. Yet he admits that he owes the first contact, if you can call it that, to all of my books, which he really enjoyed. A half-hour later, he must have realized that he had not really read much and eagerly demanded my latest work without even knowing the title.

—I am more of a Kabyle than yourself. The fact that you left the country and that I have been living here for three years speaks for itself. Three years is an incredible amount of time to live in the heart of a village surrounded by mountains with a bunch of savages. Yes, that is right, savages. I have managed to become familiar with the very depths of their psychology, their secrets, their appetites, their lives, their defects. You cannot imagine . . . I also have some friends there, real friends. Like Bekri, for instance. Poor Kaci, I am your friend. I saved your life.

—Oh, of course, I am eternally grateful and proud to be your friend.

In that instant, my bitterness towards Bekri changed into a feeling of immense pity. So when he confessed, a few minutes later, that they were here because of him and that he was the one who had thought of me—totally out of friendship—I did not get angry at him. Smiling at him with affection and sadness, I just shook my head.

—No, Captain, you are mistaken. I do not want to be a deputy. I want nothing to do with politics. I will never be a part of that. It is not for me.

—So, Kaci, you lied to me.

—No, Captain. I assure you that this is what I was told. They said he had every intention of running for election. So I suggested his name. Azem thought that it was an interesting idea. Imagine F. with Azem—that could go somewhere. I did what I could.

—But, my dear Kaci, you did not do anything, I said. You should have seen me first, consulted with me. And you think that you know me!

Yes, I was deeply shocked by the captain's arrogance when it came to Bekri. He used to put down all of his people, tell stories in which bastards mixed with traitors and cowards and in which he played the role of the magic reformer, the peacemaker, second to none except God. Bekri withdrew, made himself inconspicuous. The captain even tried using his familiar and brutal methods on me, along with his annoying display of arrogance.

—I have not come to see either the writer or the school principal but the Kabyle. Now you should be courageous enough to choose publicly, to rally your people around you. That is what you should do.

—For myself, courage means saying what you think. I have not neglected this sentiment, which is also a duty.

—You must do more. Writers are also political, at least some writers.

—Yes, a few writers. When they want to be. As for myself, I do not enjoy politics.

—For you, it is not a question of pleasure; your people are suffering.

—I cannot do anything about that. My standing for office will not change a thing.

—That is not my opinion.

—It is mine.

Then we talked about other things. About his military action in Kabylia. To tell the truth, I listened to him talk. He thought himself flawless, and I did not object.

To avoid upsetting him, I had to promise to meet him that morning with Azem, just to "discuss" the matter. But, I knew that I would not be going to that rendezvous. So this morning, at 8:00, I called him and told him not to expect me.

—Yesterday, I told him, among other things, I did not want to provoke you in front of Bekri or give him the impression that he was disturbing you unnecessarily.

—That is a shame, he answered (into the phone).

—I apologize. I have got a lot to do today.

—We will save it for another time.

—Okay.

**November 2**

I heard that the SAS captain stationed in Béni-Douala paid tribute to me at Tizi-Hibel. He supposedly said that France is proud of me, and that my village would be spared in spite of the residents' hostility.

This caused Kaci, the famous political commissioner from the area, to become deeply upset.[9] He went to my elderly parents to express his discontent. Apparently, my sisters and my parents are living on pins and needles, waiting for the FLN to condemn and execute me. This is how things stand for us. Kaci was at school with me, but he never got beyond the elementary level. He is a very audacious boy who is neither honorable nor honest. Kaci is known in our village for causing all sorts of problems. He reproaches me as well for never paying the rebel taxes. What he is really complaining about and objecting to is that I exist. And that really annoys him. I think that it will continue to annoy him until he dies. What troubles me is that I cannot do anything to reassure my parents.

**December 9**

My father died November 1, or more precisely about 8:00 the night before. He was dying at the very moment that Captain Citerne was holding forth in my office. Nobody notified me because, in Algeria on November 1st, there was a general strike commemorating the anniversary of the "Algerian Revolution." On this day it would be illegal to go to Tagt in order to telephone the children of the deceased. So the people of the village buried my father. Afterward, no one thought of informing us. No one? Well, one person did, after all. The SAS captain stationed in Béni-Douala sent me an extremely kind telegram, and for that I thank him from the bottom of my heart. "Learned of your father's death. Please accept my sincere condolences. Am completely at your service for whatever you might need." It goes without saying that one does not forget this kind of gesture, that it wipes away many grievances. I tell myself that perhaps he did not want to compromise me by talking about me in the villages. Maybe he was only estimating what he could give me as an example of what the French school system was capable of producing here. How can I be angry with him, even if it costs me dearly? In short, it was undoubtedly his way of calling me to account. In the name of France. But, ethically, does he have the right to do this? Is this good psychology? I do not think so. Are there more drawbacks than advantages in this for me? I think this is the case. So as Diderot said, this is wrong.[10] But I forgive him. His telegram saved my life.

The trip was depressing, and I remember all of the minor details. In spite of a few checkpoints that were only slightly annoying, everything went well until I got to Tizi-Ouzou.

Afterward, I had to take a taxi, go through the *oued* and then climb the remaining six miles before getting to the village just before dark.[11] The checkpoint in the *oued* was the most critical. I had my gun loaded. It was in the middle of the countryside, and the soldiers who stopped us were aggressive and suspicious. Just when they were about to grab my briefcase and discover my weapon, I showed them the telegram, and they loosened up. They released us right away. Up until that point they had calmly examined all my other papers, and it seemed to me that as they continued to check, they were becoming more and more angry. Without this telegram I was a rebel commander, and my brother, the chauffeur, and I were going to die. The spot was completely deserted and clouded over by eucalyptus trees, and the sound of gunfire would have been virtually inaudible. They would have returned to Tizi-Ouzou with my gun as a trophy.

On our way up to the village, we saw the fire's devastating effect on the fig and olive gardens. We encountered women, only women, returning from the fields. The village of Takrat was empty, with the doors to houses left wide open. I remembered the abandonned villages in the Alps that Giono talks about. But here it is power, rather than progress, that drove the residents away.

At Taourirt-Moussa I saw my former school from a distance, which—by chance—escaped being destroyed in the fire set by the rebels. My preference would have been to see the school burned down, rather than empty and abused by kids, who wanted to get even for all the arrogance it instills. We passed through the village escorted by all the women who knew us and wanted to save us from the army. How could they protect us? Everybody knows that the military does not shoot when there are women around. On the other hand, if they encounter men by themselves . . . As it happened, there were soldiers at the opposite end of the village. So we had to wait for them to leave, and we thanked the women for their kindness. In the village, the women openly took the places left vacant by the men. This is something that gives them a lot of confidence and even insolence. All one has to do to be aware of their suffering is to look at their clothing and their overwrought expressions. Dilapidated houses, here and there. We were just a mile from our village and hastened to return home.

The school in our village was occupied by the rebels. While two young strangers stared and laughed at us, we chatted with the head terrorist from Agouni. To tell the truth, they were smiling not at me but at my brother, and this is how I realized that if the SAS was speaking well of me, the others must really dislike me . . . Nevertheless, they did not become hostile at all, and I began to feel sympathy for the guy across from me who was really young, blond, and thin. He looked like a schoolboy on vacation, a totally harmless type who lowered his blue eyes shyly the minute I looked at him.

It goes without saying that my mother and my sister welcomed us with tears. But these tears were for me, and not for the old man. The villagers assessed the situation, and it was certain that the old man had to leave. As for me, I am the one who walked boldly into this trap; I was the one who my mother whispered all of her fears to while we climbed the last short, steep rise up to the house.

The people from the neighborhood had a half-hour to

come and greet us before the curfew. All of them insisted on coming. I realized that they valued me much more than they had my father. So the captain's pronouncements were indeed futile. They knew that I was one of them and that I had never betrayed them. Some of them were, of course, disgruntled that my name had been used against them. But all of them knew that I could not do anything about this and that I did not approve.

I spoke extensively with my sisters, sisters-in-law, and cousins. There is large-scale poverty in the country. Along with the harsh restrictions initiated by the military, the rebels are ruthless in their demand for taxes. None of this includes the kind of blind power wielded by the army—which tramples, dishonors, wounds, and kills—or by the vindictive and tyrannical power used by the terrorists to abuse, humiliate, and hang people.

Overall, the French are committing a grave injustice either out of ignorance or to further their own supreme interests. People are ready to suffer this unavoidable hurt because it comes from the adversary, the enemy, the one they are fleeing, the one on which they must turn their backs. The harm inflicted by the freedom fighters originates in their claim that the freedom they have granted themselves must first be exercised on the people. The contradiction arises when the freedom fighters make the people feel as if they are still enslaved, while they themselves are free. Alas! They are not only enslaved but terrorized. Nevertheless, their anger, like their despair, is immense.

Yet this does not mean that they miss the *ancien régime*. They know that they broke their alliance with the French, and they stand ready to accept another destiny. The difference is that they have less illusions about this destiny. Do they have any regrets? Who knows? Even they do not know. The only things the good people of this country know how to do are to obey those who are the most powerful, admire them, give them everything, even your life—provided that they are indeed the most powerful.

**December 22**

I am returning from Paris today. "Official Representative" from the 13th to the 20th. In fact, had an offer from Mr. Brouilley to work at the Quai d'Orsay. Met with Mr. Vimont in that particular government ministry. I turned them down. Was sent to the Présidence du Conseil, where I chatted with a nice girl who put me at ease. It was Geneviève de Gaulle. She had Germaine Tillion extend me an invitation. Saw Malraux briefly. I was immediately made a member of the Haut Comité de la Jeunesse, where I shook hands with de Gaulle. Met Kadd. Both of us signed a petition asking for the pardon of 150 people sentenced to death. On rue de Lille, saw Alquier, a lieutenant of the SAS who wrote a book on which I have commented in my notebooks. He told me that Soustelle would like to see me. But I do not want to see him. Saw the entire Seuil group, with Roblès and Nouelle. Everybody that I met knew that I was neither French nor someone who could be integrated. For them, it was enough that I was myself, and they are hoping that there are many Muslim Algerians like me. I would have liked to have told them that there is indeed a resemblance between myself, the Algerians, and the Europeans, if only to point out the absurdity of this war which France insists on prolonging.

### December 28, 5:00

A grenade just exploded right below the school in a Moorish café. Ten minutes later, I saw people running away in terror, and I went down. One poor fellow was lying on the sidewalk, the waxen color of death already upon him. He was opening and closing his mouth like an automaton as death, exceedingly slow, kept whirling around us as if it were feeling slightly repulsed at seizing this innocent victim. He was big, a little stocky, meticulously dressed in a white shirt with a large, blood-pink flower, the flaps of his beige coat were open, his feet and hands were relaxed, loose, indifferent. There was nothing left but this mouth opening and closing itself . . .

Further away, in the middle of the road, another body was swimming in a pool of dirtier, almost black blood. This one had his head cracked open on the ground and one arm completely bent around his back with his legs doubled up. Perhaps he had knelt down before totally collapsing and now his joints were refusing to cooperate. He, too, was clinging to life.

A car took away a wounded man whom I believe I know. I only saw his back. On my way down, I passed another one of the wounded. I did not see even a drop of blood on him, but he was holding his left arm with his right, screaming and walking at the same time. He had the look and desperate voice of an unlucky secondhand dealer who hopelessly holds up an old suit.

An hour later, the police, the soldiers, and the ambulances arrived, and everything quickly became solemn, stiff, and terrifying. Curious bystanders backed away out of respect or disappeared completely. Women left their terraces, and people in cars were gradually permitted to move on. The affair became official and took on its true identity: I just witnessed a terrorist bombing killing a few people and wounding a few others in a Moorish café frequented by Muslims.

# 19**59**

**February 29, 1959**

Back home. Kaci has been eliminated in his turn. It seems he was embezzling funds. It has been four years since he joined the maquis. Both of his brothers have stayed. But that did not save him. It is true that he was not worth much. Neither were his brothers. Apparently, those who regard the lives of others so cheaply are, sooner or later, repaid in kind. Tragic times and tragic Kabylia. Tragic because every day traitors are discovered, then put to death; and those who kill them also end up dead. People are talking a lot about the network of undercover agents that almost rallied all of Kabylia last June. It is absolutely certain that the maquis were infiltrated, and this explains their lack of success and the drastic cuts that the army was able to inflict each time; in every instance, the sword came down to eviscerate the organization.

When there were not any men left to help the rebels, they called on the women to take the men's place and forced them to take on all tasks and responsibilities. The army infiltrated these women's organizations, and that is why prisons and camps are now filling up with women. The fellagha slit the throats of women who betray them; the army shoots, arrests, or tortures women who work for the organization. Both sides rape the prettiest ones and make bastards with young girls as well as widows. Thank God for sparing the married women from such encounters. On these grounds people generally credit the fellagha with showing respect for customs or just plain human dignity, whereas the army is always ready to trample on it . . . A thousand times more respectful, a member of the fellagha is discreet and never forces anyone. He hides from both the townspeople and his comrades in arms. When a scandal breaks out, he is severely punished. Or he switches sides and starts attacking his brothers in arms of the previous night.

261

## 1959

There was a military assault during the night at Aït Idir. The day after, only twelve women are willing to admit that they were raped. Soldiers spent three nights at Taourirt-M. behaving as if they were in a free brothel. People have counted fifty-six bastards in a village of the Béni-Ouacifs. The majority of our pretty women back home have succumbed. Fatma's daughters and daughter-in-law were raped right in front of her.

This is now common practice, and the Kabyles have nothing left to covet in the West. Up to now, the basic objective of their social life, manners, and customs has been to jealously safeguard the sex of their women. They believe that it is their inalienable right to possess this, for their honor has been buried in the vagina like a treasure more precious than life itself. But now, they value their lives more than their wives' vaginas. So when the soldiers take the men from their homes and confine them outside of the village while they ransack their houses, they know that their wives and their daughters will be violated as well. Once the operation is over, the men are allowed to return home. They then pretend not to understand and merely talk impassively about hard times and the brutality of the soldiers who broke down their doors, overturned their jars of cooking oil, stole their hens and rabbits. Congratulating themselves for their fearlessness, they smile with pleasure when a woman tells how she almost knocked down a half-drunk soldier who dared to grab her by the arm.

The fellagha, who base themselves on the Qur'an, have explained to the women that to accept the soldiers' abuse—not to seek it out exactly—but to submit to it and then mock it is precisely what defines their fight. But certain women do not see it that way. They experienced so much pleasure that they left the village to follow their subjugators. They say that these cases are rare, but they do exist. Furthermore, people are advised not to talk about such matters and, rather than allow the enemy to believe that he has touched the living flesh of the Kabyle soul, so to speak, to act like a true patriot for whom the emancipation of the captive homeland is more important than anything else. Of course, when one begins to hold forth on emancipation, one does indeed hold all the cards, and eloquence comes easily. Unfortunately, people are becoming increasingly skeptical, and there are more and more of them wondering if their true homeland is not that void into which they are being hurled, one after the other, after having endured all kinds of suffering.

1959

### February 28

People from back home are discovering where I live and then mustering up the courage to come and visit me. After Amar, here comes Saïd, then Amar again, and once again Saïd. I cannot really do much. We must send some money to the women and children who are stranded in the village.

I found out that B. was killed. I think that the last time I saw him was last April. He was already carrying the weight of his destiny on his small shoulders. It was his classmate, H., who told me about this.

### March 12

Yesterday about 1:00 P.M., gunshots near Birmandreïs. One hour later, a rebel was brought back and put on display in the little square until about 7:00 P.M. We could see him from the kitchen, very properly dressed in military garb. Armed to the teeth. Thousands of people surrounded him and looked at him with admiration. More than a thousand of these were young students: mine. It was the Psychological Service of the Army that wanted to exhibit him like a rare bird. A strange service, strange psychology.[1]

### April 26

Situation unchanged in the interior. I mean that there has been no break or sign that the vise that is crushing people will let up. Whether it is the army or the maquis, it tightens and tightens, it violates, and it kills. Consistently. Back home, Touhami was kidnapped. And others I know at Fort-National and elsewhere. For example, Issad Lamara as well as Edouard. Now, instead of emptying the villages, the army is forcing the residents to take up arms to defend themselves. So people are escaping toward Algiers. The rebels are insisting that the refugee families return to their houses so that someone is there to host them. They have agreed that the men can flee, but the women must either remain or return. For all useful purposes. It seems that the women are quickly adjusting. For example, Akli's daughter, who was raped by soldiers, wants nothing more than to go back. The men, on the other hand, have difficulty tolerating the offenses against the women. My colleague H. told me yesterday about a fellow he knows who committed suicide after a public incident where he was tied up and forced to watch some soldiers who were sexually humiliating his wife or his daughter or daughter-in-law. I do not remember the details.

Another thing to point out is that there are rebels who ex-

263

ploit those women who are more or less consenting. They use marriage to camouflage this practice. It is an ultra-quick and short-lived marriage in which you are sure to become a widow soon after, and there is the chance to remarry right away. When you are young and in demand, this game can continue without limits. Overall, women are feeling the weight of the war: they are beaten like men, tortured, killed, and put in prison. After all that, the decrees of de Gaulle, whether or not they are inspired by Miss Sid Cara, can only propose reform. It is over; there is nothing left to reform. When that stops, the women survivors know they will have all their rights, just as they have been invariably required to take on all duties, as well as each and every instance of servitude, humiliation, and suffering. The question is whether or not there will be more of the same thing, since they are currently purging the mountains of its most ingrained, callused, representative, in a word, legitimate, elements. Yes, something will prevail: all these refugees who, in no time at all, will degenerate and be absorbed by the big city crowds where, although it would be futile to look for quality, it will be possible to discover, from this moment forward, the men of tomorrow. These are the men who are ready to disown, to compromise, to sell themselves, to love the one who beats them or the one who pays.

There was no problem finding candidates to fill in all the slots on the town councils of the ten municipalities of Greater Algiers. The Muslim voters steered clear of the polling stations. There were hardly any women. But this was not so much due to die-hard patriotism as to fatigue. When the loudspeakers started to bark orders and threats, quite a few citizens of both sexes rushed over to the ballot boxes. As a result, fifty per cent of the electorate voted.

We still have the senate elections, and people are sounding me out by dangling before my eyes the tens of millions of voters that I could have in my pocket. All right. I think that soon we are going to get beyond this craze for seeking out "legitimate men." For there are not any legitimate men except those who entered the fight, believing in practicality and the dire necessity of the struggle. These people, good God, kill and die, and that is it. As soon as they start siding with the French, they are no longer legitimate. Those, like myself, who are simply trying to live and nothing more, those who even admit they are honest, impartial, intelligent, and worthy of respect—why ask them to guarantee force in the name of justice? But do they not realize that on the day they agree to play this role, they, too, will become worthless? Moreover, this presumes that they are still worth something while they keep themselves out of the scuffle.

**May 1**

Salem's daughter is at my house. She is the same age as my daughter. She ran away from her village to avoid being raped. But I think that she already has been, just looking at her easy manner, the audacious and slightly covert expression on her face, and her fully developed body. She claims that the rebels are protecting them, showing them respect in public and are able to marry them just as openly. When they fear an unpleasant encounter, the rebels make the women accompany them on the paths linking the villages. So they simply order whichever woman they happen to see first: "Hey! Mother or sister. Put your jug down and come with us. No. Keep your jug. It is more discreet. Come with us . . ." They let her go a few miles further on. Afterward, she manages to get back. At times, the women are forced to take obvious risks. For example, when they are directed to bring supplies to passing soldiers. If the other army ran into them, they would not be raped, but machine-gunned.

She also said that the rocky and wooded valleys below the village are strewn with cadavers that no one bothers to bury any more; men, women—it makes no difference. The rebels snatch them at night right under the army's nose and then slit their throats on the banks of streams. These are men and women who have collaborated with the army. Two years ago people had no sympathy for them. Now they are beginning to refer to them as "the pitiful ones." Treason no longer means much to people, since the rebels have set the example. When it happens, they begin to uncover the most insignificant secrets and to hurt—as much as possible—those who, through fear or conviction, have served them the best.

This population's morale would suffer a hell of a blow if rebels, passing through, did not take the trouble to come and raise people's spirits by keeping hope alive and being twice as strict. And if the French were not more monstrous, more deceitful, and more dangerous than the fellagha. But since this *is* the case, it is always the fellagha who, no matter what they do, inspire confidence and win hearts. No matter what they do, they are still soldiers fighting the enemy, soldiers doomed to a certain death because they are defending the country. To tell the truth, people do not really see the need to defend the country; and they continue to concede that the French are responsive, educated, and capable of doing good. Yet, when our brothers are fighting and dying, we must, without question, help them, listen to them, bear our part of the burden, the suffering, and the anguish. It is God who has given life to each one of us. And when our time has come, He is the one who cuts off our breath.

The girl is telling heart-rending stories. Nothing else. They range from tales of physical misery, hunger, cold, disease—back there and now here—to the terrifying scenes she witnessed. As of fifteen days ago, she still had not seen the city and had only a vague notion about it. Yesterday, she stared vacantly at one television program after another and smiled disdainfully only once, at Mickey's fantastic feats. She does not seem to be making any effort to control herself, to conceal her surprise, her admiration, or her joy. In this respect, she acts like a person with a good upbringing who enthusiastically accepts your kind invitation and believes that you are worthy of her friendship. She is a good girl, nineteen years old and completely uneducated; but she has at her disposal that priceless treasure called good sense. There are all sorts of village schoolteachers bent on destroying this quality in the civilized child who manage, in the end, to create a monster in their image. It is precisely such monsters who are assaulting our girls back home. The girls understand them and forgive them, but they do not love them. This has never been the case.

**May 18**

Public officials feared that a new revolution would erupt on the 13th. Nothing happened. The city was closely monitored by soldiers who seem to be carrying out de Gaulle's orders without sulking. The reactionaries stayed home after distributing an intimidating pamphlet calling for people to turn a joyous anniversary into a day of mourning. I say mourning, because de Gaulle was called upon to take over a year ago, and he has not achieved integration, has not crushed the rebels, and has not taken responsibility for the pivotal slogans "Dunkerque-Tamanrasset," "The Mediterranean sea is a French river."[2] A day of mourning, because in essence we could not do anything else. We know only too well that de Gaulle is one of theirs, just like Delouvrier, Massu, and all the others.[3] In essence, yes; they pulled together on this 13th of May, a day marked by their sense of disappointment, one verging on despair. In their faces, I read an indescribable sadness, the reflection of a collective conscience overpowered by remorse and anguish. These were the precursory signs of defeat. It was not a defeat imposed by men, but a kind of expiation, the inevitable punishment for some nameless crime.

That morning I did not want to go out, but I saw "the crowd" watching the parade in silence. Perhaps they forced this crowd to be there, at least the Muslims. About 8:00 I saw people leaving Clos Salembier in six large cars that went back and forth. Yes, the forum was very crowded. Less so than last year. People were much less enthusiastic.

Toward 6:00 P.M., I found myself below the summer palace in a small square. From here, I admired the Bay of Algiers, silent also and beautiful. Trolleys, nearly empty, passed by; cars barreled along at full speed; the sidewalks were deserted. In the square behind a clump of flowers, just a few meters behind me, a pair of clandestine lovers took advantage of the day's sad and meditative mood to indulge in a prolonged kiss. I got up so as not to disturb their encounter and went to see the men in charge. It was the fourth time that Mr. Delouvrier had invited me to a reception, and I had declined all the previous invitations. An hour after leaving the summer palace, I was sorry I had accepted the invitation. It did allow me to rub elbows with the generals, Marshal Juin, and a few compatriots with complicitous or dishonorable demeanors: Ould Aoudia, Ouchérif, Rezzouk, Boukhroufa, Hacène, Aït Ali . . . I was also able to meet Rosfelder, whose modesty and candor I respect and who knew that I was intruding.

### July 12

My village was honored by *L'Echo*. It made the first page, if you please, three columns with photos. My village just decided to side with the French on the 7th of June. It is surrounded by barbed wire, and the intersections are monitored by police posts.

My mother wrote to me: "Here we are siding with France. The village is surrounded by a wire fence, and we are at peace. We have been set free. The general came and threw a party for us. He gave us guns in exchange for our men. They are going to create a school for girls and boys here. We are at peace. They put five families in your house, some people from Agouni Arous. You should not come here now, not until the people of Algiers arrive, not until I tell you to come. I pray to God that we will see each other soon."

Yes, I should not go home. Those who do never return.

They have a gun placed in their hands for self-defense and are forbidden to go beyond the barbed wire.

Although there are several versions about the village's alliance with the French, I know the person responsible for it who, until now, has been a fervent nationalist. Perhaps the maquis forced him to act that way. Or maybe he was feeling "nostalgic for French peace," in the words of Marie Elbe, who writes for *L'Echo*.

A few days earlier, the maquis had kidnapped more old people and slit their throats in the ravines. A few months before that, they had slapped fines on nearly everybody who could still give. It is evident that the people of the village are feeling tired, unhappy, and battered. Once inside the barbed wire, many of them must have breathed a sigh of relief. Who knows what the future has in store? Right now they need a reprieve, and they are getting one.

They improvised a djemaâ, and the few able-bodied men who stayed on had no problem accepting the hunting gun that was foisted on them. Nevertheless, two or three men refused. One of them was able to rejoin the maquis; the other two are in prison. They tell me that Ali is one of the new soldiers. Ali has played the big-time patriot and the big-time official. I have seen him change his mind several times over.

Taguemount is a neighboring village that, up to now, has been protected from adversity because the army has occupied it for the last four years. They were only waiting for our lead to join the French and provide harkis and advisers. In fact, this village has always been occupied. Of course, this excludes all those who left. This evening I found out that the president of the village is a convalescent who came straight from a psychiatric hospital. But everyone up there is more or less touched—a lunatic in charge of other lunatics.[4] In short, this would be normal if the SAS were not around the corner, with the maquis just a little further behind them.

In all honesty, the maquis seem to be in very poor health in our djebels. The steady stream of villages that have decided to side with France translates into a significant number of successful operations and victories for the army. When all of the villages will have rallied in the same way, we will find ourselves back in the "good old days," before November 1954. But all those who died will be absent. In the history of Algeria, this is a blood bath without parallel. The day of reckoning is at hand. In time, it will be possible for historians to formulate an appropriate explanation for this unjust, cruel, and pointless drama in which the madness of men succeeded in bringing down other men.

As for myself, I now feel that I can leave this story behind. It does not have a prologue, and it will not have an epilogue. The prologue had to be extracted from a century of colonialism—for us a century of servitude—and I would have to anticipate the epilogue in an uncertain future that has very little to do with me, a future my children will accept, whatever it is and however it will be. By "me" I mean my generation, and by "my children," I mean future generations.

The younger generations will accept the future because they have the right amount of experience, consciousness, and pride to forge it. Whatever the outcome of this struggle might be, it will be their future. The chance to develop and be independent will, in the end, become the legacy of our collective suffering, a victory that cost us a great deal. Yes, long live Algeria! Praise those who died for her so that others could hold their heads high and proclaim their freedom to a guilty and disgraceful humanity. Yet when Algeria becomes independent and can hold her head high, I hope that she remembers France and all that she owes her.

## July 25

Calm vacation spent at Clos Salembier. The SAU is putting forth their best effort for the young people: youth clubs, summer camps, "boy scouts." [5] Is this a return to peace? Alas! In the first place, I am getting all this information about last year's purge, groups of people keep coming in droves, and these makeshift villages are springing up almost everywhere . . . In the city, the construction industry is busier than ever. HLM, CIE, rack upon rack of rooms to house the lucky tenants; vertical shantytowns.[6] Yes, work has started up again. People in the city are not starving to death. The city and the country itself are being transformed. It is all frenetic, artificial, and deceptive. So why stop my journal? Yet, I would like to stop it and have nothing else to say. Alas, this is not the end. It is still far from over.

## August 30

De Gaulle is making a trip to the mountains to see the mountain man in his gourbi and the soldier on the mountain top. His most recent visit was to my village, Tizi-Hibel. It never would have occurred to me that, in the course of its humble history, Tizi-Hibel would play host to a man of such high standing.

Now there is an honor that will cost Da Belkacem, the man who was forced to side with France, an arm and a leg. There is a possibility that everything that has been shown to de Gaulle will lead him astray. Will he see that the soldiers or pacifying officers are wasting their time trying to "reconquer hearts?" Neither lies, nor coercion, nor trickery will work.

# 19**60**

**January 25, 1960**

Yesterday, the reactionaries organized a demonstration to protest Massu's resignation. At about 6:00 P.M., a volley of gunfire erupted in rue Michelet-Grande Poste. A state of siege was declared in the city, and the curfew was moved up to 8:00 P.M. All night long the radio broadcast Delouvrier's call to order, the chief general's communiqué, and at 6:00 this morning another by General de Gaulle.

Outcome: 19 dead, 141 wounded (8 casualties for the army).

Lagaillarde-Martel stood his ground against the universities and their troublemakers. Ortiz-Lopinto, did the same at the Bank of Algeria.

The Ultras are armed and do not intend to turn themselves in. Stores and schools are closed. The Muslims have not budged. They are waiting to find out with what sauce they will be devoured. May 13, January 24, the days go by, and "everything seems out of joint."

I am assuming that it was the reactionaries who sent me the threatening letter a little over a month ago.[1] They politely warned me to get my "death shroud" ready and to quickly finish the rebellion's *apologia* that I had intended to write.

I have to confess that I neither wrote the *apologia* nor prepared any shroud. God is good! This is what the Muslims say about my species. I am afraid, of course. Pélieu, being aware of these threats, came to offer me a refuge. My wife would have liked to embrace him.

They are preparing a demonstration this evening that could still go wrong, since the state of siege obviously implies that the formation of groups of more than three people is forbidden. Is the army reliable? We shall see.

The day before yesterday, fearing what was going to hap-

271

pen and in order to "calm the public," there was a blaring announcement about the execution of four terrorists condemned to death. It must have taken place yesterday morning.

In 1958, the fellagha executed three French soldiers, and this started what is known as "May 13th." This time four terrorists will be executed, and this did not prevent getting "January 24th" started. This caused blood to be shed. Philosophically, the Arabs think of this as immediate justice.

On the same day, someone stuck some posters on my doorway denouncing the fellagha for burning schools, killing teachers, and planting bombs. As a result, several students stayed away from school, and people realized that my school had been wired with explosives.

During a conversation, a young colleague—slightly effeminate and refined, usually reserved, polite, and well mannered—blurted out that if he had a gun he would know where to aim, pointing to the middle of his forehead. It surprised me. Whom did he want to kill? He blushed.

When I saw him this morning, he was pale and trembling. It was no longer about aiming at anyone, and like the rest of us, he bewailed the brutal reactions of senseless crowds who beat, wound, kill, destroy, and devastate. As soon as we dismissed the students, he left, like the others, to go lock himself up at home.

So today, I had to get back to this notebook, which I abandoned several months ago. It is not that I had nothing to record, concerning myself or anyone else, but the gap is always easier to bridge when there is nothing special about the details. I would have liked to speak at length about our suffering, my concerns, and the misfortunes that strike any and all of my friends every day. For example, I could talk about Camus, who died in an accident at the beginning of the month;[2] about the Roblès family, whom I saw again last in Paris in December; about Ak., now hospitalized for a nervous disorder . . . All this is sad, really too sad. So I say to myself, "What good will it do?"

I think that I am content to limit myself to an objective reporting of the facts as I see them unfolding in front of my eyes. Later on, this will allow me to re-create the atmosphere. Of course, that is if I live long enough.

### January 26

A general strike, if you could call it that. A strike brought on by circumstances and fear. Prime Minister Debré, whose visit was announced for today, arrived yesterday during the night.

He left again very early this morning, and by the time the newspaper headlines announcing his visit appeared on the stands, he was already back in Paris, his mission accomplished. What mission? The insurgents are still swaggering around behind their barricades. The center of the city is in a state of war, the European residents are visiting their heroes and feeding them supplies without much trouble. All of them feel that this is how they can win the game: "keeping Algeria French forever." De Sérigny's editorial is a masterpiece: it is full of stupid blunders but fancies itself intelligent. *L'Echo* is the most unscrupulous newspaper around. The village police who are part of the army as well as the insurrection have issued a statement that says something like this: "Why are we shedding French blood when we all agree, and when the people who live in this 'province'—regardless of religious preference—are French." No kidding! You would think that it was Delouvrier who revolted by order of an outlaw named de Gaulle.

The same newspapers are right when they state that it is completely legitimate if the rebels do not embrace the paratroopers in public while the pieds noirs look on with compassion.

At any rate, the Arabs are relaxed. Every day seems like Sunday, and from here, the insurrection looks like the bottom of a well brimming with crabs. The boutiques are all open, and as usual, people are getting provisions. They feel comfortable with each other and very relaxed while whispering rumors of terrorists and catastrophes . . . For the others, of course. Poor Algerian, "no matter what your religion is," there will come a time when you will think like a small child. On that day, they will think for you, and you will not be in any worse shape because you are quite ill and have been so for a long time.

**January 27 6:00 P.M.**

Hat. just left me. He was very relaxed. He came from Ouled Fayet to see the barricades. He found them very amusing. It is like going to the fair. People are walking all around the perimeter of the University–Grande Poste–Avenue Pasteur, chatting with the village police and saying to one another: "Okay, we can leave. Now we have seen everything." But wait, ladies and gentlemen, do not miss seeing any of the booths. Lagaillarde came out of his command post to go up to the Orléans barracks and chew the fat with the soldiers about the assault. Then he returned to "the barricades." According to Hat., everything is going very well. Amusing. No use getting riled up over nothing. We are all on the same side, right?

According to Hat. and everyone he knows, de Gaulle, being extremely arrogant, will never renounce his position on self-determination. So he will leave, and Bidault or someone else will replace him. Anyone who advocates integration will do. If not, the fair and all its chaos will go on, and the booths will stay open for business.

An hour earlier, Pélieu had come to see me again. He also thinks that de Gaulle will not give in and that the reactionaries are determined to hold out and, if necessary, proclaim an Algerian Republic modeled on South Africa. He believes that you cannot count on the army.

This morning, some village policemen visited the neighborhood. They forced the Arabs to close up their shops—but some of them reopened a few minutes later.

### January 29

Delouvrier and General Challe have settled in near Reghaïa. They televised the delegate general's lengthy speech, which he addresses to those in France, the army, the Muslims, and the insurgents "like those of the *Alcazar de Tolède*." He flatters everyone but convinces no one. He says that everybody is afraid; yet it seems as if he is more frightened than anyone else. He solicits, implores, offers conjectures and predictions, and preaches and preaches . . . in the desert. At least it seems that way. In the end, what are we talking about here? Are they going to crush a small line of insurgents or demand that the army face its responsibilities? Why are they beating around the bush and whining so much? De Gaulle is supposed to speak tonight. This will be the big night. Lagaillarde and Ortiz are waiting for it. De Gaulle will not back down. As for them, they will probably vent their anger on the Arabs in prison or any who appear suspicious. But here again, God is good. At any rate, people in the neighborhood are not worried. They are simply being cautious and staying home, as if the neighbors were having a fight. I am absolutely certain that they will not either join the barricades or shout out, "Long live de Gaulle."

This is a shame because, if they were to shout, "Long live de Gaulle," things would change to the detriment of the reactionaries. But the Arabs tend to miss every opportunity. With clear consciences, they are waiting for independence to emerge from the same old situation, which always falls short and which everyone promises to no longer impose on them. They continue to endure it with the patience born from despair.

### February 2

Thank God, everything is quiet again since yesterday at 11:30 A.M. Mr. Lagaillarde surrendered with his troops. Mr. Ortiz has escaped, and the Ultras are crying with rage because they loused up their ill-fated attempt. Friday night, de Gaulle spoke; Saturday, the army understood and decided to obey him; Sunday, the rebels of Algiers wanted to show off; Monday, they discredited themselves by giving up; and all of their supporters became turncoats—from the radio to the town council of greater Algiers, not to mention the S11. This was a sorry adventure indeed, gentlemen.

### April 21 . . . November 27

I abandoned this journal last January after the reactionaries were defeated. I could have written in it more regularly and included lots of interesting things about myself, about my compatriots, the Algerian war, France, and the world. I let it go because I was profoundly tired. I also thought it was childish to narrate—for myself and in my style—what the front pages of the press from all sides throw at us every day. What is the use? I never stopped repeating myself, and that is, in part, the reason I quit writing.

What did I want to write on this day, the 21st of April? I have forgotten already. Today, I have started to think about going back to it again. Why? It is certainly not because I do not have enough to do. But the barricades trial just started, and they will have to get out the dirty linen. I also want to say that, at this time, it is the French who are getting tired. The Arabs are again hopeful and understand that they will soon be set free. This freedom will result from fatigue and be confused with victory. Yes, I think that victory is here. By all means, this is a victory for the people who were willing to suffer and especially for the fellagha, who never stopped making their presence more or less felt, in spite of the most devastating sacrifices on their part and the incredible disparity between their evincible strength and the enemy's capacity. From now on, independence is definitively ours. Thanks to patriots and patriotism. Long live Algeria! Any regime that comes to power will be welcome, provided that it comes from the people. That is all.

In the future, those who are compelled to ponder the profound reasons for their success will suspect that the Algerians' strength came from the fact that they were forced to submit to the French for an entire century. This developed in us the habit of tolerating the worst humiliations, and at the same time, when it came to deception and trickery, we generally had the upper hand. After 1955, when they began systematically to walk all over us, degrade us, and massacre us, we went through a long period of anger, panic, and unspeakable despair. Then we settled into our misery, and each of us, to his own advantage, quickly understood that we were being plunged back into the early years of the conquest, a period about which the old people still talk and that, in our naïveté, we had considered over. So we understood that we had to live again as victims, and we accepted the life offered us. But this life was no longer at an impasse. There was hope. From behind the barbed wire fences surrounding the monstrous "French villages," the maquis were setting their inept ambushes and dying with insults still on their lips. They called on us to be patient while they wore down the enemy's patience. It is that same old reed story.[3] It is necessary that our children learn the extent to which their elders suffered and the price paid so that they could inherit a name, their pride, and the right to be called Algerians without bowing their heads like the frail reed in the fable.

We should be able to put together all sorts of stories recounting thousands of dramas. All of these thousands of deaths, outcries of rage, torrents of tears, and pools of blood have marked and disfigured this earth on which we were unfortunate enough to be born and from which they want to take us as if we were bastards. It would be best if, later on, people knew about all this and told each other, "After all, our fathers were quite commendable, and we can be proud of them."

### December 8

I have returned from Lower Kabylia, where I accompanied people from the agricultural services who were visiting the lake region. We left early in the morning, when the sleepy town would normally be waking up. We knew, however, that de Gaulle's trip to Algeria was going to cause some agitation. To avoid Algiers, de Gaulle landed at Aïn-Temouchent, then at Tlemcen.

This evening, as I was on my way back, the traffic was detoured to bypass the Polignac crossroads. This was the first surprise, the first worry. Up to that point, along the highway, my traveling companion and I simply noticed that the towns we were passing through were not very animated. The highway was almost empty. Also, it was raining quite a bit. From Alma on, we got to thinking that this was perhaps a result of the strike. Rouïba and Maison-Carrée were empty as well. Dead day. What had happened in Algiers? In Algiers? Nails! Yes. We were told that, from 9:00 on, there were nails everywhere on the roads puncturing tires, thousands of brawlers in the streets breaking windows, stopping cars, trying to make their way inside the Summer Palace. The police and the CRS fought back mainly by hurling tear gas at the protesters.[4] Hundreds of arrests. Some fifty people were slightly wounded. Not too bad, after all. A strike, indeed, that was having an effect. Starting at 9:00, everybody shut down. This time, nobody broke down doors, or destroyed metal curtains, or ransacked stores. That could be done when the FLN started the strike. Now it is the FAF.[5] It is not the same thing.

While de Gaulle is shouting himself hoarse trying to explain Algerian Algeria, those in charge are unwinding the best they can because they smell trouble. They remind me of senile tramps masturbating in a corner in order to make people think that they are virile. Nobody is taking them seriously, however.

No more seriously than Mr. Lagaillarde, "the hero of the Alcazar," who, as a matter of fact, just took off for Spain where he is to consult his friends about the best way to resolve the Arabs' fate and to topple de Gaulle.

**December 9**

There is a complacent tone is this morning's newspapers when they report yesterday's events. It was as glorious as usual for the kind young pieds noirs, who were almost having fun when they broke shop displays or shattered glass while people threw cigarettes, suckers, and candy to them from their balconies. The chap who talked about candy after describing a striking sunset concludes in DQ[6]:

The Algerian Gavroche did not capitulate . . .[7]

—Hey, someone yells, as several CRS members, who are about to be relieved, get back into their coach for a "well deserved" rest, one has to admit. Hey, see you tomorrow, you sons of this and bunches of that [*sic*].

—You bet, barks back a CRS who is still in a good mood. At what time?

Long live the so-called Algerian Gavroche with the so-called French Algeria!

Earlier in my mail, there was a so-called FLN pamphlet in which Abbas gives a so-called answer, carefully written by the Psychological Service, to the letter by Jules Roy published by *L'Express*. And this Psychological Service still thinks that I am an idiot.

At 1:00 P.M., the news on the radio confirms that today's events are quite similar to those of yesterday. I made a quick dash to Château-Royal.[8] On the way back, I saw about fifty military trucks going toward El Biar. We shall see what the radio has to say later.

Europe 1 reports that people are going down into the streets. This time it is the Arabs. The following locations in Algiers are involved: the Mahieddine housing complex, Belcourt, the Clos Salembier. (Yes, the Clos where I have not lived since October. I can well imagine, however, those poor, kind, naive, and enthusiastic guys.) In order for the Muslims from the shantytowns to come out, they had to get the green light from the SAU. And once people get in the streets, they feel free and release their pent-up feelings. So while the ultras are shouting, "French Algeria," others are responding "Algerian Algeria" and "Long live de Gaulle." This is allowed. But then, it is "Muslim Algeria" and "Long live the FLN." First, you can hold the French flag up high, and then you can do the same with the green flag. Meanwhile, de Gaulle continues traveling and creating trouble wherever he goes and even where he does not go because people shout, "French Algeria," and others answer, "Algerian Algeria." People are breaking windows, raising clubs, setting fires (a five-story apartment building in Belcourt burned down), and starting to kill others (two dead, I have heard, again in Belcourt). The FAF has decreed a continuation of the strike. The Ultras who have found refuge in Spain are now making their way to Madrid to regroup around Salan. In France, suspects are being arrested to thwart a gigantic plot that is aiming to sweep de Gaulle out of power and replace him with fascism. By the way, it is hard enough to live under de Gaulle.

And while all of this is going on, the UN is preparing to condemn France and ask for a referendum under its supervision. In the mess that is likely to occur, I firmly believe that only a powerful armed intervention can save those Algerians who are still alive.

Indeed, it seems that our young people are tired of keeping their arms crossed while the pieds noirs continue to brag.

Each group knows the other well and wants nothing more than to explain themselves. I saw some of them yesterday, walking in small groups along the ravine of La Femme Sauvage.[9] They had bright eyes and an air of mockery about themselves. Those who recognized me flashed me a big smile; and I followed them with my eyes as they walked away, one behind the other, as silent as shadows. Real conspirators. They must have had fun earlier. "You know, we are ready," one of these young men told me last year during the famous week.

And to make sure that I was convinced, he pulled a new razor out of his pocket. He was a hairdresser.

**December 11**

So today the Arabs are in the streets. These are the people "from my neck of the woods"; I mean, from the Clos. They have taken over Mahçoul and Saâda, as well as those from Belcourt and the Ruisseau.[10] There were people from the shantytowns of Nador, Scala, El Amal, Bodez, Abulker, and all the others. Kouba was represented also.

The Casbah and Bab-el-Oued wanted to join them in the streets. What was the end result of all this? It was easy to foresee. The Europeans were panic-stricken; the army got scared, or claimed to be. There was no time to play tricks, have fun, or throw candies. There was only enough time to fire automatic weapons. At 10:00 P.M., the D.Q. (*Dépêche quotidienne*) reported fifty-one dead, of which forty-five were Muslims. The army fired at them. Or the civilians.

So the situation is clear: the Arabs—whom nobody pushed and who became exasperated only when confronted with the pieds noirs and their bravado—go into the streets to shout their irritation, and they are fired on by the very people who claim to defend them, to watch over them, and to fraternize with them. Throw down your masks, gentlemen! You can massacre all of them now; you have had it. You have had it because your informers are leaving you to go back to their brothers, and your informers are becoming the most ardent of patriots. Kill them, go ahead and kill them; these people who come into the streets with sticks, who shout no more than the Ultras, who break as many windows as the Ultras, and who insult you less than the ultras.

How many people are dead, or wounded, or arrested? We will probably never know. When you kill flies, nobody ever bothers to count how many have been crushed. Poor fellows

from Clos Salembier, may you die in peace, without the benediction of your captain, who thought he was your father and
who you let think he was your father because he did care for
you. Before dying, you still had the courage to raise your green
flag over the mosque so that no one would ignore why you were
dying. Bravo.

On television, I saw a stern and impassible de Gaulle
speaking about what hardly mattered to the Kabyles of Tizi-
Ouzou. An Arab translated what he said into Arabic. People
applauded de Gaulle, but not the Arab. It might have been necessary to retranslate into French what de Gaulle was saying
through the mouth of the Arab.

The Algiers radio and television stations, whose optimism
had to be exemplary, did not let all of this affect them. They
simply advised people to remain calm. They probably were ad-
dressing the Europeans:

—Now that we are feeding on the Arabs, remain calm, you
bunch of idiots.

The Europeans got the message; already today they stayed
home. Now that the fire has been set, they have taken shelter
where it is nice and comfortable.

Schools are closed tomorrow. The Arabs will be in the
streets, and the soldiers will be there to mow them down. The
Casbah, Hussein-Dey, Maison-Carrée, etc., have all remained
silent so far. This evening, I had to take an eighteen-mile detour
to go home, even though I was, in Bouzaréa, a little more than
a mile from the house. The military had sealed off the town.

Of course, if they only have to deal with the Arabs, it will
be easy to regain control of the situation, because with the Arabs
they feel strong, and they use their power. Still it was these very
Arabs who overcame two painful years of relentless pseudo-
pacification. It feels as if we are back in the darkest days of 1957.

In the final analysis, we might further add that the work of
the United Nations should be facilitated by such dramas. It is no
longer possible to make up the truth: for six years a subjugated
people has been suffering the most unjust of sufferings. Can we
help them or will we leave them to die? General de Gaulle will
certainly not decide their fate, because General de Gaulle is not
really prepared to let them be destroyed.

### December 12

Outcome: 90 dead, 1,500 wounded in Algiers (official version). Today there were 13 dead and 70 wounded in the Lower-

Casbah area. A helicopter flying overhead shot at the demonstrators. A reporter for Europe 1 has confirmed seeing and hearing the helicopter. The official communiqué denies it and also maintains that all these demonstrations are precipitated by a handful of demonstrators who are followed by the inevitable procession of petty thieves. Yesterday, the reporter for Radio Luxembourg let us hear a conversation with a demonstrator from the Clos.

—No, the FLN has nothing to do with this. We are fed up, that is all. We want our independence. We want to shout that we have had enough. There never was any fraternization. They silenced us. We would rather die than accept this situation any longer . . .

This reaction was spontaneous, direct, and truthful.

—No, Algeria is hardworking and does not express itself through the mouths of agitators, the Psychological Services reply.

On the street, I saw dozens and dozens of military trucks pass by on their way to reestablish order by shooting into a crowd dressed in rags. What can that kind of crowd possibly do? Go home, cry for its dead, clench its fists, go back to work tomorrow to put some food on the table. That is it. It is over. Again, we have to resign ourselves. Wait, wait, and wait some more.

Earlier, my kid heard the following conversation in an arcade:

—You do not understand the mentality of these people. As for myself, I have finally made up my mind: Algeria must remain French . . .

—Come on, let us go.

They left when they saw my son. These two men were almost of the same age as myself.

Today, we could not get any bread. The baker around the corner, a Mozabite, was conspicuously serving young Europeans and European women, while ignoring the Arabs.[11] They say that fear is the beginning of wisdom. It is also the beginning of madness.

### December 13

I ran into Aoudia at Château-Royal.[12] Rezki came to visit me at home. Both witnessed up close what took place at the Clos and Diar-es-Saâda. They described entire scenes, parts of scenes. There, at least, the Muslims were killed not by the military but by civilians. Rezki says that, in the morning, the Europeans went to the top floor of his apartment complex. They found refuge in a well-situated apartment. From there, they started shooting. The Muslims had matches to set cars on fire, and the Europeans had handguns to kill. Cost of an overturned car: one Arab life.

—From my window, I saw a sixteen-year-old, a good-looking kid. He walks toward a car with a green handkerchief in one hand. With the other, he pulls on the door handle to open the car. From above, someone aims and shoots. The kid bends over. Then he straightens up, looks, raises his fist. Someone shoots at him, he falls, reaches out to pick up a flag, and waves it at the ones who shot him. His arm falls back down. The green flag is right next to his fingers.

—On the other side, I saw, through another window, a man standing up. He looked struck dumb with fear. He turned around then collapsed, like a suit that had been dropped from the jacket collar. During that day, I counted eleven like this one. Dead or wounded. The French were firing at the flies, and the drivers in cars were racing to run the flies over.

It is true that these flies were doing as much harm as they could, but they were not armed.

I also heard that the captains of the SAU gave the green light for the Muslims' demonstration. If this is really true, then it was a complete success. They say, of course, that the Muslims, who paid dearly for their demands for deliverance, will not stop there, and that the French have decided to make use of their weapons. At least we know where we are going. For a while, there will be little room for hypocrisy.

### December 18

Calm has been restored, at least until the new referendum, which will take place on January 8. Both sides are getting ready for it. The UN's political commission voted the Afro-Asiatic motion by a two-thirds majority. However, the segment recommending international monitoring of the vote obtained only 38 votes, with 33 against and 23 abstentions. What will the General Assembly decide? But that is not what is important. If France ignores this vote, how can she be forced to take notice of it?

As one can imagine, France is too ensconced in this affair to capitulate purely and simply. France is going to play games once again, to pretend and delude herself. As for the Arabs, they want independence, and they are not looking any further. They are certain that if this does not remedy the situation, neither can it make any worse a century-old evil that seems to have reached a critical point. How many victims are there this time? Nobody knows. At the Clos, the military has the situation well in hand and has started making arrests again. A few days ago, my old school was filled with suspects who were interrogated and tortured in the laundry and shower rooms. As soon as calm was restored, they started looking for the wounded, supposedly because they wanted to provide treatment. For the last four or five nights, people have not slept very much. The soldiers knock on the door, ask nicely if there are any wounded who need care and then take you away, whether you are wounded or not, if your name is on a list. So people have wised up. A wounded person will claim to be awakening from a deep sleep, and insist that he is in good heath.

—Come along anyway, the soldiers say to him, if his name shows up on a list.

He goes to the Nador school where they beat him and make him spit out what he knows.

During the demonstrations, the school and the European teachers were left alone, even though, God knows, they were Ultras to the tips of their fingernails! However, they burned the caretaker's car and manhandled her son, who had never hurt anyone. The demonstrators will never stop paying for this car, and they had never imagined that this would happen.

Yes, the newly unshackled Arabs have shown the French of the Clos and elsewhere what patriotic hatred could accomplish, and the French have understood that Arabs' feelings toward them were exactly the same as the feelings they themselves had for the Arabs.

Officials have reported plundering, but that is not true. At least, by and large. The destruction was intended as harm. That is all. Things got broken, destroyed, or burned, including bank notes.

Salah described two distressing scenes he witnessed in part. They took place in the eucalyptus area.

A European in a nice car drove up to the middle of an important group and refused to stop. Afraid, he charged the group and knocked two young men down. A demonstrator managed to get on top of the car and destroyed the windshield while the car took off with the demonstrator on top. Some people in another car started chasing the fleeing car and caught up with it some 550 yards away. By this time, the French driver had gotten rid of the Arab on his roof. He was trying to bypass a small barricade and ran over the Arab. They lynched the French fellow and burned his car. They took the Arab's body and left the Frenchman's cadaver on the spot. At that very moment, as chance would have it, a young pacifist teacher came out of his home, hoping to make it to his class. The demonstrators attacked him, burned his car, and cut his throat. Before dying, the poor fellow shouted that he was an Arab, but he was shouting in French.

I have heard that the captain at the Clos, along with the lieutenant, was carried off in triumph by the demonstrators. They made him carry the Muslim flag. During the worst part of the fighting, the soldiers of the SAU would mix with the crowd of spectators watching everything, as did the local informers. Now people are most likely assessing losses and making lists. That is why the military is constantly patrolling the neighborhood. They go, preferably at night, to the homes of people on the list who are sleeping in shifts. People have taken quite a few photographs and shot film of very familiar faces. In *L'Express,* for instance, there is a close-up of a kid from Nador-C.M. His name is Loulou Hacène, and he looks like a young hooligan.

Personally, I do not think that the SAU are handing over the population for whom they are morally and even physically responsible. Ever since they started trying to understand the Muslims, to share their concerns, and to help them, it is been difficult to say to what extent the captains have befriended them. I believe that the most honest, most sensitive among them have gotten used to the idea of independence. They were not offended by their wretched citizens letting off some steam for once. Nor by their angry shouts that silenced a privileged and unconscious minority that is, once again, trying to destroy what these captains have had a lot of trouble fixing: that is, the Franco-Algerian community, which seems to be the only reasonable means for achieving peace.

They also have every reason to believe sincerely in the success of their mission, because even under the most difficult circumstances, the Muslims have always been faithful to them.

### December 21

Last night, at 8:00, General de Gaulle delivered a new speech to open the campaign for the referendum. There was a little weariness and a great deal of disillusion in his tone. He seemed tired and skeptical—not because he no longer believes in the ideal solution, that of a "sincere" community with France, a community governed by common sense, honesty, and the mutual interest of both parties—but because such a solution is, in his eyes, an ideal one and therefore unachievable.

As a matter of fact, the fantasy is all that is left to die for, except maybe the oil.

De Gaulle is hesitant to let go of Algeria because, in the first place, it is bad for Algeria, he says. Good God, Algeria has fallen into a precipice and is only asking to get out of it. Algeria is not asking for anything else. If, later, Algeria wants to return to the precipice and jump in it of her own accord, nobody will hold de Gaulle responsible.

The best of those French people who live here are fearful of what the future holds for them in Algeria. They forget that the Muslims are also afraid for their own future. The difference is that we know that we are condemned to live and die here. They know that they will be unhappy here, and they are afraid that they will be unhappy there. Over there, in France, they will not be any happier or sadder that anybody else. They will be like the others. But they do not want to be like the others, whether it is here or over there. It is a question of habit. It would seem, however, that the time to choose is fast approaching. As for myself, I envy them the possibility of choosing. If I were in their shoes, I would not hesitate. People will say that I can choose as well. What rights do I have to choose? After all, my ancestors did not conquer France in 1830.

So both of us are on the verge of resolving a very simple problem. To solve it, all the resources of wisdom, madness, and force have been mobilized. The idea was to impose a thousand dishonest solutions on people for whom the real solution was as obvious as daylight, as soft as spring sunshine. Nobody is worried, and right now, nobody cares whether this sun turns into an inferno or not.

### December 29

These last few days, I have seen many of my French friends. They are very worried. Once more, they assure me that those who can go to France are actively working toward that goal. My colleague from Salembier has already moved her furniture. Her neighbor has filed for retirement. Members of the Rouny family are depressed. They see the time coming when people who are special cases will no longer be exonerated or spared. You are one thing or another, and that is it. From that moment on, they will be treated as such, without any other consideration. Rouny told me that the ultras really thought that the Arabs had been on good terms with them on May 13. Now they are disillusioned. Poor fellows!

I saw a man on television who was explaining why people should vote no. "You, the Muslims," he was saying, "de Gaulle betrayed you because he is handing you over to the GPRA. We promised you that we would protect you, open schools so your children could learn and factories so they could find work. We would have kept our promises. De Gaulle is against this. Understand one thing: we will never agree to rely on those who cut the throats of our wives and children. Citizen de Gaulle does not have the right to get rid of ten million full-fledged citizens. Therefore, you are going to vote no. Just like us." I think that this gentleman is a senator.

After him, the token Arab on duty came on to explain that, on the contrary, it was necessary to vote yes, regardless of one's religion, because there was no salvation outside the yes vote.

The only thing left for me to watch was a cartoon, followed by the antics of an extremely funny clown, the innocent jokes of a variety singer, or the spiteful comments of some blabber-mouth.

# 19**61**

**January 16**

The referendum ended, as usual, with a victory for General de Gaulle. In France, of course. Once again, he has been put in charge of bringing peace to Algeria. The Muslims would prefer that he left them the fuck alone. They either abstained wherever possible, or they voted "yes." The roumis voted no.[1] The "yes" vote won anyway in Algeria, as well as in France. The atmosphere is still charged with threats, and people feel the activists are capable of anything.

A rational fellow told me that the rage of the French in Algeria is out of control. Their rage is filled with hatred and fear, but not madness. They have money, and they use it to pay ruthless commandos to go terrorize the Arabs at night during curfew: they bang on doors, brutalize or kill people, and start fires. They must have lists and get specific orders. These people are killers. The Arabs fight back by yelling *youyou* and counterattack with bottles filled with water, pebbles, and sticks.[2] As soon as someone knocks on your door, start *youyouing* but do not open your door; your neighbors will cry *youyou* also, and then others will do the same. When the alert has been heard everywhere in the vicinity, you must come out and make threats. Then the black 403 Peugeot or the D. S. Citroen of the same color will hightail it into the night, with its cargo of rowdies wearing civilian clothes or paratrooper outfits.

If they are lucky enough to run into an Arab, they have to kill him to get the 100,000 old francs bonus. Otherwise, the nocturnal expedition only brings 15,000 francs for each man. Go and check if this is true or false.

**February 11**

As things stand, it seems that all bets have been placed. We will have our independence, one way or the other. Soon Bourguiba will meet with de Gaulle. Then it will be the turn of the GPRA, which now stands on its own just like a paralytic who has thrown away his crutches after a visit to Lourdes.

The other day at Chaouch's I saw a young man and a young woman, both recent liberals, openly purchase *L'Observateur* and *L'Express*. The French are affable in their dealings with us. Sometimes they let you think that they really like you, but it is better to be on your guard because that is the time when they usually trick you. Solidarity among the French has never been stronger or more unconditional; it has never been expressed with so much impudence toward us.[3]

The public services from top to bottom are infested by those expelled from Morocco and Tunisia. Preparations have been made to provide them with easy and temporary assignments. They remind me of the thrushes that come back home in October, stuff themselves with olives, and cannot leave the following March. These thrushes stay close to built-up areas and continue to fatten themselves with our small vegetable gardens. Sometimes the children find them and manage to catch them in their hands because they are incapable of flying off.

These people have too much experience not to know that it is over. I am upset by their skepticism because I know that some of them have great personal merit and could legitimately fulfill the duties assigned them. They refrain from doing so because they know that others will soon take their place and do a much better job. There is a heavy legacy of abuse that they no longer bother to hide. This gives them a bad conscience. The only thing that is left for them to do is to divide up the tawdry rags, the last favors of a whore held in contempt by everyone. As soon as they find a place to call home in France, they will rush to denounce this whore. It may be up to us to keep her memory alive—we the people she has so shamelessly exploited for a century. We could pick any day of our youth, and our memory of her would be the same: a younger whore who let herself be raped by her own bastards in front of our admiring and hungry gaze. A whore who called herself a daughter of France, and who was herself a bastard: the Algeria of daddy and an unknown mother.

—Yes, my poor darling. You are now nothing more than an old swine and me—I am no longer a child.

**March 17**

Aïd. End of fasting. Will the celebrations that have become funerals since 1954 ever regain their original look? It is quite improbable. People seem to be getting used to treating them lightly, for no other reason than modernism: you have the day off, you wear your Sunday best, and you have a good meal. Then worries take over, and the new week begins. No, this is not a celebration of joy or sadness. This celebration takes on a new dimension and creates a new face for itself, shaped more by the moments we are living and the new conditions in which we find ourselves. This celebration has become secular. So much the better.

A day of indulgence, even for a believer? In this case, I would like to retract what I have written about the new war profiteers who have come from Morocco, from Tunisia, from metropolitan France, or who have been hiding among us. Not because they must be spared, but because others do the same and do not even have the excuse of feeling they are in enemy country, among enemies. I am talking about all the opportunists, the ambitious, and the unfit ones who are Muslims and who spend their lives trying to persuade themselves first, and then others, of their good intentions, integrity, and usefulness. I prefer a straw man to these people, because the straw man will perform his new job silently and hide himself like a thief.

God! The more I frequent the great men of this world and those who have power, the less I meet men who correspond to my idea of what a man should be. Yet, I was not born yesterday, and I have never worshiped heroes or saints. If this is a sign of the times, why do we continue to kill each other for principles? We would be better off elbowing our way through life. That way, at least, the most audacious would not risk any more than a kick in the face. They do not deserve any more.

Instead of crossing out all that I have already written, I say to myself: Long live France, just as I have always loved her. Long live Algeria, just as I hope she will be. Shame on the criminals! Shame on the cheaters!

**April 24**

The day before yesterday, Algiers woke up in the arms of another master who had taken her in her sleep. Did she think, as I did, about the old days of the janissaries when the deys had their throats slashed during their sleep while others revealed themselves—covered with blood, with a torch in one hand—and had themselves cheered. To tell the truth, things happened very quietly this time. At 7:00 A.M., on our way down toward the high school, my daughter tentatively noticed and then made me hear some unusual ta-ta-ta-ta-ta honking, as well as some inexplicable traffic jams. Algiers was in the hands of the army. The army had taken power, as the radio soon announced.

I only heard about it through a colleague when I returned at 9:00. All day long, people had to stay close to a radio to try to figure out what was going on. Nothing; communications with France had been jammed, radio stations were jammed; and the rebels would do nothing more than read and reread some communiqués that announced that Generals Zeller, Jouhaud, and Challe while waiting for Salan, were in the process of . . .[4]

**July 20**

So they were taking power. They had it for three or four days. The military draftees did not want to go along with it. France did not want to go along with it. Once again, de Gaulle galvanized the entire country behind him. Challe and Zeller surrendered. Salan and Jouhaud went into hiding. The former were given a lengthy prison term after a historic trial. Recently, a high-ranking military official paid them a visit—a field marshal or general, I do not remember any more.

The other two founded the OAS, an organization that started by exhausting us, every evening, by banging "ta-tata . . . ta-ta" on saucepans. It was amusing, a bit stupid. Next, the OAS started dropping plastic explosives nearly everywhere. This made a lot of noise and a lot of damage. From the other side, terrorist attacks began to terrorize again, and the people in charge, after meeting unsuccessfully at Evian, are to reconvene at Lugrin. No doubt, they intend to part company once again without reaching an agreement.

**July 29**

It is done. The delegations have gone their separate ways. On the front page, eight columns: "Lugrin: suspension." Underneath: "At the initiative of the FLN delegation, no date set for a resumption of the talks." To the side, spread over four columns: "France refuses to participate in the Security Council debate" on the Bizerte affair. The Bizerte affair? We are talking about an attack by the Tunisians and a counterattack by the French, who shot at the Médina, the source of the gunfire.[5] Once again, Tunisia is demanding that the base be evacuated. France wants to keep it "to protect herself as well as the West." The FLN communiqué is explicit regarding the cause of the new breakdown in negotiations: the Sahara.

People generally agree that France was at fault in the Bizerte affair, which resulted in 700 deaths and 1,100 wounded in

Tunisia. It was the bad tempers of de Gaulle and Bourguiba that cost so much. And to think that any one of these deaths might be worth any living person—including de Gaulle and Bourguiba! One day, France will give Bizerte back to Tunisia, and the two countries will be friends again. Right now, none of the dead really give a damn! In spite of the OAS, Algeria will be independent, the Muslims will fraternize with the Europeans, the country will be industrialized, and its oil will be exploited. And while all this is happening, the poor wretch and the dead still will not give a damn.

### August 3

Today in Paris Captain Oudinot of Béni-Douala faced a military court. Ultra, activist, war criminal, anti-Gaullist—you name it. He has many deaths on his conscience. He knows how to make the Kabyles wail. This evening, on the news, I will find out that he has been acquitted because, after all, they would not condemn a patriotic officer for his slightly excessive love of the motherland. His colonel has just exonerated himself while being praised for his "brillant years of service." Provided that he does not send the guy back to Béni-Douala. That is my wish for today.

### August 4

I will simply note the following regarding Captain Oudinot: a Père blanc who knows him well said to me one day: "Mr. F., I believe in God, but if God ever killed a man right in front of me, I would quit believing in him, and I would say to myself: No, God in his goodness must not kill that man in front of me. A good God would no longer exist in my mind. Mr. F., I saw Captain Oudinot kill a man, and I said to myself: There you go, he does what God himself cannot do. He has not killed a single man. In Béni-Douala, there is the captain and nothing else. He is taking up all the space, even the space of . . . Oh! Excuse me, Mr. F., I do not know what I am saying any more."

Conclusion: "At the military court in Paris, five minutes will suffice to acquit the SAS Captain Oudinot." Front page of *Le Journal d'Alger.*[6] The 26,000 residents of the douar are going to be overjoyed. Give them back their God immediately, and Kabyle France will be saved! Besides, as far as I am concerned, he already saved my life. Yes, he, and his telegram in November of 1958.

### August 6

The OAS has taken an interest in this neighborhood.[7] First bomb—10:30 P.M., sixth bomb—5:00 A.M. They visited my balcony between 11:30 P.M. and 5:00 A.M. and took all the laundry. Right away Mokrane set up a metalic wire to create an electrical barrier. He aims to protect us. Ali is making sure that the revolver works. My kids love this kind of concern where you build up the danger without taking it too seriously. Just recently, they showed the film *Le Père tranquille* on television.[8] My kids were giving me sidelong glances and hoping for the impossible. That is, maybe I am one, a *père tranquille*. In an instant, I both reassured and disappointed them.

To get back to all these plastic explosives that fortunately are making more noise and causing more material damage than harm, I do not think that we should lose our heads over them. The catastrophes that they have promised us for the month of August will not occur. The organizers have no sense of the overall fatigue that is gradually being transformed into indifference. The "activists" are organizing themselves along the lines of the FLN: terrorism, extortion, peremptory demands, threats. There are, undoubtedly, among them a band of gangsters who are fishing in troubled waters. The FLN is reorganizing itself. Apparently this was necessary. It is certain that they will respond to the plastic. Why not? In the end, this will be one way of bridging the gap. What do we all have in common? Indifference, skepticism in relation to the mystics, the same stupidity, the same bad temper, the same need to crush our neighbor so we can take his place and look down on him, the same desire to do away with him if he does not share our opinion . . . and many other things that I cannot manage to express.

For the shrewd observer, aside from a few fanatics, from now on we are in a state of grace, ready to adore whatever future master is intelligent enough to offer us peace first.

**August 12**

For the Muslims, the timid patriots, the misunderstood, bitter, and powerless intellectuals, the race for a job is on. They are looking for connections, on the sly; they play the coquette and allow themselves to be duped by those who are more clever. When they do get the job they want, they start to see things from a different angle. They tell themselves that, in the end, collaboration, community, and brotherhood could all very well be the solution for the future—provided that the men of good will play their part to the fullest. They are themselves, of course, these men of good will. A long time ago, they were destined to play this essential role. So they sense their importance, lose any sense of gratitude to the underhanded protector who promoted them, eventually consider themselves wronged again, ask for more, always more, and become insatiable. Since nothing will satisfy them, they begin to wait for the "liberators of the homeland," who, they feel, will "do them justice." With the customary bow of the head, these liberators are to bring them a golden plate bearing the commission and the position that they have always deserved. Like ambition, human candor is infinite.

**August 13**

In the wake of failed negotiations at Lugrin, the army has been authorized to start up operations again in certain sectors. I am not sure if this changes much of anything on a practical level. I cannot say if the unilateral truce has really bothered the army, or if it has allowed the rebels to reorganize and take back lost positions.

In the countryside, people are living through the war in a state of overwhelming fatigue. There is no longer any hope or instruction in it for them. While waiting for the end, they know that impatience is futile and that, eventually, they will be in a position to demand accountability. Those who will be held accountable are living in the moment and doing their best to forget. Just like the civil servants who feel shortchanged, these people, at times, imagine that they will escape and that, ultimately, they will be appreciated for all the harm that they did not do. For two years they have been spreading terror throughout Tizi-Hibel, Belaïd, and Mebarek. The clan applauds them because they chase after the women of neighboring villages. The young soldiers are disgusted by the traitors who serve as their guides.

It was surely one of them who tried to save the life of poor Sadia, my water carrier. When she was with us, Sadia was about thirty years old, very robust, and beautiful. My wife was right to mistrust her, but I always respected her because I knew for sure that she had lots of men interested in her and that, as a young widow, she was freed of all constraint. I felt that she was kind and did her job. After we left Taourirt-Moussa, I learned that she had stayed on with my replacement. After the school was closed down, she became part of the resistance and was very popular within the group. She would help and help and help some more. They entrusted her with all kinds of missions, which she carried out magnificently. She was on her way to becoming a heroine of the liberation movement. When I passed through Taourirt-

Moussa about three years ago, she was the one who took me under her wing and saved me from being shot by the military.

One day last spring, someone informed on her, and she was handed over to the authorities and tortured beyond measure at Béni-Douala. The young soldier who was guarding her secretly released her after making her promise never to denounce him if she were recaptured.

— You are leaving at your own risk and peril, he said to her.

— Fine, she answered. God will repay you.

She went away wearing a simple tunic, with bare feet, bare head, no belt, a swollen face and a battered body. She disappeared into the ravines, the brambles, and the cacti. At the crack of dawn, she was not at home but was opposite the village of Tiguimounine at the rebel camp. She was going to be given a warm reception. That would have been the least they could do.

But the women seized Sadia and handed her over to the outlaws, who executed her on the spot. Sadia died as a traitor. She could not have cared less. She left behind a slightly retarded daughter who is now alone in the world.

### August 17

I have spent hours upon hours rereading all of my notes, newspaper articles, and small clippings that I have kept.[9] I have become reimmersed in a sad past, and I am leaving it overwhelmed. I am frightened by my candor, my audacity, my cruelty, and, at times, my blind spots and prejudice. Do I have the right to tamper with what I have written, to go back, to alter or rectify it?

Did I not write all of this day by day, according to my frame of mind, my mood, the circumstances, the atmosphere created by the event, its reverberations in my heart? And why did I write it like this, bit by bit, if it was not to witness, to stand before the world and shout out the suffering and misfortune that have stalked me. Granted, I was very awkward and headstrong the day when I decided to write. Whom do I know that would have been willing to do it in my place? And would I have been able to remain blind and deaf just to silence myself, just to avoid the risk of being suffocated by my anger and despair? Now that it is done, now that everything has been recorded— good or bad, true or false, just or unjust—now that we can foresee the end of this nightmare, must I keep all of this for myself? Must I forget, look ahead, look toward those who will build our future, preach oblivion, hope, brotherhood, and all the rest?

That would be a fine program for future moralists. Alas! I am not one of them, and my faith in man has been shaken enough that, from here on, I might become a hypocrite or a victim of my own naïveté.

The reason I did all of this is simple: it is appropriate that my journal supplement what has already been written about the Algerian war—good or bad, true or false, just or unjust. Consider it one more document in an extremely poignant dossier. Nothing more. And the time has come to add it to the rest. It is either now or never.

More than once, I have stated in passing that all that I have seen or known has not been faithfully, entirely, or precisely reported. I recognize in advance that certain statements are false, distorted, incomplete. However, the error or the lie, in such cases, can be attributed to my informants rather than to myself. I have explained several times why and how these informants interpreted the event. It is nonetheless true that the event itself is not imaginary; each occurrence is inscribed in the flesh of men.

Opposing the years of destruction and ruin are France's vast accomplishments of the past few years. This constitutes a positive aspect that does not appear in my journal. For this reason, people have accused me of being ungrateful or blind. My response is to say that yes, France has made a tremendous contribution. Nevertheless, this has already been sufficiently pointed out. While this huge effort at real estate investment, industrialization, infrastructure, education, and civilization unequivocally condemns a century of self-centered colonization, it does not, by any means, wipe out the memory of the price paid by both sides for almost ten years, simply because those who were tired of suffering wanted to denounce this egotism and chose violence in order to be heard. They chose? Not even. All other means were blocked.

My candor has led me to give in to anger, to argue rather than bear witness, to betray my duty as a man, to trample on noble sentiments, to abuse the trust of my friends and neighbors, and to wreak destruction on the superior interests of a noble cause. Herein lies my shame and my torment. I know how difficult it is to be fair, I know that a noble soul will accept injustice in order to avoid being unjust, and, finally, I know that silence is a heroic virtue. My people, I could have died. But for almost ten years now, I have staved off threats ten times and found shelter so that I could continue to bear witness to those who were taken by death. Those who have suffered and those who have died had the potential to say a lot of things. My goal has been to say, with some timidity, a few of those things in their place. What I have said has come from the heart and is as insightful and honest as I can make it.

If all of this is printed and published, as I believe that it must be, if this publication incites even the least bit of anger or hatred, if it increases by any amount the misfortune of an individual or the community rather than comfort, rehabilitate, and instruct, this work will be futile and detrimental. I will regret having completed it. At least, I will not have evaded my responsibility by remaining silent. This would be even more reprehensible . . .

**August 20**

Some specific facts can explain my qualms about the objectivity of my observations. It would, of course, be wise to review everything at a later time, to verify, and to discover more aspects of the same event in order to make it more specific. Yesterday, for example, I got Dahmane to talk to me about the living dead who scared his village and how he himself became a bit crazy.

—Yes, it is true, Dahmane said to me. He is a derelict. Did you know that he owes me his life? Of course, he has been disfigured by torture, and he will always be physically and intellectually weak, but, after all, he is alive.

—Did he deserve to die?

—Maybe. He helped the maquis and the FLN a lot, and he confessed everything when he was tortured. If Pastor Rolland had not intervened, they would have finished him off. That is normal.

—Normal?

—In a case like this, the army kills you, and the people accept it . . .

Let me tell you about another special case. The captain from Béni-Douala, about whom I have said lots of bad things, agreed to let Medjeber live.[10] So for Medjeber, this captain is indeed a "good God." And for many others as well, I am sure: those that he allowed to live, those that he allowed to die. Poor man. I would not want to be in his shoes. Who would dare condemn him? The military tribunal showed a great understanding of his predicament: "Five minutes will suffice . . ."

### August 21

"What a character" is the title of a note by Huron in the *Canard enchaîné*.[11] Apparently, this eccentric character became the "Frenchman from Tunisia." About four years ago, this gentleman, whom I believed was the "Frenchman from Morocco," while he claimed to be the "Frenchman from Algeria," had accused me of being a "counterfeiter" and was urging the FLN to execute me. He was an asshole, and I told him so. Well, in spite of the changes in adoptive countries, he is still the same. He waits for the decisive moment, and then, in a style all his own, he directs you toward the firing squad. He is unable to grasp his own incurable stupidity, which he views as intelligence! A good point by Huron. Thanks, *Canard*.

### August 25

While plastic explosives continue to blow up window shops, curtains, and dividers, attacks are on the rise. Yesterday, they shot and killed a notorious turncoat whom I had seen last year at the SAU of the Clos Salembier. His name was Kouara. He was a former captain in the ALN who fled to Bizerte before returning to Algeria later on. The army and the Psychological Service had been using him for over a year. He spoke to the Arabs many times, denounced his former superiors, and stressed their thirst for money and honors. He succeeded in convincing people because he sounded so sincere. He had an assistant who was less sympathetic, undoubtedly more deceitful, and belligerent in any case. He who bears treason on his face speaks like a servant. Ravussin, who was in Tunis during the escape of the two GPRA civil servants, told me that the rebels could not explain what was going on. Was Kouara sincere, at least at the beginning? It is possible, after all, but he made a mistake in wanting to play a part, and, therefore, he made himself available for a price. He was used . . . to destroy what he had once loved. When you lock yourself inside a contradiction, you accept this uncomfortable role, or else you topple over the edge . . . He died in a Mercedes. Probably a brand new one.

### August 28

I spent part of yesterday with Mermier and the Christian students for "Workers for Peace" who came from France to work on a construction site. I had to spend time talking with them. What I basically told them was that the Muslims are more upset at France and its army than at the pieds noirs. We kill the pieds noirs, we hate them, we know them. The Muslims are not afraid of them because there are fewer of them. We agree that they are Algerians like us, and we know that we will become one with them and form a new people. One way or another. All this, we think, is in the order of things. It is quite simple: thanks to France, for a century they have apparently been able to remain different from us, by maintaining themselves above us through sheer force. Now the time has come when France is about to leave them to us. It cannot be that, on top of everything else, France will make them responsible for all the mistakes and all the crimes. They are primarily the beneficiary of all the mistakes and all the crimes, at our expense. Do not let it be said that France did not greatly benefit as well.

We understand the anguish of the French in Algeria: they are responsible for all the ills that we have had to suffer. And if things can ever be mended, they will be carefully segregated, as if to forbid them any hope of living in the Algeria of tomorrow, though they have, nonetheless, contributed to its creation.

I told these young Christian students that the difference of opinion was between the Muslims and the non-Muslims. The drama blew open, the fire was set. Why did our guardian France not play the part of the arbitrator? Why did it side for one side against the other? Right from the beginning, France should have forced them to face each other and said to them: Gentlemen, put your ideas on the table, I am listening.

—Ah! Yes. For instance, Abbas-de Sérigny.

—For instance.

—Do you think that Abbas, Boumendjel, and the moderates will impose their viewpoint during a settlement?

—I think so. Or else they will agree to the opposite point of view.

—The GPRA will stand united?

—Absolutely. Algeria has suffered too much to allow its leaders to stray from the goal to be reached.

—The goal?

—Yes, peace . . .

Upon my return from Kabylia, in the evening, I hear on the radio that the CNRA has dismissed Mr. Abbas, and that Mr. Ben Khedda is the president of the GPRA. The hard-liners are now in control.

Great, I said to myself, the students will think I am either a fool or a joker. After all, did I not explain this dismissal ahead of time?

## 1961

### September 11

Two important events headline the front pages of the newspapers besides, of course, international politics. Everything is fine there, particularly the situation in Berlin, the resumption of nuclear tests, the conference of neutral countries, Bizerte and Brasilia or Rio de Janeiro, or the Congo . . .

Two important events that affect the French and the Algerians: the September 5th speech of the leader of the French state (followed by a Ben Khedda speech in Belgrade) and the attempt on de Gaulle's life the day before yesterday.

I saw de Gaulle on television. Once again he was moving and dignified, despite what people say. Whether he spoke clearly, frankly, even astutely, or naively, we could not expect anything different from him than what he said.

We were expecting him to acknowledge that the Sahara of all the Atlases belonged to Algeria, and that is basically what he did with both resentment and objectivity. It seemed to me that he reincarnated France with his discouragement, weariness, anger, and what almost amounted to be bad faith. How can one not understand the suffering of a man who carried the weight of an entire century of mistakes, egoism, grandeur, a man who comes from an old world, who clearly sees what the new world will look like, and who declares that he accepts this new world — while hiding an immense despair. Good, he accepts everything and is only thinking of disengaging France from Algeria. An Algeria that he threatens with all ills but that stubbornly refuses to play the imaginary invalid in front of doctor Too Bad. Beyond these threats, there is, once again, the futile attempt to be heard by one's own people. However, the disenchanted tone clearly indicates that, this time, all illusions are gone. People do not want to follow him down the "disengagement" road; people do not want to see this new world that is emerging almost everywhere on a planet as ebullient as a pot about to boil over. People feel that there are not enough ruins, and that they do not need architects any more than they need doctors.

This is why somebody tried to do away with de Gaulle the day before yesterday. To tell the truth, people knew that he had been threatened for a long time. There are no guarantees that he will not be eliminated one of these days. In that area also, he knows what is what. His only desire, I think, is to stop incarnating France at the very moment of his death. Because, in the final analysis, have they thought about it? Have the masters of the OAS and all the other super-Frenchmen considered whether their France would cease to exist at that very moment?

No, really, I do not know whether, at this exact moment, it is Algeria or France that is teetering blindly on the edge of the precipice.

I did not hear Ben Khedda's answer, but the press is reporting that it was restrained and intelligent, and that it left the door open to negotiations. So, we can finally hope to stop the ordeal. However, the French super-patriots want to eliminate de Gaulle to make it last longer. In reality, they are just as prepared for "disengaging" France, and also wish to leave the chaos behind them. Afterward, they will be in agreement with de Gaulle and strongly favor an association. I think that, eventually, the FLN will also lean toward this association. So this is how the fruit has ripened. This is the solution that has been found, the peace that is ready to be established in the most extreme confusion. This confusion is only superficial, and we have never been as close to each other. They want to get rid of de Gaulle because his politics are about to bear fruit after a long period of work. Others have ambitions to harvest these fruits. They are nothing more than vulgar thieves, barely able to frighten a village policeman. The superpatriots are losing their minds. It is an old habit of theirs. So much the better for the others, who may decide to react.

Among the important personalities arrested after the attempt (two generals, a countess, an important director of an Algerian mining company) appears the name of Alquier, the former paratrooper officer and head of the SAS.

Last year, before leaving Clos Salembier, I talked with him a great deal at the home of Captain Courbon. We spoke very late into the night with both intense frankness and intense reserve. For two years, I had been able to appreciate Captain Courbon, who is a remarkable man. He has known how to make himself extremely useful with an exceptional team—a lieutenant and his wife, whom a happy fate had brought together to look after the shantytown. Captain Courbon could care less about what the future has in store for him; he is only interested in being liked by the people put under his care. To be liked as an officer and as a Frenchman. He has succeeded in this. I believe that in December 1960, right in the middle of the fighting, while the Algerian flag was being waved, he asked people to shout: "Long live France," and people shouted "Long live the Captain! Long live France!"

Is this true or false? I did not ask him because he honors me with his friendship.

So, at the Courbons' I talked with Mr. Alquier, and he listened to me, too. We did not talk about everything, and we avoided any confrontation. Mr. Alquier is an intelligent man, well educated, from high society, I think. He is an intransigent patriot, there is no doubt of that. How did a man of this quality end up being involved in such a plot? How could he not understand that de Gaulle's position is the only rational and possible one for a true patriot, for the most narrow-minded patriot? That I cannot understand. Maybe he simply acted on a whim, or it was a tragic mistake of a young man . . .

When we met, he had read my books, and I had read his. That is where our reserve is rooted. I had in front of me a man filled with qualities that had been deformed by war. He seemed to be like some sort of sportsman who is entirely absorbed by an athletic exploit, the victory to be won over an adversary. The victory of a gladiator that consists in finishing off the other gladiator. Although he talked like a cultivated and well-behaved man in this living room of a Saint-Cyr graduate, the man sitting across from me was a killer. I mean a man who could kill or be killed. He had coldly chosen this role, and France had not asked that much of him. A certain France, at least.

He told me that night that he had given shelter to a young man, that he had taken him to his parents' home, that he was in the process of giving him a good education, that he intended to make him into his brother, in the legal sense of the term. Okay, fine. This was a young man who had lost his parents and his entire family. They were most likely massacred. By whom? Why? The captain and I looked at each other, and we exchanged cigarettes.

## September 16

They tell me that the OAS was not involved in this plot and that they are accusing de Gaulle of having instigated this "monstrous adventure" himself. This does not prevent the OAS use of plastic explosives any more than ever. Especially against the Muslims, who have started to fight back themselves with grenades, submachine guns, and revolvers. Innocents are falling on both sides, as well as others who are not as innocent. In Algiers, Oran, and everywhere else. For instance: "Test Garden Pub," terrorists fire from a slowing Dauphine car: among the peaceful patrons there are five or six dead and ten wounded. The following day, during the funeral, Arabs are sought out, and nine are killed. Nine who happened to pass by. Then, these nine had to be buried, taking care that this should not create other victims. It did not have that effect immediately. But how long will it be before . . .

I find out through a news item that our village policeman in Béni-Douala was shot by the rebels. This fellow got what he deserved. He is the one I have mentioned in this journal who stalks the wives and daughters of neighbors after he sided with the army. He did a lot of nasty stuff that must have disgusted everybody, from the SAS captain and the military to his own cousins, whether they were rebels or not. I say cousins because I am one of them. From afar, it seems to me that I would have been capable of punishing him myself. *De profundis*, vile cousin!

**September 17**

Yes, it was indeed my cousin Belaïd. My brother just confirmed what happened. On Wednesday evening, as Belaïd was returning from Béni-Douala, he was shot very close to the village, in front of the convent of the Soeurs Blanches. Three rebels in uniform call out to him:

—Stop!

—It is me, F. . . .

—You are the one we were waiting for.

Burst of gunfire. Seventeen bullets in his body. The kids that were carrying his purchases ran to the village to bring the news.

—Yes, my brother said to me, when he could help people, he never hesitated.

—Oh, you really think so? I have heard some bad stuff about him.

—Well, in any case, he leaves a large family behind, and his children will suffer. . .

Another one whose children will suffer is my other cousin, Ali. He had ten kids. He died in Bab-el-Oued, lynched by the pieds noirs. He is one of seven, eight, or nine, who are, in fact, twenty-five, because my brother saw the bodies at the morgue. They were among those who were killed by the Europeans after the burial of their own people. That is what you can read in the newspaper: "Brawl between the European population and the police: five Muslims dead and twenty-five wounded." When the Europeans are fighting against the police, Muslims are killed. Something else I need to mention: when Muslims bury their dead, they have to follow a timetable, and relatives are the only ones allowed to accompany the casket to the cemetery. They are warned that the army has been given orders to shoot in case of a demonstration. The day before, when the Europeans were buried, the order to shoot had not yet arrived, and nobody could oppose the demonstration during which the Muslims were killed.

My cousin was a trolley bus conductor. He was lynched near or inside his bus, in front of the police station. The driver of the bus had time to get out and find refuge inside the police station. He made it clear that the policemen tried to close the door of the police station in his face, but that he was able to save his life because of his strength: he shoved the policemen aside to get inside. Afterward, he offered to let them shoot him. They could not go that far.

My cousin had several skull fractures and his fists were puffed up. People from my hometown, who now live all over Algiers, came to see him, and they concluded that he had tried to defend his life before dying. They wrapped him up in a green blanket, and they rented taxi cabs to go wait for him at the entrance to the cemetery. Now they are going to put their resources together to help the family financially. He will become a hero in the years to come. He will have earned this status. I recall that, last year, a policeman had given him a lot of trouble. Ali lived in Mahçoul in the Comfort Housing Estate, with Europeans. That cop explained to him that living with Europeans implied certain duties on his part. He had him arrested, beat him up, and asked him to become an informer. Still feeling pain in his ribs, Ali came to see me:

—What am I supposed to do? he asked me.

—Stick to what you answered. You do not know anybody. You left your ancestral village a long time ago and do not have any acquaintances among the Muslims.

This conversation took place a year ago to the day. Both of us were far from thinking that there were other dangers lurking about for him—for everybody—dangers that would not be caused by the cops or the military. Mektoub!

**September 21**

In reference to the attacks against Muslims in Bab-el-Oued, I have to point out that if, on the one side, the pieds noirs are congratulating themselves over what seems to them like a sports exploit, on the other side, the Arabs are taking it all in without rancor but with the cold determination to avenge themselves. Specifically, my cousin was avenged because, at the Mahçoul bridge, someone cut the throat, or so I have been told, of a pied noir streetcar employee. We suppose that this is payback. Everywhere Europeans are being attacked with knives, revolvers, or grenades. By the way, the victims are always innocent. Muslim stores and Muslim and non-Muslim apartments (if one can say that) are being blown up, everywhere. Liberals are catalogued, added to police files, and condemned. A police superintendent, who was a member of the PSU and, furthermore, a Jew, was shot and killed in full daylight close by the university tunnel.[12] This is the second superintendent to be killed this year.

Even if France is successful in removing itself and its soldiers, the game is underway between the indigenous people and the Europeans, and it will terminate to the advantage of one or the other of the protagonists. It is therefore time for France to decide to use all of its might to defeat one or the other of the adversaries. Because these adversaries, in the end, are devouring each other little by little and, in the first place, are coldly putting to death innocent people. Pity the innocents! Except remember, there are no innocents. And this has been true ever since Adam ate the apple and ever since that shriveled apple got stuck in his throat so that his descendants can wonder for eternity what could have tempted him to eat this awful, dried-up fruit.

Yes, when the time came to carefully scrutinize nine million Muslims, France did indeed throw the weight of her power into the fighting. Now she is incapable of catching six hundred members of the OAS who walk wherever they want and take over the capital as soon as night comes. They quietly set their plastic explosives to disturb the unhealthy sleep of a city in which half the population is conniving with them, a city where life, fear, anger, and hate live together without decency.

### September 22

Yesterday, during the evening news, while the director of the RTF was getting ready to let the Algerians listen to an important speech, there was something like a small explosion inside the television set.[13] Then we saw a clear line appear on the dark screen. Immediately after that, we saw: This is France, the OAS is speaking to you. At first, I thought that there had been a new coup at the very time when the plan was to broadcast de Gaulle's latest speech, which he had just delivered somewhere around Rodez. But it was much simpler than that. General Salan's group had taken over the television relay station on Cap Matifou, and they were using this band to send a message to the Algerians. So this became a "good evening, French-Algeria" style for the Ultras. Tomorrow night, starting at 10:00 P.M., they have been asked to take part in a saucepan concert and, on the 25th, to go demonstrate in the streets. The Muslims have been promised another May 13th. They laid out the whole plan. This new May 13th will be Algeria's salvation. No more, no less. The most interesting part of the entire episode is that General Salan was able to rattle on for half an hour. This is surprising because the Cap Matifou area is bristling with soldiers, sailors, and pilots. So nothing could be done between 8:00 and 8:30? Does this not sound surprising? I keep forgetting that the fine-toothed comb is reserved for the Muslims. Let us wait for the end.

This afternoon, I hear from my son, who has gone to Salembier, that a captain of the mobile guard had his throat cut on the small square next to my former school. In fact, this captain had occupied the school with his guards. After the attack, they sealed off the neighborhood. The kid saw the military pick up eight men in the shantytown; they brought them out of their lodgings at random. There was an old man among them who was crying like a child. The soldier who was leading him off allowed him to go back inside his hut. A younger fellow could hardly walk. A soldier pushed him along, but in a single motion he dropped to the ground and started to shake the way an animal does right before it dies. The soldiers left this guy behind as well. That night, while listening to several attacks of all kinds, the radio announced the attempted escape of eight men who had been arrested and taken to jail. When the customary warnings were not obeyed, the military used its weapons. Were these the poor devils from the shantytown? I lost my appetite over it. Of course, these fellows and the poor captain, who may have died standing up, were undoubtedly hit from behind. Good job, gentlemen of Algeria!

**September 23**

No, it was not the fellows from the shantytown. The press says that they were prisoners either going or coming back from their trial . . .

**September 26**

The sound of these saucepans, whistles, and car horns underscoring "Al-gé-rie" [Al-ge-ria] in French is, in a way, moving. It lasted for two hours without interruption. This is no longer hysteria but an endless and desperate scream that stirs even the most callous of men. This is how one is continuously swung between two worlds that are killing each other, crying, suffering, and calling for help in vain: the pathetic sound of saucepans, the pathetic quest for an impossible miracle. This does not make me forget the others, my own people who are still falling, who are still the object of hatred and who will undoubtedly never be able to affect the people on the other side, for it has been a long time since they have been viewed as human beings. Why bring it all up again?

The Europeans are immensely discouraged. They no longer believe in a French Algeria. Everywhere one feels a sense of impending ruin, and the town is gradually sinking into an indefinable sadness. The visible sadness of the streets, of the empty or ransacked stores, the dreary sadness of public places, either empty or bustling with people in a hurry, the visible sadness of faces and of the sky, the invisible sadness of hidden suffering, of vague apprehensions, of unavowed terrors, and justified panic.

You can feel that the end is near. But what end? The most trivial one, maybe an end that will also be the most logical for each of us. It may be the most unexpected one that, after the fact, will turn out to be the only possible solution, the one that everyone will swear they expected and that therefore will not surprise anyone, will make everyone unhappy, and will allow those who are still around to start living again by beginning to forget.

Soon a sinister page will be turned, and a bright sun will rise in a pure sky to enlighten, with its eternal promise, a desolate country that has been indifferent to the sufferings of men and insensitive to its own destruction.

**December 30**

Yesterday, the president of the Republic delivered a short speech about Algeria. He asserted that, one way or the other, the end was in sight. He made it clear that Algeria will be an independent state, that either it will cooperate with France or it will not. Little by little, the army will be going back to France. "The Algerian people will deal with things the best they can," he seemed to be telling us in a disenchanted and, as expected, slightly disdainful tone.

Earlier today, I saw Mrs. G. at the Monoprix. I wanted to know how the Europeans reacted after the de Gaulle speech because it had to be discouraging for them.

—Sullen, she said. Anger is brewing. Nobody trusts de

306

Gaulle anymore. People are waiting for a miracle and are sure that it will happen.

—Otherwise?

—Otherwise, we will try to perform the miracle ourselves. Do you see how?

—Yes, I do.

We also spoke about poor C.

—He was a good man, everyone says so.

I was with him in Paris on December 2nd. We spent the day together with his trainees. We were waiting for Pelegri. O. joined us later on.

A good man, that is for sure. Why did they kill him?

The OAS kills those among its followers whom it considers as traitors: all those who consider us as equals and are prepared to live in this Arab country when it is governed by Arabs. No, the OAS feels that the Europeans must form a block and fight to the death against us, if we do not agree to live under their law. This is true fascism. Maybe they are right. However, being right is not enough. It is necessary and it is enough to be strong, to be the strongest. The OAS will never be the strongest. At least in Algeria. Every act of terrorism that has been committed here since last October is the product of absolute madness. After using plastic explosives, now they are killing people in city centers in broad daylight. They shoot people from behind, they follow people in cars, they take a thousand precautions to escape from justice and the police. They do everything they can to hurt people and to avoid being hurt themselves. Even in their anger, they do not forget that they are the masters, that is, people who are destined to hit, but not be hit themselves. And in order not to be hit, they are prepared to stop hitting themselves. Under these conditions, I am wondering if they really are dangerous.

Poor Mr. C., did you even know that you might be a target for these warriors?

**December 31**

I do not know if total chaos is going to take over. By this I mean, are we going to start dropping like flies at every street corner? Right now, it feels a bit like this. A little bit because, after all, the number of dead and wounded is still limited. Each morning, the newspapers publish a list under the headline "attacks." You can read the names, the location, and the weapon used over one, two, or three columns. This does not include who and why.

The day before yesterday, during a discussion, I met a prelate named Monsignor Duval. He told me that he feared the worst for the month of January. Yesterday evening, at 8:00, a young Arab was killed behind the house where I have been living for a month. All night long there was a concert of saucepans, whistles. They also played a record called "The Africans." This morning, an Arab was wounded by another Arab at the Clos Salembier.

I am back from the L.'s place, where I met an engineer and some young teachers. They were Christians, maybe progressive also, or maybe OAS followers. It is funny how you can no longer tell people apart. The man who says, "I am ferociously in favor of independence," realizes that we are quickly headed in that direction and that there is nothing else to hope for. So, he tries to settle into this independence by demonstrating that there is no hope for the future of Algeria without technical assistance. That technical assistance is him, and the engineer, and all the others. You have to play the OAS hand, or at least let the maniacs play it, but you have to keep the right card: the technical assistance card.

So nothing is ever lost in this miserable Algeria. Nothing. Except for those who have nothing left to lose.

As for those maniacs, I do not know if there are many of them. Everything seems to suggest that there are some, because the OAS pamphlets talk of the upcoming mobilization of anyone between the ages of 16 and 45. Pieds noirs and Muslims. Because the OAS feels that deep down, the Muslims are on their side. Of course, the Muslims are on their side. They are even in favor of anything and anyone. Good God, why don't you leave them the hell alone! Let them live, work, eat, get dressed, take care of their health, and taste a little of what is wasted and dilapidated in their names. Unfortunately, they know that the drama has been complicated by rival ideologies that do not concern them, and that the solution offered them will be forced on them. Let the OAS hurry up and be strong and show that it really wants the Muslims and the others. Otherwise, of course, it will be of interest only to the maniacs. In the end, I cannot really understand why the Muslims are the only ones who want peace. No, why the fuck don't you leave everybody alone? How are you going to do that? Everybody knows the answer to that one. Dear ideologists, is it too much to ask that you just let a man be a master in his own house?

# 19**62**

**January 6**

Yesterday, at the main post office, near the Salembier streetcar stop, one European was talking in a loud voice with another, who was nodding or answering calmly.

—Yes. B. is my village, I was born there, I live there, it is my home, you know. Who would dare disagree?

—Of course.

—I dare them to kick me out: the Chinese, the Russians, the Arabs . . .

Just at that moment, an absent-minded Arab passes by and bumps the man with his head. They stare at each other, both pale.

The Arab, realizing that the man is a European, says:

—Beg your pardon, sir.

The Frenchman, recognizing an Arab, replies:

—Do not mention it, sir. Please forgive me.

—No, it is my mistake.

—Please, no, it is mine.

Pallid and trembling, they keep on spluttering while the other quiet man discreetly slips away. Then the European and the Arab part company, both convinced of their narrow escape.

So here is where we are at, all of us. The stage is ripe for a dictator.

**January 10**

Letter from [Jean] Pelegri, sending me his wishes and his regrets at having missed me when I came to Paris. He wanted to talk to me about C.[1]

My answer:

Dear friend, yes, I was very pleased to have known C. and spent two good days with him. It was as if we had all gotten together again—Honorat, Pelegri, Moussy. I waited for you—but in your absence—we visited with a Kabyle. And then the three of us talked about our concerns, our hopes, and our memories. Please convey my sympathies and deep sadness to Honorat, because, in a sense, all of you were murdered with C., and would the same fate happen to me some day, you could weep as well by keeping in mind that it was all your brothers—those who were like you—your Muslim brothers, who had fallen. They could have been killed by any hand; the hand that killed C., or any other hand; any of which could have struck the blow . . .

There are quite sensible people who wonder why the OAS insists on suppressing everything that promotes reconciliation, peace, and practically any attempt to make the pieds noirs see the most basic of democratic principles—namely, that the minority should bow to the majority and accept its law. This has been a customary practice in France for a long time. In Algeria, more than a century ago, another practice was adopted; a minority, blessed by God, holds all the power in its hands and uses it impudently to its own advantage. For generations, people here have been unable to distinguish between democracy and fascism. But their fascism was applicable only to us, and we, the Muslims, ended up mistaking it for their democracy. This is why our fine scholars and theologians have always claimed that nothing in the world is more liberal than the Qur'an and Islam. In fact, Qur'anic doctrine is more progressive than that of Salazar and Franco. End of discussion.

In our view, moreover, "liberals" are hardly sweet lambs. These folks are simply a little sharper than others, or people who have had a change of heart.

My friends have always been perceptive. This explains why I remain loyal to them. Since they have been placed at the center of the drama, solely as the appointed victims, I have come to love them as brothers. But they should know that they are not alone; that there are many others among us who are right at the heart of the same drama.

I used to have other friends who have, perhaps, completely broken away in their hearts and now belong to the other side. Even so, I do not think that they are capable of inflicting suffering or death, regardless of whether they themselves are suffering and risking death. I suspect that, like me, they are against violence but choose to keep silent. I could never do anything but keep quiet. If this is not the case, it is too bad. They are no longer friends of mine, and I have nothing to regret.

**January 19**

Assassinations are on the rise. Every morning, you learn about the death of a friend, someone you knew, a good man, an innocent. Today, a girl came into the office. She was extremely upset.

A transportation strike has been in effect the past few days. People naively wait for streetcars that do not arrive. Or a car pulls in, slows down; a fanatic gets off, aims, shoots, kills a man, gets in, grabs the wheel, steps on the gas, and makes a daring escape. Stunned, two women faint, and then fall to the ground not far from the body . . . Trembling, the girl begins to type.

Our schoolteachers, absolute patriots, went on strike because they shot down two young guys in the street outside the school—two guys who, strictly speaking, had done absolutely nothing. It is truly indefensible that the misfortune of these young men should be exploited by educators such as these—friends of the OAS and probably active members who are used to beating up Arabs.

Madame Z. has just informed me that a Muslim student was shot down at the entrance to the university. You could call it an eye for an eye, but the two sides are neither equally armed nor equally watched. At this time, people recognize, quite clearly, the source of terrorism and the identity of its perpetrators.

**January 20**

An OAS pamphlet orders a general mobilization for "the entire French population of Algeria," thus excluding Algerians. Pirate broadcasts are advising people to hoard nonperishable goods, even gold coins. They are encouraging Muslim families to seek protection with French families living in their neighborhoods, etc. All of this is being done with the utmost gravity. It is as if from now on, the OAS is the only viable power.

Assassins continue their killing spree at eight miles per hour. Once a crime has been committed, the local district police, or the soldiers, occasionally discover a guilty Arab who trembles as they drag him to the crime scene. The idea is to rough him up and try to force him to confess to the murder. The Arab, who is always on foot, can only kill at four miles per hour. So, he does not dare. If he dares, he either accepts the penalty beforehand, or he chooses to do the deed in town, in a crowd, so that he can easily slip away. But if he has access to a car, he may do like the others. In every case, he lacks both the favor of an easy-going police force and the complicity of pals in uniforms.

The entire French population of Algeria, as people usually say, is getting ready to live through some exciting hours, days, and maybe months, whether it wants to or not. But after that, after that, by God, we will have to get back to reality.

### January 21

Some Europeans tried to murder a Muslim at Air-de-France. He was driving a 403 Peugeot, and they were trailing him in a Dauphine Renault; at the Printania crossroads, he slows down, they overtake him, shoot and wound him in the arm and knee, and flee. His car zigzags like crazy. Then another car appears with a Muslim driver. He catches up with the Peugeot, brakes, jumps, and manages to open the door and stop the 403. Just at this moment, some policemen rush in, grab the Muslim driver by the neck, stick submachine guns into his back, and accuse him of trying to murder the wounded man. The driver cries out for help from a throng of Muslims, who liberate him while throwing insults at the police. At this point, the police prefer to change neighborhoods while the Muslims tend to the victim, who sits moaning in the seat of his car.

### January 26

Nothing has happened, or not much. Not much means that almost everywhere, a few dozen miserable wretches have been murdered. For instance, some assassins went to execute a Muslim colleague who was in class; he was a school principal, a family man in his fifties. A student was also seriously wounded. Yes, they came in just like that, probably after knocking. When M. Djaffar took a step toward the window, they shot him down. He was dead on the spot. The assassins left in a Dauphine car, apparently a green one.

### February 1

Old scores were settled at the Clos Salembier. A "young" Kabyle was butchered while standing in the small square. There was a real crowd. While he was fighting back like a sheep, everyone watched the spectacle. A man fainted. The executioner proudly asked if there were any others "cut from the same cloth." Then he left in a car with his buddies. The poor bastard had fled to Algiers to hide. He had been hunted down by people from his own village. Was he a traitor, a goumier, a womanizer? All of the above? The conviction that he was guilty of all of these crimes eased the consciences of every spectator there.

1962

Of course, it makes you think of the unfortunate colleague who was slaughtered in front of his class. In the face of such events, we are thrown back into the dark ages. And one really wonders whether twentieth-century man, who can orbit the Earth in a remote-controlled rocket, is not, on another level, stuck in the distant past.

**February 5**
De Gaulle is going to give a speech to announce that the end of the Algerian war is very close. How many more victims will this war claim before coming to an end? At this point, it seems that the OAS no longer warns anyone. They kill in cars, on motorbikes, with grenades, automatic weapons, and knives. For cash, the OAS targets the coffers of banks, post offices, and firms, not unlike a production of the popular detective thriller "*Série Noire*" with its accomplices and cowards.

The latest flare-up of blind terrorism: killers are afraid that they will no longer be able to kill with impunity.

The Algerian war is ending. May the dead rest in peace, the survivors as well. Let this be an end to terror. Long live freedom!

[The following notes were found in Feraoun's papers. Before his death in March, he had already submitted the manuscript of his *Journal* to his publisher.]

**February 28**
For two days I have been holed up at home to avoid the ratonnades.[2] There was a large attack on Muslims at Bab-el-Oued, with scores of casualties and wounded, on Michelet Street and on d'Isly. The day before yesterday on d'Isly Street, I watched the gunfire. Across from the Monoprix at 11:05 A.M. — crowds, flying bullets, and the reckless flight of bystanders. On the street not far from me, state police in a jeep slowly cruise by. Indifferent, they turn their backs on the murderers. Just at eye level, on the sidewalk facing me, one of the assassins also turns his back. Wearing a light blue sweater, this young, stocky, and chubby man is firing in a rage. I see one silhouette fall while another runs toward Boulevard Bugeaud. By the time I cross over, the murderers have pursued the runner, and I see two or three of them at the end of the street. Kids run over, followed by grown-ups and some state policemen who decided to stop and intervene. I do not have the courage to approach the two

313

outstretched corpses. I run away, fear in my belly and sweat on my brow.

Later on, I listened to the radio and discovered that the incident was the "tail end" of something that had started an hour earlier at the top of Michelet Street. At that time, there were already a dozen Muslims lying on the sidewalks.

### March 2

Radio-Luxembourg is announcing a death sentence in absentia for a Mr. Achard (in absentia, because he is on the run...). Is it because he embezzled funds from the April 1961 putsch? No, because he has killed dozens or perhaps hundreds of Kabyles. Allah is great!

### March 9

Very strange. The OAS has called a temporary truce so that we can celebrate Aïd. But at the Clos, they still had a drive-by-shooting. Poor Dalibey Ali died on the street. This morning, while driving to the office, I saw a large puddle of blood on Boulevard Bru; one of my wheels ran over it; I saw it just as I drove over it.

### March 14

Terror reigns in Algiers. Yet people still go out. Those who must make a living or simply do errands have to go out. They leave without being too sure whether they will come back or fall in the street. This is where our common fate has brought us—the bold and the cowardly—to the extent that it makes you wonder whether such labels really exist or whether they are merely illusions, devoid of reality. No, of course, we no longer distinguish between the courageous and the cowardly. Unless, after living in fear for so long, we have all become insensitive and unaware. Of course, I do not want to die, and I certainly do not want my children to die. But I am not taking any special precautions, aside from those that have become habits for the past couple of weeks: limiting reasons to go out, stocking up for several days, cutting out visits to friends. Just the same, every time that anyone goes out, he comes back to describe a murder or report a victim.

[Letter written by Ali, son of Mouloud Feraoun, to Emmanuel Roblès]

Tuesday, you wrote my father a letter that he will never read... It is horrible! Wednesday evening—for the first time since we have been in the Lung house—we stayed up with my father, first in the kitchen and then in the living room. We talked about all the schools where he had taught. Then we watched television and saw the program where they talked about your novel.[3] This pleased him a great deal. I know of the friendship you shared with him. After the show, we spoke about you, and he went to bed. This is the last time I saw him. I heard him for the last time at 8:00 A.M. . . . I was in bed. He said to my mother: "Let the children sleep in." She wanted to wake us up to send us to school. "Each morning, you send three men out the door.[4] You do not think that they will give them back to you every day just like that!" My mother spat on the fire to ward off any evil spirit. Well! There is nothing that the fire could do. Dad left alone, and they did not "return" him to us.

I saw him at the morgue. Twelve bullets, but not one on his face. My father was beautiful, but completely frozen as though he did not want to look at anybody. There were fifty, maybe a hundred, like him, on tables, on benches, on the floor, everywhere. They had laid my father down on a table, in the center.

In Tizi-Hibel, we had some difficulties with the self-defense group and the French army. We had to get out in a hurry after his burial. He is buried at the entrance to Tizi-Hibel, across from the home of the Soeurs Blanches.

# Notes

### Introduction

1. Algeria was taken by conquest from the Ottoman Turks in 1830.
2. For the best analysis of the Kabyle-Arab issue, see Patricia M. E. Lorcin, *Imperial Identities: Stereotyping, Prejudice and Race in Colonial Algeria* (New York: I. B. Tauris, 1995).
3. Just prior to the beginning of World War II in 1939, about 39 percent of all troops serving in the French army were from the Maghreb, and all but 11 percent of these men were from Algeria.
4. The *sénatus consulte* of 1865 was part of Emperor Louis-Napoleon Bonaparte's imperial strategy in the Algerian colony. It recognized the difference between Muslims and French citizens and granted Muslims permission to serve in the military as well the right to work within the French civil administration; however, Muslims still were not considered French citizens. To obtain the status of French citizenship, Muslims had to renounce *shari'a,* Islamic (and civil) status under Islam, which effectively meant renouncing Islam. According to John Ruedy, only about two thousand Muslims took this drastic step during the nearly eighty years that the law stood in the French statutes. See John Ruedy, *Modern Algeria: The Origins and Development of a Nation* (Bloomington: Indiana Univ. Press, 1992), 76.
5. *New York Times,* November 8, 1954.
6. The MNA, the FLN, and the French military each accused the other groups of this "vile," "animalistic," and cowardly behavior. No one confessed to the crimes, although there are reasons to believe that the French military could have engineered it in order to destroy the Algerian nationalist's cause as it was about to be debated before the United Nations in New York in the coming months.
7. Ruedy, *Modern Algeria,* 162.
8. Ruedy, *Modern Algeria,* 116.
9. Ruedy, *Modern Algeria,* 189.
10. Although the harkis were effectively used by the French to fight against Algerian nationalists, these Muslims became despised in Algeria by Algerian nationalists and were seen as traitors. As such, the *harkis* were frequently killed and were subject to a violent purging campaign at the end of the war. Most of the harkis who had escaped from Algeria with their families fled to France, but they were shamefully abandoned by the French as they withdrew from Algeria.

11.    Frantz Fanon, *Dying Colonialism* (New York: Grove Press, 1965), 50.

12.    See Fanon, "The Algerian Family" in *Dying Colonialism*, 99–120.

13.    Fanon, *Dying Colonialism*, 30.

14.    Fanon, *Dying Colonialism*, 32.

15.    Frantz Fanon, *The Wretched of the Earth* (New York: Grove Press, 1968).

16.    Fanon, *Wretched of the Earth*, 10, 36, 94.

17.    Jean Daniel, *Le Blesseur* (Paris: Bernard Grasset, 1992), 65. It should be noted here that, according to Simone de Beauvoir, it was Fanon who asked Sartre to write the preface to *The Wretched of the Earth*. See Simone de Beauvoir, *The Force of Circumstance* (New York: G. P. Putnam's Sons, 1965), 591.

18.    Daniel, *Le Blesseur*, 66.

19.    Daniel, *Le Blesseur*, 67.

20.    Daniel, *Le Blesseur*. Daniel also wrote that Sartre was hypocritically attacking the "Occident, Europe, France, the bourgeoisie" at the same time that he denied his membership to each of these communities. It was for this reason that he looked to Fanon, in whom he found "the exemplary alienated [*l'aliéné exemplaire*]" (69).

21.    Feraoun, Camus, and Roblès remained friends through out the war, but Feraoun grew increasingly frustrated with Camus's rejection of Algerian nationalism. See Feraoun, "La source de nos communs malheurs (lettre à Albert Camus)," first published in *Preuves*, no. 91 (September 1858) and re-published in *L'anniversaire* (Paris: Editions du Seuil, 1972). For Camus's perspective, see his *Actuelles III: Chroniques Algériennes, 1939–1958* (Paris: Gallimard, 1958); and his posthumous novel, *The First Man* (*Le Premier Homme*) (New York: Alfred A. Knopf, 1995).

22.    Feraoun to Emmanuel Roblès, April 8, 1961, in Feraoun, *Lettres à ses amis* (Paris: Editions du Seuil, 1969), 181–82.

23.    Feraoun to Paul Flamand, August 6, 1961, Feraoun, *Lettres*, 187.

24.    Feraoun to Roblès, August 15, 1961, Feraoun, *Lettres*, 189.

25.    Note on the arrests kept by the Centres Sociaux. Private papers of Isabelle Deblé.

26.    *Sud-Ouest*, July 28, 1959.

27.    *L'Echo d'Alger*, December 13, 1960.

28.    Alexander Harrison, *Challenging De Gaulle: The* OAS *and the Counterrevolution in Algeria, 1954–1962* (New York: Praeger, 1989), 116.

29.    According to John Ruedy, the initial FLN estimate of lost lives was about 1,000,000, but that number climbed to 1,500,000, depending on one's source. The French claimed

that no more than 350,000 Algerians had died during the war. Ruedy also provides evidence that that number could have been closer to around 300,000. In reality, it is difficult to know just how many hundreds of thousands of Algerians died in the conflict. See Ruedy, *Modern Algeria,* 190.

30. Only Petitbon was absent. There is some speculation about the possibility that he might have known beforehand that an execution was to take place and had been warned against attending meetings at the Centres Sociaux Éducatifs.

31. Jean-Marie Garraud, "La honte . . . ," *Le Figaro,* March 15, 1962.

32. François Mauriac, "Bloc-notes," *Le Figaro littéraire,* March 24, 1962.

33. Albert Memmi, "Mouloud Feraoun: Un symbole," *Le Figaro littéraire,* March 24, 1962.

34. Jean Amrouche, "L'OAS a visé l'espoir au coeur," *Le Monde,* March 17, 1962.

35. Jules Roy, "Une partie de la meilleure France est assassinée avec lui," *Le Monde,* March 17, 1962.

36. Germaine Tillion, "La bêtise qui froidement assassine," *Le Monde,* March 18–19, 1962.

37. Feraoun did not die immediately. He died four hours later in the hospital.

38. Regardless of her past commitments to the Centres Sociaux, Tillion's public reaction to the horrible murder of her friends and colleagues, especially her solid and frank criticisms of the "murdering monkeys," appeared more than noble. It meant severe risks, considering the large number of OAS commando squads known to be at large in Algeria as well as in metropolitan France. The letters sent to Tillion, commending her for taking such an open stance against the OAS murders of her friends, testified to her courage to speak out against the OAS fascists. For example, her former colleague Vincent Monteil, comember of Soustelle's cabinet and the Islamic scholar responsible for creating the SAS, wrote in a letter: "I understand your sadness for those machine-gunned at El-Biar. It's the most odious crime of the OAS." Vincent Monteil to Germaine Tillion, Dakar, March 28, 1962. Private papers of Germaine Tillion.

Others commented as well. An employee of the World Health Organization wrote: "Bravo for your article in 'le Monde,' so courageous and so moving. But protect yourself very well from the 'murdering monkeys.'" Jean V. [unreadable] to Germaine Tillion, March 19, 1962. Private papers of Germaine Tillion.

Another wrote off the assassination's effects. A director of a secondary school wrote of the possible utility of the martyrs for Algeria's future. "The death of our martyrs is distressing, cruel, and painful, but it will not be useless." The acts of "murdering imbeciles" will come to good if they mark the end of the "seven years of imbecilic murdering." S. Bouberet to Germaine Tillion, March 19, 1961. Private papers of Germaine Tillion.

39.    *Le Figaro,* March 19, 1962.

**Preface to the French Edition**

1.    Mouloud Feraoun had asked me to make some cuts and to add the details that I deemed useful for the edition of the *Journal.* What follows is the integral text with a few fairly indispensable annotations. *Roblès.*

Emmanuel Roblès (1914–95) was trained as a teacher in Algiers and taught for a few years. He traveled extensively throughout the world (Russia, Germany, China, the United States). In the late 1930s, he formed two important friendships: with E. Charlot, who later became his publisher, and with Albert Camus, both of whom encouraged him to write. It was only after World War II that his writings were rewarded with a literary prize (Prix Fémina) and performance at the world-famous *Comédie Française.* In the early 1950s, Roblès collaborated with Luis Buñuel on the film version of Roblès's *Cela s'appelle l'aurore.* Early on during the Algerian war for independence, Roblès thought that the Algerians and the French could work out a way to live together. He began writing for the newspaper *Espoir-Algérie* and joined the committee for "civil truce," founded by Camus in December 1956. In 1973, Roblès became a member of the prestigious *Académie Goncourt. Ed.*

**1955**

1.    *Fellagha* is used to denote armed guerilla bands or outlaws. It should not be confused with the Arabic word *Fellah,* which means peasant or small farmer. *Ed.*

2.    The Aurès Mountains are located in southern Algeria. The highest elevation is Djebel Chélia (7680 feet). The ancestral inhabitants of these mountains are Berber tribes. This is the location where the rebellion first broke out. *Trans.*

3.    The *cours complémentaire* is roughly equivalent to the beginning of middle school. *Trans.*

4.    Village policemen were found in rural areas. They acted in the absence of official French policemen. *Ed.*

5.    F.'s previous position as school director before moving to Fort-National. *Roblès.*

6.    The FLN prohibited the consumption of alcohol and tobacco. In part, the FLN did this because it argued that the French government was using the tax revenues gained from the sale of alcohol and tobacco to finance the war, but it also claimed that it wanted to purge these two corrupting

forces from Algerian society. To prevent Algerian Muslims from buying these products, the FLN resorted to extremely brutal methods, including cutting off the accused's lips and/or nose. *Ed.*

7.   Feraoun's hometown. *Roblès.*

8.   This chauffeur would eventually be assassinated for not supporting the strike on November 1, 1956. To avenge his death, the chauffeur's father denounced the guerillas who were temporarily in the town and, in this way, provoked a skirmish that devastated both sides. He, in turn, would be executed while taking with him an ex-serviceman who had always done intelligence work. All of this would, in time, be revealed. (F. placed this note in the manuscript margin.) *Roblès.*

9.   *Gandoura* is a traditional North African robe. *Ed.*

10.   *L'Aïd Kabir* (literally, the great feast day) is the most important Muslim religious festival. *Ed.*

11.   *Maquis* is the French term used to describe members of the resistance. In this case, it denotes Algerians who fought against the French during the French-Algerian war. *Ed.*

12.   Mouloud Mammeri (1917–89) was a leading Kabyle writer. During the war, he joined the FLN. Toward the end of his life, in October 1988, he found himself fighting against the FLN when he advocated that the Algerian state recognize the linguistic and cultural identity of the Berber/Kabyle population. In 1988, the FLN attempted to ban Mammeri's lecture at the university in Tizi-Ouzou. In response, Berber activists protested in the streets. The Algerian authorities massacred more than thirty participants and wounded about two hundred others. Mammeri's best-known novels are *La Colline oubliée, Le Sommeil du juste, L'Opium et le bâton,* and *La Traversée. Ed.*

13.   Mr. Frapolli, the mayor of Fort-National. He was small, frail and hunch-backed. *Feraoun.*

14.   Here the manuscript indicates that this paragraph was to be "written later." *Roblès.*

15.   Here, Feraoun writes: (a paragraph [to be added]). *Roblès.*

16.   This is a reference to the night of August 4, 1789, during which the feudal privileges of the French nobility were abolished. *Ed.*

17.   Joseph uses *tu,* the informal "you" form of address, rather than *vous,* the formal "you" form of address. *Trans.*

18.   A mixed community (*commune mixte*) is the local administrative area in which Muslims are the vast majority of the population and for which there is an administrator appointed by the government. Algeria was divided into three kinds of jurisdictions: *communes de plein exercice, communes mixtes,* and *territoires militaires.* The vast majority of native Algerians lived

in the middle group. Moreover, a mixed community did not benefit from complete self-government as did a *commune de plein exercise*. *Ed*.

19.   A *centre d'arrondissement* is the administrative center for the district. *Ed*.

20.   Robert Barrat, a French journalist, published an article entitled "Chez les hors-la-loi algériens" [With the Algerian Rebels] on September 15, 1955, in *France Observateur*. Barrat was immediately arrested for not disclosing the names of the Algerian revolutionary leaders he had interviewed. After the intervention of many leading intellectuals (including Vincent Monteil), Barrat was released. *Ed*.

21.   The normal school graduates have earned a degree that is roughly equivalent to a bachelor's degree in education. *Trans*.

22.   The term *sans-culottes* refers to revolutionaries during the French Revolution. *Ed*.

23.   *Ramadan* is the ninth month of the Islamic calendar. During Ramadan Muslims are required to fast from sunrise to sunset. *Ed*.

24.   See November 24, 1955. *Feraoun*.

25.   A *marabout* is a Muslim holy person, especially known in rural areas. The marabouts are said to be living descendants of saints and to possess magical powers. *Ed*.

26.   La Kahena was a Berber princess who led the resistance against Arab Muslims in the seventh century. Jeanne d'Arc (Joan of Arc) was born in 1412 in Domrémy in eastern France. As a young girl, she heard the voices of angels who told her to kick the English out of France. She won battles at Orleans and Patay and helped Charles VII be crowned King of France in Rheims. Captured by the English army, she was burned at the stake in Rouen in 1431. *Ed*.

27.   A *chéchia* is a close-fitting cylindrical cap with a tassel; a *burnoose* is a hooded cloak. *Ed*.

28.   The *Alger-Républicain*. *Roblès*.

29.   F. was a city councilor at Fort-National. *Roblès*.

30.   A *djemaâ* is a Berber council or assembly of elders. *Ed*.

31.   *Caids* are the local Muslim officials chosen by the French authorities in the mixed communities. The caid acts as a liaison between the Muslim population and the French authorities. *Ed*.

32.   *Douars* are small villages or encampments. *Ed*.

   **1956**

1.   A Moorish café is different from a French café. Typically, only Muslim men visit Moorish cafés, and it is in such cafés that men meet to discuss politics. In a Moorish café no alcohol is sold, whereas alcohol is consumed in French cafés. *Ed*.

2.   SN stands for *Syndicat National* (National Trade Union). *Trans.*

3.   A woman that nobody wants to marry. *Feraoun.*

4.   *Amin,* in an adjectival sense, means loyal, faithful, upright; in a nominative sense, it means a chief, head, guarantor, or leader. *Ed.*

5.   Village located outside Fort-National on the road to Tizi-Ouzou. *Feraoun.*

6.   *Karouba* is an offering or a donation. *Ed.*

7.   *Fatiha* is an opening prayer from the Qur'an. *Ed.*

8.   The *muezzin* is the crier who calls Muslims to prayer. *Ed.*

9.   Muslim cemeteries are separated from the Christian cemeteries and generally are outside of the village. *Ed.*

10.   A *hakem* is a native authority in a *commune mixte. Doula* literally means "state," but in this context it probably means "colonial official." *Ed.*

11.   After Soustelle left office, the French government in Paris decided to change the post of governor general of Algeria to that of resident minister. In part, this was done to streamline government by giving the resident minister more autonomy than the governor general and to eliminate the unnecessary step of having the governor report to the minister of the interior. The new minister was directly responsible to the French prime minister and was a cabinet member. *Ed.*

12.   August 4, 1789, is the date during the French Revolution when the nobility abdicated their privileges. *Ed.*

13.   General Georges Catroux was first picked by Guy Mollet to replace Governor General Jacques Soustelle. A liberal, Catroux had been Governor General in Indochina in 1941 but went on to join Charles de Gaulle after he was replaced by the Vichy government. He had also been active in Syria and Lebanon as a representative of the Free French during World War II. *Ed.*

14.   The CRS is the *Compagnies Républicaines de Sécurité. Spahis* are indigenous North African cavalrymen in the French army. They occupied a position similar to "Buffalo Soldiers" in the American Army. *Ed.*

15.   It is impossible to fully understand these lines if one does not remember the meeting that we had organized in Algiers on January 23, 1956, with Camus. This meeting had been violently disturbed by some "Ultras." (See the text of this discussion in *Actuelles III,* NRF. An excerpt had appeared in *Le Journal d'Alger. Roblès.*

16.   *Bloc-notes* ("note pad") was written by François Mauriac in *L'Express.* Mauriac's weekly column offered an important site of criticism of French policies in Algeria. See Mauriac, *Bloc-notes,* 3 vols. (Paris: Editions du Seuil, 1993). *Ed.*

17.   *Bicot* is a derogatory word used by the French for North Africans. It is analogous to "gook" or "nigger" in English. *Ed.*

18.   The family name Durand is as common in French as Smith or Jones are in English. *Trans.*

19.   Located in the French Alps, the Plateau des Glières was the site of heroic French resistance against German soldiers in 1944. *Trans.*

20.   Mitidja is an Algerian agricultural plain known for its vineyards and citrus fruits. *Trans.*

21.   The *caves du fort* were cellars where perishable supplies and ice were kept. *Trans.* A *tarboosh* is a tasseled cap, usually red, worn by Muslim men. *Ed.*

22.   A *kouba* is a maraboutic or Sufi shrine. *Ed.*

23.   Palestro is on the western edge of Kabylia. *Ed.*

24.   François Villon (1431–c. 1463), a French poet born in Paris, led an adventurous life and was jailed on several occasions. He wrote the *Petit Testament* and the *Grand Testament* and is also famous for a poem entitled "Ballade des Pendus." He is considered the first in a long line of French lyrical poets. *Trans.*

25.   PRG refers to the *Police des Renseignements Généraux* (secret police). *Ed.*

26.   SFIO stands for *Section Française de l'Internationale Ouvrière,* which was created in 1905 from the union of two socialist parties, the *Parti socialiste français* and the *Parti socialiste de France. Ed.*

27.   The *palmes académiques* is a decoration given for services to education in France or abroad to educators who further the study of French. *Trans.*

28.   *Saracens* (a Christian term for Muslims) is a reference to Charlemagne and the events related in *The Song of Roland. Trans.*

29.   Louis XIV, the "sun king," was born in 1638 and reigned as king of France from 1643 until his death in 1715. Henry IV, the "man from Béarn," was born in 1553 and reigned as king of France from 1589 until he was murdered by Ravaillac in 1610. Raised in a Huguenot family, he converted to Catholicism to ensure his control of the French throne. *Ed.*

30.   Maximilien Robespierre (1758–94) was perhaps the best-known Jacobin leader during the French Revolution. After serving as a member of the National Assembly between 1789 and 1791, he ruled France as a totalitarian through the *Comité de Salut Public* (Committee of Public Safety) from 1793 to 1794 during the period of the French Revolution known as the Reign of Terror. He established the cult of the Supreme Being. He was toppled on July 27, 1794, and was guillotined. *Ed.* The "little Corsican" was a reference to Napoleon I (1769–1821). *Trans.*

31.    The Ottoman Dey Hussein struck the French consul Pierre Duval on the arm with a peacock feather fly whisk in 1827. In retaliation, France, under Charles x, decided to launch an assault on Algiers, the result of which was the French occupation of 1830. Unfortunately for Charles x, he was unable to salvage his government with the occupation, and he lost his crown in 1830. *Ed.*

32.    Jules Ferry (1832-93) was a prominent French statesman in the Third Republic who is known for his organization of primary teaching in France. *Trans.*

33.    General Olié was given command of Kabylia in 1956. *Ed.*

34.    A *subprefect* (*sous-préfet*) is a local French civil administrator. *Ed.*

35.    Pierre Poujade's *Union de Défense des Commerçants et Artisans* (UDCA) was a small radical movement started in 1956. The Poujadists advocated the resurrection of the Old Regime's *Estates General* and the dissolution of the National Assembly. During World War II, Poujade had been a member of the fascist French Popular Party and was known as a fierce anti-Semite. He was also a staunch supporter of French colonial interests. *Ed.*

36.    The only two gates at each end of Fort-National, a city that still has its original ramparts. *Roblès.*

37.    The reference to the nationalist flag is important because it was illegal to show it in public. It later became the flag of independent Algeria. *Ed.*

38.    During street demonstrations celebrating the end of World War II on May 8, 1945 (VE Day) in Sétif by Muslims, about forty Muslims and Europeans were killed as they clashed. Insurrections broke out in the area around Sétif and Guelma, which led to the killing of about one hundred Europeans. The French military responded by massacring thousands of Algerian Muslims. *Ed.*

39.    An excerpt from the *Journal d'Alger* is glued in the margin of the manuscript, next to these lines: "Yesterday at 4:00 A.M., the said Mansour Belkacem, perpetrator of the March 29 attack on a soldier in Fort-National, was shot as he was trying to flee." *Roblès.*

40.    Ethel and Julius Rosenberg were charged in the United States for conspiring to reveal atomic secrets to the Soviet Union in 1950. In 1951, a jury convicted the Rosenbergs of treason, and Judge Irving Kaufman sentenced them to death. They were electrocuted on June 19, 1953. *Ed.*

41.    Pan-Arabism was a powerful ideology advocated by leaders such as Gamal Abd el-Nasser. *Ed.*

42.    Paul Déroulède (1848-1914), a French poet and politi-

cian born in Paris, was president of the League of Patriots and author of *Chants des soldats* (Songs of soldiers). *Trans.*

43. He was himself assassinated by the rebels in 1958. See notebook number 12, October 2, 1958. *Feraoun.*

44. This statement has been maintained in the text although it seems to be in contradiction with what Feraoun has just written a few lines earlier when he stated that only twenty out of thirty had spoken. See also the few lines following this statement. *Trans.*

45. A *djemaâ* is a Berber village or clan council. *Ed.*

46. Ravachol is the nickname of François-Auguste Koenigstein (1859–92), a French anarchist responsible for many bombings. He was guillotined. *Trans.*

47. He was executed later in Aït-Khalfoun. *Feraoun.*

48. The clipping in question is from the weekly *Demain* (June 21–27, 1956) which recounts that before March 22, the Fleet Air Arm had bombed the village of Palestro, killing 1,200 people. *Feraoun.*

49. *L'Echo d'Alger* was a leading conservative, pro-settler Algerian daily. *Ed.*

50. BEPC, or *Brevet d'études du premier cycle* (literally, a certificate of study for the first cycle), was the exam taken at the end of the equivalent of the U.S. eighth grade. Fifty years ago or so, it was a terminal degree for many schoolchildren in the French educational system. *Trans.*

51. *El Moudjahid* is the Arabic word for holy fighter. *Ed.*

52. CAP, or *Certificat d'aptitude primaire* (literally, a certificate of primary aptitude), is a certificate delivered after examination at the end of an apprenticeship course of study. *Trans.*

53. *Jours de Kabylie* was published by Bacconier in Algiers in 1954, with illustrations by Brouty; it was reprinted in Paris by Edition du Seuil in 1968. *Ed.*

54. Throughout the war, the FLN called many strikes to mobilize the masses and in order to demonstrate to a world audience that the majority of Algerians were in support of the revolution. *Ed.*

55. *Journal d'Alger.* A clipping is glued in the margin of the manuscript. Title: "Thirty rebels killed in Taourirt-Moussa." *Roblès.*

56. A *chouaris* is a woven double basket used to transport goods to market. *Ed.*

57. Mr. Simonin, assassinated by a terrorist in 1959 at the entrance to the city, if I remember correctly. *Roblès.*

58. Ajaccio is a major tourist and commercial center on the island of Corsica, where Napoleon Bonaparte was born. *Trans.*

59. Ferdinand de Lesseps (1805–94) was a French diplomat born in Versailles. In 1869, he supervised the construction of

the Suez Canal. Later he began work on the Panama Canal but could not complete the project due to bankruptcy. *Trans.*

60. Abderrahmane Farès, a moderate Algerian Kabyle leader and a former president of the Algiers Assembly, announced in September 1956 that he would negotiate with the FLN. Observers in Algiers saw this as the end of compromise with moderate Algerian Muslims. *Ed.*

61. A copy of this pamphlet is included in the notebook. Title: Call for Algerians to boycott French schools. *Roblès.*

62. DST stands for *Division pour la Sûreté du Territoire,* or Division for the Security of the Territory. It was created by Roger Wybot during the Liberation to fight against the Nazi infiltration of the Free French forces and the French Resistance. It later became part of the Fourth Republic's police structure, and its role was similar to that of the CIA. *Ed.*

63. On October 22, 1956, the French military broke international law and seized the sultan of Morocco's private aircraft, which carried important leaders of the Algerian revolution (Ben Bella, Budiaf, Khider, Ait Ahmed, and a well-known intellectual, Moustapha Lacheraf). *Ed.*

64. Blaise Pascal (1623–62), French mathematician, physicist, and author of the *Pensées.* Pascal used argumentation based on logic and rationality to convince his readers and religious opponents. *Trans.*

65. On November 1, 1956, the Soviet army made its way into Hungary and crushed the Imre Nagy's revolt in Budapest. The incident triggered vocal opposition within the French intellectual community. *Ed.*

66. In an effort to call international attention to its struggle, the FLN ordered a general strike in Algeria. Unfortunately for the FLN, the strike ended disastrously because the French military literally forced Muslim workers back to work (often at gunpoint), which gave the impression to the world community that not all Muslims were behind the strike. Hence, in strategic terms, the strike was a tactical blunder for the FLN. *Ed.*

67. Feraoun uses the informal *tu* rather than the formal *vous* in the French text from this point until the end of this paragraph to underscore his close friendship with Roblès. *Trans.*

68. We have left this entry in its location in the original text although its date makes it sequentially incorrect. *Trans.*

69. "Intense quasi-Cornelian drama" is a reference to the plays of Pierre Corneille (1606–84). His heroes are confronted by a dilemma that forces them to choose between personal love, family honor, and defending the state. Among his more popular plays are *Le Cid* (1636), *Horace* and *Cinna,* (both 1640), and *Polyeucte* (1642). *Trans.*

70. Oradour-sur-Glane is a small village in southwestern

France. On June 10, 1944, the entire population (634 inhabitants) was shot or burned inside the local church by German soldiers. *Trans.*

71. Ouadhia is a village about eight miles southeast of Tizi-Ouzou. *Ed.*

72. *Aimée et souffrante Algérie* (Loved and Suffering Algeria). *Feraoun.*

73. Pamphlet glued in the margin of the manuscript. *Feraoun.*

74. Politician, mayor of Boufarik, president of the association of the Federation of Algerian Mayors, etc. . . . Political leaning: "Ultra." *Feraoun.*

75. Government Square is decorated with an equestrian statue of the duke of Orléans. *Feraoun.*

### 1957

1. A *gourbi* is a house similar to an adobe house. *Ed.*

2. The *Soeurs Blanches* was established by the Archbishop of Algiers, Charles Martial Allemand Lavigerie, in 1870. Along with the *Pères Blancs* (established by Lavigerie in 1869), the two were the most important missionary societies in Algeria. *Ed.*

3. "Maître Jacques" is a reference to a character in Molière's *L'Avare* (1668) who is both cook and coachman for the miser Harpagon. The term in French has come to refer to someone who has several, often conflicting, activities. *Trans.*

4. *El Moudjahid*, the paper for which Frantz Fanon wrote, was the newspaper published by the FLN during the French-Algerian war. As a state-run newspaper, it is still one of the principal newspapers in Algeria today. *Ed.*

5. After intense lobbying by the FLN's two representatives in New York, Abdelkader Chanderli and M'hamed Yazid, the FLN finally succeeded in bringing the Algerian question to the floor of the United Nations in New York in January 1957. However, French foreign minister Christian Pineau argued that the crisis in Algeria was purely an internal affair, and the United States decided to help prevent an Asian and African resolution concerning independence from coming to the floor. *Ed.*

6. *Andromaque* refers to Racine's play, written in 1667. *Trans.*

7. The *notary cadi* is, in this case, the Muslim judge who witnesses and certifies documents and takes affidavits and depositions. *Ed.*

8. Pierre Mendès-France (1907–82), a French politician with Leftist leanings, in 1954 signed the treaty of Geneva (which led to the end of French colonialism in Indochina) and gave internal autonomy to Tunisia. *Ed.*

9. In 1957, many French and Muslim educators were

accused of conspiring with the FLN. The Centres Sociaux, in particular, had many of its members arrested and brought to trial. It was extremely damaging to the reputation of the Centres. *Ed.*

10.    The *Sûreté* was a unit of the French Interior Ministry in charge of the police. *Ed.*

11.    Feraoun's publisher in Paris, the Editions du Seuil, is one of the most important publishing houses in France. *Ed.*

12.    The gray card is an annual tax levied against the size of a car's engine. The more powerful the engine, the higher the tax. *Trans.*

13.    And blind terrorism (bombs in streetcars, dance halls, cafés, etc.) made a just cause lose face. Further, it prevented us, the "liberals," from talking to the European population. *Roblès.*

14.    Camus's opinion was more qualified. He felt that there was a fascist tendency inside the Front and that it could take over. *Roblès.*

15.    *Chaouch* is the word for an usher or attendant in North Africa. *Ed.*

16.    Press clipping dated March 2: "Mr. Achard, deputy administrator of the mixed community of the Ouadhias, has left us to begin his new assignment in Batna! . . ." *Feraoun.*

17.    Hamad told me that, indeed, it seems that some people did ask for this post. *Feraoun.*

18.    Here, it is a question of selecting young men who will comprise the militia in charge of securing the village. *Feraoun.*

19.    The *harkis* were semi-guerrilla Muslim troops created by the French to fight in favor of French interests. They were considered loyal by the French and traitors by the FLN and Algerian nationalists. The harki units were directly responsible to the local SAS commander and were generally ruthless in their pursuit of the FLN. Outnumbering the FLN's ALN men, they suffered equally ruthless persecution after the war. Most of those who survived ended up relocating in France. *Ed.*

20.    In this context *mektoub* means "fate." Technically it means the "written" or "scripted," which then leads to the "pre-ordained" or "fated." *Ed.*

21.    *Le Figaro Littéraire* is a literary magazine published in Paris by the same conservative newspaper group that published the daily *Le Figaro*. Pierre Brossolette, born in 1903, was a leader in the resistance during World War II. He was arrested in 1944 and committed suicide rather than talk under torture. *Trans.*

22.    *L'Express* is a Parisian weekly magazine that utilizes basically the same format as *Time* and *Newsweek*. *Trans.* Jean-Jacques Servan-Schreiber, born in 1924, is the founder and editor of *L'Express*. He was a leading intellectual figure during

the French-Algerian War and the author of *Lieutenant in Algeria* (1957), which criticized the French military in Algeria and which was based on his own experiences as a soldier there. After the war, he became a leading political figure in France, but he has since retired from politics. *Ed.*

23. Si Kaci Yazzomène, according to a clipping from the *Journal d'Alger* glued in the margin of the manuscript. *Roblès.*

24. Clipping attached. The correspondent of the Algiers daily indeed wrote: "the proud and ardent troops lead by martial music whose strains woke in us both hope and confidence . . ." *Feraoun.*

25. *Le Monde* is a usually centrist afternoon Paris newspaper that is renowned for the quality of its editorials, analyses, and commentaries. *Trans.*

26. J. A. is a reference to Jean Amrouche (1906–62), a Christian Kabyle who was also a leading Algerian intellectual. He was from a well-known Kabyle family, and his mother was Fadhma Aith Mansour Amrouche, whose memoir, *Histoire de ma vie* (Paris: Maspero, 1968), is a classic about Kabylia. *Ed.*

27. This captain will be killed during a skirmish less than a mile away from Fort-National. Swift justice again! *Feraoun.*

28. The person who told me these things died, in his turn, two years later. He was killed by the maquis. *Feraoun.*

29. A *goumier* is a member of an indigenous North African tribal cavalry serving in the French army. *Ed.*

30. A clipping is attached. *Feraoun.*

31. A letter was included with the manuscript. It was addressed to Mrs. Feraoun. "My dear Sister Dahbia, Now our poor Chebreh Amar is dead. Yesterday, the soldiers killed him." *Feraoun.*

32. René Coty (1882–1962) was president of France from 1954 to 1958. *Ed.*

33. Sèvres, just like Limoges, is renowned for the quality of its china. It is located to the west of Paris near Versailles. The Elysée Palace is the presidential palace in Paris. Bresse is the area located to the northeast of Lyon and is renowned for the quality of its poultry. *Trans.*

34. Paper is attached. In pencil: "April 30, 5:15 P.M. Imerzoukène Abdelkader, born 11–28–36 in Taourirt-Amokrane." *Feraoun.*

35. The name "Madame Sganarelle" is a reference to a comedy by Molière entitled *Sganarelle or the Imaginary Cuckold,* first performed in Paris on May 28, 1660. *Trans.*

36. Former name of Fort-National. *Feraoun.*

37. CISL refers to the *Confédération Internationnale des Syndicats Libres. Ed.*

38. Habib Bourguiba (1903–) was the first president of

Tunisia (1957–87). He helped found the Neo-Destour Party,
which was instrumental in achieving Tunisian independence
from France. Often imprisoned, he was released in 1954
in order to negotiate the agreement that created Tunisian
autonomy in 1954 and independence in 1956. In 1956 he was
elected premier, and in 1957 he overthrew the bey and was
elected president of the republic by the newly formed constitu-
ent assembly. After being elected president for life in 1975, he
was forced from office in 1987 by Zine al-Abidine Ben Ali, his
prime minister. *Ed.*

39.    "B. M." refers to Maurice Bourgès-Maunoury, who
became prime minister following Guy Mollet in 1957. A few
months later, after the Assembly defeated the *loi-cadre* on
September 30, 1957, Bourgès-Maunoury resigned. *Ed.*

40.    Christian Pineau was French foreign minister under Guy
Mollet. *Ed.*

41.    In 1957, Raymond Aron, a French sociologist at the
Sorbonne, published his controversial *La Tragédie algérienne*
(Paris: Plon Editors, 1957), which advocated the abandonment
of French Algeria based primarily on economic considerations.
In response, Jacques Soustelle immediately published a vitriolic
critique of Aron, *Le Drame algérien et la décadence française:
Réponse à Raymond Aron* (Paris: Plon Editors, 1957). *Ed.*

42.    The mention of Sévigné's fire is a reference to one of the
letters (letter 16) written by Madame de Sévigné in which she
describes the burning of the house of one of her neighbors in
Burgundy. In this letter, she quotes Corneille's *Le Cid* (act 4,
scene 3): "The battle ended for lack of combatants." *Trans.*

43.    Afterward, this butcher was arrested and then released a
few months later. He was recently assassinated by a member of
the MNA on July 3, 1961. *Feraoun.*

44.    In reality, Medjeber was presumed dead. Everybody was
scared stiff when he returned to his village, and as a result, he
went mad. *Feraoun.*

45.    The mention of "Candide" is a reference to the
philosophical tale *Candide,* written by Voltaire. *Trans.*

46.    A *fabliau,* a French short tale in verse, was particularly
popular in the thirteenth century. *Trans.*

47.    Jean-Yves Alquier, *Nous avons pacifié Tazalt: Journal
de marche d'un officier parachutiste rappelé en Algérie* (Paris:
R. Laffont, 1957). *Ed.*

48.    The "razor-sharp knife" is a reference to the heavy
sword attached to a horse's hair and suspended above
Damocles. The wealthy tyrant Denys the Older had done this
to help Damocles understand the permanent dangers that
threaten apparent prosperity. *Trans.*

49.    Vatel, the master cook in charge of the kitchens at the

Prince de Condé's palace, committed suicide in 1671 when he realized that he would not be able to serve seafood for a meal that Condé was offering King Louis XIV. In France, Vatel has become synonymous with excellence in cooking, which explains why many French restaurants bear this name. *Trans.*

50.　Father Charles de Foucauld (1858–1916), a French explorer and missionary, explored Morocco and worked as a missionary in the Sahara. He was assassinated in Tamanrasset, Algeria. *Ed.*

51.　Antoine de Saint-Exupéry (1900–44), a pilot who was lost during a war mission in North Africa, became a hero of the French Resistance. He is also the author of several books, such as *The Little Prince* and *War Pilot*. *Ed.*

52.　*Salopards* is military slang for a Moroccan rebel during the 1920–33 campaign. The term is used in French slang today to refer to a son of a bitch or bastard. *Trans.*

53.　Here Feraoun refers to a fable by La Fontaine entitled "The Oyster and the Plaintiffs" *Trans.*

### 1958

1.　"A." refers to Algerian intellectual Jean Amrouche. *Ed.*

2.　A *rappelé* is a soldier/recruit who is called to war. *Ed.*

3.　Early in 1958, Algerian fighters based across the border in the Tunisian town of Sakiet shot at French aircraft. In response, the French bombed the town on February 8, 1958, and killed over eighty people, among whom were Tunisian women and children. The incident created a scandal within the international community and brought the Algerian question once again to the floor of the United Nations. *Ed.*

4.　Paul Roblès was mortally wounded while playing with a gun. He was sixteen years old. *Roblès.*

5.　Henri Alleg, *The Question* (*La Question*) (New York: George Braziller, 1958). *Ed.*

6.　GG refers to *Gouvernement-Général*. *Ed.*

7.　PC refers to *Parti Communiste*. *Ed.*

8.　Victim of the FLN purge of the summer of 1958 that took hundreds of lives. *Feraoun.*

9.　This poor kid was playing each side against other. Will be a victim of the purge. Has already lost his two brothers who were executed by the army. *Feraoun.*

10.　Denis Diderot (1713–84), the French philosopher, was better known for having written an illustrated *Encyclopedia*, as well as *Rameau's Nephew*. He was the proponent of a new style of play known as the bourgeois drama. He is also renowned for his *Salons* in which he developed a critical appreciation for the art of his times. His lengthy correspondence shows the insatiable intellect of one of the most important proponents of the French Enlightenment. *Trans.*

11.　An *oued* is a dry river bottom. *Ed.*

**1959**

1. Later, Jules Roy told of this incident in *Guerre d'Algérie* (*The Algerian War*). *Ed.*

2. Dunkerque is the northernmost major city in France and close to the border with Belgium. Tamanrasset is a major oasis in the southern Sahara. The combination of the two names is meant to express that there is only one country between the two of them. *Trans.*

3. In October 1958, Paul Delouvrier succeeded Robert Lacoste in a position now called the Delegate General. *Ed.*

4. The person in question is "C.," a lucid and patriotic young man. *Feraoun.*

5. SAU refers to a branch of the French military in Algiers that worked with the Muslim youth. *Ed.*

6. HLM refers to *habitations à loyer modéré*, or low-income housing—usually tall apartment complexes. CIE refers to *Centre International de l'Enfance. Trans.*

**1960**

1. Two letters in two weeks. I still have them. *Feraoun.* F. sent one of them to me; it contained the drawing of a hangman. *Roblès.*

2. Camus was killed in a car accident. *Ed.*

3. The "same old reed story" is a reference to a fable by La Fontaine entitled "*Le Chêne et le roseau*" (The Oak and the Reed) in which a strong wind uproots the tree while the reed can bend and survive. *Trans.*

4. CRS refers to *Compagnies Républicaines de Sécurité. Ed.*

5. FAF refers to *Front de l'Algérie Française. Ed.*

6. *La Dépêche quotidienne* (*Daily Dispatch*). *Feraoun.*

7. "Gavroche" is the brave and mocking street urchin in Victor Hugo's *Les Misérables* who removes bullets from dead fighters' pouches during street fighting and eventually becomes a victim of his bravery. *Trans.*

8. In October 1960, Feraoun had been appointed inspector to Sociaux, whose offices were located in El Biar, inside the estate known as Château-Royal, where the massacre of March 15, 1962, was going to be perpetrated. *Roblès.*

9. Road in the suburbs of Algiers, at the foot of the hills of La Redoute and the Clos Salembier. There is a shantytown to one side of it before you reach Belcourt. *Roblès.*

10. Diar-el-Mahçoul and Diar-es-Saâda, two new housing estates above Belcourt. *Roblès.*

11. *Mozabite* refers to a Muslim from the South Central Algerian Sahara who is a member of the Kharijite sect. *Ed.*

12. Salah Ould Aoudia is also an inspector of Centres Sociaux and will be assassinated with Feraoun on March 15, 1962. *Roblès.*

#### 1961

1.   *Roumi* is the Arabic word used by Muslims to denote a Christian or European. *Ed.*

2.   *Youyou* is a high-pitched sound, usually made by women, which would echo through the streets. *Trans.*

3.   In the margin of the notebook, facing this paragraph and the following one, joined by a bracket, F. wrote: "This is mean and gratuitous." *Roblès.*

4.   The writing stops. (Note in original text.) *Roblès.* The sentence continues in the next entry. *Trans.*

5.   *Médina* means "the city" in Arabic. Here, it means a traditional or Islamic city. *Ed.*

6.   Clipping attached. *Roblès.*

7.   Châteauneuf, between El Biar and Bouzaréa, where F. had been living since leaving Clos Salembier. *Roblès.*

8.   This 1946 French film, directed by René Clair, tells the story of an older gentleman who quietly runs a resistance network during World War II. *Trans.*

9.   This entry is to be placed at the beginning as a foreword. *Feraoun.*

10.   The "captain" refers to Captain Oudinot. Roblès added this name to the original text. *Trans.*

11.   "Huron" is the pen name of one of the collaborators who was writing for the satirical *Canard Enchaîné* published weekly in Paris. *Trans.*

12.   PSU refers to *Parti Socialiste Unifié. Ed.*

13.   RTF refers to *Radiodiffusion-Télévision Française. Ed.*

#### 1962

1.   Mr. Contensou, assassinated by the OAS in early January inside the university tunnel in Algiers. *Roblès.*

2.   *Ratonnades* are brutal attacks by Europeans on North Africans, similar to pogroms. *Ed.*

3.   *Lectures pour tous*, shown "on tape delay" on Algiers television. *Roblès.*

4.   Feraoun and his two sons, Ali and Mokrane. *Roblès.*

# Glossary

*Aït-Kabir:* Literally "great feast day"; the most important Muslim religious festival.

*Amin:* Chief, head, guarantor, or leader.

*Burnoose:* Hooded cloak.

*Caids:* Muslim officials chosen by the French authorities in mixed communities.

*Caves du fort:* Cellars where perishable supplies and ice were kept.

*Centres Sociaux:* French educational apparatus designed in 1955 and funded by the French government to offer "basic education" to non-Europeans in Algeria.

*Chaouch:* Usher or attendant.

*Chéchia:* Close-fitting cylindrical cap with a tassel.

*Commune mixte* (mixed community): Administrative area where Muslims are majority and for which there is an administrator (*caid*) appointed by the French government.

*Djemaâ:* Berber village or clan council.

*Douars:* Small villages or encampments.

*Doula:* Literally means "state," but can mean colonial official.

*Fatiha:* Opening prayer from the Qur'an.

*Fellagha:* Armed guerilla bands in Algiers.

*Gandoura:* Traditional North African robe.

*Goumier:* A member of an indigenous North African tribal cavalry unit serving in the French army.

*Gourbi:* Traditional house in the Kabylia.

*Hakem:* Native authority in a mixed community.

*Harki:* Algerian soldier who fought against Algerian nationalists for the French military.

*Kabylia:* Mountainous region east of Algiers between Algiers and Constantine, where the majority of the Kabyles live.

*Karouba:* Offering or a donation.

*Kouba:* Maraboutic or Sufi shrine.

*Maquis:* Members of the resistance; here, Algerians who fought against the French during the French-Algerian war.

*Marabout:* Muslim holy man, especially known among the Kabyles.

*Médina:* Traditional or Islamic city.

*Mektoub:* Literally means the "written" or "scripted"; can also mean, by extension, "fate."

*Moudjahid* (El), plural, *Moudjahiddine:* Literally, Arabic word for "holy fighter"; in Algeria the word for FLN "soldier."

*Mozabite:* Muslim from the South Central Algerian Sahara who is a member of the Kharijite sect.

*Muezzin:* Crier who calls Muslims to prayer.

*Notary cadi:* Muslim judge who witnesses and certifies documents and takes affidavits and depositions.

*Oued:* Desert river that is dry in the summer and flowing in the winter.

*Pied noir:* European colonial settler born in Algeria.

*Ramadan:* Ninth month of the Islamic calendar, during which Muslims are required to fast from sunrise to sunset.

*Rappelé:* French soldier or recruit who is called to war.

*Ratonnades:* Brutal attacks by Europeans on North Africans, similar to pogroms.

*Roumi:* Arabic word for a Christian or European.

*Subprefect (sous-préfet):* Local French civil administrator.

*Tarboosh:* Tasseled cap, usually red, worn by Muslim men.

*Ultra:* Extremist pied noir who refused all compromise and change to colonial status quo in Algeria.

*Zouave soldiers:* French infantry units traditionally composed of Berber or Kabyle Algerians.

# Index